THE ASCENT OF CHRISTIAN LAW

The Ascent of Christian Law

Patristic and Byzantine Formulations of a New Civilization

John A. McGuckin

ST VLADIMIR'S SEMINARY PRESS
YONKERS, NEW YORK 10707
2012

Library of Congress Cataloging-in-Publication Data

McGuckin, John Anthony.

The ascent of Christian law : Patristic and Byzantine formulations of a new civilization / John A. McGuckin.

pages cm

ISBN 978-0-88141-403-5

1. Christianity and law—History. 2. Christian civilization—History. 3. Church history–Primitive and early church, ca. 30–600. I. Title.

BR115.L28M35 2012

270—dc23

2011049615 Library of Congress

Cover image: Portrait of the Jurisconsult Ulpian from a leaf of the *Digest*, c. 1300, in the Robbins Collection, University of California at Berkeley; copyright by the Regents of the University of California, The Robbins Religious and Civil Law Collection, Berkeley Law, University of California at Berkeley. Reproduced by permission.

ST VLADIMIR'S SEMINARY PRESS
575 Scarsdale Road, Yonkers, NY 10707
1-800-204-2665
www.svspress.com

ISBN: 978-0-88141-403-5

PRINTED IN THE UNITED STATES OF AMERICA

For His Beatitude

Dr Daniel Ciobotea

Patriarch of the Romanian Orthodox Church

Scholar, Statesman, and

Renewer of the Fabrics of Civilization.

Other St Vladimir's Seminary Press Books by John A. McGuckin

Saint Cyril of Alexandria and the Christological Controversy
ISBN 978-0-88141-863-7

Saint Gregory of Nazianzus: An Intellectual Biography
ISBN 978-0-88141-864-4

Translations

Saint Cyril of Alexandria: *On the Unity of Christ* (Popular Patristics Series no. 13)
ISBN 978-0-88141-133-1

Harp of Glory (Popular Patristics Series no. 39)
ISBN 978-0-88141-054-9 (Print edition)
ISBN 978-0-88141-879-8 (Digital edition)

This Project was supported by a grant from the Alonzo L. McDonald Family Agape Foundation to the Center for the Study of Law and Religion at Emory University. The author wishes to express his thanks to Ambassador Alonzo L. McDonald, to Peter McDonald and the other Agape Trustees for their gracious sponsorship of the legal arts in dialogue with religion. The study was prepared by the author in recognition of his election as a Senior Fellow of Emory's CSLR, and special thanks are also due to the two inspiring academicians who energize that project: Professors John Witte Jr and Frank S. Alexander.

Contents

Abbreviations 9

Proemium 11

1 Gospel and Grace: Scriptural Foundations on Law, Authority, and the Exercise of Governance 15

2 Classical Foundations of Reflection On Law and Polity 27

(a) Greek Philosophical Reflection On Political Order 27

(b) Roman Conceptions of Law 39

3 Early Christian Proto-Canonical Collections: Clementine Letters of Governance, the Didache, Apostolic Constitutions, The Didascalia, and later "antiquarian" forgeries of the third and fourth centuries 57

4 The Canonical Epistles of the Twelve Eastern Fathers 77

5 Legal Theology in the Western Fathers: Tertullian, & Lactantius 95

6 A Theology of Politics in the Later West: St Augustine of Hippo 127

7 The Eastern Church's Synodical Process 167

8 The Seven Oecumenical Councils 193

9 Imperial Byzantine Codifications of State Law 237

10 Later Byzantine Canonists 255

Postludium 273

Abbreviations

AFLC	*Annali della facoltà di lettere filosofia e magistero della università di Cagliari.*
AHAW	*Abhandlungen der Heidelberger akademie der wissenschaften, Philosophie–Historie Klasse.*
AJP	*American Journal of Philology.*
ANF	The Ante-Nicene Fathers.
CQ	*Church Quarterly.*
CSCO	*Corpus scriptorum christianorum orientalium.*
FOTC	Fathers of the Church Series.
JECS	*Journal of Early Christian Studies.*
JTS	*Journal of Theological Studies.*
Pitra	*Iuris Ecclesiastici Graecorum Historia et Monumenta,* edited by Cardinal I.B. Pitra. Rome: Congregationis fidei typographia. Vol. 1: 1864; vol. 2: 1868.
RHEF	*Revue d'histoire de l'église de France.*
Rudder	*The Rudder (Pedalion) of the Holy Catholic and Apostolic Church.* Edited by Sts Nicodemus and Agapius. Athens: Nicolaides Press, 1908. English edn. by D. Cummings, tr. Chicago: Orthodox Educational Society, 1957; repr. New York: Luna Printing Co., 1983.
TU	*Texte und Untersuchungen.*

Fontes/Sources

W. Beveridge, ed. *Synodikon sive Pandectae Canonum.* 2 vols. Oxford. 1672. (Source of the Greek text in Agapius' and Nicodemos' *Rudder / Pedalion* above).

J. Darrouzes *Documents inédits d'ecclésiologie byzantine.* Paris: 1966.

F. Funk, ed. *Didascalia et Constitutiones Apostolorum.* 2 vols. Paderborn: 1905.

J. Girdley & A. Thompson *The Treatise on Laws: Gratian's Decretum DD 1–20.* Washington, D.C., 1993.

I.B. Pitra *Iuris Ecclesiastici Graecorum Historia et Monumenta.* Rome: Congregationis fidei typographia. Vol. 1: 1864; vol. 2: 1868.

Proemium

This is not a book on canon law, despite the appearances. It is not meant as such. Those who require a comprehensive manual of the Synods of the Eastern Church, or a full listing of all the canons, their practical applications, and deeper significances, will still require one having read this. Nevertheless, this is a book that reviews the ground of the legal thinking of the ancient Church, and then of the Medieval Eastern Church (for has not western canon law been interpreted so extensively that the ground is flattened enough?). I hope, and believe, that its review of these twin aspects (ancient and Byzantine) of much that makes up the Eastern Christian sense of the springs of Tradition in its formative stages will prove to the reader to be a substantive one. By that I mean that, while the book's purview is not totalist, it still sets out to offer a full and comprehensive review of the major streams of what constitute ancient and eastern Christian legal thinking.

It is not a book about canon law, however, and I would not describe myself as a canonist, a lawyer, or even a historian of law. It is probably a good thing to get that point in smartly before the reviewers get to it. I am, nevertheless, intrigued by a question that has increasingly agitated me over many decades of life as a theologian, an historian and a Byzantinist; and that is one of those great questions that seemed so rarely to be raised in all the voluminous literature that one processes in the course of a lifetime; accordingly, one of those great questions that never seem to be talked about much, despite (having once had them raised) being so great that they leave us wondering why they were never raised. It is such a question which pushed me to this book. The great question was, "To what extent did Christianity impact on Ancient Civilization?" We take for granted that the Church changed human society; and Christians would undoubtedly say, "for the better." But my question is more precise than that. It asks in what way did Christianity change the way that Civilization itself was thought about qualitatively? Did Christianity make life better?

Let us specify that one even more by adding: better for women? for slaves? for the poor and sick? Once we start asking these more specific levels of questions we can see our way out towards some kind of answer. It might be an answer that would demand many years of research in order to gather the necessary data and make more certain judgments, but at least one can see the way forward. If one were to ask what Christianity did for the poor, or the sick, one can raise the example of the socially innovative ways the Church sponsored health care programs in Late Antiquity and

Byzantine times; even being ready to strain the principles of monasticism[1] to do so. And soon enough, many examples of concrete instances could be brought together to argue the point that, for an eschatological religion, Christianity certainly did not neglect the present social fabric, but strove with great force to improve the lot of the wretched in many eras of its ascendancy. More than this, it left behind a considerable literature of philanthropy, relating that most fundamental Greek notion to the charter of its own Scriptures, its soteriological Christology, and its innermost spiritual praxis.

Great questions can thus break down when attacked discretely, as impregnable cities give way if a single gate is successfully breached. The great question agitating me: "What did Christianity do to build a Civilization?" was something that even after decades of work in ancient Christian studies I felt I did not have enough grasp on. But it struck me with some force that in this present age of ours, law has been used energetically to micro-manage human societies, human values and aspirations. If one looks across the face of the countries of the world and starts to sort countries in terms of adherence to the principle of law and rights, the principle of different conceptions of law, and the protections and freedoms the latter affords to citizens, then one can find one's ideas about degrees of contemporary levels of civilization among world societies being sharply enough focused. It became a pressing question for me, therefore, whether law worked that way in Antiquity. Of course the laws of ancient societies were not as codified as modern law, and in this book I have considered only the Law of Israel in small part, as it devolved into the canonical corpus of Christian Scripture, and Roman law, as it was transmuted into Christian Byzantine social polity. And, of course, there can be no direct comparison of past and present that does not limp. But even so, allowing for the many layers of "translating" that we are required to do in working with the past, could law be a window to the greater question of how the Christians first conceived of civilization, and how they set about managing the changes they wished to bring to it? This would be no less than the story of the "Rise of Christian Civilization," a book I would love to write, but which I think no single person could ever bring off successfully, so complex and multi-faceted would it be. But the question is, nonetheless, still so important that this latter scholarly cavil itself cannot be good enough excuse to shirk the task.

So this little book is some form of answer. It is a book on law and legal thought as it emerged in the formative ages of the Christian past. But it is not so much a

[1]Which was in many ways was defined at first as a flight from society, not a source of the chief labor for the main social welfare programs the Church offered. Further see: J.A. McGuckin, "Embodying the New Society: The Byzantine Christian Instinct of Philanthropy," in M. Pereira, ed., *Philanthropy and Social Compassion in Eastern Orthodox Tradition,* Papers of the Sophia Institute Academic Conference, December, 2009 (New York: Theotokos Press, 2010).

book of canon law as a book constantly asking what the ancient writers and theorists did with law and legal thought. It is part history, part philosophy, and, more than anything else, an introduction to issues of law and legal adjudication in the Patristic and Byzantine eras; for there are precious few such resources around reviewing the ancient and Eastern Church situation (as I discovered when I needed to access them).

I have picked up the stick of other scholars, skilled canonists, who, like lawyers throughout history, have shown themselves in their scholarly labors to be most precise, exact, and taxonomous. I might even be said to have "picked up their stick" where it was left in the lobby, perhaps "picked up" being a euphemism for "walked off with." If so, I crave their indulgence. For this is not a book on canon law; it is a book that wishes to mine the legal thinking of the Ancient and Byzantine Church in order to keep returning in a loop to the single overarching question: "How did Christianity build a Civilization?" What were the ideals and premises it worked from in relation to human value and ennoblement? The laws and the thinking they manifest are merely my grist. But in order to use them properly, I found I had to be taxonomous myself and set the story out coherently as best I could, in the best order I could manage. And for that reason I approached it historically in the main. As we progress through epochs described by the titles of the various chapters, which are trajectories, not straightforward chronological lines, we see a picture emerging.

It is my belief that the Christians did not set out with ready-made theories of what a civilization involved, but, nevertheless, made one that was most remarkable out of a constant and intelligent synthesis (a weighted and crafted synthesis, not merely a fudge or a mélange) of their scriptural charter and the social code they looked up to and admired: *Romanitas*, with its ideas of law, equity, protection and legitimate freedom. It was a civilization that had flesh and soul: an incarnate model that looked to its Incarnate Lord, whom it modeled, most pastorally, to a world with which it engaged both robustly and sympathetically. The moral and intellectual sophistication of the early Christians continues to impress me. The Byzantines explicitly claimed to have mastered *Romanitas* in an evangelical form (*Romaiosyne*) and pointed to their civilization as a world-model. That, of course, continues to inspire Orthodoxy today, and its shattered beauties can still enchant. But when so often we hear of European, Oceanic, and North American voices speaking of a "Post-Christian Culture," it is more than time to think sharply that if, indeed, Christianity has lost the tiller-hand on the making and inspiring of human cultural progress, how might it set about reclaiming the hearts and souls of the best and most educated of its societies, the culture-bearers, to whom we may offer Christ, yet again, as the goal and true *telos* of all that is good and true and beautiful in human society? It is my hope that this "mining exercise" of the legal thought of the early and

Eastern Church might provide some evidence for such a great moral and philosophical quest. This book, then, is a preliminary essay in the sources of Christian civilization building.

CHAPTER I

Gospel and Grace

Scriptural Foundations on Law, Authority, and the Exercise of Governance

Christianity as a religious and social system looks back constantly to the Holy Scriptures. It is today a cliché that these documents are its charter and perennial guide: first of all, the collation of those twenty-seven short books and letters that came to be designated as the "New Testament" (after Origen in the third century) and, secondly, that much larger and more ancient body of literature that the Christians, after the adoption of a New Testament, came to designate as the "Old" Testament, but which were previously known as the Law and the Prophets. The discussion of the rise of the canon of Scripture is not our concern here, but it may be useful to remark that the development of Christianity towards being a "religion of the book" was not a straightforward thing. We may note, in this regard, that there is no explicit reference to "the Scripture" in the whole of the New Testament that does not refer solely to the Law and the Prophets. In other words, the New Testament does not designate itself as "Scripture." Nor did the Church universally begin to see the two Testaments as a canonical collection until the middle of the fourth century. There were, certainly, "scriptural mentalities" strongly in evidence before that. All of the New Testament writings are deeply imbued with biblical thought, doctrine, and values, but there is no apparent single overriding orthodoxy of interpretation of the Scriptures. Almost all is left to presumption. If we look closely at the manner in which the Christians of the first two centuries used the biblical text, in citations and allusions, it is demonstrably random, by which I mean that the sacred text of the Law and Prophets is selectively sampled for short phrases to illustrate an argument, highlight a sermon, or give an authoritative, citable support for the author's statement.

This is basically a haggadic[1] rabbinic method that applies in most of the New Testament literature: the lifting up of an episode about Jesus or thought related to

[1]A term that derives from "telling the history" as a way of exegeting Scripture by narrating the sacred story in its reference to contemporary events. So, episodes of the People of God's story were explicitly paralleled with the sacred events from long past. The Jewish Exile is interpreted, for example, by looking back to the Exodus story (Psalms); or the sufferings of Jesus are interpreted by looking back to the story of the Suffering Servant in Isaiah (Matthew) or the sacrificial rites of the Temple (John).

him and the comparing of it explicitly to the prophetic literature in a way that says: "this is that."[2] Such a method of using the Old Testament can be called "proof-texting" and it dominates the early Church scene until the time of Origen of Alexandria, who placed biblical exegesis on a wholly new plane. Origen systematically followed three principles: first, he adopted the entire text of Law and Prophets and the Writings (including Psalms and Histories) as his definitive working canon; second, he subordinated this major collation to the authority and the interpretative lead of the Gospels and New Testament apostolic writings. Contrary though it was to chronological logic, Origen demanded that the meaning of the Hebraic Law was subordinate in both time and sense to the New Testament revelation (the meaning of time he implied was not *chronos*-time but *kairos,*[3] or eschatological time, God's process of acting which was not subject to created time);[4] and thirdly, he determined that all Christian truth was clarified by reference to the concept of biblical revelation running from the New Testament through the Old in an arc of wisdom that began in the Person of the Divine Logos and culminated in his Incarnation in time and space for the purpose of a wise pedagogy. Thus all scriptural truth had reference to the Logos (either pre-incarnate or incarnate) and was designed to lead all humankind to communion with the Logos. In this way, Origen's third hermeneutical principle[5] weaves together every text in Scripture, every verse almost, to a coherent and closely bonded "whole cloth" that all leads to the same source. Seeing the entire body of biblical texts as emanating ultimately from the same author (the Divine Logos), Origen was able to find a continuity and coherence here in a depth and degree that eluded the imagination of his predecessors. It is from his time onwards that it is possible to speak of a systematic Christian approach to the Bible. Before him, active as he was in the early and middle third century, we are in a more random position: looking at Christian authors who proof-text from the Hebrew Scriptures, or who set themselves at a distinct "angle" to it, if not in downright opposition. Marcion is one prime example of a Christian who wished to break radically with the Old Testament, refusing it any continuing validity in the Church. His "canon" was a small one that cut out all the Hebraic writings, and many of the New

[2]Brief examples may be the use of the Isaianic Suffering Servant texts to illustrate the Passion of the Lord (Mt 8.17, 12.15–21), or the application of the Jonah story to illustrate the three days of Jesus in the tomb (Mt 21.35; Acts 4.27, Mt 12.40).

[3]*Chronos* is the Greek word for sequential time; *kairos* is the New Testament theological word for "Time of Grace/Salvation."

[4]The numerous texts where he advances this argument can be seen collated together in the fourth century edition of his work by the Cappadocian Fathers Gregory and Basil, in the *Philocalia of Origen,* G. Lewis, tr. (Edinburgh: T.&T. Clark, 1911). Further see McGuckin (2003) and Idem (2004).

[5]He adopts a lot of other hermeneutical rules, such as always preferring to read the Scripture symbolically rather than literally; but these three major rules of his biblical philosophy set up the macro structure of his whole approach to what we mean today as Christian biblical theology.

Testament "Judaizing texts," which he regarded as unworthy of the Gospel of grace. Many others held positions at different angles of variance to the Hebrew Scripture. Paul is a prime example of someone deeply rooted in the Law of the Old Testament, yet also deeply ambivalent to it. One may speak of Christianity "fulfilling" the Law, thus validating it; but in an equal measure the concept of fulfillment usually connotes a profound element of abrogating the old. This deep ambivalence between affirmation and validation on the one side, and abrogation and supersession on the other side, is a tension that marks Christianity from the beginning, and is arguably still present today in Christianity's dealings with Judaism. After Origen,[6] the age of Scripture commentary begins.

Once we have this Origenian, more systematized, approach, the body of texts begins to be rapidly "canonized," that is, drawn up into lists of authorized and authoritatively received books. The books that were read (and a large body of literature that was not canonical continued to be read by Christian intellectuals[7] for several centuries to come) were really books that were "heard" in the worship services of the early Church. It is in Irenaeus of Lyons' *Adversus Haereses* that we first see this system being coherently argued by an episcopal theologian of the second century. It is this decision (which literature shall be read out at the Eucharist and prayer gatherings for the assembled faithful) which really determines the canon of Scripture in the second and third centuries. It is a formative principle over which the bishops, those earliest presidents of the assembly of prayer, have a determining role. We shall see their hand in almost every Christian development from now on, in relation to the shaping of the Christian discipline. To that extent they are the constant engine of the "rise of law" in the body of the early Church. But, before law can emerge as specific "laws" (the term that will be preferred among the Church is "canons" or rules of discipline), first we need to consider the fundamentals: how law itself was conceived of philosophically. And at the outset there remained much ambivalence among the Christians, especially as the Gentile population of the early Church started to outweigh the Jewish members, as to the abiding significance among them of the notion of "The Law," namely the Torah.

Was the Torah, considered as a sacred system of law, directing large and small matters of daily and religious life, still applicable in the Church? Although there is some indication that Christian communities living in the Decapolis region,[8] Jerusalem, Caesarea Palestina, and parts of Alexandria, regarded themselves as bound by the observance of the Law, there is also abundant evidence that Gentile

[6]Strictly speaking, just before him; for the first writer of biblical commentary we know is Heracleon a gnostic Valentinian teacher, whom Origen preserves in the process of taking to task.

[7]Not a large body by any means in an ancient society where illiteracy was the norm.

[8]Modern Jordan.

Christians of the late first century did not feel that this was an inevitable aspect of the acceptance of the Christian religion. And this despite such texts as Matthew 5.17–19 which was one of the most strenuous attempts (of the Antiochene Church in the late first century) to get the Gentile Christians to take the Torah seriously. Paul is one of those early preachers who declared that the experience of Jesus was also a liberation from the Law. Matthew 5.17–19 is a saying of Jesus, very heavily redacted so as to attack the spread of Pauline attitudes to Torah among the Gentile Christians. His Letters to the Galatians and to the Romans set out his policy on this[9] in a context where there is much controversy between those established Churches, especially in Jerusalem, which see him as something of a libertarian innovationist. The sharp conflict evidenced in his Letters (we do not have a corresponding document preserved[10] representing those who apostolically argued the contrary side: that the Law remains valid forever) reflects the conditions of the second half of the first century. By the time the Gospels are written (using historical materials deriving from Jesus that predate the apostolic letters, but composed in a time subsequent to them) we see the argument has already been won by those who see a distinctive break with the tradition of Torah in the person of Jesus the Savior.

Mark's Gospel, which is imbued with Pauline thought, takes every opportunity to present Jesus as someone who opposes the "rigidity" of the Jewish Law, with the flexibility of a new law of the Spirit, one which places the highest premium on the intentions of the heart. Small instances (for Jesus himself was undoubtedly an attentive observer of the Law in the spirit of the prophetic tradition of renewing the Torah[11]) are elevated in the Gospel as examples, or proofs, that Jesus had given his blessing to the Gentile Christian liberation from the prescripts of the "Old Testament" Torah.[12] Large sections of Matthew's Gospel also (which we may locate in the great Church of Syrian Antioch in the late first century in a context where this argument over the perennial validity of the Torah was still heated) set up the Pharisees as a target to knock down in the cause of demonstrating the Christian manner of departing from the Law in the cause of instituting a new philosophy of law.[13] The old law of external observances is here contrasted with a new spirit of seeking the inner intentionality of law: access to God's will and the implementation of behav-

[9]Rom 3.20 gives the *ethos*: "For no human being will be justified in his sight by works of the law."

[10]Which is a telling fact in itself.

[11]See, for example, B. Chilton, *A Galilean Rabbi and His Bible* (Wilmington, DE: M. Glazier, 1984).

[12]Consider for example, the sayings of Jesus about Torah observance and how they are used by the evangelist in Mk 2.23–28; 3. 1–6; 7. 1–23. In each instance Jesus is presented as rewriting the code for a more liberal interpretation. In Mk 10.2–12, he is presented as rewriting it in a stricter direction. In all instances John's Gospel sees Jesus as "greater than" the lawgiver Moses (Jn 1.17 & 5.46), just as Matthew presents him as far greater than the Law administrator Solomon (Mt 12.42).

[13]See for example Mt 23.

ior that is acceptable. This was a strong element of Jesus' original teachings about the right-interpretation of the Torah (the prophetic call to renew the observance of the Law in a heart-centered way) but in the Church of the first century it became a strong movement to call for a radical reconstitution of the Torah, giving primacy to the *scholia* of Jesus himself as collected now in the Gospel texts, affording him a far higher status as Law-Giver than Moses. Never was a personal pronoun given such emphatic and symbolic force as in the use of "your" in John 10.34: "And Jesus said to them, "Is it not written in your Law . . ."

What this amounts to, of course is a complex relationship in the Christian Church to biblical law: the Torah is simultaneously offering paradigms of behavior even for those who heavily restrict its legal range and applicability within the Church. It is not an abrogation of the Law that is actually taking place here, but a radical renovation of the Law by those who felt empowered to compose a new constitutional arrangement of it. So, although Christianity is very different indeed from Second Temple Judaism, differing precisely in its attitude to Torah observance, it in some real sense retains a claim to be an heir of Judaism, a new iteration of it albeit one that has effectively rewritten the Law. Theologically expressed, this meant that the Christians claimed that Jesus was the heart and center of all law: its Alpha and Omega.[14] One discerns in all the proto-Christian literature this radical Christocentricity as an explanation of why the Christians rewrote the concept of Torah, and also how they did so. It is a theme that accelerates and deepens into the Second Century and beyond. In short, the Church elevates Jesus as its Lawgiver in preference to Moses. As Paul put it dramatically: "The Law was our pedagogue until Christ came, that we might be justified by faith."[15] The Mosaic Torah remains as a paradigmatic guide, but two things of crucial importance happen in this earliest era: first of all, a major distinction is made by the Christians between the ceremonial elements of the Law (liturgical rules and food regulations and such like) and its moral prescripts. The moral laws are held by the Church to be still in force, if not always literally prescriptive then symbolically so (exegesis in the hands of the Christians always seeks to interpret the moral laws "spiritually" and "pastorally").[16] The ceremonial aspects, however, were widely regarded as being abrogated. So it was, from very early times, that Christians ceased observing the Sabbath, stopped the observance of kosher food laws, abandoned circumcision, and denied the ethno-centric principle of belonging to the "People of God." A new constitutional system was in process of

[14]Rom 10:4: "For Christ is the end of the law, that everyone who has faith may be justified."

[15]Gal 3.24.

[16]In other words, throughout history it has only been the real "dummies" who have thought that texts such as the Conquest of the Holy Land by Joshua's armies give a moral legitimation to "holy war," or that sinners ought to be stoned or such like. Sadly there have been, and still are, a good number of "dummies."

elaboration, rooted in the scriptural principle, devolved from it, but developing out of a new compass setting. This brings us to the second development: that the Gospels are, from the moment of their appearance, given priority. The sayings and deeds of Jesus become the highest authority for the Church (Irenaeus and Origen are the prime examples of this system in its full flowering after the second and third centuries) and all the Scriptures of Israel are interpreted Christocentrically.

Christ is indeed the "New Constitution." But since his collected sayings were either in the nature of *scholia* on the Torah, or morally pointed parabolic stories, they did not amount to any elaborated or complete rewriting of a code of law, either in reference to a New Torah, or in reference to any all-embracing code of legal conduct for the incipient Church; and so it was that the Christians in adopting the Christocentric principle gave a high precedence to the concept of the *phronema Christou* (the "mindset of Christ"; see 1 Cor 2.16) as manifested not only in his sayings but also in his deeds, his attitudes, and the *energeia* of his resurrected presence among the living body of believers. This stress on the resurrected presence of Christ remaining in his Church is high in the theological thought of St Paul, and remains a primary principle of how the Church (considered as Christ's *qahal,* or *ekklesia,* his corporate representation in history) senses itself to be endowed with the authority (*exousia*) of Jesus as a living and ongoing principle,[17] not merely a dead reference to a body of literature. In this it follows not only a spiritual aspiration (seeking the mind and spirit of Christ in the ongoing life of the Church) but also a specifically Aristotelian principle in relation to the interpretation of law: that the "mind of the Lawgiver" must be consulted in all matters of legal interpretation and development of first principles.[18]

All of this highly complex re-positioning of the early Church in relation to a philosophy of law (how it stood with relation to the Torah, but also how it understood the rule of law in its own life) was already emerging in the writings of the first century. It is present in the Gospels which give further impetus to the development of the idea in post-second-century patristic writing. But the earliest iteration of the new Christian positioning to the idea of law can also be seen developing in the later New Testament epistolary literature. From early times this has been assigned to St Paul as part of his "apostolic canon within the canon." Modern scholarship now generally places it as posterior to Paul, written after Paul's death and pseudepigraphically assigned to the name of the apostle. And thus it assigns it to a circle of Pauline Christian Churches that are starting to elaborate, quite explicitly, rules of behavior for their members, and, in so doing, laying down guidelines about the authority of their com-

[17]Understood in the early Church as the *Paradosis* (Living Tradition). See Florovsky (1972); McGuckin (1998).

[18]Aristotle, *Rhetoric,* 1.13.

munal officers. It is within this literature first of all (soon resumed in the literature of the so-called Apostolic Fathers which is very close to this late New Testament literature in both spirit and time)[19] that the Christians begin the explicit reflection on the role of law, in the wider sense of the meaning of that term, in their own communities. By that "wider sense," I mean the concept that "the rule of law" as a philosophical notion involving theories of community responsibility and representation, agreed standards, and systems of maintenance for those standards: in other words, a *politeia* governed and protected by laws. This reflection has a double interest in so far as it emerges at a time when the Churches are first attracting the hostile interest of the wider powers of law and order, which are soon bent on the annihilation of the communities under terms of specific Roman laws of "proscription." By starting to reflect on the position of law in the community, this is not to say the first Christians had an already expansive or even systematic position, nor even a consistent view of what might develop in the future. It was difficult, perhaps, for an apocalyptic movement of the late first and early second centuries, even to imagine that within two short centuries the communities would emerge as the leaders of a new empire. To have told any writer of the New Testament that the icon of the Lord would be set up in the imperial palace would have drawn out merely disbelieving laughter. The speed of the social ascent of the Church left many intellective-theoretic structures needing to be hastily assembled.[20] It is precisely for this reason that reflection on the state of law in the systems of the Church accelerates markedly after the fourth century, but the foundations are already there in the charter Scriptures.

1 Timothy and the Letter to Titus are the most interesting indicators of the Pauline communities establishing structures of legal guidance. They probably date from the late first century, and thus overlap chronologically with the earliest patristic literature, as emerging from such writers as Clement of Rome, the author of the Shepherd of Hermas, and Ignatius of Antioch; texts that also bear out much of what we see in the embryonic Deutero-Pauline texts. The letters seek the authority of Paul (as himself constituted an authoritative Apostle by Jesus)[21] and then get to the main point: the *episkopoi* of the communities are established as definitive preachers of the Jesus tradition[22] and as the overseers of church discipline. The Greek word itself

[19]Which we shall discuss in chapter three following.

[20]For example, what was Christianity's position on the legitimacy of warfare (only necessary when the Church is required to advise emperors)? Or what is the Church's attitude to secular/pagan culture (only necessary when the Church possesses resources to found institutes of education)?

[21]1 Tim 1.1–3; Titus 1.1–4.

[22]1 Tim 1.3–4 "Insist that certain people stop teaching strange doctrines . . . " Titus 1.10. "You have in your community a great many people who need to be disciplined, who are spouting nonsense and trying to make others believe in it; especially among the party of the circumcision. They must be silenced; for men like this ruin whole families teaching things they ought not to."

means "overseer," or president of a community. The Churches must have such officers to control doctrine and moral *praxis*.[23] The *episkopos* will evolve into the fully developed role and office of the Christian bishop. Both letters already show the elaboration of the threefold office of the priesthood (bishop, presbyter, deacon). So the story of the ascent of law begins in Christian textuality with the elaboration of liturgical officers. The concept of that "neo-apostolic" authority underpins the very notion of "Christian legality." It is clear from 1 Timothy that a considerable problem exists with teachers who claim to represent the Law and stand as "doctors of the Law," that is Jewish theologians who make definitive claims out of the basis of scriptural exegesis. The author(s) of the letters has no patience with them: "They claim to be doctors of the Law but they understand neither the arguments they apply, nor the opinions they defend."[24] The argument then makes a turn that for the first time, perhaps, shows the awareness that arguments about the Torah-Law, also have to be contextualized in terms of law in general:

> We know of course that the Law is a good thing, but only in so far as it is treated like any law; namely with the understanding that laws are not framed for good people, but on the contrary are for criminals and revolutionaries, for the irreligious and for the wicked; for the sacrilegious and the irreverent; for killers of their own fathers and mothers and other murderers; for those who commit immorality with women, or with boys or men; they are for liars and perjurers, and for everything else that is contrary to the sound teaching that accompanies the Good News of the glory of the Blessed God, that Gospel which was entrusted to me.[25]

This very early text demonstrates all the ambivalence towards law that there can be in the community. The sense is prevalent here that the ethic of the Spirit in the early Churches elevates the faithful above the radar of "ordinary law." The author seems to make his point tellingly, that "ordinary law" includes both the Roman legislation and the Jewish Law (Torah) in so far as they are both external systems meant to influence the behavior of people who need a law to regulate them. By putting together the Torah with the Roman penal legislation (texts that have relevance only for the dregs of society), the author is tarring the reputation of the Torah in the face of those who have (presumably) been arguing for its ascendancy in Christian communities. So far then the argument is "anomic" in spirit. But the author's context also clearly points to the need within the community for clearer patterns of gov-

[23]Titus 1.5–6. Elders (*presbyteroi*) must be established in every town to govern each community, under the superintendence of the overseers (*episkopoi*): the basic pattern of bishop and priest, to which number the diaconates (*diakonoi*) supply the third level, focused on practical (rather than didactic) ministry.

[24]1 Tim 1.7.

[25]1 Tim 1.8–11.

ernment: definitive answers to end disturbing speculations. To this extent the author calls for a strong community law, and is highly "nomic." The ambivalence towards law, therefore, is merely a rhetorical one. From the outset, the late epistles show the strong affirmation of the so-called "Household Code" of the late empire: an amalgam of civic virtue as derived from social *mores* (women to behave quietly and remain in the domestic context, men to behave honorably and seek community peace in the public forum) and scriptural injunctions to behave in a gracious and prayerful way. The scriptural version of the Household Code made a distinct new edition of the principles of common ethics in Greco-Roman Late Antiquity, but it would have been commonly recognized by many "God-fearers" who were neither Jews nor Christians in that period, and makes for some difficulty in telling apart the literature of Synagogue and Church in the first two centuries. It is within this literature that the Christian Church first starts being called the "Household of God."[26]

The Household Code lays great stress on obedience, conformity and peace. It is partially explicable that the Church should at first wish to endorse this[27] because of the external circumstances. They sensed a wave of barely concealed hostility, a wave that would break over them soon enough in the form of public imperially sponsored persecutions. In such times it is better to keep one's head down. 1 Timothy wishes to restrict the role of Christian women teachers.[28] It is the first in a long line of texts that restrict the roles and offices of women in the Church. It is also evidence, of course, that such roles had burgeoned in the earliest times, and would continue to play a massive role in the development of the Christian Church from antiquity to the present. Whether acknowledged[29] or not, the force of women's involvement in Christianity was a remarkable reversal of Hellenistic social attitudes, attitudes the author of 1 Timothy is worried that his communities are provocatively flaunting. He wants conformity and avoidance of controversy wherever this can be managed: "Remind them all that it is their duty to be obedient to the officials and representa-

[26]In echo of the title of the Temple (Gen 28.17; 1 Chron 9.13 & passim). See 1 Tim 3.15; Heb 10.21; 1 Pet 4.17; Eph 2.19.

[27]Even to the extent of advising Christian slaves in the name of Christ: "Tell the slaves to be obedient to their masters and always do what they want without any argument, without any petty thieving. So that they will be in every way a credit to the teaching of God our Savior" (Titus. 2. 9–10). The author is being disingenuous, for the sake of a general low profile for the community. However detached he may have been from Gentile secular culture of his own age, he cannot fail to have known of the massive extent of the sexual abuse of slaves that went on, on a daily basis, in the late empire. To have made the moral case that slaves in such an environment ought to respond merely by observing the niceties of personal property ownership (no petty thieving) is an extraordinary "lacuna" of moral statement that would take centuries for Christianity to redress.

[28]1 Tim 2.9–15; Titus 2.2–6.

[29]In the formal female offices of deaconess, widow, virgin, catechist, and teacher.

tives of the government."[30] It was an increasingly difficult *encomium* when the Church soon began to look on those very officials as murderous pagans.

Deacons have to be responsible men, not drunkards; men whom the outside community can look up to.[31] The president of the assembly has to be a good household manager, kindly, a good teacher, and not married more than once.[32] He ought to be an impeccable standard of good example both to those in and outside of his community. The letters also start to lay down a code of specifics (the real birth of Christian canon law) in so far as they begin to legislate for perceived (and real) problems of good order. Bishops must deal with the young women of the communities with a great sense of discretion, behaving towards them as they would towards their sisters.[33] They have to discern which of the widows they have responsibility for financially, which one is a "real widow" (he means which one has dedicated herself to a life of renewed prayer after her bereavement and has thus assumed a semi-official status within the proto-clerical ranks). If problems arise and the leader falls under suspicion he must be investigated. But then rules of admission of evidence must be enforced: "Never accept any accusation brought against an Elder unless it is supported by two or three witnesses. If any are at fault, then reprimand them publicly as a warning to the rest."[34] Here the Greek code of "honor and shame" is very much to the fore, but it is also evident that in seeking one of the earliest formulations of canonical process, the Church has turned for explicit guidance to the Jewish Law, for the admonition to seek two or three witnesses is lifted directly from Deuteronomy 19.15.

Yet, much of what we see here is most likely a creative synthesis of the rules of good order operative in several of the more dignified "associations" of the Greco-Roman world, with biblical injunctions and moral prescripts. The crucible for this fusion was, in all probability, the earliest Christian Eucharist: the context of the gatherings for the communal meals where doctrine was preached, socializing was in full force, supportive pensions were distributed under the supervision of the clerical officers; and the notion of "good order," societally speaking, was most intimately connected with the spiritual and theological conceptions of the indwelling presence of the Risen Christ in the Elect Community. It is an interesting mix: from the very beginning a synthesis of Greco-Roman legal ideas with biblical paradigms; and, above all, a particular Christian genius for immediate practical effectiveness. It is this seedling (of detailed reflection on proper social *mores*) which will very soon grow

[30]Titus 3.1.
[31]1 Tim 3.8–13.
[32]1 Tim 3.1–7; Titus 1. 6–9.
[33]1 Tim 5.2.
[34]1 Tim 5.19.

into a great tree of Christian legal reflection, always showing the same kind of constitutive principles: a synthesis of Greco-Roman legal philosophy, biblical paradigms symbolically interpreted, an immensely practical desire for the guidance of real-world communities under a high moral imperative. This is what the first glimmerings of thought about Christian legislative thought show us (as distinct from extensive arguments about Torah), and what will always be characteristic of a more abstract Christian philosophy of law in later times. In the various elements of this synthesis, Christianity thus emerges as a religion with its eyes firmly fixed on society: a religion that has definite social aspirations despite its claims to be the eschatological community. It is a religion that wishes to build a civilization, not one that is simply running to hide itself. Even if it has "seen" the New Jerusalem in another place, that very radiant vision makes the Church see the earthly city in a new light; and long before Augustine divides the heavenly Jerusalem and the Earthly City into two radically separate camps in western Christian thought, that proximity between what is aspired to as the ideal *politeia* and what is presently experienced forms a tension that drives so much of eastern Christian political theology. In no more than two centuries from this time, Christianity will assume charge of the whole empire of the Romans. Even before that dramatic ascent to power in the course of the fourth century Roman Civil War, however, Christians had long been reading the laws of the Greeks and Romans.

Further Reading

G. Florovsky. *Bible Church and Tradition: An Eastern Orthodox View.* Belmont, MA: Nordland, 1972.

R.A. Horsley, ed. *Christian Origins.* Minneapolis, MN: Fortress Press, 2005.

L.T. Johnson. "Law in Early Christianity." In J. Witte Jr. & F.S. Alexander. *Christianity and Law.* Cambridge Univ. Press, 2008: 53–69.

J.A. McGuckin. "Eschaton and Kerygma: The Future of the Past in the Present Kairos: The Concept of Living Tradition in Orthodox Theology." *St Vladimir's Theological Quarterly* 42.3–4 (1998): 225–271.

______. "Origen as Literary Critic in the Alexandrian Tradition." In L. Perrone, ed. *Origeniana Octava.* Leuven: Peeters, 2003: 121–135.

______, ed. *The Westminster Handbook to Origen of Alexandria.* Louisville, KY: Westminster John Knox Press, 2004.

A.N. Sherwin-White. *Roman Society and Roman Law in the New Testament.* Oxford: The Clarendon Press, 1963.

D.M. Derrett. *Law in the New Testament.* London: Darton, Longman & Todd, 1970.

CHAPTER 2

Classical Foundations of Reflection on Law and Polity

Greek Philosophical Reflection on Political Order

Western Christian imagination is very used to the concept of the "Two Cities" as a basic framework for approaching political theology. The writing of Augustine tends to channel the mind and its presumption of possibilities in a dominating way. His corpus never served as a lightning rod for political thought in the Eastern Christian world, however, where he remained a wholly unknown force until the high Middle Ages, and was even then a deeply marginalized theologian for all but a very few of the leading intellectuals of the Byzantine world. In the Greek Christian world, and for most of Byzantium, the Two Cities was a concept that would send their imagination straight back to the classical roots predating Christian civilization and present to their minds the powerfully formative influence of the greatest of the philosophers who shaped Byzantine Christian political thought: namely Plato and Aristotle. Both men presented significantly different, deliberately juxtaposed, theories of the political order that, by Christian times, had become the staple of the higher schools of learning, and were expected reading in the educational curricula of all learned rhetoricians. The Two Cities, as each of the philosophers delineates them, with their considerable variance and mutual tension, meant that political theology in the Eastern Christian world would be born from a polarity that was foundational; a tensile and very different origin indeed from that of the post-Augustinian West. From the outset the social consideration of polity was a shared substrate for Christian and non-Christian intelligentsia and politicians. Whether they were arguing or agreeing over interpretations of this substrate (and the different moral constructs operating between the Church and the Hellenistic Philosophical tradition often came into sharp conflict), all sides knew they were more or less on the same page of base text, and shared a common language. It is partly because of these intellectual roots that Byzantine Church polity, although often caricatured by those who have not read widely in it[1] as stiffly hieratic and mono-dimensional in its allegedly caesaro-papist supineness, is actually

[1]The caesaro-papist caricature emanates from the highly prejudiced readings of a narrow band of sources popularized by Gibbon's *Decline and Fall of the Roman Empire*. Such a reading is also very narrowly based upon

fluid and intellectually dynamic in ways that have rarely been appreciated. To understand it fully, one needs to recognize that all of the classically trained Byzantine theologians (most of the great fathers after the fourth century anyway) are developing their thoughts on political theology as extended variations on the themes presented by Plato and Aristotle. They are now, as Christian theorists, joining in the great ancient debate first started by the two seminal philosophers, and long continued in the schools. Seeing themselves precisely as the Christians inheritors of the Hellenistic tradition, it was their concern to continue the ongoing development of classical culture, though now in an evangelically colored set of *scholia*. Byzantine polity, therefore, cannot be exegeted properly until one appreciates the agendas of Plato and Aristotle, and how they were in tension from the very beginning.

Plato's City

Plato's political philosophy represented a major addressing of the issue of justice's place in the body politic for ancient society, and on into the Byzantine Christian age. It is a predominant theme of *The Republic*. The treatise, written in his mature years, has the double title in the manuscript of: "The State, or Concerning Justice." It is in this treatise that Plato sets the determining coordinates of most ancient political philosophy, for he argues that the law is more than the sum of jurisprudence and the state is more than the sum of political acts, for both are subsumed under the notion of a metaphysically conceived anthropology. Barker synopsizes this fundamental orientation of Plato's as follows: "(*The Republic*) is an attempt at a complete philosophy of Man. It deals, as it were, with the physiology and pathology of the human soul in its environment. It is primarily concerned with man *in action*, and is therefore occupied with the problems of moral and political life."[2] It is this unifying principle that explains for the modern reader an apparent disparity of the subjects treated in the work: an initial discourse on metaphysics that argues the fundamental unity of all things in the Idea of the Good; then a discussion on moral philosophy and the soul's virtues which culminates in the ideal of justice in society; then a consideration of education understood as moral training; and lastly a discussion on government and laws that are appropriate to the ideal state. This final section gives special emphasis to laws on property and marriage. The overarching tone, and intellectual concern, of *The Republic* is the issue of how a person

one or two sources (Eusebius's fulsome rhetoric celebrating Constantine's Vicennalia, or Justinian's state edicts. The wider picture is rarely sought. The Gibbonesque parody is, nevertheless, regularly regurgitated. Its racist and colonialist undertones are discussed in: J.A. McGuckin, "Orthodoxy and Western Christianity: The Original European Culture War?" in V. Hotchkiss & P. Henry, eds., *Orthodoxy and Western Culture* (Festschrift for Jaroslav Pelikan at 80) (Crestwood, NY: St Vladimir's Seminary Press, 2005), pp. 85–107.

[2]Barker (1959), p. 81.

can be made good. For us moderns this would tend to resolve it into a discourse on moral philosophy. But the ancient Greeks did not share our immediate instinct that morality was first and foremost an interior matter of conscience, but rather took it for granted that the ultimate force in moral training would be Society; and since every individual "mattered" as an individual only in so far as he[3] was a citizen of the state, then the education of Everyman into the good was a basic building block of the ideal state: the stuff of politics. The common agreement on the nature of the good (a metaphysical concern) was therefore just as important as establishing the agreed laws (a political concern) that aided the training and obedience of the citizens (a moral and educational goal). If one of the unnerving aspects of the ancient Greek approach to this is the envisaging of the human being as an element of the state,[4] it can be remembered that there is a correspondingly "humanist" counterbalance, in the way the theory of the state always tends to treat it as a moral entity.

This collectivist tendency shows itself clearly in most of Plato's thought, and runs on in the Byzantine settlement, although it should be noted that Christian theory repristinates the value of the individual as such, more than ancient Greek thought could ever do. Even so, the individualist basis of political theory had been tried by the ancient Greeks. It was descriptive of the Sophists, as Plato reads them, and their explanation of social power, as he gives it in a very critical way in *The Republic*,[5] was that the leaders of the state organized matters for the sake of their own advantage. For Plato the corruption of the state lay in the tendency of rulers to subject it to their own desires and advantages. True politics was the opposite: when the individual subjected his own desires to the service of the good of the whole. It is a core apologetic in *The Republic* that the spirit of subordinating common order to individual desire (politics as the tale of self-interest seizing power and maintaining privilege) will never work or endure for long because the laws that sustain just human relations are not merely conventional ones (subject to revision by any powerful group that wishes to extend its power base) but are rather fundamentally grounded in the nature of the human soul, and the intimate structure of the universe. To this extent Plato's idealism in metaphysics (the Ideal Good is the patterning and *Eros* of all visible good) is once again revealed as the substrate of his social theory, and one can see how, in his mind anyway, Plato's abstractions were not sim-

[3]And it did largely mean "he" in Classical Greek thought.

[4]Greek antique thought does not yet have a word for the person as individual psychic subject. It will be the efforts of the Christian philosophers, through the exigencies of the great Christological debates of the fifth century A.D., that will first bring the idea of the integral and essential "person" (*prosopon, hypostasis*) into play as a solid factor in psychic subjectivity.

[5]One device for this is to make the speaker Thrasymachus in *The Republic* the figure of a leading Sophist, and to caricature him as a dim and comic figure.

ply the panglossian[6] musings of a hopelessly disconnected academic, but were stimulated at every instance by highly practical aspirations for shaping society in particular ways, and for a theory that would strongly underpin variable human customs, with universal laws and principles of justice.

His thinking rose directly out of political passions he himself entertained. His mentor, Socrates, had been publicly rejected and executed by the Athenian state. How could democracy, governance supposedly by the will and instinct of the people, be so misled? And if the people's instinct for the good was so aberrant, how could it ever be repaired? Plato's sense of annoyance with contemporary politics is often felt in the pages of *The Republic*. He diagnosed the essential political problem of his time as twofold: first, the ignorance of the political leaders who could not tell right from wrong, or what was truly desirable in the governance of the state from what was merely short term expedient; secondly, the tendency in political organization to divide the whole up into separate sections of particular interest, and then to set these interest groups up in opposition to one another. The warring factions played into the hands of powerful rulers who would use them and their disharmony to advance the selfish interests of a small minority at the expense of the majority. In this way he diagnosed ignorance, and factionalism, as the two great diseases. His cure was to demand professionalism (the philosopher had to assume duties of philosophical governance) and harmony in all matters relating to the state. It is to the defense of these two supreme ends that *The Republic's* arguments always tend to turn, and to which the lesser arguments, examples and requirements of the treatise (commonality of wives, communistic ownership for example) are subordinated.

Plato's hostility to the level of ignorance that was characteristic of Athenian democracy in his day was translated to a wholesale opposition to the principle of "casting the lot" to administer state democracy. This was not simply a bad way to organize the allocation of authority he thought (a way to ensure that the least experienced might rise to the exercise of power),[7] but more than this it rankled with Plato as an inherent injustice. His global idea of justice was that each individual in the social whole ought to do that level of work which was most fitting for their talent and their virtue. The cobbler is a lowly craftsman.[8] It was not right for such a man

[6]The "head in the clouds" caricature of Leibniz whom Voltaire uses as his comic stooge philosopher in *Candide*.

[7]An annoyance if the local cobbler became a demagogue and swayed people from the correct path by his barrack-room arguments; but a fatality if the high offices of the state, such as leading the armies, were to be laid in the hands of such a man who then might go out incompetently to meet the professional generals of world empires. *Strategoi* (generals), therefore, were not popularly chosen by lot, but were advanced by public election campaign to ensure a short-list only of the competent. See C. Hignett, *A History of the Athenian Constitution to the end of the 5th Century B.C.*. (1952), p. 227.

[8]Behind the ranking value judgment lies the endemic ancient Greek pre-supposition that the more

to assume governance. In doing so he committed a doubly unjust deed: first in not doing his own work and neglecting his proper function in society, and then also in preventing the properly qualified man (the better man) from doing his work (governance) which he had meddled with by his unqualified seeking of office. This desire to see rule only by the wisest and the best is the chief reason why, for many subsequent theorists, Aristotle included, Plato emerged from his cantankerous diatribe not simply as an enemy of amateurism, but as actually straying into the domain of becoming, himself, an enemy of the open society. As Barker puts it succinctly: "The mistake of Plato was, that in his eagerness to deprive the masses of the right of government itself, he wrested from them the also the right of making the government, which must, as Aristotle afterward argued, in the name alike of expediency and justice, be given into their hands."[9]

Plato is also hostile to the concept of dividing the body politic into warring factions of opposed interests. So much has this spread, he complains, that each city is really two cities: the ruling minority and the ruled majority of the poorer elements. Each body is pitted against the other, and their endless strife ensures that politics runs like an engine of a constant seeking of the selfish interests of whatever faction can gain precedence. The rich used their status to advance depredations on the poor and, when the poor came into prominence, they occasionally attacked the wealthy in the form of oppressive levies (leitourgia or "liturgies") which at times were little more than wealth re-distributions that occasioned civil strife and even civil war, as political office was sought for self-protection and self-advancement.[10]

Plato's Theory of Justice

To resolve these corruptions of the body politic, Plato prescribed professional focus to overcome ignorant lack of specialization. Sparta had already impressed the wider Greek mind by its apparently successful dedication to the principle of specialization in military matters. Plato suggested that society itself should be divided into three classes of men: rulers, warriors, and farmers. Thereupon in his thought he more or less entirely forgets about the third section. The creation and maintenance of the first

lowly working classes are less than human in comparison with those who do not need to work, but can develop their minds by philosophic discourses and, as the "best," ought to have the ruling of the society as their natural function in life. The combination of the word for "best" and the world for "rule," in Greek, gave to the world the term and idea of "aristocracy." It was widespread in ancient Greek philosophical thought, as a corollary of this, that slaves and women barely ranked as human beings at all. The widely vaunted concept of Greek democracy meant, always, the vote by free wealth-owning male citizens alone. It was a political theory that demanded a significant slave population, fuelling production, on which it could stand.

[9]Barker (1959) 89.

[10]*The Republic* 521A.

two are his interest and concern: the political administrators, and the professional army on which they depend and which they must direct. To sustain this idea (what has historically turned out to be a blueprint for totalitarianism as much as any vaunted utopianism) Plato insists that education is the key factor. The state must dedicate great attention and resources to the formation of the ruling class and to their mentality and the concept of duty to which they will give their lifelong allegiance.[11] In support of this formative ethos, he argued the need for a communistic agreement at the heart of the society of rulers or "guardians." The guardians must be deprived of the ability to own property individually. All must be held in common, even wives, homes, and children. Then the temptation for a ruler to use power for his own advancement (rather than the common weal) would be removed. The entire purpose and goal (*telos*) of the education of the guardians would be to instill this sense that the good of the many is the good of the one. The different classes, by staying within their own bounds, would also, on this theory, remove the potential for internal social strife by ending that history of politics where each party sought to advance its own concerns against the other and use the concept of governance as a tool for selfish ends. The harmony of the whole system hung on the training of the guardians, so that no selfishness was allowed to enter into the governance of the ruling class, but because of their disciplined training, they constantly sought after the commonweal in all that they commanded, and constantly "saw"the true balance in society, that others with more self-interested perspective, were prevented from seeing clearly.

"Seeing" is thus a central notion for Plato's entire political thought. It is not just a matter of observation or contemplation; it involves action. It is the balanced relation of seeing truly, and thus acting wisely (justly) which is the whole *energeia* of the political system for Plato. This is why all his social thought emerges so directly from his basic understanding of philosophy as a doctrine of the formation of the soul. The line of development can be drawn exactly from his adoption of the "principle of specialization" in order to highlight the manner in which the system coheres around the concept of justice at the core:

> Beginning as it were dimly with the principle of specialization, Plato throws fresh lights on its meaning, until finally, in the blaze of the "Idea of the Good," we realize that in specialization only is Justice to be found, for Justice, being seen, is nothing more and nothing less than man's performance of the part which the purpose of the world demands that he shall play.[12]

[11]This is why pedagogical theory forms such a significant element of *The Republic*. Further see: Barker (1959) 119–137.

[12]Barker (1959) 94.

It does not diminish its political directness, therefore, to describe Plato's view of society as primarily a "psychological" one. The care of the soul is the most important good for any being; and the goal of the just society is to enable that goal to be fulfilled in common. He even takes his threefold division of the social classes from his operative taxonomy of the Soul.[13] For Plato, states are not products like inanimate things, they are extensions of the moral character of the souls that comprise them: "States do not emerge from an oak tree or a rock," he says, "but from the characters of the men that dwell within them."[14] True discernment, exercised in common by those who have been most prepared to recognize it, leads to wise judgment and just action. All in society are to be convinced, by whatever way they need to learn conviction, of what wisdom and justice are. It is self-evident, for Plato, that the guardians of society must embody wisdom and justice, before dispensing it in their rule, if the social fabric is to function.

The taxonomy of values inherent here, this interior and moral psychology that he sketches out, and to which he gives a wonderfully expansive intellectual vista, is one of Plato's great historical achievements. He sets out an ethical foundation to political theory. He basically discerns that the institutions of the State, its organs of justice and correction, its schools and academies, its economic organizations and businesses, its defense systems, are not ends to themselves or, worse, the private domains of those individuals who engage in them, but are rather concrete expressions of a single overwhelming idea: that the interior life of citizens expresses itself in its institutions. Justice is an intellectual moral commitment that must be made before the societal institutions can embody it thereafter. The great weaknesses of the Platonic system are, similarly, weaknesses of his ideas, rather than defects in his fundamental substrate. This is why his influence was taken on into the Byzantine age, although most of his political concrete suggestions were disavowed. The defect of the system (apart from the overarching Greek inability to distinguish society from state at this period) is that not all society wills the good in the Platonic version of things, only that section of society (the guardians) which has been especially trained to recognize justice and to assert it over others.[15] Politics is thus conceived *ab initio* as a benevolent despotism. Equally, the theory of communistic self-abandonment prescribed for his ruling elite was an idea that was not merely against the deep grain of human instinct, but an idea that struck at the heart of the societal communion it was supposed to protect.

[13]In his thought the soul is tri-partite: it has a lower level (*epithymia*) concerned with desires, and acquisition (the farmers); a middle level of seeking (*thymos*) concerned with bravery and sense of honor (the warriors), and the highest level (*logos*) concerned with reason and higher truth (the Guardian-Philosophers).

[14]*The Republic* 544D.

[15]*The Republic* 501A-B. "A whole people cannot be a people of philosophers."

The core element of his theory of justice, however, is that this fundamental virtue is easily recognized by all classes in society. Justice is especially that focus on the correct and appropriate function in life that nature has allotted. For Plato it is the will of each individual to do what one ought to do (*tou autou prattein*) and not to interfere in what another has been set to do. A farmer or cobbler exercises justice by performing his productive functions on which the welfare of the state depends. The soldier exercises justice by being habituated to bravery in the defense of the homeland. The Guardian exercises justice by seeking after wisdom, and protecting the common good. When all have performed their duties, the state itself is seen to be just. Plato's politics have entirely subordinated the principle of the individual (which he saw to be the bane of ancient Greek political life in the city states) to the collective. By restoring a profound sense of an external theocratically ordered standard of justice (the scriptural and evangelical charter), Byzantine Christianity, paradoxically, restored to the social order a profound sense of the importance of the individual, the person, and in this alone it made it most radical critique of Platonic premises. For Plato, the appeal to an external body of law was anathema. The wise insight of the Guardian philosophers was the ultimate rule of state. He would not have them trammeled and hemmed in by laws

Aristotle's City

Aristotle's political theory, like most of his thought on nature and ethics and humanity, is governed by an overarching idea: that all things in life have a cycle of growth, an energy within them that propels them to development. This end is the goal of all living things. It is the *telos.* All his thought is teleotic in character. One can understand the acorn only by conceiving of its *telos* which is the oak tree. An embryo makes no sense until we know what species it is that will determine its adult development. Seeing the whole life cycle and being able to categorize the various forms of life correctly are fundamental skills of the philosopher. Aristotle greatly faulted Plato's social theory for its excessively static character. He had a livelier sense of how much things had changed in politics over the years and he drew into his political criticisms of Plato a deeper sense of the teleotic movement that was necessary to characterize a just state. In his view of the true discernment of material reality, Aristotle gives pride of place to empirical judgment. The philosopher must look, scrutinize, and discern the movement and direction of the *telos* of a thing, before he can be assured of getting matters right. To this extent the concept of the *ethos* of a thing is very important for Aristotle. The *ethos* was, as it were, the ability to determine where in the arch of the teleotic development of a thing (for example that long stretch of a human or animal life from the womb to the grave) the moment came that perfectly exemplified what that particular reality was. For a human, the *ethos* would be that precise moment when all the fullness of the character was formed and energetically displayed, such that it could result in a shining moment of action that perfectly encapsulated what that individual reality was quintessentially all about. Take a Greek warrior as an example. The *ethos* of such a life could be summed up in a moment from the heroic history of the country: a fearless soldier fighting to the end without cowardice in the defense of his country. In the time of testing (such as Thermopylae, for example) the warrior's virtue (*arete*) made the act of heroism look "natural." The moment also stood as an encapsulation, the *ethos*, of all that explained the warrior to the observer, all that he had been living for up to that moment. For Aristotle it was critical, therefore, to choose that moment in the arc of a whole development of a being, or a thing, that correctly summed up its essential character. To define a human being from its infancy state, or from its dotage, would be seriously to misdirect the search for the correct definition of a human. The idea of "Man" was innately related to *andreia* (manliness) in Greek classical thought.[16] Accordingly, one could approach a proper understanding of "Man" only by studying a human being who had achieved the perfection of his state: a man exercising powerful virtue (the tasks of his appropriate condition in life), at a highly advanced level, in the full maturity of his powers.

It was just so with the study of the state. The accurate observer had to determine what was the correct moment that exemplified the state's true *ethos*, its best and most authentic self-revelatory instance. It had to be studied in action. It had to be defined from its achievement. This idea gives wing to Aristotle's critique of Plato's politics and also affords his theory a restless kind of energy. He has attracted criticism for accusing Plato of being too static in his political imagination, while he himself was not quite able to see coming down the historical road the next development of the state which was looming, namely the mutation of the city state into world empire. His ideas, nevertheless, were important, like Plato's, and had a long afterlife of influence over political thought in antiquity.

Aristotle continued the teleological aspect in his ethical reflections on the purpose of the individual in society. The function of an individual's role is the key to social cohesion. Once all understand their "place" in society, then society will operate productively and well. Each will contribute from his own skill to the common good of all. This of course reflects the privilege of his own position as a free citizen enjoying the superior benefits of his class and wealth. Bréhier pointed out that this gave Aristotle's whole ethic the character of "The morality of a middle class lady in comfortable circumstances, who is determined to make the best use of her social

[16]Again an explanation why Greek thought so consistently reduces and negates the value of women and slaves; as being "less than Man."

advantages."[17] The position of the unfree woman or the slave, as the ancient Greeks would argue, however, is not negotiable, since they are unable, precisely because of their position, to argue the philosophical case for change. As non-free, unreflective agents they live the unexamined life. Aristotle's entire premise of this inbuilt vision of inequity will be challenged by Christianity's new anthropology. The unexamined life of the working man,[18] woman or the slave, in ancient terms, is cast down root and branch by Christianity's understanding of the sacred and individual worth of all human souls as redeemed images of the divine.

Aristotle followed the intellectual agenda set down by Socrates before him, that society best functions when all understand their proper role in the social order. But behind this lies the more fundamental challenge for the leader to reflect on the proper role not of a warrior, as such, or a governor, or any other precise role of an individual in society, but rather on the proper role and function of a human being *qua tale*. The question "What is the purpose and destiny of Man?" is the underlying *aporia*[19] which needs to be answered before the political ethical theory can be established. Aristotle approaches this basic issue by positing that happiness is the goal sought after; and the highest activity on the way to beatitude is the reflective life. The achievement of *theoria* (contemplation, or what we could call here intellectual acuity) would assert (for he cannot demonstrate it otherwise) that human beings will be most happy in doing the good for its own sake and that true reason will illuminate that axiom for the thinker. Virtue (the bond of all human society) is the supremely happy state of the true human being. This state of understanding and action (*theoria* and *praxis* devolving from it) is thus the heart of the true human *ethos*, to which Man's reality ought to run, just as all other aspects of Nature run to their various and proper ends (*telos*). The achievement of that goal demands constant formative choices and all of these need to be structured in accordance with the understanding of the overarching *telos*; in other words. to be subordinated to their relative importance in attaining the overall goal. This is what underlies his insistence that the Golden Mean is very significant in ethical thought. The "mean" is not a simple searching for safety of choice in mediocrity or in base ethical averages. It signifies for Aristotle, that the ethical choice for a human being will be that which is in accordance with the fundamental goals of his anthropology: the search for balanced and happy human nature, which he posits will be attained only by the virtuous. When he sets out to give an elaborate taxonomy of vices and virtues in his *Ethics* he uses this concept of two "bad" extremes (for example, cowardice and rashness;

[17]Cited in Armstrong (1981) p. 99.

[18]The *banausic*, or vulgar, person has no leisure to devote to reflection, and is unfree, and not entitled, according to Aristotle, to be a citizen.

[19]Philosopher's set puzzle, or question, designed to stimulate thought.

or avarice and excessive liberality) to underscore his idea of the ethical golden mean in action. Christian philosophy would seize upon this aspect of his thought and mutate the beatific vision (a rightly ordered and happy life rooted in philosophical self-improvement) into the Christian sense of communion with God, on the basis of the ethics of the Gospel. Where in Aristotle the practical reflection on right-reason in ethical choices was carefully and practically elaborated, the absolute moral basis of why human beings would be motivated towards Reason's pure beauty was not so clear. In Christianity the practical "embodiment" of his moral reasoning is wedded to an incarnation of Pure Reason (*Logos*) in the practicalities of Christ's person and Gospel, and would become a strong way of advancing a refashioned synthesis of Platonic and Aristotelian principles for social thought.

Aristotle's Theory of Justice

In general legal reflection among the early Greeks,[20] the idea of justice is comparatively rare. Certainly it does not have the same robust position as justice and righteousness have in the biblical tradition (*sedaqah; diakoiosyne*) where the ideas assume central position in the theology of covenant, and there is a powerful alignment of moral concerns with those of "The Law" (*Torah*, LXX, *Nomos Theou*). The Greek sources do speak of what can be seen to be the "most just opinion" (*gnome dikaiotate*) but the concept of justice is really represented more by the term "equity" (*epieikeia*) which is prevalent even in the earliest levels of legal materials.[21] It seems to represent the beginnings of a distinction between what the law prescribes and what "ought" to be the case; in other words, to first begin to articulate the right as distinct from the legal. In Herodotos the idea is stated as a form of appeal to common consciousness: "Would not all men prefer equity rather than having to submit to the strict tenets of justice, and would they not agree that this was a more reasonable position?" [22] In his *Laws*[23] Plato has a section devoted to the way in which individuals ought not to be allowed to adapt general law so as to suit their own special "insights." He was convinced that special pleading could not be kept out of the way individuals were "enlightened" as to needful improvements in the overall system of law, and so his conclusion was simply to ban all concept of the modification of law according to circumstances; a rather wooden response which demonstrates how, even in this seminal thinker, the concept of higher ideal of justice to which law was subservient, was still a way off.

[20]Further see Barker (1959) pp. 222f.
[21]Ducos. (1984) p. 321.
[22]Herodotos 3.53.4.
[23]Plato, Laws 4.713.c; 9.875c.

It was Aristotle, mainly, who brought forward and prioritized the idea of equity in his philosophy of law, and in doing so made it possible for the later Christian synthesis of the Greek and Biblical traditions around the central notion of justice. This can be seen especially in the fifth book of the *Nicomachean Ethics*[24] which contains a major discussion of the idea of equity, and which assured that from then onwards, at least in Greek philosophical rhetoric, the consideration of law would always begin from this point and principle of the search for justice. For Aristotle, equity is the idea of justice that is often better than justice in the abstract,[25] for it is the way that a local case can exemplify what is just and be of benefit to an individual. In other words, equity is often a corrective to justice sought after through the medium of law. The law, he argues, always looks to the generic and the collective, whereas equity is the always concerned with realizing what is just in a particular instance, for people in specific circumstances. What he has presented, therefore, in this theory of equity, is another aspect of his general approach to philosophical problems where he constantly advocates seeking the "Golden Mean" in all things. By the time of Terence, the Roman playwright, the idea has become a commonplace of the stage. He sums it up sharply in a memorable aphorism: *ius summum saepe summa est malitia*: "Strict justice can often turn out to be the height of wickedness."[26] The idea of justice is taking a noticeable turn towards the local, as well as moving towards a greater interiority than it had previously. Although the Stoics had contributed much towards the discussion of the need to refine legal contracts with moral sensitivity,[27] the term "equity" had not been much employed by them. It was Cicero who synthesized the Aristotelian insights and the Stoic moral ethos, and served as the bridge to pass that insight on to the imperial Greco-Roman culture.

In his *De Officiis*[28] Cicero emphasized the necessary harmonization of justice and equity, providing an overall moral frame of reference that had an immense impact on the Christian theorists who read him, especially Tertullian and Augustine. He made the connection using the master idea of natural law.[29] It is this which he saw as the primary bond of the "Social Contract," uniting all citizens in mutual harmony and affection.[30] The code for this is *amicitia*, which will be so influential an idea for Christian theorists who will take it a stage further towards being the bond of loving-regard for the neighbor, the biblical virtue of *agape*, and, especially in the hands of Augustine, *caritas*. Natural law as Cicero approaches it in legal philosoph-

[24] *Nicomachean Ethics*. 5. 14.
[25] *Nichomachean Ethics*. 5.14. 1137b.
[26] *Heautontimoroumenos*. 796.
[27] See Ducos (1984) p. 326; Dudley (1994) p. 94.
[28] *De Officiis* Book 3.
[29] See *De Officiis* 1. 50–60.
[30] *De Officiis*. 3.6.26–28.

ical terms is synonymous with "giving to each their due."[31] It was an idea that would have a massive and influential take up among the Christians. Both these developments will be further developed in the following section when we turn to Roman ideas refining the philosophy of law.

Roman Conceptions of Law

The Origins of Roman Law

THE EARLY REPUBLIC (*Ius Civile*)

The beginnings of the Republic at Rome would see a considerable revision to the earliest form of the expression of Roman law as *leges regiae*, the sacral system of law under the kings. Politico-legal alterations, in the manner the representation of the people, was effected, introduced the first republican conception of the governance of society. Popular assemblies in the early Roman Republic, *c* 509 B.C., elected temporary leaders whom they called magistrates. There were always two of them at once, supposedly so that they could each keep an eye on the other and limit the temptation to tyranny. Their exercise of power was limited to a single year, also so as to limit their capacity and to try to avoid corruption and autocracy. The leading magistrates were designated as the Consuls. Below them ranked other lesser magistrates who formed the system of justice. Over a long course of development this established itself in the normal, or ordinary, system of magistracies: Consuls, Praetors, Quaestors, Promagistri, Aediles, Tribunes, Censors, Governors, Prefects and Procurators; and the extraordinary magistracies (called upon in times of crisis) of: Consular Tribune and Dictator. All their decisions could set precedents for further legal decisions,[32] although at first in the simper economy of the early Republic, Roman law was profoundly local in character and worked on the basis of specific cases establishing case history and precedents as the decisions of magistrates went on record. This aspect of case law, or ancient custom as it could be called, was always held in

[31]*De Legibus* 1.18.48.

[32]"The authority of matters constantly adjudicated in the same way has the force of law." Callistratus. Digest. 1.3.38; "Even if it should be countermanded by a particular judge, custom must be confirmed." Ulpian. Digest. 1.3.34; and, "Custom is the finest of all legal interpreters" *Sententiae Pauli*, Digest 1.3.37. Casuistry on the basis of precedent heavily characterizes classical Roman Law. In the later Republic, after the second century B.C., the influence of Greek philosophical treatises made itself felt to an extent, abstracting the discussions slightly more metaphysically among the jurists (issues of law's universal extension among humanity as a common standard, or Stoic-inspired issues of natural Law in the heart of humanity), but never ousting the overall reliance on case precedent (see the final section of the present chapter).

esteem, theoretically, in Roman law. It was technically designated as *ius*, or "common right."

Roman litigation evolved in three stages. The first, lasting until *c* 150 B.C., was known as the system of *legis actiones*, or the process of litigation. By the mid- second century B.C., legal administration became generally regarded as archaic and excessively rigid and was supplanted by the Praetorian "Formulary System" which held sway until the Christian imperial era (mid-fourth century). After that time the Formulary system itself gave way to the system of legal *cognitio*. The latter was a clear trend to centralize legal affairs in the hands of the state, and is part and parcel of a whole movement, throughout the era of the Principate, for centralization of power and universalization of statute.

THE SYSTEM OF *Legis Actiones*

While Roman law might be said to exist, in some sense, from the foundation of the city in 753 B.C., the proper history of Roman private law begins in 449 B.C. with the promulgation of the *Twelve Tables* (*Lex Duodecim Tabularum*). Roman law can thus be said to extend, classically over eighteen centuries, for though it comes to a major resolution and reordering under the Christian Emperor Justinian in the Corpus of Civil Law (*Corpus Iuris Civilis*) issued between 529 and 534 A.D., it was substantially the civil law of the Christian Empire until it fell to the Ottomans in 1453.[33]

The *Twelve Tables* were the result of the major political struggles of 451–450 B.C. when the Plebeian party fought to assume greater political rights. At that time the Patricians gave way to the revolutionary demands of the populace to the extent of allowing a major Plebeian principle: "Equal right under law." But they did not give way entirely, to the extent that they insisted that the *Twelve Tables* should be drawn up by a committee of Patricians only, and that it should affect only private law. In the domain of Roman public law they retained their ascendancy, and to the end of the empire, public law gave precedence to wealth and power.[34] The long enduring division between public and private law was set up as the result of this ancient political struggle. It is one of the reasons why, although law was fundamentally seen as a religious action in all times of the Roman Empire, religious matters rarely feature in the Private codes at all.[35] It is also a reason why Roman law remained, to a considerable extent, outside the channels of rapid social change. Because of this rela-

[33]The wider influence of Roman Law continues to the present in many forms. In Germany, prior to a new Code adopted in 1900, Roman Law (as mediated through the medieval western canonists, of course) was the official "subsidiary law" of the state, officially applied where there were no other specific provisions stated.

[34]Private law leaned heavily in a similar direction too.

[35]Further see: Watson (1992).

tive isolation from the Plebs, developments and changes in Roman law occurred only as a result of considerable social crisis. Its stability and continuance was assured by the most conservative elements of the most conservative of ruling classes.

The *Twelve Tables* were described as the "source of all public and private Roman law."[36] They were the subject of children's learning by rote in the schools.[37] The *Twelve Tables* have not survived except in quoted fragments among the ancients, and seem dominated by family inheritance regulation, and the determining of basic rules for legal process.[38] Johnston summarizes them as follows: "What these Twelve Tables contained was not quite a law code in the modern sense, but a list of important legal rules . . . extraordinarily laconic and . . . hard to understand."[39] Law could be added to in various manners. The earliest was by statute; which was created through votes taken by the Republican common assembly, usually under instructions from the magistrates. Two significant examples of statutory law were the *Lex Aquilia,* arising from a plebiscite of *c* 286 B.C. which concerned restitutions to be given by someone who broke another's property; the *Lex Atinia*, some time in the second century B.C., which excluded the issue of stolen goods from the principle of acquiring title to goods by possession of them for a certain time; the *Lex Voconia* of 169 B.C. that limited the ability of women to bequeath goods; and the *Lex Falcidia* of 40 B.C. which set limits on acceptable legacies.[40] The *Twelve Tables*, the statutes and the common custom, were classed by the Romans as: *Ius Civile*. This was distinguished from *Ius Honorarium*, or laws that were made by magistrates in their year of office.

The system of *Legis Actio* in this early period (up to 150 B.C.) was so named because the only actions that were legally allowable were those specifically created by the laws, or so close to them that they could be adapted to that end by the college of priests. Civil procedure at this time was thus fundamentally based around the *Twelve Tables* but worked in a way that was increasingly seen, as the Republic advanced, to be unacceptably random. *Legis Actio* was a highly ritualistic system even when it passed from out of the hands of the priests, who originally administered it as a sacred part of Roman religion, to the Praetors. Because it retained so much ritual force, minor variations from the exact ritual process were intolerable.

[36]Livy (History), *Ab Urbe Condita* 3.34.6; see also Cicero, *De Oratore* 1.195.

[37]Cicero, *De legibus* 2.59.

[38]Examples are as follows: "When parties have made an agreement, announce it. If they don't agree, they shall state their case in the Forum before noon. They shall plead together in person. After noon, let the judge pronounce. If both are present, the case shall end at sunset." Or again: "If someone is called to go to court, he must go. If he will not go, a witness should be called. Only then should he be captured."

[39]Johnston (1999) 2.

[40]Johnston (1992) 3; Mousourakis (2007) 58–59.

As times progressed the populace also grew restless with this level of imposition.[41] Under the system of *Legis Actio* a plaintiff could petition the Praetor to bring a defendant to court with sanctions awarded by the Praetor if the defendant refused to cooperate and was thus declared *indefensus*. The court appearance would begin with the laying down of a pledge (*vadium*, or "wager") by both parties, or in some cases only the plaintiff. An exonerated defendant would receive the pledge as a compensation for his inconvenience. It was meant to represent a sacrifice to the gods, but served as a remedy against frivolous lawsuits, though it made appeal to the law a costly business where the wealthy had a significant advantage. The initial hearing of a case took place before the Praetor and bore a religious character, with the initial exchange of ritual statements which were essentially the claims and counter claims of the parties and their various asseverations of honesty. This religious character of the Roman courts was a compelling reason why the early Christians often did not wish to avail themselves of the benefit of law and why the faithful were severely disadvantaged when their religious reluctance became commonly known.

In various cases the terms of the pleading were one of three types. The first was the *sacramentum*, the taking of the oath, and the standard system of litigation. Both parties had to lay down a matching *vadium* of fifty *asses*, a considerable cash sum. The second was the *postulatio*, more exactly: "*Legis actio per iudicis arbitrive postulationem*," or "Legal action by complaint before a judge or arbiter." The *postulatio* was mandated by statute in some personal cases and did not require any *vadium* to be presented. The third was *condictio*. This was the form used in cases of the pursuit of property from a debtor. A *vadium* was not given in advance, but both parties pledged one third of the amount at issue in advance. If the plaintiff won he received 133 percent of his original debt. But, if the defendant was exonerated, he received one third of the amount that had originally been demanded from him. De Zulueta characterizes the whole system as deeply ritual in its essence.[42]

The Praetor at this initial hearing appointed a judge or arbiter who was acceptable to both parties, and drawn from a list of the upper classes (*album iudicum*). The trial was assigned by the Tables to a public place, and the Forum in Rome was often favored in the capital. The burden of proof was on the plaintiff, and the customary process was to have prosecutory and defense speeches by professional advocates (those remaining by Cicero demonstrate how these worked in action) and a sum-

[41]In one case reported by the jurist Gaius a plaintiff lost a suit that involved his neighbor illegally cutting down his vines because in his written evidence he had described them as "vines" (*vites*) instead of using the word "trees" (*arbores*) as was stipulated in the *Law of Twelve Tables* (8.11). Mousourakis (2007) 33.

[42]"One may describe the *legis actiones* as highly technical rites in which the Praetor and the parties played parts fixed by law" (F. De Zulueta, "The Science of Law" in C. Bailey, ed., *The Legacy of Rome* [Oxford: The Clarendon Press, 1923], p. 189).

mary judgment was then given by the judge. Witnesses could be called but not under *subpoena*, although a refusal to give testimony made citizens liable to public declaration as *intestabilis*, a dishonorable status. It was then up to the successful party to enforce the verdict. A creditor had the right to seize the debtor if he did not pay after thirty days, and after sixty days (in ancient times) he had the right to sell the defaulter as a slave.[43]

THE FORMULARY SYSTEM

Enactment of almost all private law before the imperial age issued from the office of the Urban Praetor. He was the magistrate, ranking after the Consuls, whose particular function it was to ensure the administration of justice at Rome. It was his office, by public demand, that introduced a new system of applying the law. It began when citizens noticed how the *Praetor Peregrinus*, the legal officer in Rome who had charge of cases brought to the capital by foreigners, seemed to negotiate cases much better and more quickly than the old system for citizens. The foreign cases increasingly assumed greater prominence in the public eye when the amounts of money involved in the transactions grew in line with Rome's global expansion. The *Peregrinus Praetor* had allowed the use of standardized forms of written pleading (*formulae*) both to help foreigners negotiate the complexities of Roman law and to speed up the time required for a case to be processed through the courts. It was the success of this streamlining that soon led to the demand that the *Urban Praetor* should follow the same system for resident Roman citizens. Two significant improvements were, first that the plaintiff did not himself have to take the risk of deciding which title under the law his case fell under, and choosing it irrevocably at the start of proceeding since now the Praetor determined which formula his petition would fall under; and second, the Praetor was able to exercise wide discretion by admitting a whole range of exceptions to the strict application of the law (such as *exceptio doli* where the case under law offered clear evidence of fraud) or by inserting the clause *ex bona fide* to cover items of relevance to a case even if they did not fall explicitly into the stated terms of the formula.

The start of his time of office was marked by the Praetor issuing an Edict for the year which gave an outline of the chief legal remedies he intended to grant, listed under various "formulae." The Edict was crafted by professional jurists, while the Praetor applied the law more in the role of a politician-magistrate setting out his program in his year of office by means of the Edict.[44] Any person who wished a case to

[43]Before the reforms of the *Lex Poetelia* in 326 B.C., the creditor was able to choose between dismembering his debtor or selling him into slavery; after it his only recourse was continuing the imprisonment.

[44]In that it had to cover a large range of civil law cases, the Edict often relied on set *formulae* using fictitious cases (In the case that Arthur was attacked by Robert, etc.). This is why it is difficult for historians

be heard in the Praetor's court now had to request and cite the specific formula that covered his grievance. If it did not correspond he had to persuade the Praetor to add an existing "remedy" to the Edict. In the late second century the *Lex Aebutia* allowed the Praetor to compose new *formulae* to cover issues where the old *Ius Civile* was no longer relevant. This power immensely advanced the position of the Praetor and marked the beginnings of the new formulary system. By controlling access to the law in terms of which remedies he would agree to allow in any given year, and, therefore, which he would disallow by simply not hearing cases, the Praetor exercised a great power of procedure which directed the standard course of Roman courts without having to create much new legislation *per se*. The whole tenor of Roman Law from the time of the late Republic until the age of the Christian emperors moved decisively from legislation towards active jurisprudence.[45]

The class of jurists was thus immensely important in the history of Roman law.[46] At first the jurists had been part of the ancient priesthood (*pontifices*) and law was seen as a reserved mystery of religion,which religious character it always retained even into the era of the Dominate. But after 300 B.C. the Roman priesthoods were laid open to all. This meant, in reality, to all the noble class. To become one of the class of jurists, *Prudentes*, meant that a youth had to be belong to one of the higher families of aristocratic Rome and be inducted into the tiny circle of the legal intelligentsia. Cicero was a brilliant advocate, but even he was not admitted into the class of *Prudentes*. Since the same few noble families were also in charge of governance and the state priesthoods, the old links between law as an instrument of governance and aspect of religion were to all intents and purposes maintained in a more democratically expanded form that yet kept the reins of power tightly in the hands of the élite old families.[47] Cicero describes the jurists as an aspect of the urban militia, waging war for Rome through the pen and through their caution.[48] The opinions of the jurists held immense weight, the Praetors or Judges would hardly think to question them. Their *responsiones* to the basic facts of a case laid before them by a judge was

to distil from the surviving law codes and their cited cases hard evidence of what was going on in any era (as opposed to what was thought to be going on by the administrators).

[45]"The Praetor's Edict, an organ which on strict analysis might be considered legislative, appears to compete with the *prudentes* [jurists] in the work of development. But, apart from the fact that, like other formal sources, the Edict required interpretation, we shall see that both in its authorship and in its nature it belongs to jurisprudence rather than to legislation" (F. De Zulueta, in Bailey [1923] 188–189). Examples of how the Praetor worked practically (largely by establishing "exceptions" to the old laws) can be found in Mousourakis (2007) 54–55.

[46]Further see Mousourakis. (2007) 59–64.

[47]"The Republican *prudentes* merely represent the specialized ability of a great governing class, whose instinct was too sagacious to allow the science of law to slip into the hands of underlings. To this class, jurisprudence was a branch of the art of governing" (F. De Zulueta, in Bailey [1923] 193).

[48]"Urbana militia respondendi, cavendi, scribendi." Cicero, *Pro Murena* 9.19.

more or less equivalent to a judgment. The system explains why legal theologians from among the Christians, such as Tertullian and Lactantius, appealing to deeper principles of justice and charity in the face of persecution law, felt they were arguing before a marble slab. The weight of religious and political custom carried all before it in Rome and that weight fell upon the shoulders of the most conservative and antique class of nobles in the empire at any given period. It is this reason, of course, which accounts also for the remarkable consistency and enduring power of Roman Law, and also the manner in which it serves as a powerful outflow of a universalizing force of international culture. It was not until the process of Christianization of the Empire that this powerhouse of the jurists was effectively cracked open. The rise of centralizing imperial power would weaken it, to an extent, though the emperors generally carried on representing, in their own persons, the same principles the *Prudentes* stood for, and which they continued to recommend to them in their respective administrations. It was the move of the capital to Constantinople that really broke the power of the old pagan Roman classes, an aspect of the move which Constantine welcomed after his more than frosty reception by the old ascendancy in Rome following his victory of the Milvian Bridge. The creation of a whole new apparatus of government across the other side of the world and the deliberate establishment of a new religion seeking innovative ways to establish its rights brought new air into the old system. It was not abandoned wholesale, in any sense; for the new *prudentes* were formed in the same intellectual molds and classical reverence for precedence. but the new men of the provinces were in the ascendancy; and new ideas flourished, admitting new principles and goals for the law.

The Praetor was the theoretical administrator of all civil legislation. *Ius Civile* was meant to rank higher in honor than any other system of law. In practice, since it was also administered by the Praetor, it was almost always superseded when *Ius Honorarium* (or *Ius Praetorianum,* the official decrees of the administrators) countermanded it in any given instance. As Johnson notes: "The Edict was a flexible instrument for reforming and modernizing the law, since it could be made every year; and rejected again if need be. The greatest activity on the part of the praetors and the heyday of the edict as a source of law appear to have been in the second and first centuries B.C. In practice much of the material must have continued unchanged from year to year: stability in the administration of justice required no less."[49] In practice, the incoming Praetor could retain most of the Edict of the previous administration and tinker with a few of the detailed clauses that had been found defective in previous years, or add some particular ones for new issues that were foreseen. Although the

[49]Johnston (1999) 4. In 67 B.C. the *Lex Cornelia* explicitly forbade the Praetors to depart from the substantive part (*edictum perpetuum*) of their edicts (Mousourakis [2007] 52).

Praetor was not necessarily himself a legal jurist, he stood by the constant legal advice of the *consilium* of jurists that attended him, and himself inevitably came from the narrow ruling class that had been trained in legal rhetoric from childhood.

Under the system of *Ius per formulam* initial legal process was much the same as in earlier times, with a few amendments.[50] The parties appeared first before the Praetor who determined under what formula the case would be heard, and also decided what penalty (*condemnatio*) would be appointed to it (the value of the claim). After this informal debate had revealed to the Praetor which issue was at stake in a given case he issued a written instruction (*formula*) to the judge whom he appointed to hear it, commanding the latter to find the defendant liable or not liable according to the responses he gave to the questions contained within the *formula*. Often the matter could be settled at the stage of taking the oath (*sacramentum*) to the gods. If not, it went to trial in the usual manner, with prosecution and defense counsel. In the final settlement, the victor still had to organize his own redress, but (to take the example of ownership cases) he was now entitled to more specific legal assistance in the form of the action known as *bonorum vendito*. Thirty days after a successful claim against a debtor, the creditor was awarded, on petition, the right of *missio in posessionem* by the Praetor. This allowed him to promulgate notice of his debtor's bankruptcy and, after a thirty day period (when other creditors could assemble), a commonly agreed executor was appointed who auctioned off the property and satisfied the creditors. The real threat of the *bonorum vendito* was sufficient to avoid many delays in the system of property disputes.

The Praetor and other magistrates also heard cases acting as judges. But they were, in the main, political appointees without extensive legal knowledge in most cases, who heavily depended on the trained lawyers of the empire, the jurists. The latter were originally members of the priesthoods of Rome, but by the third century B.C. had emerged as a separate legal class of experts. As the courts became more complex in terms of judgments expected, the jurists came to exercise more and more influence. In the first three centuries of the Christian era, the jurists were responsible for developing a large body of legal writing, most of it related to practical decisions, case histories and legal theory; but also there are some examples of legally based philosophical and ideological writing. In the century before Augustus initiated the Principate, the jurists had been influenced to some extent by Greek rhetoricians, who demonstrated the potential for legal philosophy, setting a standard for sophistic writing in the Greek Christian world. It is with this latter category that the work of the first Latin Christian legal writers, Tertullian and Lactantius, resonates,

[50]Further see Mousourakis (2007) 65–75. An extensive discussion of the procedures of Roman Law can be found in L.Wenger, *Institutes of the Roman Law of Civil Procedure* (tr. O.H. Fisk) (New York: Veritas Press, 1940).

though both Latins retain much more of the grounded practicality of the Roman legal writers when compared with the Greeks.

The Principate and Dominate (27 B.C. to 313 A.D.)

The arrival of the Principate changed the Roman legal system extensively. From 27 B.C. onwards the personal role of the emperor became more and more the central crux in the issue of making and promulgating law. Augustus managed to centralize power in the single person of the emperor, while all the time attempting to present himself as the "Restorer of the Republic." He managed the change to monarchical domination[51] quietly by using a clever collection of Republican offices. He allocated to himself the proconsular power, which meant he had charge of all the armies of Rome in the frontier provinces,[52] the Consular power, which gave him supreme authority in the city of Rome itself; the powers of the Tribunate, which meant he assumed direction of the law, personally approving all the traditional magistracies; and the headship of all religious affairs in assuming, after 12 B.C., the office of *Pontifex Maximus.*

Augustus at first pretended that he was not an emperor[53] in the sense of a monarchical absolute ruler. He adopted, and the Senate clung to, the illusion that he was merely the "first citizen." For this reason he did not wish to supplant the established processes of law-making by assuming legislative powers based solely on his personal right to dominion. This remained a principle of the early Principate. Nevertheless, the emperor had personally assumed significant magisterial powers which grew over the course of time into the Byzantine system of the emperor having supreme command over the issuing of law. The two chief magistracies that formally mattered in the early imperial accumulation of Republican magistracies were the *imperium proconsulare maius* and the *tribunicii potestas.* The emperor also ruled the city through a domestic palace administration comprised of his family and freedmen, except for a few of the highest honors which were reserved for leading Senators.[54] The two leading officers of imperial administration were the Praetorian Prefect who commanded the armies (except for a few of the senatorial administered legions), and the Urban

[51]Principate refers to the early imperial myth that the emperor was merely the *princeps*, the first citizen of the Republic. The term Dominate is used to refer to the Diocletianic age and its aftermath when more radical ideas of the emperor as "Lord and Master" and the citizens as (*servi domini*) his servants was established. Augustus' policy of proclaiming his divine genius was already heading towards this end-result.

[52]The great majority of Rome's armed forces.

[53]The term comes from "imperator" or commander of the armies, and referred to his office as Commander in Chief of the frontier legions. But might is right in this case.

[54]The Senate's role was vastly reduced, though it was advanced to become a court of law for the trial of its own class, and membership remained a highly regarded honor.

Prefect who oversaw legal affairs in the city. Both of them operated as agents of the emperor in this era.

As the empire expanded dramatically at this time, so the needs of the legal system changed with it, calling for greater complexity of range and deeper sophistication of approach compared to the more rigid formalities of what had gone before. It was a highly creative era in many respects. Augustus designed the Principate on the premise that he would be the First Citizen and Senior Magistrate. Soon the emperor was seen as the *fons et origo*, the very source of law. The first main political alteration the Principate brought in public affairs was the abolition of the popular Roman assemblies that issued Statutes. By 125 A.D. the system of the Praetor controlling the administration of law by his edict also gave way, and its system of precedent was frozen in the form it had then attained, the Praetorian legal powers now passing to the emperor. A high water point of this was marked precisely in 131 A.D. when Hadrian collected and published the Praetorian Edicts and declared them to be an "unalterable" source of Roman law, with no further additions except by the personal edict of the emperor. At this time the *prudentes* had petitioned him to continue the process operative from the time of Augustus, that certain noted jurists should be permitted to give legal opinions in the name of the emperor himself. He responded by withdrawing the privilege entirely, reserving the imperial *motu proprio* to himself alone.

During the Principate, the role of the jurists continued in force. Two of the leading jurists of the early Principate, Papinian and Ulpian, are known to have served personally in the imperial administration as Praetorian Prefects.[55] The emperor issued legal *constitutiones* if they emanated from the palace, and *decreta* if they came from the law court in a case he was hearing. He could also publish general orders that were known as *edicta*[56] or send an official letter (*epistula*) containing his final judgment, or might sign at the bottom of a petitioner's formal Letter annotating his opinion and decision (*subscriptio*). After the third century both *epistulae* and *subscriptiones* came to be designated as "receipts" (*rescripta*). After the late second century imperial *rescripta* had the force of establishing legal precedent. The imperial staff dealing with legal affairs were headed in two sections by the Secretary *Ab Epistulis*, whose office was concerned with answering letters and questions, and the Secretary *A Libellis*, who dealt with petitions. The emperor would have been involved person-

[55]Both were assassinated while in office.

[56]Edicts outlasted the life of the emperor who issued them. They covered a wide range of issues; private and criminal law, the arrangement of the courts, grants of citizenship (Mousourakis [2007] 108). Imperial mandates (*mandata*) were instructions he issued to members of his administrative staff. The most important of these, such as decisions he communicated to Provincial Governors on major issues of administration, were collected; but were regarded as legislatively significant only during the emperor's lifetime. They had to be renewed to have enduring force.

ally only in significant and political cases.[57] The major and most interesting issues would probably be dealt with by the secretaries themselves with the assistance of jurists. These were often the very cases that found their way into the summary legal codices of the later age. Matters of lesser moment or interest would normally be delegated to the lower staff.

It is undoubted that the application of centrally issued laws varied to the degree one left the center. The often repeated demands in the Codes for the same law to be observed suggests that Roman legislation was neither absolute nor assured everywhere. The patchy application of penal laws against Christians in various provinces also testifies to that quite clearly. But the intent was there, nevertheless, to establish the law as a uniform pattern of good standard throughout the empire's provinces, though much depended on the provincial governors. In 1981, in the Roman hamlet of Irni, the tiny village of El Saucejo between Estepa (*Ostippa*) and Sevilla (*Hispalis*) in Andalucia, which was in Roman times only a little less obscure than it is today, a set of six bronze tables was unearthed. These turned out to be copies of the Flavian Municipal Law, reflecting some local variations as could also be seen in copies known from the law codes of Salpensa and Malaga, nearby. The code had been validated by Domitian, and dated to 91 A.D.[58] Even when there existed useful and applicable local laws, the inhabitants of Irni are specifically instructed by Domitian's jurists to reserve a long list of matters, so to give precedence to the Edicts of the Provincial Governor. The ninety-third chapter of the *Lex Irnitana* states that "for all matters for which it is not expressly written or determined in this statute which law the citizens of this municipality of Irni should use among themselves, then for all these matters let them use the *Ius Civile* which Roman citizens use . . . " Reflecting on this, Johnston notes: "This is very remarkable. The provisions of Roman law were not merely displayed, laboriously engraved in bronze, but intended to be applied."[59] Admittedly, Spain was already considerably Romanized in Domitian's time, and Seville (*Hispalis*) was a major administrative capital, not far away from Irni. Even so, the *Lex Irnitana* suggests a pattern which must have been echoed throughout the empire, with Roman contemporary prescripts always taking precedence over local legislation until the provinces inexorably became more and more Romanized over time. The idea of Roman law spreading out over the different nations to consolidate a trans-national whole was at the center of the "imperial Roman idea," and after 212 A.D., when citizenship was granted to almost all the inhabitants of the empire by Caracalla's Edict, that dream was moved further to its realization.[60]

[57]See Honoré (1994) 1–56.

[58]A. D'Ors, *La Ley Flavia Municipal (Texto y Commentario)* (Rome, 1986).

[59]Johnston (1999) 10.

[60]One of the problems after Caracalla's extension of citizenship so widely (*Constitutio Antonina*) was

The Legal System of Cognitio Extraordinaria

One of the characters of this centralizing movement, one that started to look to legal rescripts more as a universal charter than a simple record of cases (thus prefiguring the final reforms of Justinian), was the shifting of the whole Roman legal system, by the end of the third and into the early fourth century, away from the formulary system to the system of *Cognitio Extraordinaria.* What this meant in essence was that, while most private Roman law hitherto had been essentially a common form of "witness to disputes" most clearly seen in the way that the victor in legal decisions had to enforce the verdict himself, and the inability to have a case tried "in default," now the state, in the person of the emperor as supreme source of law, assumed greater powers in its own right. The older system had offered to disputants a formula whereby they could resolve differences. They met and agreed the basis of the case which was then handed over for third party adjudication. Now the state assumed the right to prosecute the case from beginning to end. The emperor himself was now the *fons legis* and the sacred guarantor of the well-being of the imperial commonwealth. It was a major part of his imperial administration to extend a massive oversight of the legal system through his appointed magistrates. The change in the system not only continued the centralization aspects of the Imperium, but also underlined that it was now the state's duty, not that of individuals within it, to prosecute justice.

This was a movement that was taken to new heights by the Christian emperors after Constantine, a trend undoubtedly influenced by theological reflection on the sacral role of the emperor mediated through biblical lenses of the centrality of "The Law" for the health of the Elect Nation. By the late fourth century, with generations of Christian interpretation of the Scriptures in place, "the Law" as it appeared in biblical sources, no longer connoted the Jewish ritual law at all, but the Christian polity in the widest sense, especially as this came to refinement in an evangelical moral lifestyle. The civil law was understood as something now far more than merely civil, or secular. At its simplest level it was the fence around the righteous life, the protection of the innocent and the correction of the wicked. In more sophisticated forms, it was (in a typologically extended way from the thought forms of the Old Testament) an integral part of the process whereby the Byzantine empire occupied on the face of the earth, the place of the Elect Nation. Its manner of life, in accordance with

that local law in the provinces was rendered antiquated (not necessarily superseded) and often two systems ran on local customs and the assertion of Roman law proper, which at first was understood and applied frequently in garbled ways. It is thus difficult to know in any instance whether Roman law, as such, is being applied in the distant provinces, or whether a mingling of Roman law and local custom. This was the confusion that the Justinianic reform would later aim at eliminating by establishing one law for the (Christian) Empire of the Romans.

God's Law, determined its military and social extent. This represents in a real way a remarkable symbiosis, or dynamic synthesis, of much that underpinned the philosophical understanding of the importance of law both for the pre-Christian Roman Empire, and for the Jewish nation in the time of their political independence under the kings.

In the pre-Christian legal system of *cognitio* a complainant could lodge a charge in the courts and a court officer would set out to ensure the defendant attended at court. If he was unwilling, the court would arrest him. If he managed to avoid attendance, but was called for over three sessions of the court, a judgment against him would be made *in absentia*. We can see this process in full swing at the Oecumenical Council of Ephesus in 431, held by rescript of Theodosius II, when Nestorius (the accused Archbishop of Constantinople, and resident across the street) was summoned to attend the synod three times but refused to acknowledge the legitimacy of the tribunal, and was thus deposed from office.

Under the *cognitio* system the trial was held before a magistrate who was generally fairly skilled in professional legal affairs. He was not bound by the formulary of a trial and so his discretion, according to the statutes, held much greater sway. The magistrate could decide on his own authority, seen as a reflection or extension of that of the emperor, and thus as a sacred and God-given role, to admit whatever evidence he deemed appropriate. The magistrates tended to give precedence to written over oral presentation.[61] After hearing evidence in what was now a much less adversarial environment, and which somewhat curtailed the scope of the rhetorical performances that used to be critical in the earlier process, the magistrate would hand down his decision in a statement accompanied by a written decree to both parties, who were then bound to accept it. Appeals were possible though not encouraged, and difficult to arrange. They basically ran through a system of higher tribunals, perhaps even as far as a hearing before the emperor himself for very compelling cases. In questions of debt, court bailiffs would assist the creditor by seizing goods that were due and auctioning them off publicly. Courts also issued several forms of penalty, such as confiscation of goods, exile, and various forms of physical punishment.

Available Sources of Roman Law

The tidy assembling of Roman Law is a difficult task, as might be expected in the face of such a vast and sprawling human record, extending over such an enduring span of time. The main sources are the jurists' writings and the official Codes.[62]

[61]Indeed, no written source of evidence could now be overthrown by oral evidence alone.

[62]There are also many important sources for Roman legal history in epigraphic remains, and papyri evidence. Cases include the *Lex Irnitana* which demonstrates civil law in use in the Spanish province at the time of Domitian; and the *Archive of Babatha*; see J.C. Greenfield et al., *The Documents from the Bar*

LEGAL WRITINGS

Chief among this genre is the *Institutes of Gaius*,[63] which is an introduction to the study of the law written in *c* 160 A.D., and which is notable for its clarity and usefulness. Its author was an important jurist who lived between 130–180, an older contemporary of the Christian legal apologist Tertullian. He shows a conservative and antiquarian spirit, and the work from the outset probably served as the common law text book of its day, and for several centuries after, until it was superseded by the revisions of the Byzantine sixth century. It is commended as a standard in the later Codex Theodosianus, and comparative studies have shown that the Justinianic *Digest* incorporated large sections of Gaius almost word for word, although omitting the context of decisions which Gaius offers, since the latter was important in Gaius' day and no longer operative in Byzantine times. The *Institutes* of Justinian are also structurally based upon Gaius in terms of their arrangement of materials and method of analysis. What Gaius' *Institutes* shows, in a way that the Justinianic *Digest* and *Institutes* obscure, is the extent to which Roman Law in the Principate worked on the basis of trying cases according to rigid *formulae*. In the time of Justinian there is a movement in Roman law away from this system of individual highly positioned legal officers manipulating the old formulae by means of personal discretion as to what constituted an equitable adjudication, and towards a system of stating laws as universal principles. This is why the Justinianic sources tend to omit the context of the formulae which are so essential to the very working of law in the time of Gaius, and around which Gaius sees the whole matter and value of the jurist's work revolving.

Another important source is the *Pauli Sententiae*, collected adjudications, in all probability fathered retrospectively onto the renowned jurist Paulus. It is a work that is focused on private law and derives from third century Africa.[64] A third is a short compendium of decisions attributed to that other famous classical jurist, Ulpian. It is known as the *Ulpiani Epitome* and dates to *c* 320.[65]

Kokhba Period in the Cave of Letters (Jerusalem: Israel Exploration Society, Hebrew University, 1989) which makes a similar case for the Near East in the first and second centuries; and there are many legal tablets surviving from Pompeii and Herculaneum. See Johnston (1999) 13–14.

[63]Discovered in Verona in 1816 in a palimpsest manuscript of St Jerome. See F. De Zulueta, tr., *The Institutes of Gaius*, 2 vols. (Text and Commentary), Oxford: Oxford University Press, 1946, 1953. An *Epitome of Gaius* also exists from the fifth century, probably written in Africa

[64]D. Liebs, *Römische Jurisprudenz im Africa* (Berlin, 1993), 32–43.

[65]From the same period comes the *Fragmenta Vaticana* which is what remains of another collation of legal decisions and opinions by jurists, and formal constitutions on a number of topics. See D. Liebs, *Die Jurisprudenz im spätantiken Italie* (Berlin, 1987), 151.

LAW CODES

Known to history only by references to them in the sources are the *Codex Gregorianus* and the *Codex Hermogenianus*. These were both issued in the Principate of Diocletian (284–305 A.D.) as part of his extensive reforms of the empire. Neither of them have survived. Extant, there is the better known *Codex Theodosianus* of the Christian Emperor Theodosius II, issued in 438 A.D. Its focus is primarily on public and municipal law, how the imperial administration functions, and the application of new regulations to aid the spread of Christian religion as the "religio Romanorum." The most famous of all of these great renovationist collections and updates of the legal system of Rome is the *Codex Justinianus* of 534 A.D.[66] Both these extensive Christian codifications of the law,which remain profoundly indebted to the classical Roman legal sources, will be discussed more fully in the chapter dedicated to the later imperial reforms.

Roman Legal Reflection on Justice and Equity

In the period at the end of the Republic, and on into the early Principate, Greek philosophical ideas had culturally penetrated Rome, including Roman legal thinking, to such an extent that even this most traditional and impermeable aspect of Roman life begins to show the signs of new issues raised and new horizons of thought being considered by the jurists. Nowhere is this more significantly represented than in the classical theoretical debates on the difference between equity and justice, which we briefly touched upon earlier, in the context of when they had first been raised by Aristotle. It is this discussion of the relation between these two cardinal concepts which Christian patristic writers will also register and reference in their own works. Accordingly it is an important notion to return to, and with which to end this current section introducing Roman law.

The reflection on the significance of Law and Equity (their harmony and their potential disparity) is a topic that first appears in Roman thought as early as the poet Ennius discussing the case of Priam, King of Troy, in a dramatic tragedy.[67] The pairing of both concepts also occurs also in the poets Plautus and Terence.[68] For the late Republic, however, it is Cicero as philosopher who most extensively reflects on the nature of law and justice in Latin literature, especially in his treatise *De Officiis*.[69] In Book Two of this work he comments that the historic reforms of the land laws by

[66]See Johnston (1999) 14–24.

[67]*Hectoris Lytra.* fragm. 19: "Justice and equity keep far away from evil men."

[68]*Curculio* 64; *Menaechmi* 580; *Mostellaria* 682; *Persa* 399; *Sticus* 423, 559 & 726; *Trinummus* 97; *Andria* 901; *Phormion* 450, 637; *Heautotimoroumenos.* 642

[69]Relying in Book 3 of his *De Officiis* on the moral works of Panaetius and his disciple Posidonius, cf. *De Officiis* 3.6.

the Gracchi meant that many occupants of land who had enjoyed possession for generations were thrown off. And he concludes: "What equity was there in this?"[70] The theme of the relation between law and equity became a significant *topos* of Stoic moral theory in their discussion of the relation between right and utility. It appears formally in the Stoic school disputation between the followers of the two sages, Diogenes of Babylon and Antipater of Tarsus. Cicero discusses this key issue and what it stands for. The first of these Stoic thinkers had argued that a seller of goods had the moral obligation to disclose defects in his merchandise to the extent that the law explicitly required disclosure.[71] The latter argued that a seller had the moral duty to disclose all substantive issues of defect [72] in his goods for sale, regardless of the limits of the explicit terms of the law, because private interest was never as compelling as the public good. In the case of the wider disclosure, justice is given precedence over the letter of the law, a justice that has a wide social remit, and which is based upon "the natural bond which exists between all mankind."[73]

It is thus in Stoic thought that equity (*epieikeia, aequitas*) is clearly defined as a form of justice (*suum cuique tribuere*), [74] a principle that Cicero holds high in his system. It was not among these Greek Stoics, however, that the theme enjoyed any extensive development. They were predominantly content to add variations on the topic of *Epieikeia* as it was first distinguished by Aristotle.[75] It was Cicero himself, from his vantage point as amateur philosopher and late synthesist and codifier, who was the one who really and extensively opened up the discussion in the late Republic. More than others he stressed the essential need to preserve the force and honor of law by reference to its ethical value. For Cicero there could be no question that justice was "the sovereign mistress and queen of all the virtues."[76] Beyond any questions of legality and social benefit from law, he argued, there were higher moral issues of right and wrong, justice and equity, that lay beckoning beyond them. If

[70] *De Officiis* 2.22.79.

[71] *De Officiis* 3.50–53.

[72] Excess price in relation to true market value is the case in hand.

[73] *De Officiis* 3.12.53.

[74] "To give to each their due" (*De Inventione* 2.53.160).

[75] *Nicomachean Ethics* 5.10.8; see M. Ducos, *Les Romains et la Loi* (Paris: Belles Lettres, 1984), 323–324. Aristotle says: "What is equitable, apart from being superior to a certain type of justice, is itself inherently just" (*Nicomachean Ethics* 5.14). In his *Rhetoric* 1.13, he connects the pursuit of equity with the need to seek the true "spirit of the law" in terms of seeking the original intent of the lawmaker. For Christians this principle was applied directly by St Gregory the Theologian, in his legal comment on the Christian assimilation of Roman law of marriage, and his refusal, in response to a *quaestio* by Theodosius the Great in 380, to allow that the Greek Church should adopt the Roman Church's strictness in terms of not allowing divorce (*Oration* 37, PG 36.284). His ruling thereby became the basis of Byzantine Christian law on marriage regulation in the Church; see J.A. McGuckin, *St Gregory of Nazianzus: An Intellectual Biography* (Crestwood, NY: St Vladimir's Seminary Press, 2001), pp. 332–336.

[76] *De Officiis* 3.28.

society did not pay attention to them, then the very foundations of law itself would crumble. In making this important move, Cicero was aided by his readings in Pythagorean thought, for it had long been an emphasis of this school that equality was a primary foundation for justice.[77] It was Cicero who used and extended this notion first to argue that Roman law had to look beyond the narrow perimeter of the interests of "citizens and friends,"[78] so as to become a universal standard of just behavior for all humanity. If this happened, he says, then the individual interest and the civic good would coalesce, so as to form the strongest bond possible for the good society.[79] Equity demanded, by terms of logic and by virtue of the natural law, that the gods had set in the hearts of human beings, that where equal circumstances applied,[80] then all human beings ought to be treated equally.[81] For Cicero, it is the binding force of the natural law, set within the inmost heart of the rational being to function as moral conscience and compass, that is the primary force that demonstrates both the harmonization of law and equity, and the motivating force for how this can be accomplished in society. Only with this moral basis, can society as bonded by friendship (*amicitia*), stirred in the individual hearts of all towards others seen as significant moral agents, function peacefully and progressively. In other words, without civic moral foundations rooted in agreed moral categories, even the rule of law itself will perish, and civilization will degrade. Law itself cannot provide them, but must depend upon them rooted in the fabric of society at the deep level of the individual's inner awareness. *Amicitia* has to be demonstrated and developed by its exercise in mutually beneficial behavior. Thus (and it is a concept the Christian theorists will extend religiously), Philanthropy is the social face of Equity functioning as the root of social bonding. This is the law which Cicero says is "written in the heart of man."[82] Cicero argues that it is precisely because it is a part of natural law that equity is inseparably related to justice. They have a systemic relationship: "Law and all that is honest should be sought after for their own sake . . . .. for all good men love equity for its own sake, and law for its own sake, because the law

[77]See Ducos (1984) 328; G. Ciulei, *L'Equité chez Ciceron* (Amsterdam, 1972).

[78]*De Officiis* 3.28: "Others again who say that regard should be had for the rights of fellow citizens, but not of foreigners, would destroy the universal brotherhood of mankind; and, when this is annihilated, kindness, generosity, goodness, and justice must utterly perish; and those who work all this destruction must be considered as wickedly rebelling against the immortal gods, for they uproot the fellowship which the gods have established between human beings."

[79]*De Officiis* 3. 27: "This, then, ought to be the chief end of all, to make the interest of the individual and that of the body politic identical. For, if the individual appropriates to selfish ends what should be devoted to the common good, all human fellowship would be destroyed."

[80]That issue of "equal circumstances," of course, left a large leeway of moral maneuver for ancient society, not least in terms of the issue of slavery.

[81]Cicero, *Pro Caecina* 21.59, and *Topics* 4.23. See O. Roblerda, "L'Aequitas en Ciceron," *Humanidades* 2 (1950) 31–57.

[82]*De Legibus* 1.16.44.

ought to be sought out and honored for what it is in itself, and along with law, the same applies to justice."[83] Thus, natural law and its energy which is set in the human heart, holds all his systematic thought together, and transforms Greco-Roman legal philosophy, and the social polity that derives from it, into a deeply ethical concern on the very eve of the Christianization of the empire.

Further Reading

A.H. Armstrong. *An Introduction to Ancient Philosophy.* Totowa, NJ: Littlefield & Adams, 1981.

E.R. Barker. *The Political Thought of Plato and Aristotle.* New York: Dover, 1959.

J. Barnes. *The Cambridge Companion to Aristotle.* Cambridge and New York: Cambridge University Press, 1995.

M. Bretone. *Storia del diritto romano* (7th edn). Rome, 1999.

W.W. Buckland. *A Textbook on Roman Law.* Cambridge: Cambridge University Press, 1963.

D. Daube. *Roman Law: Linguistic, Social and Philosophical Aspects.* Edinburgh: Edinburgh University Press, 1969.

M. Ducos. *Les Romains et la Loi.* Paris: Belles Lettres, 1984.

D.R. Dudley. "Blossius of Cuma." *Journal of Roman Studies* (1941) 94f.

A.M. Honoré. *Emperors and Lawyers.* Oxford: Oxford University Press, 1994.

L.T. Johnson. "Law in Early Christianity" pp. 53–69 in: J. Witte Jr. & F.S. Alexander. *Christianity and Law.* Cambridge: Cambridge University Press, 2008.

D. Johnston. *Roman Law in Context.* Cambridge: Cambridge University Press, 1999.

J.M. Kelly. *A Short History of Western Legal Theory.* Oxford: The Clarendon Press, 1992.

R. Mayhew. *Aristotle's Criticism of Plato's Republic.* Lanham, MD: Rowman & Littlefield, 1997.

E. Metzger, ed. *A Companion to Justinian's Institutes.* Ithaca, NY: Cornell University Press, 1998.

G. Mousourakis. *A Legal History of Rome.* London: Routledge, 2007.

B. Nicholas. *An Introduction to Roman Law.* Oxford: The Clarendon Press, 1996.

M.P. Nichols. *Citizens and Statesmen: A Study of Aristotle's Politics.* Lanham, MD: Rowman & Littlefield, 1992.

O. Robinson. *The Sources of Roman Law.* London: Routledge, 1997.

F. Schulz. *Principles of Roman Law.* Oxford: The Clarendon Press, 1936.

______. *History of Roman Legal Science.* Oxford: The Clarendon Press, 1963.

A. Tessitore, ed. *Aristotle and Modern politics : The Persistence of Political Philosophy.* Notre Dame, IN: University of Notre Dame Press, 2002.

A. Watson. *The State, Law and Religion: Pagan Rome.* Athens, GA: University of Georgia Press, 1992.

F. Wolff. *Aristote et la Politique. Paris:* Presses universitaires de France, 1991.

H.J. Wolff. *Roman Law: An Historical Introduction.* Norman, OK: University of Oklahoma Press, 1951.

[83] *De Legibus* 1.18.48.

CHAPTER 3

Early Christian Proto-Canonical Collections

The Rise of the Christian Synodical Movement

It is often said that the meeting of the Apostles (Acts 15) to discuss large questions arising out of the mission of St Paul, not least whether circumcision was required of Gentile converts, was the primary model of the Church's practice of leaders' meetings for debate and resolution of more than purely local problems; in other words, synodical practice. But the example of this first "Council of Jerusalem" is not alluded to in this way before St John Chrysostom, and the idea was not taken up in any other patristic writing before the fifth century. Nevertheless we know episcopal Synods happened much earlier than this. Synods gained their name from the Greek term for "coming together," and from the outset this meant, in ecclesiastical terms, the coming together of the bishops of a province to discuss pressing and urgent matters where common polity was felt to be required. We first hear of them textually, by report, from the Latin theologian Tertullian, who, in the second century, is curiously observing "good practice" in the Eastern Churches, and recommending it as a way to settle problems in the West more democratically than by simple episcopal authority; he had large issues with the leadership of Pope Callixtus of Rome at the time. Tertullian spoke of how the Asia Minor bishops had an established custom that the church leaders of their large geographical territory would meet occasionally to discuss controversies (*On Fasting* 13), and, by being able to repeat this news in North Africa, he suggests to us that already by the second century the gathering of the eastern bishops into provincial synods had become something of a regular way of life. The biblical symbol of the apostolic council was, therefore, a later afterthought; a tropological way of connecting the now established and authoritative method of church government by synodical process–after the fifth century–with biblical precedent. So too was the notion of "Apostolic Constitutions," thought to have grown out of these gatherings. For, as we shall see, the majority of the latter,holding a significant place in the collected canons of the later Eastern Church, are pseudepigraphical.

It is more likely, therefore, that the Romano-Hellenistic world (organized as a chain of cities in dependence on the emperor, with each city having a surrounding hinterland of country areas feeding into them and in turn dependent on the cities both economically and politically) provided a ready example of the need for provincial leaders to establish common policies by meetings of neighboring town councils (the *curia*). Such an imperial system set the terms of reference for the early Christian communities: a pattern of communities representing each of the larger towns, with town councils largely being independent under the leadership of a single president in a wider "council" of *curiales*,[1] and occasions when delegates from each *Curia* could represent the town to the Provincial Governor concerning regular fiscal and political affairs. The Church from earliest times, regularizing this as a formal process in the canons of the Council of Nicaea in 325 when church and civic boundaries were commanded to be synchronized, thought it best to reflect the processes of the imperial city administration in its own affairs. Deliberate policy did not play the lead role in this; surely it was more a matter of seeking round for common examples of good practice of leadership models. The first example of how Christian bishops, who assumed for the Church the position of the president of the town *Curia*,[2] echoing the symbolic office of the Apostle, practically conferred with one another, is provided in the custom of extending letters of communion (*eirenika*) and recommendations for Christians travelling between various city churches (a common event in the vast network of trade relations that comprised the Roman Empire). One of the first examples is given to us in the exchange of letters St Ignatius Theophoros (or Ignatius of Antioch) had with St Polycarp, his younger episcopal counterpart in Smyrna, when Ignatius was being brought to Rome for trial. The reception of one Christian bishop by another is regarded as a commonplace courtesy in Asia Minor at this period, the dawn of the second century. What is more, Ignatius was regarded as a living martyr, a confessor of the faith in an era of persecution. The bishops exchange more than hospitality, of course. These letters are important sources of how the Church moved towards the establishment of a monarchical (single) episcopate, and Ignatius gives Polycarp, and the other neighboring large-town churches on his route towards Rome, practical advice on matters of doctrine and Christian practice. We are not yet at a stage of canons issuing from a formal assembly of bishops in synod (we have no written evidence of this that survives), but we are here witnessing the embryonic stage of how such decisions could be arrived at: a mixture of the "auctoritas" of notable figures (such as Ignatius) and local dignitaries (such as Polycarp).

Another major step can be seen in the writings of Clement of Rome at the end of the first century. Here in this dossier of letters we see the emerging strength of a great city Church, an imperial capital, whose Christian life is already "setting the

[1]It was an easy step to reflect this in the rapidly established proto-Christian pattern of a single presiding elder (*episkopos*) in a council of elders (*presbyteroi*).

[2]The head of the town Curia in pagan cities would often lead the senior "priesthoods" of the old gods.

tone" for the Christian customs and practices of many other places that looked to it for example and for "good practice," the two chief aspects that account for the spread of an international pattern of behavior among early Christian communities at this embryonic stage. We shall return shortly to the writings of Clement as an illustration. To his evidence we shall also add on the examples of the early Church's first attempts to collate lists of "canons" or rules of discipline. But before we do so let us complete, as it were, this global and rapid history of the earliest form of the synodical process up to the time of Gregory the Great.

It was the emerging Montanist crisis[3] that would put this Asia Minor synodical practice on the public Church map as a highly efficient way of resolving ecclesiastical problems, and one that did not rely on the single authoritative voice of a leading see that, indeed, might have wisdom and maturity on its side but equally might be seen at times to be bearing down on others with too heavy a hand. It was Rome, the greatest of all the ancient city churches, that seems to have moved the hands of the clock in this regard. Pope Victor's treatment of the Montanists had been seen by some other Churches as too severe, and an alternative system of church order as provided by a larger gathering of bishops began to prove more popular across a wider area of the Church in both East and West. In response to Pope Victor's subsequent call[4] to settle the date of Easter coherently (the Quartodeciman Controversy), a series of councils was convoked across the Christian world,[5] and this significant departure truly internationalized the Asia Minor synodical practice, starting a process of development that would be capped, symbolically, by the Great Ecumenical Synod held at Nicaea in 325. At this stage, an equally large-scale gathering was orchestrated by a mix of ecclesiastical and imperial authorities, and patterns for the fully emergent synodical structure were laid out clearly as paradigms to follow.

In the mid-third century, in the later part of Origen's life, he had been called by the collective of Palestinian bishops as a theological specialist[6] to help them resolve several problems of theological interpretation. His records of the meeting show that the earliest conception of gathering (*synodos*) was a genuine dialogue seeking com-

[3]See Eusebius, *Ecclesiastical History* 5.16.10; also *Ecclesiastical History* 7.7.5 concerning Dionysios of Alexandria on the synodical treatment of Montanism. They were an "enthusiastic" prophetic sect.

[4]He was clearly following an old-established practice of Rome to see itself as having an international governance role among the Churches (see the discussion of Clement of Rome's letter below) as exemplified in both the Montanist controversy and Quartodeciman dispute.

[5]Eusebius, *Ecclesiastical History* 5.23, 2–4

[6]Our understanding of these interesting events from the mid-third century is provided by the recently discovered treatise *Dialogue With Heracleides*, where he is shown engaging in debate with an Arabian bishop, disputing various interpretations of the Scriptures, and helping the assembled bishops of the region to come to a common accord on Christian liturgical practice. Heracleides had been arguing (on the basis of a literal reading of the Old Testament), that members of his church ought to refrain from eating blood (i.e., observe kosher rules).

mon agreement and consensus through study. At the end, the dissident bishop Heracleides is reconciled to the majority by admitting he had been convinced by the evidence. Only later did the councils, or synods, assume the character of "trials" of dissidents.

One of the first examples of this is provided by the case of Paul of Samosata, a high ranking official and philosopher who served the royal court of the city who was elected by the local Christian community as their bishop. When he started to develop a speculative theology of his own, the Church and the council of presbyters became increasingly alarmed, but he acted, with the queen's support, as if he were a leader of a philosophical school whose students had rebelled, and he refused to give way before complaints that his theories were "heretical" in terms of Christian tradition and practice in other Churches. The Christians could not move against him legally, and either ask him to step aside, or reclaim the church buildings. Therefore, the bishops of the surrounding towns and cities, with international support, were called together to declare Paul "deposed," no longer the authentic bishop of the Catholic Church and no longer in communion with the provincial bishops. So it was that, although they could not reclaim their buildings, they set aside Paul's leadership and declared his religious assembly to be henceforth sectarian and proceeded to elect a new member of the council of presbyters as the bishop of the Church in Samosata, recognized as such by the surrounding synod. From notorious cases of troubles such as this, there soon derived the practice that the ordination of each bishop of a local Church had to be attended and celebrated by several bishops from the neighboring Churches. So, it was presumed, a coherence of doctrine and liturgical practice could be assured across a more than merely local domain.

By the third century the principle of annual meetings of the bishops of a province had become common. St Cyprian, bishop of Carthage in North Africa, came into that role after a life of service on the highest council of the Curia of Carthage, as lawyer and politician. In his letters he shows that the North African bishops were now meeting regularly to decide disciplinary matters in their Churches.[7] This movement to common agreement over the high significance of synodical concord, soon enough established councils,at least in the Eastern Church, as the supreme source of canon law. The disciplinary decisions which the Synods published became known simply as "the canons." After stating an agreement over the doctrinal or disciplinary issue that was the motivating cause of the particular synod, the acts of the councils almost always proceed to issue these specific disciplinary guidelines. After the fifth century the papacy increasingly issued law as from the Roman See itself, and based upon the written dictate (*decretal*) of that see's ruling bishop. From this time onwards there would be a growing friction between the

[7]Cyprian *Epistles* 55; 67.1.

three domains of ecclesial authority that had now been established structurally: first, the issue of the authority of a "ruling" bishop in his own diocese; second, the authority of a Metropolitan bishop, that is the head of a large and important super-city of the empire, such as the authority vested in the papacy as bishop of the senior see in the West, or the authority of the eastern senior bishops in Antioch, Alexandria, and from the late fourth century onwards, Constantinople; and thirdly, the authority vested in a synod of bishops meeting together to adjudicate issues. This tension would grow into major developments shaping the whole tenor of subsequent Western and Eastern Christian canon law. The history of the papacy and reactions to its increasing authority, the western conciliarist movement notable among them, can be charted along this route; but it is a topic not our main concern here, and much ink has already been spread on the scholarly page in telling the story of western canon law. We shall retain a primary focus on affairs governing the rise of Christian law in the early and eastern provinces.

Pope Leo I, in the fifth century, issued a set of guidelines in several of his letters, explaining how the authority of councils was vested in the inspiration of the Holy Spirit, in the foundation of Scripture, and in harmony with universal tradition. He also went on to say that the council, to be authentic, had to agree with its predecessors, be popularly received (the consensus of the faithful) and be approved by the Roman See.[8] Apart from the last item, the East concurred entirely. If the idea of conciliar authority being the final court of appeal was conflicted in the West, because of the extraordinary rise of the power of the papacy, it was not so in the East. The council was always given precedence in authority over the bishop or Metropolitan, or Patriarch, and that remains today the accepted principle of the entire eastern Church; though it has to be noted that there has not been an agreed General Council in the East since the eighth century and, in that context, the authority of the Metropolitan (or Patriarch) and the local (provincial) synod has risen to fill the gap in the "real world" of church governance.

So much for a very rapid survey of the rise of the synodical movement. It is from the synods, of course, that the law of the Church really starts to accumulate. If synods are not the sole source of Christian law (the Gospels remain the charter for all things and there always were several other sources of Christian norms) they were, nevertheless, a major factor in accumulating and arranging Christian law. As we have noted already, to most of the synods in history belong a series of resolutions, usually appended to the end of the synodical acts (where acts exist) and known as "the canons." The Greek word means a "rule" or "measure." It signifies, in reference to the regulation of church life, the kind of behavior that is regarded as normative for producing a properly Christian set of behaviors in Church. Bishops were regarded

[8]Pope Leo, *Epistles* 13; 14; 106; 119; 129; 145–147; 162; 164; 166.

as the primary administrators of church law and, as such, they were the primary agents issuing the rules for behavior in the Churches that seemed right to them after their communal gatherings in the Synods. So, while many later scholars have tended to look at the ancient conciliar meetings primarily in terms of the doctrine they expressed (not unsurprisingly since many of these great councils establish major theological statements such as the divinity of Christ, as at Nicaea, 325, or the Holy Trinity, as at Constantinople, 381). Even so, we ought not to be led astray by our modern preconceptions, for it is clear enough that the bishops in their own time saw their work producing canons to be just as important as their theological statements. They themselves regarded the canons as simply another way of doing what they had just done theologically: reaffirming the faith of the Church, and ensuring that the Church's life was constantly oriented towards purity of worship. This is why, from the beginning to the end, the synodical canons deal with moral standards and the discipline of pure worship. In future chapters we shall see this system unfolding dramatically after the fourth century. It took this amount of time simply to establish a body of work, a collation of canonical suggestions from across the synods of the Christian world that started to be known and have enough substance to make people think there could be a viable collection made of them for general guidance. The earliest collections of canons are mainly pseudepigraphica and are attributed, vaguely so, to "the Apostles." By the third century this pseudepigraphical process was gaining higher visibility and greater public dissemination with deliberately archaizing books of canons. We shall review them shortly. By the end of the first century, however, there can be traced the first glimmerings of this system in an era where the leading bishops of the city churches were truly overlapping in antiquity with the age of the Apostles. Figures such as Clement of Rome give us our first view of Canon Law's emergence embryonically in this way. He and other writers of his era are often called "the Apostolic Fathers."

Clementine Letters of Governance of Rome (*c* 96)

Clement was one of the early leaders of the Roman Church, at a stage when it was poised between its origins as a series of smaller house churches (in different regions of the ancient capital, especially Trastevere where many congregations of Jews and God-fearers gathered) and its development into one of the most organized and prestigious Christian communities of the Christian world: "the Church of Rome." Clement flourished around the year 96 of the first century. He is commonly classed as one of the most important Apostolic Fathers, and has long been regarded as one of the first historically notable "popes" of Rome. He officiated as a leader in the

Roman Church between circa 88–97. He is the author of a *Letter to the Corinthians*, which is a striking piece of evidence for the organization patterns of the early Christian communities, and something that opens out for us some of the most embryonically formative ideas of the ancient notion of inter-church governance, if that is not too strong a term for what is observable at this stage. The letter's very title has unavoidable associations with the Apostolic New Testament letter of the same name; and such associations are not accidental. Apostolicity is specifically evoked as an issue of authoritativeness from a Church which was already positioning itself in the wider Christian Oecumene as the site of the paradigmatic labors and glorious martyrdoms of the two most famous Apostles, Peter and Paul.

Clement probably wrote his Epistle during the persecution of the Emperor Domitian, and it was still being read alongside the Pauline Letters at the Church of Corinth (paralleling the reception as Scripture in that Church) as late as 170. Domitian is recorded in history as the second persecuting emperor, after Nero. His repressive measures against the Church were initiated in the year 95, and were largely aimed at the Roman nobility who were showing a degree of attraction to "Jewish ideas" in morality and worship, a movement Domitian despised as eroding Roman values and traditions. The class of "Judaizing ideas," of course, included the early Church at this stage. Domitian's purges show the manner in which Christianity had already permeated to high social circles in a very short time. Domitilla, the emperor's own niece was probably already a Christian, and was exiled to the island of Ponza at this time, where her "cell" finally became a Christian cult center in the fourth century.[9] Her husband Flavius Clemens was executed, for, among other things, "Jewish sympathies." He was, for a long time in Church History, himself presumed to be our Clement of Rome, the leader of the Church. But it is now generally thought that Pope Clement was more likely a different individual related to his clan, perhaps as a freedman client. Domitian's desire to deify himself confirmed the worst suspicions of Christians that this persecution was more than a passing political problem. It raised among them the deep sense of an eschatological foreboding that, as the Church was gaining visibility, so too were the powers of evil in the world, actively raising the earthly powers to destroy it. Clement's context is thus one that is going to be apocalyptically charged. The persecution is reflected in several Christian sources, not only in Clement's own writing[10] but also in the closely contemporaneous work, the *Shepherd of Hermas*. It can also be seen reflected in the works of Tertullian,[11] Melito of Sardis,[12] and not least in the Book of Reve-

[9]Eusebius, *Church History* 3.18.4; Jerome, Ep. 108.7.

[10]Clement, *First Letter* 7.1; 59.4.

[11]*Apologeticus* 5.4.

[12]See Eusebius, *Church History* 3.17–18 and 4.26.9.

lation.[13] It was the cause of the Apostle John's exile to Patmos and the curious case of the summoning of the last known surviving relatives of Jesus for magisterial examination at Rome.[14] Christianity was lumped in straightforwardly with "Jewish practices" at this period, though by the end of the first century Roman law would start to make a clear distinction between the two religious systems, a distinction greatly to the detriment of Christianity since it then lost any claim it previously had for special consideration under state law as *religio licita*. Christianity thus became targeted for increasing political purges through the third and fourth centuries, until it took control of the political system itself, with Christian emperors and senators.

In his *Letter to the Corinthians*,[15] Clement pleads for the restoration of peace in a divided community in this major city of Greece. He offers support for Corinthian church leaders who appear to have been ousted in some kind of local power struggle. It may have been related to the persecutions, which normally caused a large tidal wave of trauma in their aftermath and sometimes generations of institutional divisions in the Church. One of the key issues of a community under pressure, where membership in the Church could amount to a death sentence, is that one's leaders have to be relied on utterly. If there is a lack of confidence in the leadership, such large-scale crises often stressed the structures to the point of implosion. This may have been the cause of what seems to have been a younger and more robust set of leaders ousting an older set. The old leadership seems to have been literally "old men." The first title we have for Christian leaders, "priests" as they finally came to be called,[16] is *presbyteroi*, or elders. In all probability the Christian leadership (the council that organized worship and church financial administration) was made up in the earliest times from the old people of the community. But in a time of crisis the principle of talent often superseded the principle of priority by age. The appeals of those who were ousted, however, seem to have been sent to Rome, and the Roman leadership under Clement firmly sympathized with the old ways of doing things. This was, for many centuries to come, to be the habitual practice of the Roman Church: careful conservatism in all matters ecclesial. In holding to this view

[13]Rev 2.13; 20.4.

[14]See: Hegesippus, in Eusebius' *Church History* 3.19–20.

[15]A second *Letter to the Corinthians* was also attributed to him in the 4th century. It is not authentically his, but still has great interest as, perhaps, the earliest surviving example of Christian homiletic from a liturgical context (based on Is 54.1). Clement's name soon began to be a receptacle for much other literature from the early Church that was seeking an authoritative home. Chief among this *corpus* of the so-called *Clementine Literature* are the *Clementine Homilies* and the *Clementine Recognitions*. In his legendary development in this early romance literature, Clement became seen as a major theologian whom the Apostles used to transmit their teaching to the later Churches.

[16]The English word "priest" is a Saxon development of the Greek "presbyter."

it was reflecting things that Rome was world-famous for,above and beyond its Christian life and culture: namely, a classical way of observing the order characteristic of *Romanitas*, Roman "good order and style." This cautious conservatism has sometimes been called the "Roman Household Code." It can be observed in several of the Pastoral Epistles of the New Testament where there is a call to good order and good discipline as a virtue to be preferred highly. In the code (at once a religious and a civic duty), wives are to obey their husbands, slaves are to be docile to their masters, and all are to be obedient and dutiful.[17] The Household Code has a horror of *res novae*. This literally means "new things," but it is revealing in so far as it is the primary Latin term for "revolution."

The old leadership probably appealed to Rome,[18] and expected to gain redress. Only a very small minority of the local Church had remained loyal to them. Most felt that the new leadership was a far better thing. The hope for support was not disappointed, but what we see emerging in Clement's letter, above and beyond the general encomium to good order, is one of the first times a Christian writer has acknowledged that there ought to be an international gold standard of good order in the affairs of the Churches, and that they, as Roman leaders, have a right and duty to remind others of what that amounts to if local passions cloud any particular Church's clarity of judgment. To that extent, the Letter is primary evidence for a ministry of oversight from one Church to another. Rather, not any Church, but an "old" and prestigious Church, which can *de facto* act as an "elder" to a "younger." Clement's letter begins by recalling to one and all how exemplary was the peace of the Corinthian Church before all these troubles arose. It goes on to become a general homiletic exhortation, using the Scriptures to deprecate incidents of discord and envy raising up numerous examples of humility, before it presses its argument from the example of the Roman army; namely that an institution that does not respect its officers will never flourish and that Roman soldiers understand strong discipline. It has made the army powerful. In the Old Testament, Clement says, there are numerous examples of the good order of the hierarchy of priests, and to them has been committed authority. Finally, Clement argues, Christ instituted authority in his Church. He gave it first to his Apostles, and these in turn delegated it to the Elders. To overthrow Elders is a thing unheard of in Christianity, which above all else is a religion that prioritizes charity and humility.[19] "We deem it, therefore, an injustice," he says in his key passage of argument,[20] "that persons so appointed

[17]Eph 5.22f; Col 3.18; 1 Peter 3.1f; Eph 6.5; Col 3.22; Titus 2.9.

[18]It may also be the case that Rome simply heard of the problems from travelling members of its own community and decided to intervene without being asked.

[19]He thus uses two arguments for his polity: precedence from local custom and principle from the scriptural charter denoting the primacy of love.

[20]Clement, *First Letter* 44.3.

should be ejected from their sacred ministry." If authority has been passed from Christ to the Apostles and thence to Elders, then their priestly role should never be taken from them while they live. When they die is the time to appoint other proven men to follow in their steps. Clement ends by calling on the new leaders to do penance and restore their former leaders. He hopes, he says, that he will be gladdened by a return letter sending news of how their troubles have been resolved according to his advice and how peace has been restored to the Church's affairs. Whether or not they listened to him is not known.[21] Clement himself says that what he has sent to them is "Written by us through the Holy Spirit." As a chief priest of the Church, he thus claims the hieratic authority to speak on behalf of God: his letter is a prophetic oracle. Thus, if the community refuses to listen to him, the sin will be theirs, not his.[22]

What Clement's letter demonstrates, for our purposes in this present study, is an embryonic form of canonical regulation of Churches. Who in the Church has authority over others and how can that authority be exercised? What are its limits and who enforces it? What Clement demonstrates more than anything else is the principle of *auctoritas*. *Auctoritas* is moral authority in Roman legal theory. It carried weight by virtue of its own logic, by virtue of its inherent rightness, and by virtue of the high standing of the person who voiced the argument. It was not to be equated with *potestas*. *Potestas* was the power to be able to compel others to one's will. It could be effective even if one was wrong: brute force can still demand assent to a wicked regime or ideology as any invading army can testify. *Auctoritas* is more difficult to negotiate, but has a longer reach. And the juxtaposition of two of its important characteristics, clear rightness of the argument and a high moral standing of the person making the case, were very significant in the evolution of international codes of standard in how the Christian Churches would henceforth negotiate their international relationships. To the principle of local autonomy was added the concept of international fraternity under a system of certain authoritative church leaders setting standards for emulation. Over the next three hundred years the Churches of Rome, Antioch, Alexandria, andfinally Constantinople by the early fifth century, would emerge as the chief centers which could assume this mantle of international *auctoritas*. Each one, for different reasons (but all of them for the same reason in the sense that each one was a major capital which attracted immense resources to their side), emerged as a recognized authority for certain things for which other Churches ought to, and indeed did, look to them and take note. Thus, Antioch was a vivid and immensely important center for liturgical development. It stamped its patterns on

[21]They were, however, sufficiently impressed as to preserve his text and read it in the Church, like Scripture, for the next eighty years.

[22]Clement, *First Letter* 59.1–12.

the whole Christian world. Rome was a renowned center for legal adjudication, for good order, for the establishing and maintaining of precedents. This can be witnessed, even in Clement's time, as the first in a long series. Alexandria was the crucible of theological thinking. All the great doctrinal developments of ancient Christianity in the first five centuries were born in Alexandria. Finally, when Constantinople appears on the scene like a Benjamin, it serves as the great Imperial Byzantine clearing house. It consolidates in itself all the older resources of the different capital cities that had preceded it and amalgamates them all into a vast powerhouse of influence whose authority was felt as far afield as Britain and Ethiopia. This is the seed of the principle of Metropolitan Churches, with senior archbishops in them presiding over local synods comprised of all the leaders of the province, synods of bishops whose collective reflections can have an undisputed authority. The collection of the "oracles" of the high priests of Christendom was seen as a paradigm of inspiration, and the model of establishing good codes of discipline, namely "canon law."

Clement's authority is unavoidably tied up with the prestige of his Church. The large city Churches exercised a great sway over the smaller Churches of the rural provinces surrounding them in much the same way that great sea-going ships pulled smaller craft after them in their wake. The Christian Churches always developed with a view to "good practice" prevailing in visible and prestigious sites. While we do not know the results of Clement's appeal to the Corinthians, we do know that the hieratic and life-long view of ordained ministry became standard across the Christian world of antiquity. The concept of larger Churches' authority also became generally recognized, and the growing idea of provinces corresponding with one another to ensure a degree of uniformity became more and more part of the international Christian agenda after the third century. The large synods that start to happen more regularly in the fourth century are a major marker in this regard. But before we arrive here, there is yet one more piece of the puzzle which is necessary to observe. This is the creation of books of "Church Orders," the first literary examples of the principle of collating canons of guidance for liturgical and governance matters. Many of them were pseudepigraphical, trying to claim that the Apostles themselves had composed them; another testimony to the desire, perhaps anxiety, to tie in practices of authority and discipline to a direct apostolic precedent. Not all of these books falsely claimed the authority of an apostolic author. The earliest of them stood on their own legs as being virtually among the class of Apostolic Fathers, and they clearly attempt to establish a gold standard of discipline that can be widely emulated. It is the later ones which more and more adopt the mantle of pseudepigraphy. There are five of these "Church Orders" which stand out, and they cover the second, the third and fourth centuries, respectively. Looking at them gives us another window into the rise of the proto-canonical system of the governance of Christianity.

The Didache–Second Century

The most significant of these ancient books of discipline is the *Didache*. The Greek word means "teaching" and it is the abbreviated title of a very important treatise on church discipline rediscovered only in the late nineteenth century: *The Teaching of the Lord Through the Twelve Apostles to the Nations*. It comes from the late first to mid-second century, and is more in the style of a compilation of practices for a group of Churches than the work of a single theologian-author.. Its context shows that it originated, probably, in Syria, although some scholars have thought that conditions mentioned might also evoke the Church in Egypt. In the fourth century the book was still mentioned and was highly respected, but it was increasingly becoming obsolete. It survives today only through a single manuscript which is a sign of how it simply ceased to be reproduced once it was not practically useful, despite the venerability that attached to it. The fourth century historian and theologian, Eusebius of Caesarea, mentions it as a venerable book, but one, he insists, that was not canonical Scripture.[23] Earlier, Clement of Alexandria had thought it was Scripture, however, and, in the fourth century, St Athanasius of Alexandria[24] specifically recommends it as a useful text to serve as a guide for catechumens. In doing this, he, at one and the same time, attests to its venerability but ensures that it shall be sidelined as a *pro paideusis* rather than as a centrally authoritative text: something useful for beginners (catechumens), but not necessarily for standard Christian use. The *Didache* had a strong influence on another Church Order of the late fourth century, namely the *Apostolic Constitutions*, which reproduces much of it in its own Book 7. The *Didache* gives a picture of a Church still closely bonded to Jewish religious thought and practice. The communities, however, now have some pagan converts among them and clear prospects of more coming, and these they are anxious to instruct in the basics of the "God-fearing" life.

The first six chapters of the *Didache,* setting out an example of moral catechesis for baptismal candidates, speak of the "Two Ways" (life and death) that stand before the believer. This is a form of *paraenesis* (moral exhortation) which is typical of late Jewish literature, and has parallels with the *Shepherd of Hermas* and the *Epistle of Barnabas*. One of the few specifically Christian elements of this material is an extended interpretation of Jesus' commandment to love (chs. 1.3–2.1). Chapters seven through

[23]Eusebius, *Church History* 3.25.4.
[24]Athanasius, *Festal Letter* 39.

ten give instructions on baptism, prayer, fasting, and the *Agape*, or common meal. The Church's fast days are determined to be Wednesday and Friday. Baptism is to be generally by triple immersion, although effusion is permitted in cases where no deep water is available. Prayer is to be offered in the form of the Lord's Prayer every day. The eucharistic prayers in the book (chs. 9–10) are based on Jewish table blessings. It is still not universally agreed whether they reflect a Christian *Agape* (Love Feast) or a Eucharist, or a combination of both. In chapter fourteen of the *Didache* the synaxis[25] of the Lord's Day is mentioned, and reconciliation among the community is given a high priority as the only fitting preparation for the reception of the Eucharist. The Churches to whom the book is addressed still witness what must have been an ancient pattern of ministerial order, in so far as they are apparently visited from time to time by itinerant "apostles and prophets," who are "your chief priests." The local ministers are instructed to give way to the prophets for a short time, but the prophets are not to linger in one Church for more than a few days. Chapter fifteen gives a very early instruction on the process of election of deacons and bishops. It ends in chapter sixteen with a warning about the coming of the antichrist and the imminent parousia. The setting out of regulations (protocanons) is not something that the book's collator feels it is necessary to argue about or elaborate. The text simply tells the reader what is the case. Presumably, it was published within the Church on the authority of the episcopate (clearly a group sense is already indicated, not just an individual perspective), and reflects their "executive orders" for the arranging of worship rituals. The *Didache* is an *ordo ecclesiae*, or a description of church order, that has already been established by custom, and which is being set down in writing as an induction guide to community practice for neophytes. Yet again the issue of *auctoritas* is present as the kernel of Christian polity. What is good is what has been established by longstanding practice and precedent. This is how Christians do things. This is how new catechumens ought to be formed. The authority of the bishop, however, has also emerged from the mist of an earlier age. It is now possessed of a clear executive character.

The Didascalia Apostolorum–Third Century

The next important church order book, also presenting itself as an authoritative guide to international practice, is the early third century Syrian book,originally written in Greek but surviving complete only in Syriac, and partially in other Latin and Greek versions, called the *Didascalia Apostolorum*, or "The Teaching of the Apostles." The *Didascalia* continues the genre style of combining general moral exhortation

[25]Liturgical gathering together.

with specific rules for church discipline. The *Didascalia* is aware of, and uses, parts of the D*idache*, The *Shepherd of Hermas*, and the *Letters* of Ignatius of Antioch. It bears the title in Syriac: *Catholic Teaching of the Twelve Apostles and Holy Disciples of Our Savior*, but is more generally known by the shorter reference above. The text argues a very important point for the developing legal systems of the Church, that only the moral prescripts of the Old Testament remain binding for Christians; its liturgical, political, and ceremonial prescripts are all superseded. The office of bishop is put forward prominently in the book. The bishop is the authoritative source of all church order, administering the Church and its sacramental life. There is here perhaps an echo, albeit a faint one, of the Roman legal argument that the *Imperator* is the source of law (*fons et origo legis*), not least because the authority that the bishop holds, as high priest, is that of Christ himself, the King of Kings. Instructions are also given about family life. The structure of ministers in the Church reveals that widows and deaconesses were still active at this period and in this area, the territory of Antioch.

The book advocates a six week Lenten fast before Pascha, and, in its baptismal instructions, the practice of anointing in the name of the Trinity takes place before the immersion, even a two-fold anointing, a common practice in Syria at this time. The doctrine of the Church's forgiveness of all sins (even adultery, apostasy and idolatry) is advocated, except for the "sin against the Holy Spirit," although as to what that actually is, is left unclear. The *Didascalia* was incorporated into the first six books of the *Apostolic Constitutions* which we shall look at below, and thus had an afterlife into the next century and beyond. What is becoming a common pattern in these books of order is the focus of canons of discipline related to liturgical practice. It is not so much that these books,which have long been regarded as the mainstays of professional liturgists and historians of liturgy, are actually trying to shape a liturgical commonality. Rather, I think, it is that they reflect the anxiety of the senior clergy about the holiness of those approaching the sacramental mysteries. They are deeply concerned with the sacral purity of the altar and in establishing a common sense of right behavior in Church. It is because of the holiness of the altar that the lives of the faithful are increasingly going to be regulated. We see the first signs of this in the establishment of a wider and more inclusive sense of Church penance in this book. Permanent exclusion for serious sins is no longer going to be the norm of the community, as it was in the earliest days, but in relaxing the rigor to some extent, the discipline is actually stepped up in the sense of extending its remit into more domains of the lives of the faithful. This becomes an increasingly obvious characteristic of canons after the third century and may also explain why the canons are particularly concerned with the regulation of the lives of the clergy, the ministers of the altar.

The Apostolic Tradition–Early Third Century

From the same era comes another of the books of church discipline. It was formerly known as the "Egyptian Church Order," but is now generally recognized to have been the composition of the theologian Hippolytus, an important early third century thinker and leader (an anti-pope) of the Roman Church. The book has been reconstructed in modern times from its appearance in several other church order books. The text includes rituals for baptism, ordinations, and Eucharist, as well as instructions about morning prayers, burial, fasting, and the services for the evening lamplighting (the early Vespers service) attached to a Love Feast (*Agape*). The work has many duplicated passages which have been taken as a sign it was a compilation of two very similar previously existing treatises, with a later scribe combining both and duplicating only those passages which had variants. Hippolytus broke communion with the Roman Pope, probably Pope Callixtus in the early third century, whom he accused of both theological ignorance and moral laxity,[26] and then led a separatist community. The *Apostolic Tradition* was probably his attempt to show how Callixtus' policies (such as the reconciliation of public sinners) were not "traditional", while those of his community were. His example of the Great Eucharistic Prayer (*Anaphora*), as well as his other liturgical information, cannot necessarily be taken as a sure guide to traditional Roman church practice in that period. It has been suggested, for example, that the written-down *Anaphora*[27] that he gives is just as likely to be a free composition of his own, illustrating (in an era when the prayer was still commonly made up spontaneously) how eucharistic prayers "ought to be made" by a presiding bishop. The book was heavily used in the Roman Catholic Church's liturgical reforms of the late twentieth century, sometimes under the impression that this was a definitive guide to early practice.[28] It is a book full of important historical information about the liturgy. For our purposes here, it is worthy of note that the ordering of the liturgy once again is the occasion of (this time implicit) claims to authenticity of authoritative leadership. The link between the issuing of canons of behavior and the chairmanship of worship is immensely close in this formative period. It suggests a perspective that has often been neglected in the later study of Church law, that the canons themselves ought to be seen in an eschatologically liturgical light. This connection between liturgy and eschaton is

[26]Not entirely fairly. Callixtus enraged Hippolytus by advocating a more liberal process of penance and also advocating that the Church should recognize degrees of marriage forbidden by the State: such as slaves marrying freeborn.

[27]The central eucharistic prayer of thanksgiving.

[28]Its eucharistic prayer was the basis for the contemporary Roman Liturgy's "Second Eucharistic Prayer."

something that has tended to slip away in much of the thought of second millennium Christianity, but was profoundly there in the first. [29]

The Apostolic Church Order–Early Fourth Century

The Apostolic Church Order once again claims the authority of the Apostles for its instructions. It is an Egyptian discipline book of the very early fourth century, and is also known as *The Ecclesiastical Canons of the Holy Apostles*. The book imaginatively ascribes sets of rules to individual Apostles, supposedly during a meeting they had with Mary and Martha present. We start to see here the accelerating evolution of the liturgically focused order books, into the collection of canons that we shall later see emerging from the episcopal synods. Sections four through fourteen reflect the sermon on the "Two Ways" that begins the *Didache* and present moral exhortations much in line with the other second and third century church orders that preceded it. The second part of the book, sections fifteen through thirty, legislates on ministerial affairs. It specifies there should be a single, monarchical, bishop in each community, with several presbyters, a church reader, deacons and an order of widows. It explicitly argues that women should not participate in the sacrifice of the Body and Blood of Christ, indicating, perhaps, a rejection in Egypt at this period of the eucharistic aspects of the office of female deacons. Originally written in Greek, it was also translated into Latin, Syriac, Coptic, Arabic, and Ethiopic. It enjoyed a high authority, since its ascription to the Apostles was long taken as authentic, and through the medium of the last book of order that we shall now look at, the *Apostolic Constitutions*, it provided an important list of canons abstracted from it. Almost all the ancient authors of the East took its claims for apostolic authorship quite seriously and therefore gave to its rules and regulations apostolic weight. They became, although late in the day, paradigmatic of how episcopal synods would now compose "newer" canons.

The Apostolic Constitutions–Late Fourth Century

The *Apostolic Constitutions* is one of the very last of this genre of books of church order. Its pseudepigraphy was recognized in antiquity. It was a late fourth century book of Church Order compiled, probably by an Arian theologian, who wanted to give a more solid basis to his own Church's particular, and perhaps peculiar, liturgical practices. Arians, for example, did not baptize three times in the threefold name

[29]To study it further one needs to begin with that paradigmatically liturgical eschaton depicted in the Book of Revelation 4.1–8. 5.

of the Trinity, but singly in the "Name of Jesus" This was lifted up against them severely in the fourth century as a manifestation of why their theology of the person of Christ and the role of the Trinity was as wrong as their worship forms. To appeal to apostolic authority, therefore, was a useful apologetic ploy. It is, like many of the others in its genre, a deliberately archaizing and antiquarian collection, based explicitly on many older materials, especially three previous church orders which it heavily reuses (the *Didache*, the *Didascalia*, and the *Diataxeis of the Holy Apostles*, the last being a version of the *Apostolic Tradition* of Hippolytus). The book gives many instructions on liturgical matters, notably the ordination rituals, proper eucharistic forms, and the ritual of baptism (three versions no less). Although its liturgical materials are of very high interest (it contains an extensive excerpt from the early Antiochene liturgy), it is now generally regarded as not being a sure guide to real or standard practice in the fourth century. It offers much pastoral advice on the Church's assistance for widows and orphans and advocates prayer and almsgiving. The reconciliation and forgiveness of penitents is encouraged. It has, appended to it, a final list of canons. They are eighty-five in number and have been known separately, for centuries as the *Apostolic Canons*. They became paradigmatic for the later Church, though at the time they were no more innovative than much else in the book. Canon 85 gives the list of the received biblical books which is almost exactly the one currently received today, except that the *Book of Revelation* is not yet admitted, and the *Apostolic Constitutions* is itself included as a scripturally weighty authority. The Trullan Synod of 692 first recognized that there were clear Arian elements in the book, but still could not free itself from the lure of its pseudepigraphy, and concluded that it was indeed an apostolic book that had been interpolated by Arians.[30] It thus set aside all its liturgical rules but retained its canons as authoritative. The Trullan Synod's important endorsement of its canons propelled them to the fore (in the sense of standing first in the line of supposed origin and *auctoritas*) of Christian legislative decrees. As it was of supposed apostolic origin, this list was chronologically put at the head of all lists, and fourth century legal discourse was thus given a first century precedent, emphasizing that this would be a paradigm for future canonical composition. The Apostolic Canons remain to this day with a high authority in eastern canon law. The whole work is now seen by scholars generally to be entirely a product of a pseudepigrapher (some say Julian the Neo-Arian bishop of Cilicia) using some ancient materials interpolated with his own instructions and opinions. The Canons themselves probably had an independent life as church regulations operative in the Church of Antioch, circa 380. Julian was not making them up, but rather was giving a local Syrian discourse a wider remit. They gained a further new momentum when the eastern theologian Dionysios Exiguus was given the

[30]Gaudemet, 1985.

task at Rome of collating a guide to canon law, and included them in his sixth-century collection of rules for universal church observance. Even at the time there were doubts about their apostolic original and universal validity by Roman theorists. The scholar known as Pseudo-Gelasius was one of the first to voice his doubts in a work entitled *De libris recipiendis et non recipiendis.*

Conclusion

By the time we arrive at the third century this emerging movement towards the consolidation of Christian law, at first originating with liturgical codes, but soon extending with a moral remit to cover more and more areas of the lives of the faithful, has gathered pace and visibility. It showed signs from the very outset of being in the hands of those capable administrators, the bishops, whose office progressively attributed more and more domains to itself as the Church entered the third and fourth centuries. This development can be clearly seen in what was the next logical stage of development of canonical collections. It witnessed the abandonment of subterfuge: the cessation of making pseudepigraphical dictates from invented apostles and the acceptance that the episcopal office was the inheritor of the apostolic authority. Bishops became thus the heirs of the Apostles. It meant that their decrees could carry weight without having to seek antiquarian weight. This meant in turn that their decrees could keep pace with contemporary problems: the law of the Church would now be able to live in the light of the day and legislate for real-world issues. It also meant a certain limit was placed on the authority of the bishop. The monarchical principle was partly accepted. This bishop, as Ignatius of Antioch had argued in the early second century, was possessed of the authority of Christ himself. There was no higher authority than that in the Church. But the progress of the community through the political and intellectual difficulties of those three earliest formative centuries meant that it was also impossible to ignore the fact that individual bishops were often fallible guides. The massive controversies of the fourth century would underscore this even more. So it was that the monarchical episcopal principle was eventually offset by the synodical principle: checks and balances, group consensus hopefully ironing out individual idiosyncrasy. For Christians, law was about establishing good order; and that was primarily effected by charter texts (the Scriptures and their exegesis), stable precedent, and good practice; things which seem always to have been at the heart of developments in Christian affairs. The next stage in the story, however, was well and truly set in place. The third century bishops increasingly began to realize the potentialities of their office. By the fourth century the new Constantinian dynasty would legally and civilly endow them with magistratial power as well, reinforcing the trend they had already initiated themselves. From the third century onwards, therefore, we begin to see the rise of the legal phenomenon of authoritative episcopal letters of discipline, known now as the "Canons of the Fathers." To these we shall now turn.

Further Reading

Primary Texts

J.P. Arendzen. "An Entire Syriac Text of the Apostolic Church Order." JTS 3 (1901) 59–80 (with ET).

R.H. Connolly. *Didascalia Apostolorum: The Syriac Version Translated and Accompanied by the Verona Latin Fragments.* Oxford, 1929.

J. Donaldson, tr. *The Apostolic Constitutions.* ANCL vol. 17. part 2 (1870); Also in ANF vol. 7 (1886) 385–505.

J.B. Lightfoot. *The Apostolic Fathers.* London, 1890.

Studies

P.R. Amidon. "The Procedure of St Cyprian's Synods." VC 37 (1983) 328–339.

J.V. Bartlet. *Church Life and Church-Order During the First Four Centuries With Special Reference to the Early Eastern Church-Orders.* Oxford, 1943.

B. Botte. *La Tradition Apostolique de Saint Hippolyte: Essai de Reconstitution.* Munster, 1963.

B. Bowe. *A Church in Crisis: Ecclesiology and Paraenesis in Clement of Rome.* Philadelphia, 1988.

P.F. Bradshaw. *The Search for the Origins of Christian Worship.* Oxford, 2002: 73–97.

R.H. Connolly. *The So-called Egyptian Church Order and Derived Documents.* Cambridge, 1916.

K.P. Donfried. *The Setting of Second Clement in Early Christianity.* Leiden, 1974.

D.A. Fiensy. *Prayers Alleged to be Jewish: An Examination of the Constitutiones Apostolicae.* BJS 65. Decatur, 1985.

G. Florovsky. "The Authority of the Ancient Councils and the Tradition of the Fathers." In G. Muller & W. Zeller. *Glaube, Geist, Geschichte.* Leiden, 1967.

______. "Eschaton and Kerygma: The Future of the Past in the Present Kairos. The Concept of Living Tradition in Orthodox Theology." *St Vladimir's Theological Quarterly* 42, nos. 3–4 (Winter 1998) 225–271.

J. Gaudemet. *Les sources du droit de l'église en occident du 2ième au 6ième siècle.* Paris, 1985.

S. Giet. *L'Enigme de la Didache.* Paris, 1970.

A. Harnack. *Sources of the Apostolic Canons.* London, 1895.

C.N. Jefford. *The Sayings of Jesus in the Didache.* Leiden, 1989.

R.A. Kraft. *Barnabas and the Didache.* The Apostolic Fathers: A New Translation and Commentary. New York, 1965.
C.H. Turner. "Notes on the Apostolic Constitutions." JTS 16 (1915) 54–61, 523–538.
F.E. Vokes. "The Didache: Still Debated." CQ 3 (1970) 57–62.
A. Voobus. *Liturgical Traditions in the Didache.* Stockholm, 1968.

CHAPTER 4

The Canonical Epistles of the Eastern Fathers

The Canons of the Twelve Holy Fathers

The Fathers of the Church[1] become increasingly significant as a collective body of authorities in the Eastern Christian tradition after the great crisis of Arianism in the fourth century. The amount of synods during that century which contradicted one another as the battle for influence over the doctrinal tradition waged to and fro, between Nicenes and various stripes of opposition, with the imperial family intervening heavily and tipping the balance towards a state-favored Arianism,[2] gave the Orthodox Nicenes a certain sardonic view as to the utility of general assemblies of bishops when the majority seemed at times to be heretical in intent. It was at this period, therefore, that the concept of "patristic testimony'" rose to the fore; the notion that even in times when state authorities fostered a majority view that was unacceptable to Orthodoxy, there could still be great heroes of faith who defended true doctrine and whose works were a sure guide to Orthodoxy for later times. After the fourth century had settled down, with the reaffirmation of the Nicene creed and faith (forumulated in 325) at the Council of Constantinople in 381, the retrospective elevation of who these great authorities were started with the appearance of collections of their works as the definitive commentaries on Nicene Orthodoxy. Chief in this first rank of patristic collation were the Nicene defenders Athanasius of Alexandria, and the Cappadocian theologians, Basil and the two Gregories.[3] In the second wave came Cyril of Alexandria, and the later "conciliar fathers" whose works and reputations, after the fifth century when Cyril began this process formally at Ephesus in 431, were regularly assembled in the proceedings of an oecumenical council and promulgated along with its decisions. So it was, for example, that Cyril at Eph-

[1]A collective title for the leading bishop-theologians of the early Church.

[2]Eusebius of Nicomedia, who finally baptized Constantine himself, was a kin member of the Constantinian dynasty, and highly favored by the imperial court. He used his influence extensively to damage the Nicene cause as long as he lived. The imperial cities (Nicomedia, and then Constantinople) where he was the ruling bishop, were Arian until the reign of Theodosius I.

[3]Basil of Caesarea, Gregory the Theologian (of Nazianzus), and Gregory of Nyssa.

esus elevated St Athanasius as a sure guide to faith (along with several other patristic guides), Chalcedon (451) elevated Cyril, and Nicaea II (787) lifted up St John of Damascus, in such a way associating the patristic and synodical traditions together so that the one amplified and underlined the other.[4] A similar process can be observed happening in the Syriac sources, though sometimes with different authorities being cited, between the fifth and eighth centuries. After the alienation occurring subsequent to the Council of Chalcedon, the Byzantine and Syriac traditions largely grew up in parallel dimensions.[5]

To the extent that the greater synods had already established themselves as a chief source of the creation and governance of wider church affairs, through the means of the issuing of canons and rules of discipline and order, it was a natural step that the works of the fathers who rose up in significance alongside the synodical process, would retrospectively be "canonized." This did not just mean that their authority was recognized as highly significant in all matters concerned with doctrine and spirituality; it also meant that their corpus of works was often scrutinized so that rules of discipline could be extracted from it and added to the burgeoning canonical lists that were growing up as a result of the synods. This process of distilling "canons" from the writings of the Fathers was easy in one sense, when famous writers of the past, whose names were now safely enshrined in the patristic lists of authoritative writers, had actually written letters concerning discipline and church order in their own lifetimes, as several of them had.[6] These letters were now given canonical authority by being included in synodically-approved lists. When the writers had not actually written specific letters addressing canonical matters, but had significant things to say anyway, often later editors went through their works digesting lists of canons from them. In both cases these canons derived from the Fathers became known as patristic canons, or "Canonical Letters of the Fathers." As we have noted, the formal process began with St Cyril's digesting a list of theological propositions from the works of major theologians of the past in the form of an anthology of authorities at Ephesus (431), and by the time of the Quinisext Council *in Trullo* in 692,[7] which focused explicitly on the collation and arrangement of what authorita-

[4] See McGuckin (1998).

[5] The Syriac sources are in *Synodicon Orientale,* a collection of canons for the Church of the East compiled between 410 and 775. The critical edition is Chabot (1902). The *Synodicon* was composed by the Catholicos Timothy I (780–823). It covers the usual canon law issues but also spreads out to inheritance legislation not normally found in Byzantine sources–probably because the Syriac bishops, liminally located, often had to adjudicate these matters in their episcopal courts far more often than a Byzantine counterpart in a see with many civil magistrates available. See Erhart (2000).

[6] Their role as local bishop-magistrates involved them all in at least some form of legal adjudication; and often there were significant disciplinary matters that involved special appeals to their judgment.

[7] Canon 2 of the Quinisext Synod; literally the "Fifth-Sixth" Oecumenical Council, so named because it was a synod that was called retrospectively to add disciplinary canons to the decrees of the Fifth and

tive canon law the Eastern Church should look to, the "Canons of the Twelve Holy Fathers," as cited in canon 2 of the same, have been elevated as universal legal authorities. After this point, the listing of patristic canons was established as a core part of the material. The process of adding new historical data was more or less coming to a close by this stage in the seventh century.[8] The patristic canons are placed in the literature immediately after the conclusion of the synodical canonical collections. The chief items in the patristic canonical genre are as follows:

St Dionysios of Alexandria (d. 265)

The canons of Dionysios[9] come from a renowned figure in patristic history, a disciple of Origen who became archbishop of the See of Alexandria (248–265). He was one of the most learned clerics of his age and came to be known as Dionysios the Great. Dionysios was born into a wealthy pagan family and had come to Christian faith from his extensive reading in philosophy,[10] and governed his Church through the persecutions of the Emperors Decius and Valerian. He wrote many letters, expressing his opinions on a wide range of doctrinal and disciplinary questions affecting the Church of his day; notably, the issues attending on the early trinitarian terminology, and controversies arising from the Novatian schism. The disciplinary chaos consequent to the cessation of persecution in the Church of Alexandria called for great pastoral tact. From his letter to Bishop Basilides of Pentapolis (Libya) in 260, four canons were later abstracted to enter the universal code of eastern canon law.[11] They generally relate to liturgical rules for cleanliness, or sacral purity, and

Sixth Oecumenical Synods (the Councils of Constantinople II and III); and it did not wish to claim a separate existence within the pre-existing scheme of the "Oecumenical Councils," but aimed rather at attaching itself to the two previous ones, and claiming their authority for its own moral reforms. The synod met in the domed hall (*Trullo*) of the imperial palace at Constantinople in 692, and from this location it is sometimes known as the Synod in Trullo, although this is a very confusing designation since the same title also describes the 6th Oecumenical Council of Constantinople III held in 681.

[8]The *Letter of Tarasios* would be added, but the Byzantine era sees no substantive new additions, and the process of new adjudications in the form of Episcopal Chancery decisions (*Eratopokriseis*) is conducted with care so as not to make them appear "new" in any sense.

[9]Rudder (1983) 714–723; Pitra (1864) 541–550.

[10]Eusebius, *Church History* 7.7.1–3. Eusebius dedicated almost all of the seventh book of the *History* to him.

[11]The first concerns the correct time for the ending of the Paschal fast. Basilides had noted that the Gospel accounts did not state the time of the Resurrection very clearly, and Dionysios gives a commentary on how the different accounts are to be synchronized. He resolves that the practical liturgical issue is clear enough: that the feasting should not begin until the time of Resurrection is celebrated, but that those wishing to commence the festival earlier (late Saturday night) but who have only observed a two day fast (Friday and Saturday preceding), are not to be used as models–rather a four day fast ought to have been observed. The second concerns the prohibition of women in their time of menses from attending public

Dionysios generally assumes the position that the law ought to respect freedom of conscience, when the conscience is sufficiently educated. Pitra's collection also includes other canons from Dionysios' *Letter to Conon*, which concern the process of rehabilitation that can be assigned for lapsed Christians. Dionysios offers to them what may seem to moderns a rigorous path to reconciliation, such as certain numbers of years standing outside the church building where the Eucharist is to take place, but also allowing immediate restitution to communion for those on their deathbed. He arranged this system of reconciliation, however, in the face of many rigorists of his day, Novatian among them, who insisted most strenuously that the showing of mercy to the lapsed was a decadence in terms of church discipline and forbidden by the terms of orthodoxy. Dionysios courageously stood for the principle of mercy in the Church, and the ordering of laws for the end of pastoral care for the good order of people, more than their punishment, and did so even at the cost of personal criticism. He demonstrated a fine pastoral spirit of generosity to the weakness of generally good people whom he knew had been forced back into the pagan rites largely through fear of torture.

St Gregory Thaumatourgos of Neo-Caesarea (d. *c* 270)

Gregory was a contemporary of Dionysios (and also a disciple of Origen), who had followed his course of advanced studies at Palestinian Caesarea. He was the Apostle of Cappadocia, evangelizing large regions of new territories towards the Armenian border and establishing many Churches, for which he wrote on matters of law. Gregory sent a letter on church discipline to the Christians of Pontos by the Black Sea. Twelve canons were digested from it,[12] mainly relating to manners of disciplining serious offenses against social order. Gothic raiders had pillaged Church communities there and the local bishop was asking how to proceed with the restoration

church services, an item which shows the close alignment of Jewish liturgical ideas in the Church of Alexandria at this period. It was reaffirmed by the seventh canon of Timothy of Alexandria, and Novel 17 of Leo the Wise made it a state law for Byzantium that women should not attend public church services at this time. The weight of the Old Testament Law was decisive on this matter in Christian Antiquity. Nicodemos of Athos in the late 18th century (Rudder [1983] 720) completely misinterprets the reason for the prohibition of blood flux in the ancient texts reading it (in the narrow censorious limits of an early modern Greek monk) as equivalent to something "disgusting, unclean, and abominable in common understanding" when in fact it carried a high charge of fearfulness because it was regarded as a highly sacred thing, cultically debarring the Israelite woman from common society. Nicodemos even uses the canon as a reason to explain (we can hardly say justify for it is a specious exegesis) why the office of Christian Deaconess was abolished by the Church. The 3rd and 4th canons are also liturgical decisions relating to what constitutes issues of sexual defilement. Dionysios advocates the application of common sense and advises that husband and wife ought to be left to decide how they themselves regulate their approach to the altar.

[12] Rudder (1983) 725–737; Pitra (1864) 562–566.

of discipline. Were captives forced to eat with pagans to be held guilty of eating food sacrificed to the idols? Were Christian women who were raped to be held guilty in some way and debarred from the sacraments? The response is that the moral issues ought to be separated from the practical circumstances. Was it a matter of moral collaboration or not? If the eaters at the Gothic banquets were simply there by necessity, the issue of where the food came from is hardly significant. If the women were not sexually complicit, then they share no blame in anything. For Gregory, the heart's intention frees the Christian; this ought to be established by the local bishop taking into account the quality of the moral life before the barbarian raids and making his adjudications accordingly. Looters and profiteering carpet-baggers among Christians, however, ought to be debarred from communion. Those who joined in with the raiders and refused to return property they too stole, receive a heavier sentence of banishment from the Church communion. The last canon in this series, describing how the degrees of lesser banishment from communion are to be ordered for Weepers, Listeners, Hearers and Co-Standers, is not derived from Gregory's writings but is actually written by St Basil. This canon presents the arrangement of repentance processes in order to clarify Gregory's remarks, which have been elevated to a series of judgments as a way of censuring different levels of community injustice.[13]

St Peter of Alexandria (d. 311)

Peter of Alexandria was also a renowned figure in the early Church and demonstrates the manner in which the early canonical code of Alexandria had a dominant influence over Eastern Christian affairs, especially given that it was the leading see of the whole Christian East from the third century until the fifth. Peter became Archbishop of Alexandria *c* 300, and presided over the Church during the Diocletianic persecution which began in 303. He too, therefore, had to cope with a Church in massive turmoil, making his legislation relevant as the way in which a large Church dealt with a particularly severe persecution, during which many local believers had lapsed into idolatrous conformity but then repented and wanted readmission. His *Homily on Repentance* and how Christians could be rehabilitated was the source of the fourteen canons extracted from it.[14] In all of them he outlines the ways appropriate for returning to active Church life, by degrees meant to demonstrate sincerity. In 307, the fourth Pascha after the ending of the Persecution, he ordered that those who had lapsed after tortures, who "still bore on their bodies the wounds of

[13]Rodopoulos (2007) 51–52.

[14]Rudder (1983) 740–756; Pitra (1864) 551–561

Jesus" (canon 1), ought to be admitted to communion after spending the final forty days of Lent fasting. Those who lapsed with lesser reasons are given longer penances. Those who pretended to the authorities that they had sacrificed to the idols,as required by state law, when they had not done so, are still to be penalized by six months of debarment from the Eucharist, for the bad example they gave (canon 5). Those who used their capital resources to buy off the persecutors are not to be penalized, Peter says, since they used their money in a right fashion (canon 12). The principle is set out with great pastoral care: let the severity fit the offense and let mercy and the principle of rehabilitation be paramount, especially for those who bore great sufferings before they capitulated. But clergy who denied the faith must not resume a teaching position. Only those who refuse to repent at all are to be disbarred from the Church. To the fourteen canons were added a fifteenth, taken from his homily on Pascha, which sets out the need for fasting on Wednesdays and Fridays (an early sign that distinguished Christian liturgical practice from Jewish custom in the city), which thereafter became universal Orthodox custom in honor and commemoration of the Passion of Christ.

St Athanasius the Great (d. 373)

Out of the many theological and ecclesiastical works of this great fourth century father, three writings became important for the later canonists.[15] The first was a letter to the monk Amoun in 356, who had asked him for advice concerning the unconscious sexual movements of the body and whether or not they were defiling for an ascetic. The second was his thirty-ninth Festal (Paschal) Epistle, written in 367, concerning the canonical books of Scripture. The third, from 370, was his letter to Bishop Rufinianus in response to queries raised as to how to receive Arians back into communion if they stated a desire to reconcile with the Church.[16] These indications, from a prestigious Father, were especially important in establishing processes of negotiating re-union with dissidents, and from this basis went on to have a distinct and powerful impact on the ecclesiological stance of the Orthodox Church as a whole. His judgments were affirmed at the Trullan synod, and went on to enter the Byzantine *nomokanons.* These Athanasian rules for negotiating union with dissi-

[15]Rudder (1983) 757–770; Pitra (1864) 567–575.

[16]He argued for a condition of practical realism to guide local episcopal decisions: If Arian clergy were sincere they could be admitted and retain clerical rank; if it was a matter of political time-serving then more barriers ought to be set up. The decrees emanate from the time after 362 when he had instituted a reconciliation Synod of Alexandria to bring the eastern episcopate together, as many as could be formed into brotherhood, in defense of the Nicene Creed. It once again demonstrates the highly practical and philanthropic nature of the early canons, designed for positive ends

dents who were seeking reconciliation have determined many of the attitudes of the contemporary Orthodox world to the modern ecumenical movement. His first canon, from the *Letter to Amoun*, shows Athanasius in his pastoral role as archbishop, dealing with the anxieties of the rising number of celibate ascetics in the Egyptian desert who wanted guidance about sexual psychology as it related to issues of liturgical cleanness. He establishes the principle for Amoun, an important monastic abbot, that the issue of "uncleanness" is not a physical matter, but a moral concern. The unmentioned "opponents" of Amoun, against whom he is seeking the support of Athanasius' opinion, seem to have been arguing that sexuality inherently defiled. On the contrary, Athanasius argues, marriage and sexuality, *per se*, are not to be held in dishonor by the ascetics and every moral act must be considered precisely in its context. The law in this instance again supports the freedom of rightly-educated conscience as supreme moral arbiter. It was in the course of this argument that Athanasius raised up, as a rhetorical example, how context determined rightness or wrongness in individual acts, arguing that a soldier in time of war killed and was praised for it by his community, whereas in time of peace such an act would be accounted as murder. Many later commentators misread this, often reading it blatantly decontextualized as an argument for the morality of killing in the course of a just war. In fact, Athanasius was not addressing this question at all,[17] and his words cannot be taken as an early defense of Just War Theory in any way.

St Basil of Caesarea (d. 379)

St Basil's canonical writings[18] assumed the highest of all patristic authority, just as in his own lifetime he had a massive reputation as the leading Orthodox spokesman for Nicaea (after the death of St Athanasius) and one of the most vigorous and far-sighted of early church politicians. Ninety-two canons derived from his writings,[19] taken from his Treatise *On the Holy Spirit* and from his numerous *Epistles*. The first eighty-six of the Basilian canons come from his letters of advice to a close friend of his family, the young bishop Amphilokios of Ikonium, who regularly wrote to him for his pastoral opinion in matters of discipline. His first canon concerns the manner in which to receive schismatics and heretics back into communion, and how to tell the two apart. It amplified the similar reasoning of St Athanasius' rules about reunion and provided a generous and open-hearted process of allowing for the establishment of Church unity in a difficult time. Basil's wide and embracing eccle-

[17]Further see McGuckin (2006).

[18]Rudder (1983) 771–863; Pitra (1864) 576–618.

[19]Sometimes even ninety-five, although the smaller number is the standard listing.

siology (though he does not blur the necessary lines in refusing to acknowledge any bonds of unity surviving with the greater heresies[20]) provided an important counterpart to the narrower and more rigid thinking along the lines of who belonged to the Church, as provided by Cyprian of Carthage. In the later history of the Church they have proved to be very important in determining what the "limits of Christian belonging" were. Once again, they demonstrate a profound sense of pastoral concern behind his desire, as a bishop, to establish good order in a tumultuous border province of the Church. His metropolia's rules of good order came to have a massive international influence partly because his Church was the founding missionary base for the evangelization of Armenia and Georgia; and also because his own monumental patristic status carried on to give his canonical rules an extraordinary weight. He is largely responsible for setting that tone and character of careful pastoral concern that illuminates the best of the eastern canonical collections thereafter. The second canon established an important principle of compassion towards women seeking abortions, though it might read with great severity today, for it imposes not a lifelong ban on the procurer, but a ten years suspension from communion, accounting the crime both a reckless endangerment of the woman's life (which it certainly was in antiquity) as well as moral act towards the fetus synonymous with murder. In this context, however, Basil decrees that the canonical penalties of murder *qua tale* shall not be applied, for reasons of pastoral compassion. That allowance is not afforded to women who abandon their infants to death on the streets. That pagan Roman practice is definitively barred from the Church by his canon 33.

Many of the other Basilian regulations were concerned with setting up standards of marital law. Canon 8 treats domestic violence against the wife with extreme severity, showing that the fourth century Church was attempting, against great odds, to rid the Church of the scourge of the violent and patriarchal standards of late Roman family life. Canon 87 derives from a lengthy instruction forbidding marriage within close kindred degrees and was originally addressed to Bishop Diodoros of Tarsus, who had credited to Basil the authority of an earlier (Syrian) sage with whom Basil has no hesitations disagreeing, whatever his reputation. Canon 13 concerns Christian men who return from wars after having spilled blood. In it Basil admits that in defending the Christians from barbarian raids (hence with appeal to a just cause of belligerence) these men had done their duty; even so the spilling of blood, under whatever species of just cause, is a serious matter and those guilty of it should remove themselves from communion for three years. This adjudication, so modest in the few lines in which it appears, and seen by many, perhaps, as an example of

[20]Nevertheless advocating that in such cases petitioners could still be admitted to the Church through catechesis and baptism.

tentative thinking, was a milestone in Eastern Orthodox reflection, refusing to allow the Orthodox to elaborate any theory of Just War, such as the Latin Church erected, via Augustine, on the basis of Cicero's philosophy. The Byzantines regularly absolved Christian soldiers from the actual stricture (not going to communion for three years after a war had concluded) but, along with Apostolic Canon 66, they were careful to preserve the sense that the Church ought to guard, in all strictness, the principle of the sacredness of life, the enormity of shedding blood, and the unjustifiable nature of glorying in slaughter even on the pretext of national right. Basil legislated that a willful and unjustifiable killing should be sanctioned by the Church with debarment of the offender from communion for twenty years (canon 56). In canon 84, after having enumerated multitudes of years of debarment from communion (five, ten, fifteen or twenty years, in order to signal degrees of seriousness in the various moral crimes he enumerates), Basil tells Amphilokios that he is doing this not to insist on the exactitude of the penalties but rather "So that we provide the opportunity to test the sincerity of repentance. I am not so concerned with matters of time in each of these cases, but we should pay more attention to the manner of the repentance that is being witnessed." In this he bears witness, once again, to the important overarching principle that the law serves for the shepherding in to salvation of the flock entrusted to the bishops. He thus underlined two abiding characters of canon law: that it was designed for the spiritual correction and ultimate health of the community (and thus, any penalty had to be reconstitutive in nature), and that it had to be applied with pastoral discretion. Later eastern canon law devolved from those two standards its pastoral legal approach of "economy"; in other words, allowing the bishops a wide discretion in applying the law that had relevance to personal moral failings.

The last two in the long series, canons 91–92, derive not from his letters, but from his renowned treatise *On the Holy Spirit.* The Quinisext Council in Trullo (692) adopted many of Basil's canons as its own. His collection was so wide-ranging (covering matters of a bishop's regulation of clergy and monastics, and his supervision of standards of marital life in the context of liturgical and eucharistic access) that it had a very strong effect on later collections. It marked the the Church's transition from a time of persecution (the earlier collections had been designed to govern Church life in the aftermath of major traumas) to a time of greater stability and urbanized domesticity, conditions which were more reflective of the long ages of the Church when it enjoyed political peace and stability.

St Timothy of Alexandria (d. 385)

Timothy was a disciple of Athanasius and his brother Peter's successor as Archbishop of Alexandria. He answered queries put to him by subordinate bishops and eighteen of these "Questions and Answers" formed the nucleus of a collation of a list of canons.[21] They are predominantly of a personal character relating to issues of sacramental worthiness. There are one or two marriage regulations contained within them. One canon (15) decrees that a wife's "possession by a demon" is not sufficient grounds for divorce. This was underlined by the later civil Byzantine marriage legislation in Leo's *Eclogue* and set out a significant principle that (what we today would approach as) mental illness did not invalidate a marital bond whose capacity for compassion ideally was meant to exceed such problems.

St Gregory the Theologian (d. 391)

Of all Gregory's writings, which had immense authority in Byzantium, only a few poetic verses have been extracted as canons.[22].They largely consist in thirty-four verses lifted from his poem about the canonical books, "On Which Tomes of the Old and New Testaments Should be Read." He composed this mnemonic poem at the time when the Emperor Julian the Apostate had decreed that Christians must no longer teach any classical literature in their schools. Gregory and the two Apollinarii decided to meet this hostile attempt to deprive Christian schools of independent existence by composing "new classics" for them using the best of Greek rhyme schemes so as to illustrate high rhetorical principles. With Julian's fall shortly afterwards, the need for a parallel curriculum disappeared, but this poem on the canon was preserved as an addendum to Athanasius's dogmatic letter on the same subject. Several of Gregory's theological works were also digested and received the highest accolade from the Council of Chalcedon in 451, as a perfect summation of Trinitarian orthodoxy. They thus became known as the "Five Theological Orations."[23]

His archiepiscopal judgment, composed and issued on the question of divorce and remarriage, probably requested by Theodosius the Great at the time he assumed his eastern capital at Constantinople in 381, became the standard way in which the Eastern Church approached the issue,[24] but it was not ascribed to Gregory in terms

[21]Rudder (1983) 889–901; Pitra (1864) 630–645.

[22]Rudder (1983) 883–884; Pitra (1864) 654–659.

[23]Orations 27–31.

[24]One marriage intended as norm; a second allowed for weakness; a third for extreme cases only; and a fourth never permitted. See McGuckin (2001) 332–336.

of canonical authority, although he presented the argument (as he did so much else in his *opus*) in an exemplary intellectual way.[25] In arguing the principles of how the law ought to be interpreted, Gregory assumes and justifies the significant premise that the "mind of the lawgiver" ought always to be sought after in each case of conflict of interpretation. In this case, where there was a conflict of interpretation between Christ's words forbidding divorce and the established Church practice of his day allowing divorce, what would be the solution? Gregory says that it would be to give priority to the mind of Christ as lawgiver, a mentality, he says, which was always governed by his desire to demonstrate compassion on earth. In this instance of human life, Gregory says, Christ the Lawgiver can be interpreted as wishing to err on the side of latitude, not severity. The Emperor Theodosius had probably been pressing him to decree that Roman Canon law (forbidding all divorce) should be adopted in the Greek East. Gregory disagrees with him: severity is not synonymous with fidelity to the Gospel. His letter and his character in general, are a remarkable testimony to the compassionate, philanthropic, nature of so many of the patristic mandates. Gregory's Last Testament was also included in many canonical collections as a model legal agreement for bishops,[26] though it never assumed canonical status *per se*.

Amphilokios of Ikonium (d. 395)

Amphilokios, who was Gregory's cousin and a close friend of St Basil of Caesarea, also wrote on the nature of the canonical (scriptural) books to Seleucus, setting them out in verse. Sixty-none lines extracted from his poem have been taken out as canons[27] and appear very widely in later collections.

St Gregory of Nyssa (d. 394)

Gregory was the younger brother of St Basil of Caesarea (Basil the Great) and was appointed by him as bishop of the small see of Nyssa in Cappadocia (Nevsehir in modern Turkey). He was soon ousted from his position by Arian opponents on the specious grounds of maladministration of finances. His elevation to the see was an attempt by Basil to amplify the number of bishops in his Metropolitan district, by ordaining hierarchs to small towns which hitherto had not been thought large

[25]His works became for centuries after him, a standard "how to do it" manual for use of bishops in the Byzantine Church.

[26]Pitra (1868) 153–160.

[27]Rudder (1983) 885–888; Pitra (1864) 655.

enough to merit an incumbent bishop. After Theodosius' reclaiming of the empire for the Nicene cause after 381, however, Gregory rose to great prominence as the chief surviving defender of the cause [28] and was invited by the court to give notable memorial orations. His theological writings were extensively studied in the twentieth century after many years of neglect in antiquity. Of his numerous works (mainly theological, ascetical, or rhetorical in character), a single Letter to Bishop Letoios of Armenian Melitene has been given canonical status.[29] It was divided into eight canons related to penitential practice.[30] The prelude is a discourse on how a leader ought to practice discretion and care in the guidance of men and women in the living of a just lifestyle. It is an early and remarkable psychology of governance that takes its pattern of legal regulation from the state of the human soul, cognizant of its innate desires as well the tendency for these sometimes to be disordered. Gregory is insistent that the words of governance from the bishop have to be applied with immense discretion so that they effect a "change for the good rather than making situations worse than they already are." We might call it a philosophy of psychological realism applied in the context of his pastoral legal guidance. His overall conclusion is that the "sins of the mind and soul," heresy, apostasy, are far more serious than those committed because of the weakness of the body. His third canon instructs that the presiding judge should make enquiry as to the state of intentionality of those accused of various crimes. And in the fourth canon he applies the same "principles of interiority" to settling various canonical penalties for the infringement of marriage regulations. Gregory instructs that those who manifest a more sincere state of repentance should be permitted greater leniency in terms of canonical penalty. His was an important authority for advocating the principle of proportionality, based upon the moral principle of the "intention of the heart" having priority (Mt 5.28; 15.18–19).

St Theophilos of Alexandria (d. 412)

Theophilos was a powerful archbishop in Egypt and uncle of the great Cyril who succeeded him. Fourteen canons were abstracted from his writings,[31] mainly from the Festal Epistles, which it was the custom of the Alexandrian bishop to write annually, and the Canonical Letters he wrote to his hundreds of auxiliary bishops as occa-

[28]The older generation of his colleagues, Athanasius, Basil, Gregory of Nazianzus, Meletios of Antioch, and Eusebius of Samosata, having largely passed away.

[29]Affirmed by canon 1 of Chalcedon 451, canon 2 of Constantinople 681, and canon 1 of Nicaea II, 787.

[30]Rudder (1983) 865–881; Pitra (1864) 619–629.

[31]Rudder (1983) 903–914; Pitra (1864) 646–649.

sion and controversy demanded. The Archbishop of Alexandria governed the only large see of a vast geographical territory, one unlike any other ecclesial organization in the ancient Church. This is why most matters of any significance were referred to the Alexandrian episcopal chancery. Canon 2 of the Quinisext Council in Trullo (692) gave his canons universal force. His first canon signals Sunday as a day of observance for Christians and separates it out as a festival day on which fasting is not appropriate. Several of the regulations relate to the qualities that ought to attend on the clergy, setting them up as irreproachable in the sight of the people. The final canon (14) demonstrates how the force of church law carried with it, in the villages at least, a weight equivalent to civil law. The presbyters of a town in Upper Egypt had excommunicated a Christian woman, Kyriadon, who had been acting unjustly (one presumes in terms of a wealthy woman oppressing her workers) and after a mission to Theophilus on her behalf by the emissary Eustathia, she promised to reform if she was admitted back into the local communion; a thing which the presbyters had refused to do. Employing the archbishop as a court of appeal, therefore, both parties in the local dispute were able to ensure that the church canons had some local force above and beyond their application in liturgical matters. The canons carried deep moral authority, in other words, and were thus important factors in social engineering towards a Christian moral norm.

St Cyril of Alexandria (d. 444)

Cyril of Alexandria is one of the greatest of the early Church's theologians and presided over the Council of Ephesus in 431[32] which established international standards of Christological orthodoxy. His theological writings concerning the unity of the person of Christ were given oecumenical status at Ephesus in 431 and at Constantinople II in 553, and were highly influential in forming the Chalcedonian *Ekthesis*[33] of 451. Two of his letters were also afforded patristic legal status and were abstracted into five canons.[34] The first source writing was his letter to Domnus, Archbishop of Antioch, who had forcibly retired one of his auxiliary bishops called Peter. The first three canons come from this letter. Cyril has had an appeal addressed to him from Peter, an old bishop from Syria, who felt he had been badly treated as a result of accusations of financial mismanagement (or incompetence; it is not clear) laid against him by several Syrian ecclesiastics. Cyril tactfully suggests to Domnus that his judgment (to retire Peter and allow him to use the title of bishop but not to

[32]See McGuckin (1994; 2004).
[33]Conciliar creedal definition.
[34]Rudder (1983) 915–922; Pitra (1864) 650–653.

have church income) is not a fair or useful decision. He recommends that, if Peter was thought fit to retain the title, despite accusations which could have been synodically tried, then he is presumably fit to continue his episcopal ministry. If not (if there is something of substance in the charges) then he should be tried or deposed from office altogether. To offset what might "appear to be harshness," Cyril says, he gives this opinion because he wants to make the point that canonical regulation must be done in an orderly, legal way. As it is, Cyril says, it would be good to "stop the old man's tears." It is clear from the letter that Cyril is advocating a merciful dispensation; but if Domnus thinks the matter of the accusations ought to be looked into, then he should hold an episcopal synod from which any hostile accusers are recused. The letter gave excellent advice on due process for the removal or exoneration of bishops by disciplinary action, advocating clarity at every stage of the process.

The second letter that was used canonically comes from his Epistle to the bishops of Libya and Pentapolis concerning the problem of young monks who had left monasticism but then, after being married and ordained, returned to serve as priests in the churches near the ascetic communities. The Egyptian monastics had expressed a sense of scandal, and the bishops are warned that greater care must be taken in future over the selection of ordinands.

St Gennadios of Constantinople (d. 471)

Gennadios became Patriarch of Constantinople in 458, and in the following year he convened in the capital a synod of eighty-one bishops which published an encyclical letter, composed by him, against the corrupt practice of offering religious ordination for financial favors. It was sent to all the metropolitans and to the pope. As it was ratified by canon 2 of the Quinisext Council in Trullo (692), it was afterwards included in all the canonical collections of the Orthodox Church as a standard warning against simony.[35]

To the canonical decrees of the "Twelve Holy Fathers" we may also add a note on two other sections of canonical patristic material in the sources: notably the Encyclical Letter of Tarasios Patriarch of Constantinople and the so-called "Monastic Canons," both of which are often published along with the lists of the Patristic Canonical Epistles. The Letter of Tarasios has assumed a significant canonical status for the importance of its regulations concerning simony. The monastic canons are generally applied more as spiritual *epitimia* for ascetics by their spiritual fathers and mothers.

[35]Rudder (1983) 923–928; Pitra (1868) 181–189.

St Tarasios of Constantinople (d. 806)

Tarasios was made Archbishop of Constantinople by Empress Irene in 784 and was energetic in trying to re-establish good relations with the Western Church. In 787, he secured the agreement of Pope Hadrian I for a General Council to discuss the issue of Iconoclasm at Nicaea, over which he presided, and which became the seventh Oecumenical Council of the Universal Church. Afterwards, he fell into political difficulties at the court, with many monastic critics also charging him with not taking a stronger stand against its lax behavior. After being accused of uncanonical behavior by rigorists in the capital's monasteries, he wrote a detailed letter to the pope, seeking his support and outlining the strong stand that the imperial Church would take regarding simoniacal ordinations, thus also providing a code for excessive political interference in the higher offices of the Church. Henceforth, such ordinations would be regarded as utterly null and void. The text is widely known as *The Letter on Simony;* it received authority in the Orthodox Church by being included as part of the canons of the Seventh Oecumenical Council.[36]

Para-Canonical Materials Concerning Monastics

The writings of the monastic fathers Antony and Pachomius, via Greek and Latin translations, and especially of Basil and Theodore the Studite, assumed a significance as major legislative authorities (canons) for the monastics of the Eastern Church. A large list of 222 canons was abstracted from the ascetical authors. They have never been formally or synodically included in the canonical system of the Universal Church as such, but continue to hold a high moral authority as practical paranetical regulations among the monastics.[37] Several canonical manuscripts, presumably those originally produced for monastic communities, incorporate this material.

Pseudepigraphical Patristic Canons

The canons attributed to Nikephoros I of Constantinople (806–815) are largely not by him. Many collections have them though they never received synodical ratification and later Orthodox canonists did not give them high authority. In this criterion also fall what are known as the "Penitential Collections," governing what type of *epitimia*, or penances, ought to be applied to defaulting monastics by their con-

[36]Rudder (1983) 953–962; Pitra (1868) 301–313.
[37]See Pitra (1864) 660–662; Rodopoulos (2007) 55.

fessors. These were often collated together (as in the West where such Penitentiaries were popular among clergy) and attributed, often pseudepigraphically, to the name of a great father from the past. In the case of the eastern canonical collections, Saints Athanasius, John the Faster, and John Chrysostom were the chief designees. The collections were not given synodical authority, though they were widely used in medieval times by confessors.

Conclusion

It is difficult to sum up in a short paragraph or two what the significance of all this patristic material is, given its massive range of content and the wide disparity of the situations that occasioned all the texts. Certain things, however, might be abstracted before we go on to consider the later Byzantine environment, because there is no question that the attaching of the names of the great Fathers of the Church, legitimately or not, served to strengthen the process of canonization of the laws of the Church. Synodical weight was here allied with historical patristic authority and each buttressed the other, allowing the codes of canon law to serve, in a certain sense, in place of both the synods (which ceased having universal import after the eighth century) and the Fathers of the Church who similarly "dwindled away" at the same time. From the ninth century onwards, the great ecclesiastics of the Church looked more and more to the established authority of church law as preserved in the canons, contenting themselves, in terms of disciplinary matters, with organizing what they found and trying to bring some sense of priority into the ancient materials. Just as the civil lawyers regarded themselves as the heirs of the ancient Romans, so, too, the later Byzantine churchmen felt bound to retain and observe the patristic decrees, even when they had to amend some of their aspects. Certain characters of the patristic codes were thus established as having a very long-term of influence. One negative aspect of this was that canon law was rarely abrogated in the East. Canons never "went out of date," even when they were evidently appropriate to a time long since vanished. This had a slowing effect on certain aspects of the development of social consciousness. When the medieval canonists are still reading patristic queries about the degrees of moral collusion possible for nuns who had been raped in time of war, they were unconsciously being deeply influenced by attitudes of Late Antiquity and the social conditions of that era which sometimes reflected more of Aristotle's ideas on womankind than the Gospel insights. Homer could nod, but it was a rare thinker in Byzantine times who expressed the opinion that so, too, could a Church father.

Eastern canon law, therefore, in a sense, accumulated like a great and sprawling forest: it was collated and arranged but it never witnessed the deep prunings and systematizations that were brought to bear on western canon law. Although this led to many headaches in terms of the applications of church legislation, it had a powerful effect in elevating to the fore the principle of episcopal discretion. The discretion of the magistrate was always a powerful factor presumed in legal administration in late Roman Antiquity. Its use in the Church was an important way of balancing out the negative effects of the accumulation of so much material from antiquity continuing to be given legislative priority into later ages. Therefore, the bishops were trained to exercise discretion as a fundamental part of their pastoral office. Together with this discretion we can also point to the way that the great Fathers of the Church manifestly witness pastoral compassion in their legislation. This pastoral attitude also came over into the praxis of the later bishops who studied the patristic canons very closely. It was a leaven of great force in eastern canon law: that the rules of Christian governance were first and foremost for the benefit of the Christian people and that their regulatory force was pedagogic in form and meant to be for the salvific benefit of all. It was this spiritual and merciful philosophy at the root of all Christian legislation that prevented canon law from growing into a body of law that could be used to tyrannize. The continuing prevalence of Byzantine civil law, under separate magistrates and officers of state, also prevented eastern canon law from assuming an overburdening weight or allowing any claim for absolutist authority on the part of the higher clergy. In this sense, the patristic canons represent three very significant factors in the development of Christian philosophy and practice of law; namely, that it must be therapeutic in character, compassionate in scope, and merciful in application.

Further Reading

Primary Texts

J.B. Chabot, ed. *Synodical Orientale.* Paris, 1902.

P.P. Joannou. *Codice di Diritto Canonico Orientale.* Rome: Grottaferrata, 1962.

Sts Nicodemos, Agapius, eds. *The Rudder (Pedalion) of the Holy Catholic and Apostolic Church.* Athens: Nicolaides Press, 1908. English edn. by D. Cummings, tr. Chicago, IL: Publications of the Orthodox Educational Society, 1957 (repr. New York: Luna Printing Co., 1983).

I.B. Pitra, ed. *Iuris Ecclesiastici Graecorum Historia et Monumenta,* vol. 1. Rome: Congregationis Fidei Typographia, 1864; vol. 2. Rome, 1868.

G. Rhalles & M. Potles. *Syntagma ton Theion kai Ieron Kanonon.* Vols. 1–6. Athens, 1852–1859.

Studies

L.D. Davis. *The First Seven Ecumenical Councils: Their History and Theology.* Wilmington, 1987.

V. Erhart. "The development of Syriac Christian Canon Law in the Sasanian Empire." In R.W. Mathisen, ed. *Law, Society, and Authority in Late Antiquity.* Oxford: Oxford University Press, 2001.

J.A. McGuckin. *St Cyril of Alexandria and the Christological Controversy.* Leiden: Brill, 1994. (Reprinted Crestwood, NY: St Vladimir's Seminary Press, 2004).

———. "Eschaton and Kerygma: The Future of the Past in the Present Kairos. [The Concept of Living Tradition in Orthodox Theology.]" *St Vladimir's Theological Quarterly* 42, nos. 3–4 (Winter 1998) 225–271.

———. *St Gregory of Nazianzus : An Intellectual Biography.* Crestwood, NY: St Vladimir's Seminary Press, 2001.

———. "Non Violence and Peace Traditions in Early and Eastern Christianity," in K.K. Kuriakose, ed. *Religion, Terrorism and Globalization: Non-Violence–A New Agenda.* New York: Nova Science Press, 2006.

P. Rodopoulos. *An Overview of Orthodox Canon Law.* Orthodox Theological Library 3. Rollinsford, NH: Orthodox Research Institute, 2007.

Rudder (1983). See Sts Nicodemus and Agapius above.

There are very useful notes and text resources available for public access on the Internet, on the website of Catholic University of America, prepared by world class canonists Kenneth Pennington and Heinz Ohme. See: *http://faculty.cua.edu/Pennington/Canon%20Law/ShortHistoryCanonLaw.htm* And: *http://faculty.cua.edu/pennington/OhmeGreekCanonLaw.htm*

Heinz Ohme gives a good bibliographical review on the CUA website, providing detailed data for the best critical sources for individual canons from the different synods and collections. Joannou's text is the closest to the best overall critical edition currently available.

The text of the canons offered in the *Pedalion*, although often unreliable, is perhaps the most accessible of the versions.

CHAPTER 5

Legal Theology in the Early Western Fathers: Tertullian and Lactantius

Quintus Septimius Florens Tertullianus (*c* 160–230).

Tertullian is rightly celebrated as one of the most significant theologians of the early Latin Church. His sharp mind and brilliant rhetorical style of writing combined to make him one of the leading intellectual apologists for early Christianity. His deep legal training is evident in almost everything he wrote. Being immersed in a period of intense persecution, his reflections on the legal rights of Christians, as well as larger scale ruminations on the place of Christianity in contemporary culture, make him a "constitutional" thinker whose thought had a long-term influence on nascent Latin Christianity. The Byzantine Eastern Christian world later passed him over,[1] retaining him simply as a vivacious witness to the age of the resistance of persecutions and as a vivid apostle of the intense manner in which Christianity was ready to offer dissident protest to the prevailing political culture. The Latin Church, however, afforded him more the status of venerable authority. He was the thinker who more than most invented a Latin technical theological vocabulary for Christianity, and as such, the terms of his theological structures had a long afterlife in the domains of Christology, Soteriology, Ecclesiology, and Trinitarian theology. All of the major Latin thinkers up to Augustine owe him a debt; and it is really only in the time of Augustine that Latin ecclesiastical thought is able to move out of the pull of his slipstream.

That such a dynamic legal mind should articulate so much in these conflicted early centuries resulted in the whole of Latin theological thought being cast in a certain legal master-structure. This often noted juridical aspect of Latin theology can be found strongly in his work and shaped much that was to come after. But apart from the juridical approach to issues of doctrine and discipline, his robust engagement as a "defense lawyer" for the Church at-large in time of persecutions made him have to face up to issues of Christianity and enculturation in a way that was not witnessed in many of his predecessors.

[1]The scholarly Eusebius of Caesarea is the only major Greek theologian who notes his writings.

Tertullian, though he has left us a fairly large body of work, did not leave much in the way of autobiographical material. When, in the fourth century, Jerome came to write his account of previous Christian litterateurs,[2] it is obvious that he too knew little about him. Tertullian was born into a pagan household in Carthage, the North African provincial capital, *c* 160, and probably lived and worked there all of his life, with the exception of a short visit to Rome as a young man. His father was a ranking officer in the Roman army, with a reasonable education and a good income, who was able to sponsor his son's training in rhetoric, at that time a vibrant mixture of public speaking, legal advocacy, and literary aspirations; the kind of training required of everyone who aspired for public office and the passport to the upper echelons of Roman society. Jerome says that he lived into *decrepitatem aetatis* which in that age probably meant his seventies. Sometime before 197, when he published his two earliest works of defense of the Christians, the *Adversus Nationes,* and the *Apologeticus,*[3] it is obvious that he had converted to the Christian movement in a time when that was a courageous act. He put his intimate knowledge of pagan culture and religion to work, however, drawing sharp and telling contrasts between what he calls the "culture" of Athens and that of Jerusalem. It has been thought that he was a priest of the Carthaginian Church,mainly from the way his works after 200 set out to instruct catechumens and speak about a more internalized ecclesial agenda;[4] but this point is not clearly established.

By 207[5] Tertullian starts to show increasing sympathy in his writings for a movement of rigorism that had begun in Asia Minor but progressively moved westwards and which struck a resonant chord in the rigorist climate of Latin North Africa, not so much in the more urbane Christianity of the capital at Rome. This was the prophetic-charismatic sect known as Montanism. The Montanists tended towards a more stark "other-worldliness"than other parts of the Catholic West and their rigorism attracted the puritan temperament of Tertullian. By around 213[6] he probably broke ties with the Catholic establishment because of its continuing opposition to Montanist thought and patterns of church organization. He cited the reason for the tension as the growing laxity of the Catholics as evidenced particularly in the increasing readiness of the bishops of the main Churches to negotiate systems of

[2]Jerome, *On the Lives of Illustrious Men* 53.

[3]*Treatise Against the Pagans,* and *A Public Defense of the Church.*

[4]The extant works from this period are: *Concerning the Games, On the Prescription of Heretics, On Prayer, On Baptism, On Patience, On Penance, On the Dress of Women, To His Wife, Against Hermogenes, Against the Jews.*

[5]In the so-called "semi-Montanist" period, with works such as: *On the Veiling of Virgins, Against Marcion* (first issued in 200 but radically revised from his new perspective later), *On the Pallium, Against the Valentinians, On the Soul, On the Flesh of Christ, On the Resurrection of the Flesh, Against Marcion Book 5, Exhortation to Chastity, On the Military Crown, The Scorpion, On Idolatry, To Scapula.*

[6]With works after this date such as: *On Flight in Times of Persecution, Against Praxeas, On Monogamy, On Fasting, On Modesty.*

penance to reconcile the lapsed, and systems of forgiveness for those guilty of marital or sexual irregularity. Tertullian's mind was cast in a vividly eschatological way, and these "laxities," for him, were not so much signs of pastoral realism, as Rome and other major Churches interpreted and explained them, but rather indications of end-time infidelity that weakened the Church facing its eschatological test by the "Great Beast" and its servants, the persecuting Roman authorities. Most of his doctrinal writings now start to take the Catholic Church to task, rather than the pagans or heretics. After 220, he enters literary silence and we know no more about him. In his political theology this change can be discerned. His earlier writings are more ready to adopt a reasonable attitude to Rome's power, culture, and society.[7] It is a God-appointed system of human rulers with authority over human affairs (a stance he takes directly from the Apostle Paul[8]) and Christians offer the empire loyalty in all that does not directly touch upon matters of faith or conscience.

In his later work, however, he is more caustic, perhaps because he has also seen what little effect his call to reasonable discussion actually had, and more apocalyptically doom-laden. His earlier writings were at times ready even to be a touch unrealistic, partly because he is bent at this stage on putting the best face possible on all things to do with Christians and the Roman State. In the *Apologeticus* he tries to maintain that the wise Roman rulers had always protected and defended the Church, citing Marcus Aurelius, Tiberius, and Septimius Severus as friends of the Christians, whereas Nero and Domitian, he alleges, persecuted the Church. In his later Montanist phase, he is more ready to dismiss all of Rome's imperial attitude to the Church as demonically inspired.[9] Rome is once again (as in the Book of Revelation) the "Servant of the Beast." Eastern Christian tradition never followed Tertullian in this late move to elevate such a strident political theology. Montanism had been rejected from the Greek Christian provinces quite early in its manifestation (originally in Asia Minor) and it was only in its late second phase, when it had arrived in North Africa, that it had a larger impact on the mainstream Latin Christian tradition, chiefly in terms of this ongoing dalliance with apocalyptic terms in political theology which had largely been marginalized in other forms of theology.

[7]See Braun (1992) 57–66

[8]1 Tim 2.2. Rom 13.1; *The Scorpion's Sting* 14.1; *On the Military Crown* 13.4; *Apologeticus* 32.

[9]In *Concerning the Games* 30.3. He calls out for all the gods of Rome to be cast down into the dust; but again this is not so much a "hidden agenda" of anti-Roman sentiment as some have thought, as much as a return to highly eschatological sensibility, which saw the gods as the terrestrial demons whose fall was a sign of the impending apocalypse. Braun (1992) convincingly demonstrates that Tertullian is, through all his career, consistent with the political theology he first set out, with caveats on the extensive "corruption of manners" that had come into Roman life because of its idolatry. The sharpening of a hostile tone does come in later works, but not to the extent that he ever denies a Christian cannot fully enter into the heart of the social fabric. Only aspects of the normally-expected cultic life of the soldier are incompatible with Christian vocation.

The later history of the Christian West, for example, would frequently show this tendency to political apocalypticism, and social theory emanating from it, in various stages of its history. In many parts of the Christian West, the Book of Revelation is still a primary source for political judgments, whereas the Christian East had long since settled definitively on the Pauline compromise. In all the voluminous liturgical sources of the Eastern Church, the Book of Revelation hardly appears; it has never been a heavily influential book in the Byzantine Christian world.

Tertullian's Theological Approach to Legal Polity

Tertullian is not a Roman jurist in any technical sense of that term. His legal knowledge and the legal cast of his mind can be found woven throughout all his work, and it is arguable that Tertullian, as one of the founders of technical Latin ecclesiastical language, is one of those most responsible for giving Latin Christianity its "legal cast" that would endure for millennia afterwards. His demonstrated knowledge has led many commentators to think that he practiced as a lawyer, either in Carthage or Rome, but this is not a necessary conclusion. He was a leading educated member of the Christian community at a time when they were suffering bitterly from unjust laws, and it follows that his pleading would need to be focused around this central issue. Many of his works demonstrate a legal framework of understanding. For example, his large attack on heretics in the *De Praescriptione Haereticorum* takes it starting point from the legal principle of prescription; namely, that in dealing with a corporation or a case of testamentary bequest, only those who are members of the corporation or named as legitimate heirs can be considered as part of the case. All others not directly and intimately related have to be excluded from legal consideration and their voices must not be allowed to distract from the hearing of the affair in court. They suffer legal prescription. In the case of Christian heretics, he argues, it is not worth while engaging with them to debate which set of believers (Catholics or Gnostics) has the correct version of any given aspect of Christian life. To engage in such a debate would be to recognize the validity of the claim of the other group to be considered a genuine part of the corporation or family which is the Church. On the contrary, he argues, as heretics these dissident groups have departed from the truth of the Catholic family, and in so departing, they have lost all moral, rational, and legal claim to be called Church after that point. This stark view fully represents the exclusivist ecclesiology that characterized the early Church, and was taken to a further refinement in his later Latin compatriot St Cyprian, whose views on the matter became standard for large areas of early Christianity.[10] Tertullian was

[10]Tertullian himself followed St Irenaeus in elaborating this argument for the Church's absolute integrity. Irenaeus had argued in his *Against the Heresies* that the possession of the Apostolic Succession (of

also very influential on the development of all subsequent Latin thought on the person and nature of Christ and depicted this in a highly legal framework of a matter of possessions (law of property). A person, in his approach, was that which possessed a nature of its own. In setting out the technical terms of two natures and one person with which the Latin Church would thereafter describe the Incarnation of the Word of God, Tertullian framed all of later Western Christology in a certain kind of objectivist modality because of this legal analogy focused around "owning."[11]

However, his main reflections on law, justice and society evidently appear in his great work of *apologia* for a Church under persecution, his master work which he called *Apologeticus*. Here he set out to defend his community which was in mortal peril. His task was first of all to reverse the concept of *praescriptio* itself and argue that Christians, by virtue of their religion alone, had not forfeited the rights afforded to them by law and natural justice. The argument arose from the sacral character still attached to classical Roman law. Ancient law regarded crimes in the sense of sins having been committed against the order of justice established by the gods. To offset the outlaw's breaking of these sacred obligations an expiation had to be made– a religious sacrifice of some kind to repay the debt. At first, for great crimes, the sacrifice in antique Roman society was required to be the life of the offender. Later this severity was reduced and exile and confiscation of goods were substituted. Such an exile was literally an "outlaw." He was outside the scope or protection of Roman law. He stood as an *homo sacer* and anyone finding him on Roman soil was regarded as having fulfilled a religious duty to avenge the sacrilege committed.[12] In Tertullian's day this religious character still attached itself to Roman law, albeit in an extended sense. But the root of the imperial persecutions of the Christians, however politically motivated, or explicable on the grounds of ethnic scapegoating, always demonstrated a profoundly religious character to them: the Christians had, by refusing honor to the gods who supported Rome, definitively set themselves apart from Rome. By living in the midst of the empire yet offending the Roman gods day by day, they were a threat to Rome's continuing greatness and were thus a cancer that had to be extirpated. Their similar refusal to honor the divine genius of the emperor was simply a particular example of the overall and relentless dishonor the Christians offered to the gods (whom they regularly called wicked demons). By virtue of this fundamental character of their religion (the refusal to worship any but the Christian God) had not the Christians declared themselves to be *de facto* outlaws? It was

true teaching as well as episcopal guidance) was the defining character of the *ekklesia*. To lack this meant a group lacked the defining element of being Church.

[11]Many of the Greek Fathers avoided the concept of legal possession in favor of the analogy of dynamic interpenetration, like the lily and its perfume.

[12]Mousourakis (2007) 36.

against this type of prescriptive argument that Tertullian was forced to make one of the Church's first, philosophically considered legal cases.

The problem was not that the imperial law system was simply arbitrary and brutish. This was an all too understandable perspective and an argument that was made, of course, by those educated Christians who were suffering its legal punishments as criminals. Another common argument that circulated among the Church in the time of persecution, to explain the savagery roused against them, was that the Roman gods were, in fact, demons and had stirred their worshippers to a level of sub-rational frenzy against them. But in fact, the law's position against those being persecuted was politically reasoned and traditionally longstanding. The Christians would later share the major premise with it, namely that the type of religious worship celebrated in the state determined the moral quality of the body politic. This experience of suffering persecution at the hands of a self-righteous state machinery led the Christians to articulate a major departure from the ancient religious attitudes of Roman and Near Eastern society. It can be seen clearly in the writings of Tertullian, which amount to one of the first appeals for freedom of conscience in all matters relating to religious practice and belief. This was a monumental departure from the usual theology of divine providence that applied in ancient societies (it applies alike to Jewish or pagan sources); namely, that the people's veneration of the electing deity (deities) covenantaly secured the protection and flourishing of the state. Religion thus mattered politically and militarily: there could be no such thing as private devotion. The Christians in the time of Tertullian are one of the first ever groups to argue strongly for a certain disconnection between divine providence (let us say as discerned in this case as the manifest will of God for a nation) and fidelity to the cult. The roots of that theology, making the discernment of God's true will a more complicated matter than the tendency of self-identification of ancient societies as divinely-elect nations, is found, of course, in Jesus' own complex theology of providence.[13] But after Tertullian, Augustine takes it to a new pitch in his *City of God*, which we shall consider in due course.

To the Roman claim that Christian refusal to honor the gods of Rome is fittingly a capital charge because it cosmically undermines the divine honors on which account the gods granted Rome's political ascendancy, Tertullian answers with the acerbic response: Rome never flourished on this earth because it was religious, it gained the world precisely because it was irreligious,[14] always ready for war and raping. Straightforward providential readings of history are ridiculed in this stance. It was not the gods of Rome which dealt favors to Italy, but, on the contrary, it is the

[13]See Lk 13.1–5. The Cross itself is the most stark challenge to the notion that the faithful believer will be assured divine protection in terms of this earthly society (Mk 8.34–35).

[14]*Apologeticus* 25.

supreme God of all history, the one God of all mankind, who allots and takes away kingdoms.[15] Tertullian often comes back to this insistent setting of earthly history into an apocalyptic frame of reference. It gives much of his work an interesting socio-political edge. In this instance it implies that if one is to read history aright, one cannot simply read it as a story of this or that particular nation's rise to dominate others and then claim divine permission to continue the dominance. On the contrary, it argues that the oneness of the true God who is the sole Lord of History makes of human culture both a search for harmony and fraternity, and also a moral test. What did one society do with their moment of ascendancy: extend their rapinage, or seek to raise the common good?

Because of his dislocation of simplistic providence theology it followed that Tertullian can make what would have appeared to ancient contemporaries as a very startling conclusion. Religion, Tertullian says, is a matter of private conscience. He is one of the first Christian theologians (sadly not a voice that was afterwards high in the memories of Christian leaders when once in their ascendancy) to argue that the peace of a diverse society demands that every human being has an inalienable right, by virtue of being a rational and moral creature (on which basis human society is founded) to freedom of worship. It is a privilege of our nature, he says, that each one must worship according to their deepest conviction. He goes on to say, pressing the point that legal compulsion of religious matters is therefore counter-rational and contrary to morals, that one individual's religion can neither harm nor help another: "It is, assuredly, no part of religion, to compel religion, to which free will alone must lead a rational being."[16]

Here his philosophical position owes much to his Stoic education. The Stoic reliance on the notion of the natural law to be a synonym for conscience is what Tertullian regularly alludes to as the power that underlies the bond of human society. It is this foundational energy of harmony and consensus that law merely binds together on the surface. If the underlying rational fundament of consensus should disappear, law would not be enough to sustain human society. It is imperative, therefore, that law should foster and sustain the springs of this natural moral harmony and due order in society. In his own thought, Tertullian often makes the natural law a synonym for "conscience."[17] In Christian hands this is more potently charged with individual religious overtones of grace and sinfulness than ever it was in the Stoics and much more religiously rooted in both than it is in modern appeals to the social utility of natural law, but it undoubtedly served in

[15] *Apologeticus* 26.

[16] *To Scapula* 1.

[17] "Neither God nor nature lies" (*On the Soul* 6.1). Conscience is the "primordial gift of God to mankind" (*Against Marcion* 1.10.3).

the ancient world as a commonly recognized *lingua franca* among those who, for many centuries past, had been arguing that law was the servant of justice and equity, not the other way around. Tertullian commends the progress of Roman law through the ages precisely on this basis, that law conforms itself more and more to justice as society matures.[18]

This is a trend that can be witnessed as far back as the great classical Roman jurists Ulpianus and Paulus, who had been heavily influenced by Stoic moral philosophy in their reassessment of Roman law[19]. It is abundantly evidenced in Cicero, too, and Tertullian thus stands in a long line of juristic philosophers who are basing their appeal to legal reason, or good moral common sense, on the grounds of a natural law operating in society. It would have been an argument easily recognized by any well-educated jurist of his day and would have evoked a certain sympathy. The problem with Tertullian's position, however, is illustrated in his claim that the ferocious determination of the Christian martyrs not to make any compromise at all with Roman authority was simply a manifestation of the calm determination of the Stoic sage.[20] This was unquestionably hard for most of the local magistrates to swallow. The legal convention of distinguishing the classes into *nobiles* (who merited different punishment) and *vulgares* (who merited only burning or throwing to the beasts if they demurred from the values of their betters), meant that much, if not all, of Tertullian's argument was destined to fall on deaf ears.

The theoretical problem was that Roman law had traditionally excused certain categories of heinous crime from due process, just as today societies deal with dangerous categories of dissidence under "special considerations."[21] In the persecutions, Christians were being treated generally (if we consider the judicial executions imposed in times of persecution as distinct from the many cases where mob rule and sporadic local violence can be discerned as the causes[22]) under that extra-ordinary system of adjudication by the provincial governor without full process of representation by counsel. This removal of cases from due process was reserved by the state for serious crimes that fell into the specific categories of sacrilege, lèse-majesté,

[18]See Fredouille (1972) 246.

[19]A. D'Alès (1905) 407, citing P. Kruger, *Histoire des sources du droit romain* (Manuel des antiquités romaines, vol. 16) 167–169.

[20]*Apologeticus* 49.6. Ibid. 50.

[21]Laws to deal with terrorism for example.

[22]It is sometimes difficult to tell whether execution of Christians in any provincial town was the result of simple mob violence, which was rife in the empire, or an officially sponsored movement. For the suffering local Christians the matter came down, in the end, to a global theory of persecution: the Roman state gravitated to persecute the covenant community because that state was the servant of the Great Beast, and followed the will of the gods it honored, who were in reality demons bent on the destruction of Christ's society. This basic theory applies from the earliest times (vividly seen in the Book of Revelation) through the *Pax Constantina.*

illicit political association,[23] or the practice of magic. The charges of lèse-majesté and sacrilege were the favored ones made against Christians, and these two *foci*, which are very closely associated in Roman legal thought,[24] thus become the structure of Tertullian's *Apologeticus*.[25] Such crimes were instructed to be dealt with by summary expedited process and carried with them the severest penalties.[26] What we read, in later Christian history, as the extraordinary (sometimes romanticized, but generally horrendous) tortures of the martyrs, were simply the second and third century standard penalties for dealing with what was seen as systematically organized opposition to the state. Tertullian's problem in posing a legal defense of the Church was how to mount the argument without convicting himself in the first sentence.

He sets out a case that Christians deny the existence of the gods of Rome, certainly,[27] but do not deny the existence of a supreme God who rules the affairs of mankind. Nor–and this is to the point in the legal case against the Church–are the Christians alone in denying the existence of the pantheon of gods. He thus raises the concept that if everyone who denied the reality of the Roman pantheon was guilty of treason there would be few people left safe. He is playing to the gallery here of the Roman upper classes, the administrators of law, who, for many centuries, had taken a sardonic view of the old rites of Rome. Cicero is a prime example, in his *De natura Deorum* expressing personal leanings towards a philosophically based monotheism (because the existence of such gods is incredible), while advocating the public utility of "superstitions of the plebs" in sustaining public morality standards. Tertullian simply says that to apply the legal prescription brutally, that all deniers of the gods are worthy of execution, is an unworthy refutation of reason, which a rational discussion, should the Christians ever be allowed time in court to set out their religious beliefs, would be able to dispel.[28]

But if the gods are at issue, Tertullian goes on, there can be no issue at all about the question of the loyalty of the Christians. "A Christian'," he says,"'is an enemy to no one, and least of all to the Emperor of Rome, whom any Christian knows to have been appointed to that place by God, and whom he thus cannot but love

[23]Which is closely associated with armed rebellion and occupation of a temple (hence sacrilege) and given the same legal penalties (*Digest* 47.22.2; Ulpian 1 6; *On the Office of Proconsul,* D'Àles [1905] 385).

[24]Digest 48.4.1; Ulpian 1.7. *On the Office of Proconsul*: "What is called treason is very close indeed to the concept of sacrilege. Lèse-majesté is that crime committed against the Roman people, or against its security, and they are guilty of it who have initiated matters by malicious counsel, or actual association" (D'Àles [1905] 385).

[25]"Let us deal with the charges of sacrilege and treason; for this is the chief accusation against us; indeed the sole charge" (Tertullian, *Apologeticus* 10).

[26]*Pauli Sententiae* 5.29.1: "The lower classes are to be thrown to the animals, or else burned alive; and the nobler classes are to be decapitated" (D'Alès [1905] 385).

[27]*Apologeticus* 11.

[28]*Apologeticus* 11.

and honor."[29] The Christian duty to love and obey the emperor does not mean, however, that the Christians do not have the rights of citizens to criticize or correct abuses. The Lord's command to "Give to Caesar what is Caesar's" also means that they are duty bound to withhold from him what is not his.[30] But the emperor, if he is a true "Emperor of the Romans," will himself recognize the limits of what is just and right. God, Tertullian says, has appointed him to power in order to enforce just laws. This is his primary duty, his *raison d'être.*[31] He must preserve the peace and punish the wrong-doer.[32] If he should ever reverse this divinely-appointed natural order and, instead, punish the just and reward the wicked (as the persecutions demonstrate), then he would preside over a major revolution in short order. Law must sustain the foundation of all society which is reason. Persecution of the innocent Christians[33] is counter-rational.[34] But if the emperor fulfills his true function, then he deserves the obedience of all citizens,[35] and in this respect the Christians will not be lacking in showing their loyalty.[36] In this, of course, Tertullian departed knowingly from a certain tendency in earlier North African Christianity that glorified the martyr's resistance precisely because it spurned the earthly city. Such an attitude can be found in the stark "other worldliness" of the *Passion of the Scillitan Martyrs*, written after their executions in 180. Here there is little common ground between Christianity and empire, little awareness of any Christian expectation to do much more in this cosmos than witness to its passing away.[37] But such texts probably represented the simpler village mentalities of men and women who had never looked beyond the boundaries of their small holdings and never felt the need to articulate a wider Christian social vision in the way Tertullian did.

Tertullian lumps together, albeit unrealistically, the "wise emperors" who sheltered the Christians, and contrasts them with the blatantly wicked persecutors such

[29] *To Scapula* 1.

[30] *Apologeticus* 32.

[31] *Apologeticus* 32.

[32] *The Scorpion's Sting* 14.1.

[33] He goes further, of course, and demonstrates to what extent Christian morality and philanthropy have benefited the state: *Apologeticus* 36; ibid. 37.8; ibid. 39.

[34] *On the Military Crown* 4.5.

[35] *Apologeticus* 30–32.

[36] *Apologeticus* 33.1; Ibid. 36.2.

[37] On July 17, 180, a group of 12 Christian youths was brought before the Proconsul Publius Vegellius in the African town of Scillium. One of them, Speratus, spoke for all of them and his dialogue in court was written down. The Proconsul asked them to "come back to their senses" so as to receive clemency from their lord the emperor. Speratus replied: "We have never done anything wrong, or committed any crime. Even when people mistreated us we gave thanks, because we honor the emperor." When the Proconsul asked them to swear before the divine genius of the emperor, Speratus went on: "I do not know the empire of this world. The one I serve belongs to God."

as Nero.[38] Weigh up the case, he challenges the emperor. Whose side would you like to be on, that of your predecessors who found no harm in the Church, or that of the likes of Nero?[39] Augustus is pointedly praised because in his wisdom he did not insist on receiving divine honors.[40] At the local level, Tertullian says, many magistrates demonstrate their humanity and wisdom by dismissing cases brought against Christians, simply out of their own love for justice and law.[41] For the illumination of the unconvinced he gives particular attention to Trajan's rescript to Pliny who had investigated the Christians in Asia Minor and declared them basically innocent. By recorded rescript, Tertullian argues, the Emperor Trajan declared that they ought not to be sought out any longer, but those who had been brought to the attention of the authorities ought to be punished. What inconsistency, he concludes. If they are innocent, why should they be punished at all?[42] Even when Tertullian is promising the Romans his loyalty, there is always the important and necessary *caveat* that underlies all Christian judgment on social polity. The allegiance is never to be absolute, unthinking: it always depends on the giving of allegiance to a God-appointed authority whose duty it is, pagan or Christian, simply to sustain that which is right. Accordingly, the root of the Christian social duty is always to remind the leaders of this limit of their authority–the reason why they will so rarely be liked for exercising it.[43]

Law, Tertullian argues, must be by its very nature transparent; patently rational and defensible and applied equitably, or else it fails to be a good law, and society suffers. In a famous dictum he presses the point: *legis injustae nullus honor:* "An unjust law deserves no respect."[44] Transparency of due process demands that the procedures under which Christians are being summarily executed without a hearing must be declared a miscarriage of justice. If a law wishes to hide in the darkness, it is a clear indication it is evil.[45] Let the workings of justice be in the light of day. Let Christians make a case in court. If they are wrong, then reason will prevail and at their condemnation the law will be all the more held in honor by all. But if they are seen to be unjustly persecuted, then the law must be changed, for this is what improves law: its constant openness to being improved in the light of culture's progress towards justice and equity. The very system of ancient Roman law bore witness to this in the manner in which later rescript was always ready to improve on

[38] *Apologeticus* 1.5.
[39] *Apologeticus* 5.
[40] *Apologeticus* 34.1.
[41] There was wide latitude for local judges in hearing cases; cf. *To Scapula* 4.
[42] *Apologeticus* 2.9.
[43] Osborn (1997) 85–86.
[44] *Ad Nationes* 6.
[45] *Apologeticus* 4.

old and decayed practice. The present conservative attitude, Tertullian argues, witnessed in the era of persecutions, of justifying an unbending attitude with regard to legal changes (law as "unchanging truth"), is hostile to the central cultural principle that law must not clash with morality.[46]

The role of reason underlies all his wider thought on legal polity, and it derives directly from his deeply rooted theological anthropology. For Tertullian, God has established an order in society,[47] which is an apex of that which he has established as the rational system underlying all creation. Mankind is the high point of that creation and emerges as Lord of the Creation in *mimesis* of the Father-Creator, to the extent that mankind demonstrates *Logos* on earth; that is, a way of life that is consciously lived out in accordance with the dictates of reason and order.[48] Moral order is chief among these aspects which put human social systems in harmony with the natural orders of the creation. The rational life of society is, in short, the highest manifestation of natural law, not something opposed to it. It can be perverted, however, and when mankind acts out a lifestyle that is disordered, given to selfish and immoral activities rather than philanthropic social care, then not only is society disrupted, but the whole creation is unbalanced, since its God-appointed head, the human race, has lapsed into sub-human irrationality. A reasonable and mutually philanthropic lifestyle brings about social harmony and the peace of society which allows all civilized art to flourish. This is precisely why the emperor has been set up by God to preside over the administration of reasoned justice on earth,[49] and why he commands the allegiance of the Christians.[50]

Tertullian consistently argues throughout his writings that of all forms of human existence, it is that of the Christians which will bring peace into the heart of the human system most fully and most effectively, since it is a revelation of a lifestyle built upon the premise of love. Within Christianity, Tertullian says, love is for the first time ever in history elevated as the supreme rule of society, the highest vision of social communion.[51] It is both the perfection of an individual life and the perfect flowering of God's desire for society. This law of love is the universal law estab-

[46] *Apologeticus* 4.

[47] The Empire of Rome has a part to play in that evolving system. Despite many who have (perhaps carelessly) read Tertullian as innately hostile to Roman politics, more recent careful analysis has demonstrated that the pagan cults and their embeddedness in the political system is his constant target. He envisages the system of imperial government itself as a cultural force that has been God-blessed with immense potential for human good. His political theology is set within a biblically rooted apocalyptic vision of God's overarching judgment of human affairs. See R. Klein, *Tertullian und das römische Reich (*Heidelberg. 1968); also A.Z. Ahondokpe, *La Vision de Rome chez Tertullien*, 2 vols. (Lille, 1991).

[48] *On The Soul* 17.11; *Apologeticus* 4.5; Osborn (1997) 86.

[49] *Apologeticus* 30.2; *To Scapula* 14.1.

[50] *Apologeticus* 30–32.

[51] *On Patient Endurance* 12.8; *On Flight* 14.2.

lished as a natural order within humankind, though it has struggled to emerge; first growing in the social code of Ancient Israel which was set by God to teach the world, but never belonging solely to Israel, since the law of love was set in the heart of that first law God gave to Adam and Eve from which the Law of Moses later developed.[52] The way Christianity has gone on to bring this natural law to its divine perfecting within society is, for Tertullian a major revelation of truth to the world of his time. The law of universal love is taken, in Jesus' command, to the pitch of loving even against the grain. "Our perfect and unique form of goodness," Tertullian comments, "is not something that is shared with any others. All love their friends. Only Christians love their enemies."[53] But all the laws of humankind, for Tertullian, in so far as they are explicit attempts to lead society to virtue, devolve directly and divinely from the Law of God as their ancient model.[54]

The higher standard of the Christians' moral lives in the empire, and their reasonable and peaceful behavior, he says, will lift the empire to a purer standard of culture. But, it is exactly this higher standard which has in his current era annoyed the Christians' neighbors, who prefer to live a brutish life, and who thus wish to annihilate the Christians from among them. His argument returns full circle, insisting that the persecution is the perfect example of social disorder, a profoundly irrational movement initiated at a simplistic level by unthinking and socially destructive mobs, yet sustained at a more damaging level by Roman legal officials. These officials ought to have seen that the Christian lifestyle is deeply attached to reason and morality and, de facto, ought to be protected as society's benefactor. It is only the prayers of the Christians, Tertullian argues, that restrain the anger of God from bursting out on the corruptions of Roman life. It is their prayers that have often secured Roman victories in times of war.[55]

Even though so much of Tertullian's writings and reflections were produced under duress, as occasional answers to direly pressing problems, it is extraordinary how wide-ranging his reflections on theological polity were. He sets out, in the course of mounting an immediate claim for legal equity, reasonableness and moral balance for the benefit of his suffering co-religionists, a deeper understanding and a broader vision of what would constitute a truly just society. Tertullian himself is deeply rooted in Stoic moral philosophy, but his vision is far more than that; it takes social polity beyond the generalities of a sophistic appeal to natural law as a putative societal bond. Such an appeal still sustained the more basic distinction of class, benefitting the elite, and presuming always that "men of finer feeling" (the *nobiles*)

[52] *Against the Jews* 2.4.
[53] *To Scapula* 1.3.
[54] *Apologeticus* 45.
[55] *Apologeticus* 42; *Apologeticus* 5.4; *To Scapula* 4.1

would be approachable on these terms, but the common masses always needed to be held in check by severe laws and treated with summary violence whenever necessary. Tertullian is able, by appealing to the theology of Christian love, to set in place a truly equitable vision of a commonwealth, in which the supreme leader, the emperor let us say, is an adjudicator, not a tyrant; someone who rules in accordance with a system of values, and whose task it is to elevate social values as widely as possible. More than this, we find for the first time in a serious Christian theologian, a profound defense of the value of individual conscience and freedom of religion. Tertullian gives to all subsequent Christian reflection on law and social theory a significant benchmark. For his immediate Latin successors Lactantius and Augustine, he set a bar and determined an agenda that they both recognized had to be elaborated extensively in the new era of the Christian ascendancy in the *Pax Constantina.*

Further Reading

PRIMARY TEXTS

P. Holmes & S. Thelwell, trs. *Works of Tertullian.* ANF vols. 3–4. Edinburgh, 1885.

E.J. Daly. *Tertullian: Apologetical Works.* FOTC 10. New York, 1950.

STUDIES

A. D'Alès. *La Théologie de Tertullien.* Paris, 1905.

T.D. Barnes. *Tertullian: A Historical and Literary Study*. Oxford, 1971.

R. Braun. *Deus Christianorum: Recherches sur le vocabulaire doctrinal de Tertullien* (2nd ed.). Paris, 1977.

______. *Approches de Tertullien,* esp. pp 57–66: "Christianisme et pouvoir impériale d'après Tertullien." Paris: Institut d'Études Augustiniennes, 1992.

C.B. Daly. *Tertullian: The Puritan and His Influence: An Essay in Historical Theology.* Dublin, 1993.

J.C. Fredouille. *Tertullien et la conversion de la culture antique*. Paris, 1972.

R. Klein. *Tertullian und das römische Reich.* Heidelberg, 1968.

J.Morgan. *The Importance of Tertullian in the Development of Christian Dogma.* London, 1928.

E. Osborn. *Tertullian: First Theologian of the West.* Cambridge, 1977.

R. Roberts. *The Theology of Tertullian.* London, 1924.

Lucius Caecilius Firmianus Lactantius (*c* 243–320)

Lactantius, a layman, is one of the most intriguing figures of the early Latin Church. His fame has been largely overshadowed. Tertullian was much louder than he, perhaps less subtle, and far more dramatic, which was always a benefit in the process of historical transmission, and which is why Tertullian seized Western Christendom's imagination, even despite his Montanist lapses later in life. Moreover, Lactantius was followed by Augustine, and that literary fate (to be preceded and succeeded by such luminaries) was a hard one. The Church retained his memory as a supreme stylist, but as an intellectual he had a limited range of influence. The fact that he was a binitarian so late in the day,[56] on the very eve of the Council of Nicaea, was not a theological lapse that could be forgiven as easily as those of his predecessors. So, while his friends, especially Jerome, graciously "lost" his incriminating theological letters, his work was retained mainly for the wonderful style and literary elegance with which he refuted attacks on the rusticity of the Church, turning the joke back on his pagan contemporaries whose writings could not match his own for purity of diction and rhetorical verve. That his ideas had less acceptance than the more commonly known Latin Fathers is not to say they were unimportant, for it is clear that Augustine read him fully and carefully and used him as a source in constructing his own political theology in a slightly different mode. More than this, however, Lactantius represents a door to the understanding of ancient Latin thought that is unique in its character. He is highly eschatological in tonality, yet closely focused on the conditions of society, and is one of the first Christians to advance a political theology. He was interested in Christianity's reaching out to the educated non-Christians of his day, and advocated a broad Church of spiritual affinities to make that possible in practice. To argue his case he has universalist ideas that must have sounded alarming to the more conservative Christians of his day. He held that Christ was a universal priest for human culture and religion was the universal aspiration for human justice. The Sibyl and Hermes Trismegistus were valid prophets, like those of the Jews. Christianity is entirely a matter of the heart and conscience, with no external trappings. Religion can never be coerced. Dissidence must be tolerated and disagreements resolved by rational exchange. Life is so sacred that that even capital punishment is a crime against God and humanity. Few possessions are really needed to make us happy, so one ought to be content with a simple life. The rich ought to divest themselves of their surplus by generous support of the indigent. These were interests and ideas that did not, generally, find a ready welcome in the more clericalized voices of the later Fathers, who from the fourth century onwards

[56]The Father and the Son were divine; the Spirit simply another way of referring to God generically.

were almost all bishops and priests, with vested interests in clerical themes, internal Church arguments over Orthodoxy, and views about policing it.

Lactantius did have one ear, however, that listened to him at great length and was sufficiently impressed to want to make him (by that time a grand and very old man) the tutor of his own eldest son. That ear was the young Constantine's. In fact, Lactantius can be said to have been the Christian political formation of Constantine, whose tutor he possibly was for several years in the time of the young prince's residence at Nicomedia as a hostage of Diocletian. If it is true that Constantine's mother, Helena, was a life-long Christian, and also true that his troops at the famous battle of the Milvian bridge included a predominance of Christians (which is why a Christian or "Christianize-able" battle-sign was necessary[57]), then we look too late to discern Constantine's pro-Christian religiosity from his Milvian Bridge experience, or from his later legislation. Rather, we need to look earlier. It is precisely in the universal type of sophic-religious aspirations, for a world where sacrificial thought would be morally internalized and justice would be used to bond together societies in peace (the new *Pax Romana* of the fourth century's New Order) that we can see the confluence of Lactantius and Constantine's socio-religious agendas. It is Lactantius who is one of the first to acclaim Constantine's reign as the Golden Age returned, an ancient theme that held together much of Roman legal philosophy on the nature of justice. It is very probable that it was Lactantius who, in the time he was at Augusta Trevirorum (Constantine's western capital before the civil war with Licinius brought him to supreme power in both halves of the empire), encouraged Constantine to see his own reign as the "New Golden Age," himself as the new agent of God who would raise him to monarchical power in the future, and the Christian Church as the supreme medium for bringing a universalized sense of morality and justice to the dominions through a new form of rationalized and moral cult. "Monotheism, morality, and central imperial paternalism" was Constantine's vision for a new society. Insofar as a Christian theorist may well have been agentive in this polity, Lactantius deserves our attention.

What can be told of Lactantius' history can be quickly recounted. He was born in Latin North Africa as Lucius Caecilius Firmianus,[58] a youthful prodigy who wrote a *Symposium* that gained Jerome's admiration,[59] and, from the extent of his classical

[57]That the *Labarum* of Constantine was a Chi-Rho cipher for Jesus' name, and that his priestly vision at the Milvian bridge (for as *Pontifex Maximus* he had to take the auspices before battle) was a cross, are things that are "interpreted" for us by Eusebius and Lactantius, the two great Christianizers of the Constantinian conversion narrative.

[58]The family name was found on an ancient tombstone in the excavations of the African city of Constantine; cf. G Wilmans, ed., *Corpus Inscriptionum Latinorum*, vol. 8, pt. 1 (Berlin, 1881) no. 7241, p. 649. "Lactantius" is a sobriquet.

[59]Jerome, *On the Lives of Illustrious Men* 80.

rhetorical training, he was evidently from a well-positioned family.[60] He studied under the rhetorician Arnobius (who later became Christian himself) at the school in Sicca Veneria. Jerome tells his readers that Lactantius became tutor to the Caesar Crispus "in his extreme old age" when he was imperial *Comes Clarissimus*. Crispus probably engaged his rhetorical studies in his seventeenth year, the same time he was proclaimed Caesar in Gaul, on March 1, 317. If we imagine that Lactantius was around seventy at this period, then he must have been born sometime around 243. His rhetorical studies are evident in the manner in which he combines philosophy with practical religion in an overwhelmingly legal context. The ancient rhetor was, of course, first and foremost a political lawyer. In Lactantius' time that had also evolved into being, of necessity, a political and moral theorist. The Greek East would push this more and more into a form of Sophism. In fact, the Greek patristic ideal is born from it, since almost all the major Greek theological writers between the fourth and eighth centuries were trained as rhetoricians first and foremost and adapted their studies to accommodate their philosophical and religious argumentation.

Later in life, when theological ideas dominated him, Lactantius looked back slightly ruefully on his earlier profession as legal rhetorician, saying that the proclamation of the Gospel is a far sight more useful to society,

> And ought to be considered more glorious by far, than the kind of oratory I was so long engaged in, the training of young men, not to virtue, but in cunning wickedness.[61]

He is a legal convert, however, who is not going to deny the value of his training:

> For that practice in fictitious law suits which I have had, has been of great advantage to me, because I am now able to plead the cause of truth with greater fullness, and facility of language. The truth can be defended, of course, without eloquence; and so it often has been defended, by many. But it also needs to be explained, and, to a certain degree, discussed with clarity and elegance of diction, that it might flow more readily into the minds of men, and then have its own force as well as the adornment of rhetorical brilliance.[62]

[60] If he is related to the Caecilii Metelli, then from a very high ranking family indeed. They had been the greatest patrons of North Africa in earlier times.

[61] *Divine Institutes* 1.1.8.

[62] *Divine Institutes* 1.1.10.

The connection between Lactantius' own legal ideas and aspects of Constantine's early legislative process have long been noted,[63] especially the early Constantinian attempts to regulate the selling of children and the unsuccessful effort to ban the public spectacles.[64] Lactantius' major work is entitled *The Divine Institutes*, a concept which is directly borrowed from contemporary Roman law manuals,[65] and his theology abounds throughout with juridical imagery. He certainly influences Constantine's writings even much later in the emperor's life, when he was resident in the East and listening to the teaching of Greek bishops.[66]

The Emperor Diocletian, hearing of his fame, summoned him, around 290, to assume the post of chief Latin rhetorician at his new capital of Nicomedia.[67] Holding a very high social position at court, he was notable already for his Christian philosophical commitment, in which he embraced voluntary poverty[68] and thus advocated a radically simple lifestyle as the heart of the Christian witness to the return of compassionate justice to the earth.[69] There were several other Christians in a similar position at Diocletian's court. It is possible that Diocletian's own wife, Prisca, was a catechumen, and remained so until about 303 when it became an impossible position to maintain and live. Lactantius himself describes how the outbreak of the great persecution under Diocletian was prefigured six years before it happened by the presence of Christians in the imperial entourage who would not take part in the ritual of state auspices[70] that were arranged to seek guidance on the

[63]E. Backhouse, *Early Church History to the Death of Constantine* (London, 1899) 219; C. Ferrini, "Die juristischen Kenntnisse des Arnobius und Laktanz," *Zeitschrift der Savigny-Stiftlung* 15 (1894) 343f; J. Gaudemet, "La legislation réligieuse de Constantin," RHEF 33 (1947) 25–61; A. Wlosok, "Laktanz und die philosophische Gnosis," AHAW 2 (1960) 199f, 211f.

[64]Compare *Codex Theodosianus* 5.7.1 and *Divine Institutes* 2.20.1 f. and 6.20.2.

[65]And would later supply Calvin with a model.

[66]It can be clearly seen in comparing Constantine's *Address to the Saints* 3 with *Divine Institutes* 1.2–3; *Address to the Saints* 16–20, and *Divine Institutes* 4.15; and *Address to the Saints* 24, with Lactantius' *On the Deaths of the Persecutors* 4–6. See F. Heim. "Influence de Constantin sur Lactance," in J. Fontaine & M. Perrin, eds., *Lactance et Son Temps* (Paris, 1978) 55–74; R.P.C. Hanson, "The *Oratio ad Sanctos* attributed to Constantine and the *Oracle to Daphne*," *Journal of Theological Studies* (New Series) 24 [1973] 505–511; D. De Decker, "Le Discours à l'assemblée des saints attribué à Constantin, et l'oeuvre de Lactance," in J. Fontaine & M. Perrin, op. cit., 75–89. Where Lactantius had addressed to the pagan world a plea for tolerance, Constantine here finds himself using Lactantius' ideas and phrases to make the same argument to the bishops he had chosen to structure the magistracies of the eastern provinces, but this time pressing the need for tolerance of pagans.

[67]Jerome, *On the Lives of Illustrious Men* 80. This was a prestigious post that put Lactantius into high court circles. Diocletian was intending to make Nicomedia a world centre of legal and rhetorical study. To gain an idea of the financial implications we can consider the case of Constantine's own father, Constantius Chlorus who, when attempting a similar initiative to revive the rhetorical schools of Autun, summoned the rhetor Eumenius at a salary of 600,000 sesterces, a very princely sum.

[68]Gennadius, *On the Lives of Illustrious Men* 15; Eusebius, *Chronicle* (for the Year 2330).

[69]*Divine Institutes* 6.11.6–7.

[70]*Divine Institutes* 4.27.4; *On the Deaths of the Persecutors* 10.

Persian expedition of Caesar Galerius. Galerius was the real enemy of the Christian party, and it is understandable that the Christian faction at court would not wish to be associated with any "prayers" for his safety, let alone the issue of taking a rain-check on the pagan practice of reading the auspices from the entrails of birds. The pagan faction at court blamed the Christians present for making the sign of the cross during the ritual and thereby defiling it, so that the gods withdrew in anger. Receiving this report, Diocletian ordered that a test of faith (by offering sacrifice to the gods of Rome) should be applied to the imperial household and to the army.

Six years later, Sossianus Hierocles, the local Governor,[71] and another leading rhetorician at court, a pagan rival to Lactantius,[72] joined in the urgings of Galerius[73] and persuaded Diocletian to make empire-wide moves against the growing power of the Christian party. Lactantius derided the oppressive religious policy:

> Who could ever be so arrogant, or who could ever be so full of themselves, as to dare to forbid a person to raise their eyes to heaven? Who could ever try to impose on another the obligation of worshipping what they do not wish to worship; or of not worshipping what they do so wish?[74]

This was the beginning of what came to be known as the "Great Persecution" in 303. Lactantius was one of its first targets. He resigned his official position and began two large works of defense of the Christian movement. The first, *The Divine Institutes*, was a generic study of why Christianity was necessary to the building of a new civilization. This study was built around the idea of how Rome had always aspired to be the principle of justice in the world, but had not been able to accomplish it, whereas Christianity was able to do so because it could speak at once to the intelligentsia and to the common folk, offering the heights of wisdom, and the commonalities of moral codes for the masses. The second work, *On the Deaths of Persecutors*, was a sustained set of political *philippics*, naming names and recounting the disasters

[71]*Praeses* of Bithynia in 303, a philosophical politician who had an axe to grind (literally!) against the Church. Lactantius regards him as a much more dangerous character than the boorish Caesar Galerius, and wonders (because of Hierocles' detailed knowledge of Christian practices), whether he was a disillusioned apostate. Elizabeth Digeser has also argued recently that the overall philosophical underpinnings of the Galerian-Diocletianic move against the Church was provided by Porphyry's *Philosophy From Oracles*, whereas the *Divine Institutes* were meant to provide a Christian (and Constantinian) opposite polity.

[72]Lactantius describes his role in organizing the series of propaganda lectures against Christian religion that the imperial court instituted. Lactantius and other Christians used to attend them. He says that he found the man's hypocrisy more memorable than his philosophy (*Divine Institutes*. 5.2.8–11).

[73]Lactantius explains that it was Galerius himself who insisted on the anti-Christian moves, which involved a major change of Roman religious policy: repealing the toleration edict of Gallienus, and re-enacting the laws of the disgraced Valerian (*On the Deaths of the Persecutors* 11).

[74]*Divine Institutes* 5.13.18. He gives as the answer to the pagan cry that the "gods demand" the Christians should be compelled to worship them, that: "This is the chief reason they ought not to be worshipped, who wish to be so worshipped" (*Divine Institutes* 5.20.8).

that fell upon the imperial persecutors as God's agenda of justice was not deflected by the tyranny of oppressors. Modern readers are often put off by the harsh tone of the judgments "against the pagans" in this smaller work, but they fail to take into account two springs of that book's composition, the first that it was written in the immediate aftermath of bitter suppression of the Church, when many of Lactantius' friends had been executed and accounts were now being rendered in the Constantinian *Pax*; and the second, that the work was directly modeled on the biblical *Book of Maccabees*[75] (whose canonicity Lactantius accepted) as a form of the "continuation" of Church history as revelation (comparable, perhaps, to the relation of the Book of Acts to the Gospels) where the enemies of God's people, in biblical fashion, met their due punishment even in this life.

At the height of the persecution in 305, a time coincidental with the resignation of Diocletian and Galerius' assumption of supreme power as Augustus in the East, Constantine decamped, fled the city, and sought to join his father, Constantius Chlorus, one of the imperial Tetrarchs with the rank of Caesar then based in the garrison camp at York. It had been Diocletian's policy to keep the Caesars from their families precisely so that inheritance by kin would be excluded from the imperial succession system. This is why Constantine's flight from Nicomedia is more or less a declaration of civil war. Lactantius, who in his years at Nicomedia had served as Constantine's tutor, also disappeared from the capital at the same time. He was in Nicomedia early in 305, for he describes the forced recantation of a leading Christian under torture in that year; but his material about the capital after that point is no longer based on personal reminiscence. We do not know exactly where he went, but as he next reappears just over ten years later as a senior advisor to the emperor in his time in the West, and as tutor to his eldest son Crispus, it is a reasonable supposition to imagine him throwing in his lot with Constantine's new court in the West from the time of the famous flight from Nicomedia. The rhetorical schools of Gaul were not only still flourishing, but were under Christian patronage and protection. The story of the accession of Constantine is well enough known to merit only a few lines here. When Constantine arrived in York, his father passed away and he was acclaimed Augustus by the troops.[76] And so the civil war began in earnest. Its outcome was to be the historic victory of the Christian faction and the ascent of Constantine himself to sole power.

The pagan persecutors had made the case that religion could not possibly be separated from politics and could not be left as a matter of private conscience as the Christians had long been arguing. Religion was a civic affair, and if harmony of

[75]J. Rougé, "Le *De Mortibus Persecutorum* et le Vième livre des Maccabées," *Studia Patristica* 12, TU 115 (1975) 135–1443.

[76]The site is now preserved as the under-crypt of York Minster.

belief and action were not shared in the body politic, then Rome's integrity would be lost and a failure of its command over the affairs of lesser nations would inevitably ensue.[77] The Christians, therefore, were not simply religious dissidents, but a cancer in the body politic. As was the case with ancient Hebraic theology, if the covenant sacrifices were not sustained, the blessing of God over Israel could not be assured. For the Diocletianic dynasty, if the sacrifices to the gods of Rome (who sustained and blessed the regnant emperors in particular) were not honored above all, then the religious-political integrity of the empire was deeply threatened. Augustus had shown the way to hold together diverse and sprawling dominions: one divine emperor, representing on earth the power of the Roman gods who blessed the emperor's dynasty and rule. Christian calls to freedom of religion undermined all of this and were thus regarded not so much as dissidence, but as treachery to the very idea of *Romanitas.*

It was Lactantius' urgent concern to answer the argument. He wishes in his work to demonstrate that the Christians have a greater claim on *Romanitas* than the pagan dynasty presently persecuting the Church, because civic loyalty does not depend on adherence to false mythical systems or ideologies, but rather on fundamental springs of political coherence that are demonstrated in the basic building blocks of wisdom (a society seeking to live rationally and discursively[78]) and justice (a society striving to live equitably). It is the latter virtue which is gifted by God to all mankind as a kind of absolute standard and which underlies all attempts by human beings to build a society in which it is worth living. In the *Divine Institutes,* Lactantius wishes above all else to show that the Christians have greater claim on justice than anyone else (he means Roman pagan nationalists of the party of Diocletian-Galerius), because their understanding of divine compassion and ethical principles are better than anyone else's by being more universal in application, and thus meet the deeper aspirations of Roman inclusiveness. The alternative would be to leave the claim for *Romanitas* in the hands of colonizers whose only aspiration for Rome's expanse in the world would be as financial extortioners. Lactantius may have been a closet politician, without much real experience of the brutality that underlay claims for power,[79] but he had his dream: his view of the expansion of Rome (in a renovated

[77]The same argument would later be the basis of Julian the Apostate's *Edict on the Professors of Rhetoric* which attempted to reverse the Constantinian favoring of Christianity, and to which Gregory of Nazianzus would provide the definitive answer for the Christian East: namely, that Christians had to engage with secular culture which so often had tangential or diametrically opposite values to it, not by renouncing culture and its achievements, but rather by approaching it as a bunch of roses: First clip the thorns, and then enjoy the flowers. See Norris (1984).

[78]That is, by shared discussion and agreement rather than by political oppressions.

[79]He overlooks Constantine's slaughter, but takes careful note of the executions of the other emperors. Rhetoricians traditionally used to "pass over in silence what ought not to be commented on" (as St

Christian form) as the outreach of a universal force of culture based on a humanitarian international community held together by common veneration of the highest ideals and the protection of human dignity by law. To this extent, in his argument, it is the Church which fulfills the ideas of *Romanitas,* not the imperial cult or any of the pagan religious traditions.

Justice and its apprehension on earth are thus key concepts to his work. To this extent, Lactantius' appeal for toleration of dissidence in times of stress (denying the right of the emperors to penalize religious difference) is certainly not the same as a general plea for toleration of religious diversity on the grounds that it is of no matter to the state. Lactantius demands freedom of conscience for all, but knows that the religious system determines the moral character of the state as its articulation of its transcendent ideal, and therefore the basic form of its standard ethical pedagogy.

Book Five of the *Institutes* is almost a separate treatise *On Justice.* It may well have started off life as an independent monograph written to present a legal and moral justification of the Christian system.[80] It is certainly a very early and elaborated form of Christian reflection on social justice, and the role of the Church as a factor in society. He tells his readers, early on in the book's dedicatory pages, that he envisages his work as a legal *institutio,* a kind of charter to show how a new order needs to be built on new religious premises. Like the great legal theoreticians of Rome (he is thinking about Quintilian, Cicero, Seneca and the like), who turned their pens towards philosophy at the end of their careers, he too will now discourse about theoretical issues:

> For if some skillful writers, who were once arbiters of justice, finally turned to composing and publishing their "Institutions of Law," in the hope that they might quiet the strife and contentions of discordant citizens; how much better and more fitting it is for me to follow up by writing Divine Institutes. For here I shall not argue about crop and water rights, or the pressing of claims, but shall speak about hope, about life, salvation, immortality, and God. It is thus my hope to set a term to disgraceful errors, and to superstitions that have proven to be quite deadly.[81]

In his *Institutes*, Lactantius advances a general thesis that Christianity is the world's universal moral culture and, as such, it is the universal force that Roman civ-

Gregory of Nazianzus once put it in the *Oration on the Death of his Sister*); for Lactantius the motive of the former, restoring true order under Monotheism, was a sign of election, and seemed to justify what in the latter was simply laid to the door of bestial cruelty.

[80]Cf. H.J. Lawlor, "Notes on Lactantius," *Hermathena* 12 (1903) 485. Lawlor sees chapter five of the *Divine Institutes* as a first major reaction in 306, to the persecution of Diocletian, when Lactantius goes to the heart of the philosophy of justice to articulate a defense of his Church.

[81]*Divine Institutes* 1.1.12.

ilization was seeking for, whether it knew it or not, to give it enduring value by an inner spiritual coherence that it lacked. His argument is that the ancient world was frustrated in its civilized progress because its religion was divorced from wisdom and its wisdom traditions were hostile to religion. The adherents of the common cults were uninformed polytheists whose cult was bound up with material and sensual selfishness.[82] The adherents of the schools were religious relativists whose skepticism divorced their *mentalité* from active and moral lives. In the face of this impasse and divorce between religion and wisdom in *Romanitas*, he describes Christ, the Incarnate Wisdom of God, as the High Priest who is simultaneously the true Philosophical Teacher of the world. As High Priest and Philosopher, Christ offers his new movement to the world as the exemplification of a new society that is religiously humane and which expresses its active and dynamic philosophy in a cult of wisdom that gives social unity and direction under the aegis of justice.

As someone well versed in Roman jurisprudence and philosophy, Lactantius the Christian makes an interesting weave between biblical ideas of justice and Classical Roman traditions. In biblical thought, justice is primarily a character of the holiness of God. It is *sedaqah*, righteousness, the divine character of mercy and justice given to the earth through the elect community which serves the divine law and thus the divine will in covenant fidelity.[83] Lactantius reflects all that basis in his presumption that justice can only flow from the right worship of the One True and Merciful God, since true worship is synonymous with a fundamental training in compassionate ethics:

> Our religion is firm, and solid and immutable, because it teaches the principles of Justice, which is ever present among us, and which is altogether rooted in the heart of the worshipper, namely that person who offers up his own mentality as the sacrificial gift. In other religions all that is needed seems to be the blood of beasts, and smoke, and useless libations. All we think necessary for worship is a good mind, a pure heart, an innocent life.[84]

[82]False cults degrade because they subordinate a transcendentally insightful human creature to inanimate idols and unreal myths (*Divine Institutes* 2.2.17–24); true cult, on the other hand, which is found in the Church, elevates the worshipper to a transcendent destiny and awareness. It is moral in character and trains a society in intellective and moral awareness (*Divine Institutes* 2.18.1).

[83]Following the statutes of the Law was righteousness for Israel (Deut 6.25). It was the supreme duty of the Judges or the King to execute righteousness in the form of true legal judgment over the covenant people (Deut 16.19; 1 Kings 10.9); it was a fundamental character of God himself, his covenant faithfulness (Ps 5.8; 31.1–5; 35.24, 28; 89.14; Is 5.16); and the harmony that kept the covenant together, and thus Israel in existence (Ps 85.9–13). Righteousness was the primeval force for the peace of God's covenanted society (Is 32.17; Ho 2.19; Jer 22.3–4). It is ideas such as this that are behind Lactantius' reworking of the Roman social theory of the Golden Age.

[84]*Divine Institutes* 5.19.27–30. See also: *Divine Institutes* 4.3. 2, 4–6; 5.8.3; 5.8.6–9; 6.25.12.

To this extent, Lactantius never tires of repeating that "true" worship has to demonstrate a fundamental character of high level morality seeking after justice. If it cannot demonstrate this character, it is neither worship, nor religion, simply irreligious prejudice. Worship worthy of the name, and accordingly only that which is worthy of the attention of the good state, is that system of religion which is concerned with the formation of a human conscience in just action: whatever produces "a good mind, a pure heart, and an innocent life." Christian worship fulfils all these requirements. Its distinctive "sacrificial gift" to the deity is *opus iustum*,[85] deeds of righteousness. For Lactantius, it is this kind of religion alone that can stand as the *fundamentum* of a social polity. Paganism, despite all its vaunted claims for being the antique glue of Roman society, has nothing to offer society, for it fails to develop inner values in its adherents. For Lactantius, when Constantine encouraged the supremacy of monotheistic worship in his New Roman Order was the supreme moment when justice was manifested once again in human affairs;[86] for only when there is true worship can justice be consciously developed between humans.

Yet he also echoes this biblicizing moral approach by appealing to the tradition that the goddess *Justitia* fled from the face of the earth horrified at the mounting crimes of an inhumane humanity. Classical Roman poets referred to this period before the flight of justice as the Golden Age, and, both in the Augustan and in the Constantinian eras[87] (both occasions of the immediate aftermath of bitter civil wars), there was widespread nostalgia and hope that a new political order might restore it. Lactantius, however, is severe against those who merely languish in aspirations, believing social justice to be an impossible dream:

> Why do you keep thinking to yourselves that justice is so feeble as this; why wish that it would just drop from heaven as in the wall paintings? Look around you. She is under your eyes. Take her into your heart, if you are able. Do not imagine that this is something difficult, or not appropriate to our time and age. Start to be just, and the justice you long for will start to follow you of her own accord. Root out every evil thought from your heart and the Golden Age will immedi-

[85] *Divine Institutes* 6.12.31.

[86] *Divine Institutes* 7.26.11; 1.1.13–16. The moment when monotheistic worship was lost to society, he argues, was when selfish violence began to flourish as a rule of life among humankind (*Divine Institutes* 5.5.13).

[87] Constantine was referred to as "The Father of the Golden Age." Lactantius makes two dedications of his book to him at various times in the re-publication process. In the first at *Divine Institutes* 1.1. 3–16, he celebrates him for bringing justice to earth in his defense of the Christians, and also because he allowed justice to flourish since he encouraged the worship of the One God as the heart of his new society. In his second dedication in *Divine Institutes* 7.26.11f. he lauds Constantine's rebuilding of the "House of Justice" in the Roman dominions because of his defense of Christian worship.

> ately return to you. But there is no other way to do this than by the worship of the true God.[88]

Justice is not simply a randomly ethical lifestyle, therefore, but a system of moral positions that grow directly out of a prior religious understanding of the place of humanity in the social order, what we might today call a sense of transcendent imperative in human affairs. Lactantius uses extensively the Stoic *topos* that the human being is "the creature that alone can stand up," though he reapplies it to Christian ends by changing it to a cultic focus: the creature that alone can "look up to the heavens." Religion, for Lactantius, is the marriage in a human individual's life of true worship (which by definition has to be rational and moral in character since it is the worship of the Divine Wisdom that created all order within creation) with true understanding (by which he means a reflective and philosophically simple lifestyle). This is what he means by his constantly repeated theme in the *Institutes* that society can only find balance when it represents the union of religion and wisdom; *pietas* and *sapientia.* As he puts it in his customary lapidary form: "Knowledge is defined by the knowledge of God. Virtue is defined by the veneration of God. In the first lies the root of wisdom. In the second lies the root of justice."[89]

Worship is given this key role in the Lactantian system because it recognizes worship as the force in society which trains men and women in attitudes of righteousness. In his experience of the Diocletianic persecution, it is the first principle, that of the freedom of conscience,[90] that is subjected to attack by the tyrant in society. But in more general terms, it is the quality of a society's understanding of the ordering of worship that is the quality of its ethic, for where the aspirations of the most reverent of its members lie, so too will its social values be enshrined. Accordingly, Lactantius argues that for pagan "sacrificers"[91] who live in a materially obsessed cult and follow mythic stories of immoral deities, their *cultus* will lead them inexorably to an immoral lifestyle.[92] On the other hand, for those who worship a single sublime deity, justice is a natural corollary of spiritually transcendent worship.

> Worship is the root of all justice because it teaches a human being to look beyond himself, to look upwards: reason teaches us that man is born mortal, and becomes

[88]*Divine Institutes* 5.8.3.

[89]*Divine Institutes* 6.5.19.

[90]"Nothing is so much a matter of free will as religion" (*Divine Institutes* 5.19.23). This is also why he acclaims Constantine as the restorer of justice on earth, since he defended the rights of Christians to worship the true God in peace (*Divine Institutes* 1.1.13–14).

[91]Lactantius shared Constantine's deep distaste for blood sacrifice and may have influenced the emperor's insistence that while pagans were free to continue their own systems of religion apart from Christianity, they were no longer to continue blood offerings within the Roman borders.

[92]*Divine Institutes* 5.19.27–30.

immortal, that is when he starts to live by God, or in other words to follow after justice. And justice is contained in the worship of God, since God raised up man to look upwards to heaven, to look at God himself.[93]

He profoundly appreciates the significance of moral *paideia* for the construction of a harmonious social polity. Indeed his entire Christological understanding is based around this master theme of incarnational *paideia*.[94] This pedagogy of being lifted up to realize that a human being is more than a mere social animal is the way in which worship educates an enlightened society into justice, which, for Lactantius, is based upon the primary understanding that a human being is a divine icon. This is why, he argues, religion is the only societal force that compels man, by a sacred bond, to hold his fellows dear as holy things. It is this which brings the "Golden Age of Justice" back to the earth:

> When Justice was banished from earth, she took with her Truth; and men were left in error, ignorance and blindness. This loss of the Golden Age and the expulsion of Justice was simply the laying aside of divine religion, which is all that makes one human being esteem another as dear to him, and which instructs him in the common tie of brotherhood, since God is the common Father of us all. In this way we learn to share the gifts of our common God with those who do not possess them. We learn to injure no one; to oppress no one; never to close our door against a stranger; never to close our ear to someone begging us; but instead to be generous, kind, and liberal; those traits which Cicero thought were characteristic of a King. This is the reality of Justice. This is that original Golden Age which was corrupted under Jupiter.[95]

Lactantius contrasts the variability of human law codes with the universality of that law which is written in the heart, that common standard of justice which God has established as the fundamental cohesion of society:

> For civil law is one thing, and it varies almost everywhere according to custom, but Justice is another thing altogether, and it is this which God has set forth to all mankind as both uniform and simple. It follows then, that whoever is ignorant of God, must also be ignorant of Justice.[96]

For Lactantius, justice is not an abstraction but a way of living. It is a conglomeration of all the virtues harmonized in a rationally defensible system:

[93] *Divine Institutes* 7.5.22.
[94] *Divine Institutes* 4.11.7
[95] *Divine Institutes* 5.6.10–12.
[96] *Divine Institutes* 6.9.7.

> For Justice embraces all the virtues together, but there are two which are foremost, and which can never be separated from Justice. I mean equity and reverence. Things such as faithfulness, moderation, goodness, innocence, integrity and the like may be witnessed (as they always have been) in the characters of those who are ignorant of Justice; either by natural endowment, or because of parental training . . . but reverence and equity are the veins of Justice, and in these twin fountains the entirety is contained. The source and origin of Justice lies in reverence. The force and method of Justice lies in equity . . . and by this I do not mean the equity involved in good judgment (although this is also praiseworthy in a just man) but I mean the principle of a man making himself equal to all others. It is this which Cicero calls equitability. But it is God who gave breath to man who willed that all should be equal and equally matched . . . In his sight no one is a slave, no one a master. We have the same Father and all thus all have the same right to be children. No one is poor in the eyes of God, except the one who is poor in justice. No one is rich in his sight except the one who is rich in virtue . . . It follows then that Greek and Roman society could not possess Justice since it had men differing from each other in many degrees; from the poor to the rich, from the humble to the powerful; from private persons to kings. But where all are not equally matched, there can be no equity. This inequality excludes justice, whose very force is to fashion equality.[97]

This is an extraordinary and radical claim, of course. And it is a standard of equity against which the Church either of his own time or today would be uncomfortable to be measured. But Lactantius is here reflecting a radical part of the eschatological message of the Gospel and the Apostles,[98] and presenting a charter of what a society governed by those premises might look like, a society where the ideals of the Church were taken seriously. He himself is said to have elected, in a life condition that could have commanded riches, to live in radically simple poverty. A generation after him the monastic movement commandeered this insight and charism of radical detachment and simplicity, but in Lactantius' day monasticism had not really established itself so deeply in the imagination of the Western Church. When it did, its vision of freely chosen personal poverty was played out on a different basis to Lactantius' ideas of the need for social equity.[99] In his constitution for the New Order Lactantius puts the Christian vision of aequitas at the very pinnacle, a concept almost incomprehensible to ancient Roman society and a standard of eschato-

[97] *Divine Institutes* 5.14.9–20.

[98] Mt 23.8–12; 2 Cor 8.14; Jas 1.9–11; 2.1–9.

[99] Monastic poverty is articulated in the later classical Christian ages as part of an eschatological renunciation of the world-order, not so much as an attempt to reconstitute it on different, and more equitable, terms.

logical *renovatio* that established Christianity has frequently declined from. He foresees the arguments that will be sent back, of course, for his next section of the *Institutes* is an answer to critics who point the finger at inequalities already abundantly visible among the Christians.[100] His case here is that there may be differences of condition among Christians, but there exists in principle a single mentality wherein all true believers:

> Regard and speak of each other as family in spirit, for we have no servants, but in our religion we stand as fellow-servants. Riches do not make our members more illustrious among us, except in so far as they allow individuals more scope to stand out by good works. Being rich does not mean having great monetary capital, but rather spending lots on works of Justice . . . Each is more elevated according to their greater degree of Justice.[101]

If society cannot demonstrate equity (at the very least this appeal to the fundamental notion of a moral meritocracy) at the heart of its system, it cannot claim truth. Lactantius takes several cases in point, notably the theory of war on which the Roman Empire was built, dismissing it as a whole ethics "based upon immediate concerns and the convenience of social institutions certainly not upon virtue or justice."[102] In fact, he argues, the two greatest signs of the presence of the Golden Age in human affairs were the marks of innocence: the lack of war and a pacific ethos that accompanied it in society, allied with a liberality of spirit that did not wish to hoard goods but ensure an equitable distribution, especially to those in need.[103] Once the Golden Age had passed from the Romans, according to Lactantius, in the time when polytheistic cults were introduced, then false worship brought with it immediately a turning to violence and war, as a chief way to enshrine the spirit of cupidity, private gain, and selfishness:

> When the worship of God disappeared from earth, mankind lost the knowledge of good and evil, and the common intercourse of life perished among men, and the bond of human society was destroyed. It was then men learned to fight and plot against one another, and think of gaining glory from the shedding of blood. The source of all this evil was cupidity . . . for not only did those who had excess fail to give a share to others, they even started to seize other men's property, drawing everything into private gain. Then it was that things that even individuals used to labor for, in the cause of the common good, were now carried off to the houses

[100] *Divine Institutes* 5.15.1–5.
[101] *Divine Institutes* 5.15.3–5.
[102] *Divine Institutes* 6.6.24.
[103] *Divine Institutes* 5.5.1–7; 5.22.7–10.

> of the few. In order to reduce others to slavery they especially began to hoard and reserve the necessities of life and keep them firmly under lock... Under the name of Justice they passed most unequal and unjust laws designed to defend their plunder and avarice in the face of the multitude's power... And since there was no longer any trace in them of Justice (whose offices are humanity, equity, and pity) they soon began to rejoice in a proud and boastful inequality and made themselves higher than other men . . . Justice was banished, and took with her into exile the Truth. Men were left to error, ignorance, blindness.[104]

Having lost the Golden Age on Earth, Roman society, for Lactantius, was completely unable to restore it because of the vested interests (human self-interests on the small scale) that are always hostile to justice. These individual tendencies to live according to self-interest, if allowed to accumulate on the larger scale (as tolerated social policy for example), have enough momentum in them to overturn any global aim that a society may have to live according to principles of justice and equity. In Lactantius' argument, only Christ was powerful enough to serve as the Universal Priest (initiating society into a moral cult) and Sage (illuminating the masses with deep wisdom traditions that revealed the way to a new commonwealth). Although the flourishing of injustice seems now to have the upper hand (since it is part of the charism of justice to seek a humble and enduring path[105]), Lactantius calls out to his readers not to despair or think that it is absolutely hopeless to imagine the restoration of a just society: justice has its own inner power, too, just as selfishness has. It convinces and argues for itself, with a certain "divine force." It has a power that is greater than the merely "local" character of the individually self-centered drive to succeed even at the cost of others. That force even flows from the transcendent nature of man's essential condition:

> Do you suppose... that Justice is so irrelevant, and so God-despised, that it has no power or influence of its own, that will serve for its own preservation? Those who are ignorant of the mystery of man[106] and can think of nothing beyond the evidence of this present life cannot understand the great energy inherent in Justice.[107]

It is the seeking after this law, the Law of God made concrete in the constitution of Christ's Church,[108] that will restore society to the Golden Age of peace and mercy and justice.[109]

[104] *Divine Institutes* 5.5.14–5.6.11.
[105] *Divine Institutes* 5.14.2; 5.21.7–10.
[106] He means the transcendent character of man as the image of God on Earth.
[107] *Divine Institutes* 5.17.14.
[108] *Divine Institutes* 4.3.2 & 4–6; see also *Divine Institutes*. 6.6.25, & 28; 7.11.14, & 18.
[109] *Divine Institutes* 5.8.6–9.

Lactantius had few readers in antiquity, and few since. But reading him today is extraordinarily illuminating and refreshing. His is a rare patristic vision of theology which is at one and the same moment a charter for a new civilization. He does not have much time for the niceties of bishops, ecclesiastical politics, or even the *minutiae* of what might or might not constitute Christian Orthodoxy, and to that extent, later Christian ages, wearing themselves out with the details of Orthodoxy and episcopal politics after the later fourth century which he just missed, looked at him askance. Even so, they never withdrew the reverence they felt for him as an antique and venerable figure. His pure-hearted idealism perhaps deprived him of a school of disciples necessary to extend his thought. Historically, his socio-political theology suffered a supersession in the East by that of Eusebius of Caesarea and in the West by that of Augustine. Augustine had read him, of course, and there is more Lactantian politics in Augustine than meets the eye. The great African bishop would learn from his two mentors, Tertullian and Lactantius, and attempt to bring them both into a larger synthesis. If Lactantius' idealism casts a shadow of doubt over the realism of his social vision, it is, I think, important to remember that the idealist is not just a dreamer, even if he is proved to be a dreamer); and certainly this extraordinarily pure and prophetically poetic vision carries in it a force that can recall one to sobriety. His sparse sketches of Christian social polity, as a sustained project in mutual justice, have about them the power of simple line visible in a great master of drawing, such as a Picasso. He spoke, archaically perhaps, for his own age, couching his theological horizons on the base of eschatology. But in our own day Christian social polity needs to rediscover just this element of eschatological urgency, to temper the flattening out of horizons which inevitably came with Christian political ascendancy. That ascendancy has been radically challenged in recent centuries. It is perhaps the astringency of a Lactantius that can help us think back to the springs that once motivated the Church to found and pursue a New Order.

Further Reading

PRIMARY TEXTS

M.F. McDonald. *Lactantius: The Divine Institutes.* FOTC 49 (Washington, 1964).
———. *Lactantius; The Minor Works.* FOTC 54 (Washington, 1965).

STUDIES

K. Aland. "The Relation Between Church and State in early Times." *Journal of Theological Studies* (New Series) 19 (1968) 115–127.
T.D. Barnes. "Lactantius and Constantine." *Journal of Roman Studies* 63 (1973) 29–36.

J.R. Bowlin. "Tolerance Among the Fathers." *Journal of the Society of Christian Ethics* 26 (2006) 3–36.

E. De Palma Digeser. "Lactantius, Porphyry, and the debate over religious toleration." *Journal of Roman Studies* 88 (1998) 129–146.

______. *The Making of a Christian Empire.* New York, 2000.

C. Ferrini. "Die juristischen Kentnisse des Arnobius und Laktanz." *Zeitschrift der Savigny-Stiftlung* 15 (1894) 342f.

J. Fontaine & M. Perrin. *Lactance et Son Temps.* Paris, 1978.

J. Gaudemet. "La legislation réligieuse de Constantin." *Revue de l'histoire de l'église de France* 33 (1947) 25–61.

R.P.H. Green. "Doctrina as 'Culture' in Lactantius' *Divine Institutes.*" *Studia Patristica* 31 (1997) 302–306.

J.R. Laurin. *Les Orientations Maitresses des Apologistes Chrétiens.* Rome, 1954, pp. 186–304.

V. Loi. "Il concetto di Iustitia e i fattori culturali dell'etica di Lattanzio." *Salesianum* 28.4 (1966) 583–625.

______. *Lattanzio: nella storia del linguaggio e del pensiero teologico pre-niceno.* (Diss.) Zurich, 1970.

______. "La giustizia sociale nell'etica di Lattanzio." AFLC 37 (1974–75) 71–78. (*Augustinianum* 17 [1977] 153–160).

J.A. McGuckin. "The Non-Cyprianic Scripture Texts in Lactantius' Divine Institutes." *Vigiliae Christianae* 36 (1982) 145–163.

______. "Spirit Christology : Lactantius and His Sources." *Heythrop Journal* 24 (1983) 141–148.

______. "Lactantius as Theologian. An Angelic Christology on the Eve of Nicaea." *Rivista di Storia e Letteratura Religiosa* 22.3, pp. 492–497.

F. W. Norris. "Of Thorns and Roses: The Logic of Belief in Gregory Nazianzen." *Church History* 53 (1984) 455–464.

M. Spanneut. "La non-violence chez les pères latins." In *Kyriakon. Festchrift fur J. Quasten*, vol. 1. Munster-Aschendorf, pp. 37–38.

L.J. Swift. "Lactantius and the Golden Age." AJP 89 (1968) 79f.

U. Val. "El Senequismo de Lactancio." *Helmantica* 23 (1972) 291–323.

J. Vogt. "Toleranz und intoleranz im constantinischen Zeitalter. Der weg der lateinischen Apologetik." *Saeculum* 19 (1968) 344–361.

CHAPTER 6

A Theology of Politics and Law in the Later West: St Augustine of Hippo

St Augustine (354–430) is someone who needs little introduction in one sense. He is a cultural artifact of the West, though the sophisticated nuances of his thought have often been presumed to be known rather than studied. His influence on Western Christendom cannot be over-emphasized. Whereas in the Greek-speaking Eastern Church, there were always a considerable number of outstanding lights in all the generations of the formative centuries, so that the towering genius of an Origen would be muted, moderated, and synthesized by his brilliant commentators and critics, the same cannot be said about the intellectual evolution of the West. Augustine is a lighthouse whose incessant flashing enthralled all ancient western Christian thought, determining almost all Latin writing in the Church down the high Middle Ages, and beyond. But it was not Augustine who made this impact himself. In his own lifetime he was relatively obscure, living in as out-of-the-way corner as one could find. His works circulated mainly among a small circle of élite friends and "God-seekers." It was after his death that his international reputation began to grow, at first slowly, and not without criticism,[1] but finally like a wildfire. The irony of it was summed up by the letter that arrived for him shortly after his death, an imperial summons to take part in the Oecumenical Council of Ephesus in 431. The western emperor, Valentinian III, seeking (on the advice of Pope Celestine) to have representation at the council called by Theodosius II, could hardly have thought of anyone else. Augustine's impact was to break over the western world like a wave, only after it had been simplified and packaged for mass consumption. This task was to be accomplished by Gregory the Great, who moderated Augustine's political views in ways Augustine had never originally imagined, to fit a new situation where the popes were the virtual replacements for the western emperors.

In his own writing, and on his own terms, Augustine was more complex than could easily be compressed into a vade-mecum of a political handbook. His ideas were heavily eschatological, and as such they were as much deconstructive as they were affirmative of political systems. Despite his great elevation as the authority par

[1]Such as John Cassian, the great ascetic at Marseilles.

excellence of the medieval Western Church, it is important to remember that what Augustine wrote on the nature of law and equity was predominantly practical and immediate. This is especially seen in his *Letters*, as distinct from, for example, his great monograph *The City of God* which we shall discuss shortly. In their edition of several of the *Letters*, Atkins and Dodaro remind us of the very local nature of his theory:

> He was . . . before else a Christian pastor. As a bishop he struggled with the daily reality of political life in a society in which church and state had never been, and could not conceivably be, disentangled. In this context "Justice" referred not to the rise and fall of empires, but to the decision whether to punish or to pardon a Donatist thug who had beaten up one of his priests. War was not merely a theological construct, an instrument of divine wrath or divine education. It was happening in the next province, where one of Augustine's old acquaintances was responsible for warding off the barbarian raiders. Civic power may have been symbolically embodied in the emperor in distant Rome, but here in North Africa it was men like Augustine's correspondent Apringius who made the decisions that mattered.[2]

So many subsequent political theorists, from Aquinas to Niebuhr, have made neo-Augustinian syntheses in his name that owed more to their own anachronistic understandings and altered contexts than to any careful exegesis of the originals,[3] that we ought not to forget this principle. Augustine is monumentally important for a future that changes him at many instances (Gregory the Great is a prime example), but in his own writing he is predominantly local, deeply patristic, biblically inspired (and thus eschatological), and often "working it out" as he goes. He stood out from his patristic predecessors in the range of his imagination. This was a benefit afforded to him because, unlike them, he did not have to deal with state persecution, and could have the leisure to reflect on questions of Christian culture. But Augustine belongs to their world, not ours.

We know a great deal about his life both because of his autobiographical writing, and from his extensive correspondence. His devoted disciple, Possidius, also wrote a *Vita* shortly after the saint's death. Augustine was born in Thagaste, near Madaurus, in Roman North Africa. His father Patricius was a pagan and remained so all his life until his deathbed. His mother, Monica, enrolled her infant son as a catechumen in the Catholic Church. The child's talent was noticed early and a wealthy patron, Romanianus, sponsored his education. He studied rhetoric at the

[2]Atkins & Dodaro (2001) xi.

[3]Scott (1999) ably demonstrates how much Niebuhr's very influential analysis of Augustine as the root of his own adherence to "political realism" was very much a Protestantizing *eisegesis* of the original works.

local capital, Carthage, where at the age of nineteen he was powerfully attracted to the vocation of rhetor-philosopher by reading Cicero's now lost treatise *Hortensius.* His mother pressured him to enroll for baptism, but Augustine had already set up house with a concubine (whom he never names) to whom he was deeply attached, and he was not willing to threaten that relationship or to submit himself to the doctrines of the Catholics which he had now come to regard as simplistic and based on archaic and silly sacred texts. He attached himself to the Manichean movement, in the rank of auditor, and belonged to that party for the next ten years. The Manichean Church funded his teaching career; first at Rome and then in the prestigious chair of Rhetoric at Milan, which he had to abandon on eventually becoming a Catholic in 387.

While he was in Milan he became increasingly disillusioned with the Manichean religion[4] and a series of crises shook his personal and intellectual security, beginning with increasing asthmatic troubles (a devastating setback for an ancient orator) and his agreement with his mother's plan to dismiss his partner, now of fifteen years' standing and the mother of his son Adeodatus, so that he could make an advantageous marriage to an heiress, one that would advance his career *de novo.* His ready agreement to her dismissal was soon followed by heartbreak at her loss. She returned to Africa and nothing more is known of her, except a small reminiscence from the ageing bishop to the effect that he believed she never married anyone else. After that point, his mother held less sway over Augustine, but his rapid employment of a live-in sexual surrogate in Milan caused him to regard his philosophical aspirations with a depressed skepticism. At that period celibacy was regarded as *de rigeur* for a serious philosopher and Augustine's thoughts were turning more to the philosophical life of quiet contemplative writing and reflection.

At this time, he had increasing contact with intellectual church circles, by the mediation of the priest Simplicianus, a theologian-philosopher and friend of Marius Victorinus, who worked in Bishop Ambrose's administration and was particularly interested in Neo-Platonic thought. Joining the philosophical circle of intellectuals associated with Simplicianus opened up new vistas for Augustine, especially easing his mind on the view of Christianity as an intellectually bankrupt system. Augustine was greatly impressed by Ambrose when he came to know him and began to consider the possibility of a similar career as an ascetic Christian philosopher. He describes his own psycho-sexual and spiritual struggle in a famous autobiography, *The Confessions,* which he wrote many years later. In that story he depicts the turning point of his life[5] as occurring dramatically in a quiet garden in a

[4]A crisis that is reflected in his treatise *Against Faustus the Manichee.*

[5]A bishop when he wrote this tale, it was a conversion to Christ that was his focus, of course. Literary critics have suggested that when he did undergo baptism in real time, it was as much a "*conversio*

Milanese villa, when he abandoned his destiny to Christ and subsequently petitioned for admission to the Church. For a while he stayed with Christian friends who formed a scholarly college around him. Soon, however, he returned to Rome, where Monica died. He made his way back to Africa, in 388, where he intended to live with his companions and found a philosophical *collegium* at Thagaste.

One day in 391, while making a visit to the seaport of Hippo Regius, he was apprehended by local Christians and forcibly ordained priest by Bishop Valerius, so that he could help the old bishop in church administration. He and his companions accepted their forced initiation into church administration and Augustine moved his community to the town where he served as the assistant priest. In 395, Augustine was consecrated as Valerius' episcopal assistant and soon afterwards became his successor. Adjacent bishops in Africa regarded his promotion as canonically dubious, and even his baptism as somewhat irregular, for the news of his early life (both his sexual liaisons and his membership of the heretical Manichees) was common gossip in a Church much troubled by the rigorist dissident party of the Donatists. To defend himself, Augustine composed treatises against the Manichees shortly after his priestly ordination; and after his consecration as bishop, he wrote the *Confessions*, an exercise in how self- scrutiny can be a salvific reading of the story of God's providence in creation and in a human life. It was a brilliant answer to his local African critics who complained against him for being baptized in Italy, and thus slipping through the rigorous sacramental "scrutinies"[6] of the African Church.

As bishop, Augustine made moves to resolve the schism of the Donatists, which led to his enunciation of important principles that would form the basic substructure of Western Catholic ideas on sacramental theology and ecclesiological self-definition.[7] His works greatly developed the Latin Church's understanding of itself as both a heavenly and earthly body (like Christ himself, he argued, whose body it was, a complete and perfect synthesis of flesh and divine spirit). The Donatist movement regarded the Catholics as a degenerate form of the Church, with invalid orders and sacraments. Radical elements among the Donatist laity (Circumcellions) organized violent protest groups which roamed the countryside applying force to those who resisted them. Several Catholic clergy were targets for street beatings. Although at

morum" or a conversion to the celibate philosophic life that was in his mind. Celibacy was not required by the Church of baptismal candidates. It was expected, by academic society, of the *Sophoi*, those aspiring to be public sages.

[6]Public confessions of all one's past sins in detail, during a lengthy time of repentance and preparation preceding the reception of the sacrament.

[7]The Donatists were a "pure Church" movement that had resulted in the aftermath of persecution. They accused the Catholic clergy of having lost the validity of their orders because of the apostasy of several of their bishops. The Donatist issue essentially revolved around the question: "Just who was the real Catholic Church?"

first opposed to applying secular pressure on these dissidents, Augustine reluctantly came to a position by 411 that allowed for the partial legitimacy of a church policy that could call on the assistance of state repression. That decision has been regarded as monumentally symbolic for the later history of Christian repressive politics. In its origins, it needs to be interpreted parochially. After Constantine, Christian bishops were empowered to act as local magistrates and had judicial power (subordinated to the coercive power of the civil magistrates) in all affairs relating to church life. Circumcellions exercised considerable violence in the country areas in their resistance to Catholic clerical claims, and (so it would seem, to many aspects of Roman law in relation to slave plantations and the rich exacting payment of loans).[8] In later generations of the Church, forgetting Augustine's immediate and local context, where the bishop's legal work was very limited and particular,[9] his immense authority seemed to have been placed behind the overarching principle of state-aided religious compulsion "when necessary," and it was an authority much evoked to justify forms of ecclesiastical oppression in later centuries.

The publication of his *Confessions* had caused some outrage in Rome, where a moralist preacher named Pelagius was appalled by his reading of Augustine's autobiography, chiefly for what he saw as its passive resignation of salvation as a matter of God's extrinsic grace, not the honest moral effort of the penitent sinner. Pelagius called for a more robust personal commitment and effort for personal repentance, stinging Augustine intimately; thus began a controversy that was to mark all of Augustine's later life and cause him to elaborate a profound and careful doctrine of grace that would become determinative for Western Catholicism. Augustine regarded humanity as having nothing on which it could base its salvation: all was a free gift of God. Humanity left to itself could only slip into the slavery of sin and corruption. His ideas were meant to be set out within the overarching structure of a theology of praise for God's merciful providence, but in some, more negative,

[8]In both these regards they have habitually been dismissed as "heretics," being seen only through the lens of Augustine's ecclesial theology which marginalized their bishops' positions, and their own lay recourse to what he saw as unjustified violence and crimes against good order. Recently there has been much revision. After all, the out-and-out rejection of slavery as incompatible with Christian brotherhood, and the application of punitive measures to Christians who demanded usury, were both entirely reasonable Christian mainstream positions (albeit "the road less travelled") and when Donatist bishops permitted the flogging of the rich for extortions against the poor they were doing no more (it could be argued) than Constantine had allowed them: to apply Church law to a recalcitrant community. It was not so much the violence Augustine objected to in theory, it was the principle he invoked in his arguments with higher civil powers against Donatists, namely that the poorer classes punished the superior classes, that reveals his mindset and which also drew the immediate attention of the military ruling classes, for it contradicted a major principle in Roman law.

[9]Except for obscure liminal parts of the empire where the civil administration was correspondingly weak, and the episcopate subsumed much of the role of "local law and order."

readings of his legacy, the pessimistic tone predominated in an unbalanced way and Augustine in a real sense has to be seen as the author of a marked tendency in Latin theology to focus on the notions of Original Sin, and the corruption of the material world along with an ever-present bias of the whole race towards depravity. This argument with Pelagius would have a large impact not only on his views of personal morality and free divine grace in the soul, but also on his views of society and politics. Augustine's pessimism as to the possibility of a righteous society would father much subsequent Protestant thought on Church and State. Greek Christian writers never laid such stress on this pessimism and never adopted as elements of the faith (unlike subsequent Western Catholicism), what they regarded as peculiarities of Augustine's local Church (*theologoumena*).

After the sack of Rome in 410, Augustine began a work of large scale apologetic to answer those who laid the blame for the decadence of the western empire at the door of the Christians. Between the years 412–427 he produced a monumental work called *The City of God* where he elaborated the first extensively considered ethical and political view of what Christianity conceived of as a civilized order, in distinction to pre-Christian Roman theories. He stresses the earthly city's (human society's) radical dissociation from the true City of God (the eschatological realization of the Kingdom) but makes a case for how the earthly city is informed and guided by heavenly ideals. Slavery is a prime symptom, for Augustine, of the inherent corruption of the world's affairs. In the midst of endemic violence and disorder, the Church has the destiny to represent mercy and reconciliation, guiding society to a perfection it might never attain, but to which it is inexorably summoned.[10] It is in this work that his major outlines of political and legal thought are sketched out, and we shall return to it for an extended discussion in due course.

To stand with the *Confessions* and *City of God*, in his triad of "world-classics," we should add Augustine's monumental work of theology *On the Trinity*, composed between 399 and 419. In this he constructs a major anti-Arian apologetic around the Nicene faith in Christology and Pneumatology. He demonstrates from a wide variety of triadic cosmic patterns the reasonableness of the Trinitarian doctrine of three divine persons subsisting in one single divine nature. Much use is made of triadic patterns of human psychology (the soul as the image of God); and Augustine emphasized once again his deeply-sensed connection between self-scrutiny and theological method, something common to Augustine and the Platonic tradition.

His vast corpus of writings became, of course, his own form of ascetical exercise. The great extent of his work made him function as an encyclopedic theological authority for the next millennium in the West. His spiritual writings gave a great

[10]In the recently discovered Divjak Letters of Augustine he can be seen actively intervening for slaves and oppressed children in his role as Bishop-Magistrate. See Dossey (2001).

impetus to monasticism as the organizing structure of the Latin Church, something which Gregory the Great later picked up and developed. This monastic focus ought to remind us that Augustine's social theology is essentially that of an ascetic analyzing social order primarily in terms of consumption and resistance to consumption. But an especially dominant theme of all his thought is the primacy of *caritas*, which we can only with difficulty render as "Love."[11] *Caritas* is brought by Augustine to the very heart of political judgment. In this lies his essential genius as a Christian political theorist. He particularly stressed the element of true faith leading to a deep desire of the heart for God, an affective spiritual tradition that made him an attractive and highly approachable Christian writer: aspects that still appear from engagement with his work.[12]

Augustine died as the Vandals were besieging his city on August 28, 430. One of his last instructions was to have his favorite Psalms written in large letters around his walls so that he could read them as he died. Augustine's friend and monastic companion, Possidius, wrote a biography soon after his death and in it placed an invaluable list of all his writings, most of which are still extant. At the same time, Prosper of Aquitaine began a process to lobby for Augustinianism as the standard theological system of the Latin West; a movement that slowly gathered momentum, despite several at the time who had strong reservations. This movement was brought to a completion in the late sixth century with Pope Gregory the Great's enthusiastic endorsement of Augustine as the pre-eminent Latin theologian and church authority.

The Political Influence of the "City of God"

"*Glorious things are spoken of you O City of God. But I will be mindful of Rahab and Babylon knowing me.*"[13] So Augustine begins this monumental work that contains the heart of his social and political theory. The chosen text from the Psalms gives the game away immediately. He is thinking from the outset about missionary strategy: the Church's outreach to pagan society, which, in his day, was still far from exhausted or superseded.

[11]Since "Love" has been so heavily romanticized as a notion, and to that extent robbed of its *force majeure* in Augustine's system.

[12]Many modern Christian political commentators in the Augustinian tradition tend to lament the disappearance in today's discourses on civilization of the organizing principle of *caritas*, that so inspired Augustine.

[13]Ps 86.3–4, Old Latin Bible (*Vetus Latina* as used by Augustine). The Catholic and Orthodox "numbering" of the Psalms is often one psalm "different" from the Hebrew and Protestant numberings. For the former reference cf. Ps 87.3–4.

The text *On the City of God* is one of Augustine's largest writings. Barker, in his introduction to the Everyman edition, puts it touchingly : "The student who wishes to acquaint himself with the thought of St Augustine may well be dismayed by the many pages of the De Civitate Dei."[14] It was composed over a large space of time. Commissioned in June 412, it was not finished until 427, and by the time it was ended it was simply not the work Augustine had begun to write so many years previously, but had evolved into a much greater conception. Its historical impact after Augustine's death has been phenomenal. It became a constitutional guide for Western Christian thought and determined much of the social-political agenda of the Medieval Church, later becoming something of an "eye of the storm" in the great religious and political conflicts of the Reformation Era, determining much of the presuppositions (in different "takes" of course) about Church and Society in the Catholic and Protestant worlds. In the traditions of Eastern Christianity (Byzantine, Slavic, African, Armenian, and the wider Orthodox world), Augustine never gained a following at all, was not even read until well into the high Middle Ages, and only by a very few intellectuals; and so his ideas never took hold in the same way.

Immediate Origins of *The City of God*

In 412, two years after Alaric's shocking sack of Rome, the Imperial Count Marcellinus asked Augustine to make some kind of formal reply on behalf of the Christians to the disaffected criticisms that were being raised against the religion and its adherents who were currently in the imperial ascendancy. The Roman province of North Africa where Augustine was a significant figure had become an emergency refuge for many of the capital's aristocrats who had fled there to their estates after the difficulties of 410. After that, Augustine had been quite involved in organizing relief for the many displaced persons. Marcellinus, however, was concerned that mutual friends, such as the pagan intellectual Volusianus, had taken the occasion of the sack of Rome to point to the scandal of the central weakness of the empire after the Christian administration's very short time in power. In the second century a pagan intellectual philosopher named Celsus had been one of the first academicians to take note of the early Church, and he ridiculed Christianity in a book called *The True Word*.[15] He seems to have read some of the Gospels, and concluded that if such a system was ever adopted it would bring ruin to the empire by its peace ethic. This constant criticism that Christianity could only ruin the imperial world order con-

[14]John Healy, tr., *The City of God*, Introduction by Ernest Barker (London: Dent & Sons; and New York: E.P. Dutton & Co., 1945) xxii.

[15]It received no answer until more than a century later when the great Alexandrian theologian Origen made a substantial response to all its points. Origen, *Against Celsus*; cf. J.A. McGuckin, ed., *The Westminster Handbook to Origen of Alexandria* (Louisville: Westminster John Knox Press, 2003).

tinued to be laid at the door of Christians, even though by the middle of the third century it was clear that they were a rising power at the center of imperial affairs.

Parts of the Severan dynasty already encouraged Christian philosophers. Julia Mammaea employed Christian rhetoricians, and Philip the Arab, emperor in the mid-third century, was possibly a Christian soldier who had assumed the purple. By the fourth century, of course, the Christians had achieved ascendancy (with the exception of the rule of Julian the Apostate) and Christian emperors of Rome were the norm. To the society of the mid-fifth century, however, this was by no means an assured thing for the future.

By the end of the fourth century, the Danube and Rhine had ceased to be the natural barriers they once were to the nomadic peoples of the North. In 380, massed Germanic tribes had crossed the borders and demanded relief within the empire. The ensuing war resulted in a disastrous defeat of the armies of Emperor Valens, and the political affairs of the empire were conducted for the next three centuries with a policy of the emperors in the East (Constantinople) constantly deflecting the impact of barbarian invasions to the West. It was presumed, and proved to be the case, that the imperial infrastructure could not withstand such long-term weakness. Those who lived in the western imperial provinces, that is North Africa, Italy, Gaul, and Spain, were less than pleased with the new political order centering on Constantinople. The resonances of all this unhappiness of migrations and invasions, and a general sense that the old world order was coming to an end, is reflected in the historical and political ideas of *The City of God*. It was a common anxiety among Christians of the West, even as it was a deeply felt resentment among the pagan sections of society, especially the more literate and higher ranking classes who were dismayed by the decline and laid the blame at the door of the Christian inheritors of imperial glory.

Augustine's pagan correspondent Volusianus voiced that dissatisfaction mildly when he wondered aloud if the Church's peace ethic was not the real cause of such social disintegration, as evidenced in the sacking of Rome by such a small group of barbarian warlords in 410. The invaders did not have the capacity to conquer Rome. They only had the resources to mount a dramatic raid, taking off its movable goods and jewels, and engaging in widespread rape and murder. The point was not so much that the sack of Rome was a shattering long-term disaster: rather that it showed that Rome no longer could hold up its head as a world city. What lay underneath the critique of Volusianus, therefore, was more than just the symbolic element of nomadic tribes on the rampage, but the strategic decision of the first Christian Emperor Constantine to relocate the real capital of world empire to Constantinople on the Bosphorus, a capital that was truly militarily defensible and strategically central for both conquest and trade. Rome had been declining for generations when Alaric's war party broke apart its defenses and so publicly humiliated it.

Time and Society in *The City of God*

After the sack of Rome it had been mooted that the old gods had so long fostered Rome's ascent whereas after their neglect, it seemed, the Christian God did not appear to hold Rome in any esteem at all. This is why Augustine begins his work with a large-scale critique of Roman religion, comparing and contrasting it to Christian attitudes in the cause of showing the superiority of the latter and considering the processes of Roman history and politics in the light of biblical ideas of theocracy, providence, and the meaning of history in the light of eschatological judgment. The underlying significance of the biblical understanding of the world order is of fundamental importance for Augustine the bishop and the very foundations of his whole political theology.

The biblical conception of time that underlies the New Testament writings was formed in the apocalyptic era of Judaism, roughly two centuries before the time of Jesus. It involved a reworking of the older prophetic notions of God's judgment on history being transmitted through the insights and warnings of the prophets. If the covenant people of God had sinned, the prophet would admonish them that judgment was not far off. The great disasters that befell the ancient nation of Israel were explained, in this sense, as just punishments visited upon the people for their sins. National catastrophes such as the exile of Northern Israel under the Assyrians, or the exile of Judea to Babylon, were prophetically "explained" to society in terms of this cycle of sin and punishment within the general conception of a line of history that unfolded according to the will of God. In this straightforward and commonly graspable scheme, politics and religion were a single line: the societal covenant of Israelites with one another was simply an extension of their common obedience to the terms of the religious covenant; sacrifice kept all in balance. The great cult at the Temple in Jerusalem sustained Israel in God's blessing. If Israel's cultic obedience faltered (if it laid reliance on horses and chariots more than in its Lord, or if it cultically defiled itself with the rites of other gods, or abandoned the terms of covenantal morality), then the political favor God showed his people would be withdrawn. In this sense state-funded worship was the equivalent of a functioning foreign policy office.

Nevertheless, in the centuries preceding Christianity, this straightforward providential theology of the Old Testament had come into some degree of crisis. The so-called Apocalyptic movement was a form of its repristination and rehabilitation. In the Apocalyptic literature, a genre of theological discourse still extant in parts of Ezekiel, the Book of Daniel, and most of the intertestamental literature,[16] and, of

[16]Most of it, the religious literature of Israel current in the time of Jesus, did not make it into the scriptural canon of either the Synagogue or the Church. Both phased out strict apocalypticism. For the Syna-

course, so much of the New Testament, the conception of history is no longer that of a great cycle of events, waxings and wanings, as the affairs of humanity unroll. Rather, time is conceived as the cycle itself cut and unrolled. Archaic ideas of time as a circle of progression and decline were abandoned. This was a decisive intellectual event. For the ancient world, the cyclical nature of time was a commonly shared notion, axiomatic in several of the great philosophers. It formed the substrate of Stoic ideas of the Cosmos and providence, for example. This cyclical notion can still be seen underpinning much of Indo-Asian religious cosmology. With the Apocalyptic movement the circle of time had been cut and rolled flat. Now time became seen as a dynamic line. This had massive societal and political implications. Time now started somewhere, the creation point, and shot forward in a progressive dynamic that also, presumably, led somewhere; to no less than the ending of time, Christians would confidently say, though others were not so sure where it led or why.

This end of time event, known to the Greek Jews and the Christians as the *eschaton*, was not simply the end of a series but the *telos* of history, that is "the end" considered as the ultimate goal of a process. In late Second Temple Jewish and Christian thought is it is quintessentially the *telos* of judgment. If Creation was the beginning of God's design for the world, the whole unfolding of progressive history was now seen as an attempted fulfillment of the plan of God for the world. Events and world powers that did not fit into the plan, that tried to frustrate the plan, were powerful only in their own day, but would never control the ultimate fulfillment of history. At the "End of Time," God's will would be all in all.

The biblical code word for this overarching plan of God within history is the "Kingdom of God" (*Basileia tou Theou*). It immediately demonstrates the electric nature of this central idea for political theology and gives a sharpness to Jesus' laconic saying "Give to God what is God's and to Caesar what is Caesar's."[17] The Kingdom of God, and its approaching nearness,[18] is an idea central in the late Jewish apocalyptic writings such as the *Book of Daniel*, and is clearly seen in the *Apocalypse* or *Book of Revelation* at the end of the New Testament; it underlies as well the whole conception of God's plan and world history within the Gospels themselves.

gogue the defeat of Simeon Bar Cochba in the mid-2nd century of the Common Era was a definitive spur to depart from apocalyptic models, and for the Christians, by the 4th century apocalyptic literature was also on the wane, though it remained more in the Christian bloodstream than in that of the Synagogue.

[17]Mt 22.21. It is a saying that has often been "de-eschatologically" rendered as an advocacy of disestablishment, but which, if understood as part of Jesus' own Kingdom of God eschatology, is explosively different from that. Jesus does not clarify what actually does belong to Caesar in this world. He deliberately left that to the wit of his correspondent, as he does to us today.

[18]The idea of the imminence of the Kingdom (the *Parousia*) is an extension of apocalyptic thought. The Kingdom is, in itself, always seen as inexorable and absolutely transcendent; but in the hands of the eschatological preacher it is often said to be "impending even now," in the sense that the long-awaited redress of God for the saints (his rebuke of the ascendancy of the powers of evil) is about to happen.

The concept of the approaching Kingdom is, of course, the central gist of the main prayer Jesus gave to his followers: "Father, let your will be done on earth as it is in heaven. May your Kingdom come!"[19] In this eschatological understanding of history, *istoria* itself becomes *theologia.*

In the teachings of Jesus in the Gospels, the doctrine of the Kingdom of God is presented in the modality of short paraenetical exhortations; encouragements to live as if the Kingdom were near and as if it was significant to you personally. These exhortations were delivered in short stories or parables and rabbinical comments on the law, rather than in the form of an extended discourse. Accordingly, much Christian thought of the first three centuries, in so far as it was biblically focused, had followed this atomistic pattern and had not produced large systematic reflections on the nature of history and culture. Augustine, therefore, is not doing anything new in establishing this idea at the heart of his thought, but he sets it on a new plane of philosophically polished reflection.

It is a constant motif of this type of eschatological literature that a great prophet would announce the meanings and times and destinies of history, from their (heavenly) vantage point of prophetic insight. This pattern is witnessed in the *Book of Daniel,* where Daniel is caught up into heaven to see things not given to other men, and also in the *Revelation of John,* where the seer is given a synopsis of the meaning of the world order and then given the charge to announce it to "those who have ears to hear" in the latter ages of the world. This is substantively what Augustine does in his own presentation of Christian history and philosophy of history. In functioning as an apocalyptic prophet he is fulfilling the expectations of his episcopal office in fifth century Africa, where the Church's "high priests" were still expected to be able to announce the oracles of the Lord, and where their particular office of expounding scriptural exegesis in the liturgy was commonly taken as a Christian extension of the ancient prophetic charism.

Within the apocalyptic scheme the events of the world order are cosmic dramas of salvation. The chosen people will make forward progress, even if the powers of the world gather in hostility around them to attempt a frustration of God's plan which has prioritized the destiny of the faithful community on earth. Chief among the great cosmic episodes that delineate this plan are the fall of some of the angels, God's first and powerful helpers. It is common in the literature that some angels resent the favoritism shown to human beings, and so rebel against the plan of the Kingdom. In their rebellion they fall from grace and decline into dark and malicious beings who try, with the reserves of their once great power, to frustrate the flourishing of the covenant nation on earth, particularly by raising against them various persecutions by wicked earthly rulers. Persecutions occur around the storm-center of

[19]Mt 6.10.

the cult of the gods, which the early Christians all unanimously attribute to these apocalyptic demons, masquerading as the gods of old Rome and embittered at the way the Christians denigrate their status by refusing them worship.

The eschatological literature also stresses the need for the regular repentance of the covenant community, and its need to observe a constant caution in relation to the "world," which is never there to assist it, and, at worst, can be drawn against it as a servant of the "Great Beast," the ultimate dark angel who is determined to crush the people of God on the earth. Demonology and the call for purification greatly appealed to Augustine's ascetic instincts. In the *Book of Revelation*, Rome is explicitly called the "Whore of Babylon" who is the "Servant of the Great Beast" (we are reminded of Psalm 86, cited above, that gave Augustine his title for *The City of God*). Readers who wonder why Augustine seems to roam so far and wide in his treatment of world history, so as to include extensive considerations of the nature of angels, need themselves to be reminded that, as far as Augustine was concerned, he was by no means wandering from a central conception of world political history in discussing the unseen powers that control the destinies of the lower earth.

The Apologia against Roman Paganism: *The City of God*, Books 1–10

Augustine's initial impetus in writing *The City of God* was to work up a relatively simple castigation of Roman religion as outmoded and irrelevant for explaining human affairs. As he had learned from Tertullian and Lactantius, the best primary sources to use in such a critique were the Roman philosophical writers themselves: Varro, Cicero, Seneca, and echoes of Euhemerus as cited extensively in Lactantius, provided a ready quarry of controversial arguments. He also does not have to go too far to find more of the same in the extensive library of other African Christian apologists before him, such as Minucius Felix, Optatus, and Arnobius. This desire to answer and refute pagan charges that Christians had broken the cycle of the world order by abandoning the worship of the gods of Rome, thus causing the decline of Roman power which they had sustained in their heavenly majesty, is the spark that incites him to write Books 1–10, and it directs his agenda. But he got fed up with the argument, as he often did when writing a large treatise. He could see the terminus of his thesis by book three and it tired him to write through to the logical end. For this reason, he abandoned his original conception of *The City of God*. He set his disciple, Orosius, to finish the *Apologia* against pagan religion, which the latter did in many more long, unreadable, and unread, books of his own.[20]

[20]Orosius, *Seven Books of Histories Against the Pagans*. To restore his honor it should be noted that it was the most widely read book of history throughout the Latin Middle Ages.

Freed from the tedium of continuing a harangue against pagan religious cult and morals, Augustine changes his tack mid-course and redirected *The City of God* to make it a more encyclopedic review of the significance of world culture under the eyes of God. It was from here on that he really set in motion some of the first considered Christian political theory, even though the earlier apocalyptic chapters are fundamental for understanding his general context. *The City of God* becomes from here on a mystical philosophy of history. This too was not new in itself. As we have seen from the other major African patristic theorists, it was a sophisticated Rhetorician's "translation" for a wider audience of the biblical idea of history as a record of salvation which he had inherited from the Scriptures. Lactantius, in the *De Mortibus Persecutorum,* had especially prefigured him, although Augustine's imagination is on a grander scale. This decision to change direction, however, left a deep mark on the structure of *The City of God,* letting it stand as almost two treatises bound as one. Books 1–10 consist of a critical engagement with Roman religious culture.[21] Books 11–22 are his own, more positivistic, ideas on what Christianity means by history, politics and culture. It is in these later books that Augustine the intellectual emerges more forcefully.

In dealing with the *apologia* against paganism Augustine had a lot of material at hand to attack the crudities of ancient cults and their frequently loose association of religious practice and personal morality. Here he was on the high ground and acts accordingly. But the underlying idea in ancient society that religion was more than just securing favors from divinities satisfied with blood offerings, and was actually an attitude of conservatism that seamlessly unfolded into patriotism and transnational imperial identity, was something that he could not so easily deal with by simple ridicule. This close association of Roman religion and national pride was related to the idea that the gods protected Rome. Christians had to be subversives, therefore, who treasonably ridiculed the Roman pantheon. Augustine attacks the problem squarely, like Tertullian and Lactantius, dealing with it in terms of a legal defense.

The notion that Christians had abandoned the gods and thus called down disasters on the heads of the Romans was an idea that was suited for more simplistic folk, he suggests. There were many of those around then, as now, of course. But to reflective monotheistic thinkers, whether Jews, Christians or pagans, the idea that world events always followed a providential order straightforwardly had long since

[21]They fall into two distinct sections. Books 1–5 are addressed to those who worship the gods thinking that they thus secure their earthly happiness and the security of the fatherland. Books 6–10 are addressed to those who think that their worship of the gods will secure a more elevated beatitude, a transference into a blessed afterlife, or at least the purification of the heart and soul. The first five are a diatribe against paganism. The second group of five are a missionary effort to win over intelligent converts to the new Christian society.

been doubted. Judaism had, in the later biblical books, itself already questioned the theological theory suggested by the earlier prophets that Israel's sin was always the reason it suffered political setbacks. The *Book of Job* is a sophisticated, if enigmatic, consideration of that issue; so too the Wisdom literature and the opaque treatment of providence in *Ecclesiastes*. Among the Christians there were many who held to simplistic views about God's rewards for the just and his condemnations of the wicked. But the whole tenor of the Gospels, showing a Lord of Glory who was crucified and rose again to a non-earthly dominion, cast the shadow of a cross over all subsequent Christian theories of direct and simple providence. Providence there was; clearly discernible it might not always be.

Among his Roman non-Christian religionists there were similar complex reflections that the old cult, with all its myths of divinities looking after their worshippers, was not quite how reality was. Augustine takes much time to show how the best of Roman religious writers themselves (for him Seneca and Cicero) were of the opinion that the old rites, such as auguries and sacrifices, were useful only for the simple-minded. For Augustine, true thinkers among the Romans had already abandoned the gods as their mythologies had proclaimed them. Christians, with their severe critique of the old religions, he argues, are doing no more than formalize what the best of the pagan thinkers had already voiced, but were afraid to state openly in case they undermined social morality. Augustine presses the point home: divine providence is not a thing that can be easily explained. Even if one were a devout pagan worshipper engaged in the Roman cults, the turbulent history of Rome, with its innumerable political collapses, shows that Christianity cannot be reasonably blamed, when most of these grand-scale roman disasters occurred long before Christianity appeared. So much for his attack on paganism as a system of religious and civic piety in Books 1–5.

In the second section of this first part of *City of God* (Books 6–10), Augustine turns to consider the position of those who say they worship the gods not for a crude motive of rewards, but for the finer destiny of being conformed to the gods, of being rendered divine as much as a human being can be, in a purified state of soul and mind that would render the élite fit for a transcendent afterlife. Augustine is more respectful of this type of Roman religion, but not too much more. Having already alluded to the instance of Cicero acting as *augur* who, in his private writings, deplored the crass superstition of taking auguries,[22] he now turns to Seneca,[23] who could only pretend respect for a civic religion, which he laughed at in his private correspondence. Augustine takes as his main argument from this the inability of Roman religion to deliver on those things that even their best religious philosophers

[22]Cicero, *On Divination* 2.37; Augustine, *City of God* 4.30.
[23]*City of God* 6.10.

had hoped for: purity of heart and purpose and an elevation to the company of the divine. Such religion, he implies, has not led a Cicero or a Seneca to their wisdom; it has rather been a cultural chain on their mind restraining their true potential for ascent and forcing them into hypocritical stances.

Augustine is very conscious, however, of a strong argument, underlying Roman hostility to the new religion. From the earliest persecutions mounted against the Church in the first century, the attitude had been that the religion of the Christians might be foolish in scope, though relatively harmless in morals, but was civilly dangerous in its "misanthropy." Misanthropy is a charge very commonly raised against the Church in the generations before Augustine. What was meant was that the withdrawal of Christians from the cultural and religious *mores* of the people undermined the coherence of society as a whole. Refusal to worship the gods of Rome suggested a less than enthusiastic endorsement of the divine dream that was Roman domination. Equally, refusal of any form of worship of the genius of the emperor gave a *frisson* of anxiety when this could easily be read as resistance to the emperor's authority and rights. Not least symbolic was the attitude of Christians to war and bloodshed. Their longstanding custom to refuse baptism to those engaged in the active military life (for its inherent paganism as well as its bloodiness) seemed to the Romans to indicate that they were a passive crowd that could not be counted on to defend civil rights. Accordingly, when they were not seen as an anti-military fifth column, they were generally despised. The idea that Christians who constantly looked to a "higher country than this" might be undermining the unarguable and direct claims the local city made on citizens in Late Antiquity, was to a large degree correct. Augustine writes at the same time that the ascetical movement was catching the imagination of Christians: monks renouncing society to live in the desert. Did not all this spell out loud and large that Christians could not be trusted with the governance of the state or the city? Augustine himself, in two private letters, admitted that some of his closest Christian friends delayed their acceptance of baptism because they believed that the Church's demands of pacifism were contrary to the duties their Roman patriotism imposed on them.[24] If even Christians thought this, who could blame the pagans for charging it to the account of the Church?

Should not Christianity forgive its enemies rather than militarily destroying them? And who would ever vote for a truly Christian general to lead the forces in times of crisis? It is partly because he knows he is on weak ground here that Augustine makes one of his strongest arguments that Christianity does have a position in relation to patriotism. In fact, as is often the case, we might even suspect that he makes the case so adamantly because he knows it is his weak point. He made the point so emphatically, however, that it afterwards became fixed in the firmament of

[24] *Epistles* 136.2; 151.14.

medieval polity and has lain like a heavy hand over much of western Christian political theory ever after. His answer was to protest that the Christian religion elevated patriotic duty to the status of a religious obligation. The manner in which social laws in biblical times were advocated as the will of God (a theocratic paradigm given in the Old Testament) was held up by Augustine as having been fulfilled in the New Testament, not abolished by it. Thus, he says, whoever resists civil authority and the laws of one's country "resists God's ordinance and . . . incurs God's wrath," using the words of St Paul.[25] Aware that his constant theme of preferring the true fatherland of heaven to the illusory fatherland of the earthly city may have undermined this argument for his readers, Augustine all the more insists upon it. What Christians may lack, he argues, in relation to civic and political fervor, they more than make up for in overall terms by their generally higher standards of community morals. The only thing that Christians can genuinely absent themselves from is immorality. In all other matters Christianity will adapt itself to local custom and practice.[26] Nevertheless, his highest praise is that, defective as earthly society may be, unfulfilling as it may be, and ultimately frustrated as it may be, it is still, nonetheless, the greatest good of its kind that human beings possess.[27] Like the vice-presidency, it all sounds as appealing as a "bucket of spit."[28] But since the proper goal of the earthly city ought to be the pursuit of peace and social welfare, that is something in which civic minded pagans and Christians can certainly be of one accord.

Perhaps Augustine's most baneful argument here is in his reply to the reproach that Christianity demands pacifism of its adherents. His predecessor Tertullian had severely warned against the military life outright as a profession that radically endangered one's Church membership. Augustine now changes the position and, in so doing, gave authority for generations after him in the medieval Church to develop a theology of war that had been unthinkable in earlier times. The Gospels, Augustine argues, do not denounce the military profession as such, but commend various soldiers for their righteousness (one thinks of the centurion whose servant Jesus heals, or Cornelius the centurion, or the soldiers addressed by John the Baptist who are told to be content with their lot). Following from this, he surmises, the command to give back good for evil[29] does not mean exactly what is says. It really means that, if war has to be waged (and he takes that as an inevitability), the Lord commands that its effects must be moderated. It ought, that is, to be carried out with limited aims, and with a concern to be ended quickly, to avoid as much evil as pos-

[25]Rom 13.2.
[26]*City of God* 19.17.
[27]*City of God* 15.4.
[28]The office was so described by John Nance Garner, Roosevelt's vice president from 1933 to 1941.
[29]Lk 6.27; Mt 5.39.

sible, and seek to punish the unjust and protect the innocent. Augustine thus sketches out the theory of the "just war" (*ius in bello*). It was a monumental step forward in Christian thought, accommodating itself to political realities, a step which the Christian East refused to take with him.[30]

The theory of the just war makes the declaration and pursuit of war permissible, when it is necessary and when it is designed to establish peace (*ius ad bellum*). This has shaped modern Christian destinies in more ways than are imaginable and can be clearly seen, of course, in most modern western political theory. Augustine is logically coherent, according to his own principles, when he concludes that the common soldier has a duty to obey orders. He himself is not answerable for crimes that may be committed in those instances where the orders themselves have commanded things that were of dubious quality. That principle, of course, was substantively rejected at Nuremberg after the World War of 1939–1945, but remains to tug at the sleeve of the international justice theory, usually in the aftermath of atrocities.

At the end of his apologetic reply to his pagan critics Augustine begins to sketch out what will be ever afterwards the definitive medieval Christian reception of "Roman History" as well as the fundamental working definition of polity. Cicero, he says, was right in defining a city or commonwealth (*res publica*) as "a group of rational beings bound together by a common acknowledgement of right and a community of interests."[31] The problem, however, was that, although the city is the natural home of justice, in practice justice could rarely be found in a city under Roman rule. In recognizing this, the Roman philosophers had themselves testified to the impotence of their system and had taken refuge in the idea of a small élite group of intellectual purists. For Augustine this partial solution allowed a privileged élite to enjoy the benefits of civilized society while excluding the common person. The Church, on the other hand, envisages society, true society that is, as a universal communion offering salvation to the world. The Church is the model and goal for a genuinely universal plan of human culture founded on justice as the eye of God sees it.[32] When the idea of Roman civilization is probed, as for example the core-value

[30]Eastern Christian theory on war refused to follow the path to a coherent Just War Theory. It retained the older canons of St Basil of Caesarea (died 379) who had written to his own soldiers advising them that while they had a moral duty to take up arms to defend the homeland, nevertheless any who shed blood would be canonically debarred from communion in the Church for a specific number of years until they had done penance. In this "economic" position the Eastern Church acknowledged the inevitability of war, but refused a theological sanction for it.

[31]*City of God.* 2.21.2. Further, see J.A. McGuckin, "Non-Violence and Peace Traditions in Early and Eastern Christianity," in K.K. Kuriakose, ed., *Religion, Terrorism, and Globalization: Non-Violence–A New Agenda* (New York: Nova Science Press, 2006).

[32]Throughout his work Augustine is conscious of the chasm operating between secular pagan notions of *justitia* as a legal right and property, and biblical Christian conceptions of *Justitia* in the biblical sense of "righteousness" (*dikaiosyne*).

patriotic narratives such as that of Scipio Africanus,[33] it turns out to be a sham. The glories of Rome amount to its greater success than local bandits, in internationally significant rapinage and brigandage.[34] Rome, therefore, was never a *res publica,* in its vaunted sense, in any of its history.[35] It never valued *concordia.*

If the first ten books of *The City of God* present Augustine as the last great Latin Church apologist, his new beginning in the second major part of the work (Books 11–22) show him in the light of a positive exponent of Christian social thought who is synthesizing his predecessors and going beyond them in his range. After handing over the apologetic task to others, he now dedicates his argument as an invitation to the ancient world,whose core values he has exposed as defective, to come to the sources, to learn a correct conception of how religion, morality, politics, history and world culture can be systematically combined in new ways. It is a dramatic Christian vision of universal polity, uniquely vivid and spacious in scope. When Seneca and Cicero continued to give mere lip service to the old religion, Augustine argues, they did so only for fear that world order would morally collapse. The insincerity of the best of men showed the rottenness of the whole system. Christianity now has the power to openly declare that rottenness, because it can offer an alternate system: the revelation of true social order in the "Last Days" of history: the "Age of the Church."

The *Politeia* of the Two Cities

In this most important part of *The City of God* (Books 11–22) Augustine tries to establish two important ends: first, he wishes to present the substance of Christian faith and cultural ideas to the open minded pagan reader,[36] and second, he is writing for his Christian readership and obviously wants his arguments to establish a common understanding of theological polity among them. This long section is itself divided into three parts with a double theme: the Origin, the Development, and the End, of the City of God (*civitas dei*), and the same for its counterpart the earthly city (*civitas terrena*). Books 11–14 discuss origins. Books 15–18 give a survey of histories from the vantage point of biblical narrative, showing the perennial interweaving of the two cities in human and sacred history. Books 19–22 present a summary review and point to the final destinies awaiting the two cities.

[33] *City of God* 2.21.4.

[34] *City of God* 4.4–6.

[35] *City of God* 2.21.4; 19.21

[36] He reflected on his own change of method in *The City of God* in the later writings: *Letter to Firmus,* in Bibliothèque Augustinienne 33 (Paris, 1950) 170; and in *Retractations* 2.43.2.

In using the concept of "City of God" as a major political cipher, Augustine canonizes,and simultaneously overturns and redefines, a Stoic conception of political morality. The term is already found in the political writings of Marcus Aurelius. The "City of God" signifies for him the ideal and intimate fusion of all life under the gods and explains why religion, morality, and civic virtue are, for the Roman, as one. This harmony of virtues will bring stability and success to the state that is beloved of the gods. Marcus Aurelius thought that all citizens' lives would be hierarchically positioned in the City according to their degree of justice, from gods and daemons, to wise beings who assume positions of leadership, and even the foolish, who have their contribution to make. Augustine affirms this vision of *civitas* as *concordia* but he also takes a strikingly different position by introducing (from biblical sources) a stark polarity and a vivid sense of judgment into the concept of society (twin elements that define the eschatological genre). His key argument is that the whole cosmos is not the City of God in all its variety, rather there is a pure City of God and a defiled earthly city constantly grinding against one another, overlapping, often getting in one another's way. His Christian polity is thus far from seamless, far from the apparently flawless harmony of Marcus Aurelius' dream society.

Into the idea of foundational cosmic and social architectures Augustine has introduced the razor-sharp notion that God will exercise judgment on the justice-righteousness of every single effort. As are angelic beings, all of humanity is classified by Augustine as belonging predominantly to one or the other camp. *The City of God* has as its biblical "type" (or revelatory symbol), the Heavenly Jerusalem.[37] This means that Augustine will find much revealed about the nature of the true Jerusalem in the biblical statements that refer to Jerusalem (City of Peace) in the Psalms and historical books of the Bible, for example; but the real Jerusalem is that heavenly city spoken of in the *Book of Revelation*, which is, far more than a geographical place, the moral destiny of the saints in the glorious Kingdom that will only come after the eschaton, the end of all earthly history. The earthly city, likewise, is not first and foremost a place (it is not a capital such as Rome, or even the world considered as the global domain of secular culture), but it is rather a mystical symbol.[38] The earthly city also has its biblical type, or symbol, in the term Babylon; sometimes he calls it the "city of the devil."[39] This aspect of Augustine's dualism will have a monumental effect on almost all subsequent western Christian theories of Church and society, and theories of the relation of the Gospel to culture, where a tendency towards separatism becomes the rule rather than the exception.

[37]The earthly type of the City of God is Israel in the prophetic era, or the Church in the contemporary era: but it is simply a sign of the City of God, not its realization, which can only come at the Eschaton.

[38]*City of God* 15.1.1.

[39]*City of God* 17.20.2.

For Augustine the heavenly city is the ultimate destiny of the universe that God has placed within the pattern of creation: that all rational life should ascend to divine communion, and the immortality that was once associated with Adam's knowledge of God in what the created state was before the Great Fall. The earthly city with its enslavement of humanity to the forces of pride and lust, violence and lovelessness, is both a corruption of true human reality and a continuing plot of envious dark angels to deprive earthly creatures of benefits they formerly lost through ancient rebellions. By adhering to Christ's Gospel, Augustine argues, humans have the possibility offered to them once more to bring about the ideal city. This ideal dream is, for Christians, rooted in a concrete moral and political order of reality. It is, he says sardonically, not a Platonic concept of city (the most celebrated example of political thinking in antiquity), since Plato's city, Augustine adds wittily, could exist only in our heads because the ideal for him had no material substrate.

By contrast, Augustine sees the earthly city as guided only by self-love and material pleasure. As the Heavenly City sets out the goal of divine transcendence and communion of the saints as its highest ideals, so the earthly city sets out self-glorification and self-promotion as its most important goals. The Heavenly City (partly exemplified in the struggle to become the Church of Christ on earth, although the Church is not the synonym of the heavenly city as it is also in process[40]) is comprised of those who struggle to become a communion of justice and love, bonded together by reverence for the God of justice and peace. The earthly city prizes its independence and regards self-satisfaction to be the highest of its goals. It has no desire for communion, or service. Whereas the Heavenly City is fashioned from repentance, the earthly city despises this as mere weakness, looks down on the humble, and scorns the poor. The end of the one is an ever deepening ascent to the sublimity of God's love; the end of the other is to be cast down in to the darkness with the other spirits who mutated themselves from angels of light into demonic forces of darkness. What Augustine draws for his reader here is a wonderfully vivid polarity. It is a masterpiece etching, but one in black and white; grey does not work so well. It serves his ends in answering Roman complaints about Christian administration of the world-wide empire. It became in its afterlife a seminally important approach using polarized forms, that would build the architecture of medieval Christian polity. The very polarizations that make for the vividness of a stark and memorable picture, of course, can also serve to set fast limits on alternative possibilities of political imagination. Augustine's rhetoric here may well have made western Christianity more rigid in its approaches to pluralism than it needed to be in later ages.

[40]*City of God* 8.24.2; 13.16.1; 16.2.3.

In Eastern Christian political theology, the legal principle, philosophically articulated by Cicero, that society was bonded together by adherence to law and that law itself was an extended set of principles based around natural rights (*ius gentium*), was a generally accepted premise, acceptable as far as it went in a society that still counted, until well after the seventh century, a considerable number of non-Christians at its core. Augustine in *The City of God* is not so much interested in practical collaboration with the pagans as in offering a vigorous apologetic against them and all their philosophies. Accordingly, he is not at all happy about canonizing law as a workable fundament of true society. He says that law, most of time, primarily reflects human desires and ambitions and does not represent a true search for justice. Law, therefore, can frequently be far less than the standard of justice to which God has called human beings to aspire. It is Augustine's contention that law always represents a certain compromise with goodness, one that bends to accommodate the unjust and ingrained habits of society.[41] According to Augustine, to be part of the heavenly city one must never mistake law for love or justice and must always seek to live by a higher standard than that which is acceptable to the majority. The task of the citizen of the Heavenly City is to strive constantly not to be conformed to this world, and the earthly city, but to bring the values of Jerusalem into the forum of Babylon.

Political Archetypes Augustine Establishes for the Western Church

Augustine's City of God is often acclaimed as the classical Christian position on the transcendence of the City of God over all earthly political structures. This treatise, along with the *Confessions*, established his reputation as a political thinker. Yet it is important to remember that he never set out to write a specifically political treatise. All his writing is an eschatological theological account of the struggle of the human soul to attain to its divine destiny. His work is an overarching narrative of the great pilgrimage of the soul through history and space. Its journey through this world is but one phase. His angular approach to political theology has led to several differences of opinion among the commentators as to his intended meanings and political judgments. Not least in this respect are foundational differences in the manner in which Catholicism and Protestantism have approached the notion of politics and culture on Augustine's authority. Western Catholicism would tend to assert the transcendence of the world order by the Kingdom of God in terms that argued the superiority of the Church over secular rulers, ultimately instanced in the super-monarchical authority of the papacy, a stance that explains much medieval

[41] *On the Spirit and the Letter* 36.65.

political to-ing and fro-ing and which itself led inexorably to the great divide among Latin Christians we now call the Reformation. Protestantism, in its turn, has tended to emphasize the distinction, even a necessary separation, between the Kingdom and the world order, seeing the affairs of the Church (understood primarily as an eschatological mystery of pure believers, not coincident with the ecclesiastic structures here visible) as ever under threat from hostile oppressors or, at best, uncomprehending and insensitive interferers. Augustine's hint in his early books that empire might not be as well suited to *concordia* as a federation of nation-states was seized on by both Catholics and Protestants, to the dismay of Byzantine Christians who regarded that as a sacrilegious idea, inimical to the trans-global unity (world Catholicism) which they saw the Christian Roman Empire as having a destiny to bring to mankind.[42]

The American Constitutional separation of Church and State (alleged separation in cultural terms) partly grew out of a desire to see the end of centuries of religious fighting in the blood-stained lands of old Europe and an earnest wish not to import the contagion to the New World: but it expressed a profoundly Augustinian spirit when it presumed that a (basically) Christian government (as it was at that time) should not imagine itself as having any role in creating the culture of the Church. The idea is at once so seminal for Western Christian political thinking, and so patently at odds with the reality, that Augustine's book still demands serious consideration from contemporary readers. Western Christianity has had many frictions with the Eastern Christian world over basic disagreements with this political theory. The Byzantines, for example, presumed on the continuation of the religio-political paradigms presented in the Book of Psalms, or the Books of the Kings of Israel, namely that the extent of the dominion of the righteous covenant people on earth would be synonymous with the extent of the dominion of God's Kingdom on earth; and thus the boundaries of the Christian empire would be political lines of separation with the infidel and the foe of the Kingdom. God's righteous king, as far as Eastern Christian political theology was concerned, was the earthly lord that the heavenly Lord had selected to rule as his agentive power on earth: the "God-Beloved Autocrat of the Romans," as the Byzantines now called the Augustus of (New) Rome. The West, by contrast, favored Augustine's suggestion (it is nothing more in *The City of God*) that a confederation of nation-states would be a better way to preserve freedom by limiting the extent of an evil ruler's possible influence. Today, of course, we have reason for skepticism with both models, and have been as much plagued by nationalisms as we have been by global imperialism.

[42]Further see J.A. McGuckin, "The Legacy of the Thirteenth Apostle: Origins of the Eastern Christian Conceptions of Church-State Relation," *St Vladimir's Theological Quarterly* 47, nos. 3 & 4 (2003) 251–288.

Augustine's characteristic pessimism about political systems never being other than endemically and profoundly flawed by human sin gives his political theology a different cast to that of the classical Byzantine religious synthesis which, despite many occasions of lively criticism of the incumbent monarch, tended usually to see the Christian emperor's role as that of the righteous king typified in the Psalms. The Augustinian pessimism, on the other hand, spoke consoling words to generations of western Catholics through the Dark Ages when the practical collapse of the universal idea of Roman imperium in the occidental provinces and the rise of tribal leaders thence devolving into monarchies was regarded with a raised eyebrow by many leading clergy. It received new enthusiasm again in the Reformation era when strong moves were being made to disestablish Church and politics in the aftermath of bitter wars of religion, and once more received close scholarly attention in the latter part of the twentieth century, when Catholic and Protestant historical theologians were again world-weary with global war and the many other international conflicts of the era. In short, "Augustinianism" (and this understood as the revival of modern scholarly interest in the great African thinker, but mediated heavily through medieval and reformation matrices of thought) "as a discourse and worldview speaks directly to the crisis of late twentieth century culture and was to become a favored weapon in the arsenal of cold war political commentators."[43]

Augustine as a Local Bishop-Magistrate

However much Augustine was to have long-term definitive influence over the Western Church's understanding of religion and culture, of Gospel and law, of freedom and restraint, the fact remains that in his own day his reflections on these matters grew out of immediate and limited cultural and political experiences. Even something so extensive a set of meditations as *The City of God* is conceived in order to answer an immediate apologetic need: the request of the educated élite of Roman Christians to give some kind of answer to the caustic criticisms of the pagan Senator Symmachus, and the queries of Volusianus' educated circle, that Christians were not fit to guide an international and mature empire. Most of Augustine's developed theory of politics and culture lies here in the local domain, and understanding the pressing and intimate nature of that part of Augustine's office as Bishop-magistrate will help us understand the peculiar nature of such local "adjudication" experience that grows in his mind into principles of how humans work, need governance, and

[43] J. Scott (1999) 658 (my parenthesis). See also R.R. Ruether, "Augustine and Christian Political Theology," *Interpretation* 29 (1975) 252–265; and J.B. Elshtain, *Augustine and the Limits of Politics*. (Notre Dame, IN: Notre Dame University Press, 1995).

how the Church should be involved in this. The occasional and *ad hoc* nature of his involvement in the systems of Roman justice and penal law, often illustrate not only how tentative Augustine really was in relation to Christian political theory, but also how different were the application of the principles of Roman justice and order between the capital and the provinces, between the rich and poor, between the upper and lower classes.

A vivid window, albeit a small one, has been opened for us in recent years with the discovery in 1981 by J. Divjak of forgotten and misplaced letters of St Augustine. This newly published cache shows Augustine predominantly in his role as administrator-organizer. He is involved with the flood of refugees coming to North Africa to escape the invasion of the early fifth century, and he is actively involved trying to organize relief works. His offices as pastoral magistrate also emerge clearly. But here we also have recorded cases where Augustine has to exercise discipline over recalcitrant clergy and laity, specific legal cases dealing with child enslavement, clerical rape of nuns, and other serious offenses requiring Augustine as a bishop to act as a magistrate. How he approaches the issue of inflicting legal penalty is instructive.

Eastern Church law was significantly changed when Constantine, in the early fourth century, decided to elevate Christian bishops to the status of local judges,[44] especially in all cases that referred to church affairs. If a citizen had recourse to an episcopal court (*audientia episcopalis* as it was known in the West), then recourse could not be had back to the civil courts if the bishop's judgment did not please one of the parties. Constantine's law basically meant that bishops were henceforth to be classed as those who had judicatory rights according to *privilegium fori* of upper class community leaders.[45] This elevating of local bishops to some form of recognized decurion status was meant to do two things in the age of Constantine: to give some redress back to the Church after years of persecution, property confiscation, and civil disability and also to allow Christian communities a stronger degree of self-determination. Constantine and his successors strengthened the Church's legal capacities to act as a corporation, but it was never intended that the church courts would ever replace the imperial legal system: merely to serve as a refinement of level within it.

Gregory Nazianzen, one of the most educated bishops of his age, had a father who was a bishop in a small town in the deepest recesses of Cappadocia. In his funeral oration for the old bishop, one of the first to enjoy the *privilegium fori qua*

[44]With laws as early in his reign as 306–307. See Dossey (2001) 98, fn 2. Constantine again in 333 commanded the Praetorian Prefect to enforce episcopal judgements (*Codex Theodosianus*. 1.27.2 [408]). Further see: Lenski (2001) 83; also Gaudemet (1978); Nonnoi (1934); Cimma (1989); and Lamoreaux (1995).

[45]See J. Harries, *Law and Empire in Late Antiquity* (New York: Cambridge University Press, 1999) 191–211.

bishop, although as a local magnate and millionaire he had clearly fulfilled this legal leadership role independently as landowner, his son Gregory praises his moderation as a Christian, reminding the locals that his father "liked to threaten the lash more than use it."[46] It is a clear and chilling reminder to us how extensively the bishop's powers moved. Augustine himself shows evidence in his letters that he knew he had the legal power to inflict interrogation under torture, excommunication, or lashing: perhaps even lashing with the infamous lead-tipped scourge, which was tantamount to a death sentence considering the physical irreparable damage it inflicted.[47] There was some movement of retrenchment after Constantine. In 399 Honorius, emperor in the West, assured the proconsul of Africa, for example, that bishops were meant to judge only ecclesiastical affairs. The local civil magistrates are presumed to be entirely competent, and the proper authority, to apply penal law everywhere.[48] And in 408 an imperial edict (again from the western court) decreed that bishops could only serve as judges if both parties agreed, although this was simply a reiteration of a standard element of Roman civil arbitration law; and it went on to state clearly enough that the civil officials were meant to enforce that episcopal judgment once it was given. It was clear enough that the civil legal authorities saw *audientia episcopalis* as local supplementary administration only.[49] But there was no backing off the basic principle. In 409, for example, and in response to growing problems of ecclesiastical governance in Africa (the Donatist crisis) the western emperor, after specific petitions from the Catholic bishops, offered military assistance to clergy in Africa. The message was abundantly clear.[50]

More and more in the post-Constantinian age, the local bishop emerged as the leading rhetorician-lawyer-landowner, and more and more his functions as administrator of law and defender of the Roman peace came to be paralleled with his priestly duties. The less developed legal system in the western provinces afforded greater scope to the western bishops. Africa is an interesting example. At an early stage eastern canon law had seen the difficulties that would come without regulation. The Apostolic Canon 27,[51] one of a collection emanating from fourth century Syria and reflecting the ascendancy of the Church in the post-Constantinian era, specifically forbids bishops from physically disciplining people, and does so under the high canonical threat of deposition. It obviously reflects widespread concern that bishops had assumed their new judicial powers too strenuously. This was a

[46]Gregory of Nazianzus, *Oration 18:* "On The Death of His Father" given in 374 A.D.

[47]J. Divjak, *New Letters of Augustine*, *10 (CSEL vol. 88 [Vienna, 1981]).

[48]Cod. Theod. 16.11.1 (399).

[49]Cod. Theod. 1.27.2–3 (408).

[50]Cod. Theod. 16.2. 31 (409).

[51]Also echoed in *Didascalia Apostolorum*, Canon 7.

church law that was generally adopted universally among the eastern clergy (though with continuing and numerous local exceptions), coming to the West as a cited canonical authority only after the sixth century, and to North Africa not until the seventh. In the Greek-speaking provinces, however, it reflects a growing consensus. Bishops and priests who have charge of communities that include unruly and disruptive members are required to make efforts to control them. They have the duty to "name and shame" offenders (not to be underestimated as a form of control in ancient society that was so ordered by concepts of honor and disgrace), and if the bad behavior does not improve they can apply spiritual penalties, such as exclusion from the Church. But generally speaking they are not allowed to go further and apply physical punishments. If they feel the disruptive behavior has become a threat and shows no sign of improving, they are instructed to bring the offender to the attention of the civil powers, who will apply the full (and violent) force of the law against them on behalf of the emperor. So, clergy are related to the imposition of legal order, but are not to be directly involved in it. Such an involvement in violence was regarded as a defilement of their priestly, sacral role.

Of course what happened in the years after Constantine's death is that the Church organization grew exponentially and often its infrastructure was the highest and most developed form of civic administration available, especially in the provinces. Lenski makes this telling comment about the extent of Roman judicial organization away from the large centers: "The state, therefore, was hardly a real presence for the enforcement of justice at the community level [in North Africa]. In the state's absence the Church filled the void."[52] So, where the civil arm was weak, as in the more obscure villages and provinces, such a clean-cut separation of Church and state activities was not always observed. Also, when bishops assumed large retinues, such as those of the super-bishops of Rome, Alexandria, and Constantinople, they usually acted as great magnates, with their own police force. In the fifth century, Cyril of Alexandria had a police force of some five hundred at his personal disposal.[53] Nestorius, his counterpart in Constantinople, was once heckled in his cathedral by a dissident monk and, to the cat calls during his sermon, shouted back that, if the reverend sir would attend his palace the next morning, he would give him a full answer that would completely satisfy him. The dim monk took him at his word, only to find waiting for him the archbishop's personal guard, who administered a severe beating. Even so the monk's case was regarded as something scan-

[52]Lenski (2001) 92.

[53]And this was as officially restricted as a curb to his pretensions, though the number was allowed to grow to 600 two years later. See: J.A. McGuckin, *St Cyril of Alexandria: the Christological Controversy* (Leiden: Brill, 1994) 15 (repr.: Crestwood, NY: St Vladimir's Seminary Press, 2004). These "parabalani" vigorously and often violently defended the bishop's interests in the city affairs of Alexandria.

dalous, and the beating was itself used as a canonical charge against Nestorius (by his opponent Cyril of Alexandria) in the process that culminated in the Council of Ephesus in 431. This beating up of a monk would not have been sufficient in itself to bring about Nestorius' downfall, but it was capable of being used as grist in an already moving mill, because more ancient Christian sentiment still felt strongly the need for a sharper separation of the bishop's pastoral role and any new social judicial function.

The Donatist crisis which saw Circumcellion gangs roaming the countryside burning slave-owning estates and beating up Catholic clergy as colonial oppressors as well as alleged heretics, caused widespread outrage among the Christian aristocracy and made them ready to come to the aid of what they saw as a dangerous precedent in the African province, where the lower classes seemed to have taken the advantage over the landowners. It is interesting to see the catholic hierarchy early in the dispute appealing to the proconsul of Africa, Septimius, to demand that the Donatist hierarchs should be forced to address this abuse among their lay followers and should engage with their own synod to resolve the larger dispute by debate.[54] But dissatisfaction with their opponents' compliance led the same Catholic synod in 411 to appeal to, and rely on, imperial landlords and special agents to force the reluctant Donatist laity back into the Catholic Churches after their cause had civilly been declared illegal.[55] Augustine, writing to Petilianus of Cirta, himself argued that clerics should not use clubs to defend their churches against Donatists but should have ready recourse to legal protection from the civil powers.[56]

In the seventh century Pope Gregory the Great publicly criticized the Patriarch of Constantinople for flogging a theologically dissident priest. In a letter he told him "What the canons say about bishops who want to be feared for their blows, you well know. But in truth we have been made pastors, not persecutors."[57] But he was not always consistent in this pacific attitude. He later demanded, in what he evidently expected to be a legal ruling of his own dominions in which presumably he would not stand any intrusion from outside, that the bishop of Naples should have his own senior subdeacon publicly flogged and then expelled from the city for having laid false accusations against his own Roman colleagues.[58] The same pope also ordered a bishop in Sardinia who had discovered pagan idolaters hiding among his congregation to "castigate with blows and torture" those among them of servile birth[59] and

[54]Acts of the Council of Carthage in 403. Sources Chrétiennes, vol. 224, 11–20.

[55]See P. Brown, *Religion and Society in the Age of St Augustine* (New York, 1972) 301–331.

[56]*Contra Petilianum* 2.19.43.

[57]Gregory the Great, *Regest.* 3.52.

[58]Gregory the Great, *Regest.* 11.53.

[59]He refers to country folk, and thereby signifies those in the rank of the *coloni*, or serfs, working the land.

to imprison the freeborn involved, "so that agony of the body might be able to bring them to the desired state of health of mind."[60] When Augustine of Canterbury asked his opinion on the correct treatment of people who stole money and goods out of the churches, he sent the advice that Augustine should beat them heartily: "For even a father would beat his well-beloved sons."[61] In 675 the Spanish Council of Braga found it necessary to urge priests to stop beating up their parishioners, "except in the cases of the mortal and most serious sins."[62] Benedict's Rule, widely regarded as exceptionally lenient and kind in its time, shows some of the ambivalence when it allows for the beating of dissident monks in communities, but urges that it be done "with fatherly kindness."[63] The Rule of the Master, which Benedict's Rule set out to revise and adapt, had sounded another note when it advised that recalcitrant monks should be beaten "to the point of death" before they were thrown out of the monastery.[64] In the Eastern Church, the widespread monastic Rule set out in the *Typikon* of the Stoudios Monastery at Constantinople regarded physical violence in the monastery as "suitable perhaps for those who live in the world, but it was judged an unacceptable procedure by our fathers."[65] But this was a monastery that was imperial in many respects and had noble aspirations. Across the Eastern Christian world, beatings of monks and laity administered by abbots or bishops must have been common enough. The rule that was always observed carefully (or else there would be legal fallout of a large order) was the principle of social rank. A social inferior could not, under any circumstances, order violence against a social superior. It did not matter whether that inferior held the rank of bishop or not. If a member of the upper classes was mistreated there would be a serious row to follow. The treat-

[60]Gregory the Great, *Regest.* 9. 205.

[61]Gregory the Great, *Regest.* 11.56.

[62]Council of Braga, Canon 6. J. Vives, ed., *Concilios visigoticos e hispano-romanos* (Barcelona, 1963) 377.

[63]*Rule of Benedict* 2.28. CSEL 75, p. 24.

[64]*Regula Magistri* 13.69. Sources Chrétiennes. vol. 105. p. 46; Cassian's Monastic *Institutes* also advocated the utility of beatings in a monastery; see J.C. Guy, ed., Sources Chrétiennes 109, p. 142. Pachomian monasticism applied the beating of monks as a regular discipline. Monks who stole, tried to flee to other places, or engaged in illicit sexuality, were subject to thirty-nine lashes and exclusion until they had performed penance (*Rule of Pachomius* 84; 120). Palladius speaks of three palm trees at Nitria where miscreant monks and robbers were tied up and scourged (*Lausiac History* 7.15–19). Further up the Nile, the Coptic monastic leader Shenute was widely known for his violent form of community governance. He himself says that with regard to a disobedient monk: "I would strike with canes or with my hands those whose minds were inflated with pride" (De iis qui e monasterio discesserunt, in H. Wiesmann, tr., *Sinuthii archimandritae vita et opera omnia,* iii, CSCO, Scriptores Coptici, series 2, vol. 4 [1906] 86). He had thought out this position as justified by Scripture (Prov 3.11; Heb 12.6.), and did not hesitate to extend his violence to laity, especially the rich who oppressed the poor of his locality (David N. Bell, tr., *The Life of Shenoute by Besa*, 81, Cistercian Studies 73 [Kalamazoo, MI, 1983] 65). Pagan shrines were often a focus of his monks' violence. But Shenute, nevertheless, was on the fringes of the empire and his behaviour was regarded as an uncomfortable oddity even then, and often by local clergy near him.

[65]*Typikon of Stoudios* c. 25, PG 99.1713.

ment of the poorer classes was largely left to local procedure. Nevertheless, one sees that the role tensions between pastoral care and good governance (between the duties of reform, and the invocation of just punishment) was not one that was perfectly resolved in Christian antiquity. All in all, the Church avoided the widespread use of physical coercion and applied to the state for redress when it was felt necessary. But the conflicted ambiguity of a fifth century Syrian canon on this subject speaks volumes: "Do not scourge anyone, O priest; but if there is a reason by virtue of which you are compelled to scourge, then either scourge them only to frighten them, or send the guilty ones to the judges of this world."[66] This, of course, was trying to invoke the distinction that the clergy must not inflict a death penalty and their punishments must only be applied as corrective measures. From the early fifth century the local bishops regularly employed a local official *defensor ecclesiae*, whose duties paralleled the civil post of *defensor civitatis*, a kind of chief of police who ran a local gendarmerie, when funds allowed. Otherwise, the town watchmen or local garrison stood in, or, in some cases, the priests and deacons turned out in force. The bishop used this body of local men to enforce his decisions practically.

It was one such case of a mistaken degree of rank that brought Augustine out into the light of day as a practical legal administrator. A decurion-ranked priest in his diocese had raped a local nun. The outraged clergy, with the aid of local police acting under their direction, tied up the priest and beat him with rods (a lesser form of punishment than scourging). He appealed over the head of Augustine, directly to Pope Celestine in Rome, demanding redress since his rank precluded him from this kind of treatment. The pope, when he eventually replied to the letters, advised that as the man had suffered *injuria*, the local Church should afford him compensation. Augustine was deeply annoyed by both the intervention and its tone. He was appalled that the rape of a nun should have been committed by a priest in the first place. The action of the local clergy was regarded by him as appropriate even if not entirely in accordance with law. Celestine's decision upset him because it was in accordance with law but not in harmony with justice or the standards the Church ought to uphold. Augustine expresses dismay that no one in his society seems to care about the crime of rape or the laws governing it, except the church authorities. He himself instructed that his own monastic clergy ought to be beaten even for simply conversing with nuns.[67]

The Divjak letters that relate to Augustine as judge show that he clearly tended to reserve his judicial dealings to matters that concerned clerical misconduct. The one exception to this was his intervention in the case of a family of orphaned chil-

[66] *Rabbula's Rules for the Clergy*, c. 23. See A. Voobus, tr., *Syriac and Arabic Documents Regarding Legislation Relative to Syrian Asceticism* (Stockholm, 1960) 45.

[67] J. Divjak, *New Letters of Augustine* *20.5 (CSEL vol. 88 [Vienna, 1981]).

dren who had been unjustly enslaved following their parents' death. The children's father had leased them out as hired labor to a local landowner. After his death shortly afterwards, the landowner claimed them as his estate slaves. Augustine, writing on this matter to his close friend and clerical colleague Alypius, suggests to him that the latter should go to the court at Ravenna and present a case for stricter laws to be passed covering such enslavement of freeborn children. Here Augustine acted as defender of the rights of the freeborn poor and gained the children's manumission largely because of the close interest he took in a wider environment that suggests the local civil magistracy did not care much about what happened to poorer people far away from the capital. It was actions like this that earned many of the early Greek bishops the title of *Philoptochos* "Friend of the Poor."

One of the other cases in the letters concerned Augustine's having to intervene in a dispute between a local diocese and an auxiliary bishop named Antoninus. The latter emerges as clearly a crook who was on the make. He had applied his powers, as a suffragan bishop in an out-of-the-way rural area, to extort extensively. He had defrauded people's property, applied unjust fines, and threatened violence to anyone who stood against him. Eventually the local Church had had enough, and, after he defrauded a widow, it accused him before Augustine's episcopal court, calling for his deposition as a bishop. Augustine heard the evidence and, although here was a scoundrel who had merited deposition and exile from the community, Augustine evidently wanted to "hold back" from the main penalty that was within his power, deposition and excommunication (a ruination of the man). So he instead allowed Antoninus to continue as bishop, subject to repentance and restitution of the property in question. Immediately Antoninus appealed against Augustine's judgment to the papal court at Rome. The outcome is not known, but Lenski (2001) concludes that the episode shows that Augustine was something of "a soft touch" and may indicate that these episcopal courts were regarded as a softer option than the civil ones.

Augustine tells his readers that his rhetorical training was from the outset undertaken with a view to practicing law.[68] It is equally clear that he viewed those legal duties as a bishop with an increasingly jaundiced eye. Several times in his later writings he complains of the legal burdens of his episcopal office. In a letter *On the Works of Monks* he praises monastic withdrawal compared to the bishop's need "to endure the highly tumultuous perplexities of other people's legal cares about worldly business."[69] His close friend and biographer Possidius tells us[70] that Augustine regularly spent all morning in hearing legal cases, and sometimes even the afternoons, too.

[68] *fora litigiosa:* see *Confessions* 3.3.6.
[69] *De opere monachorum* 28 (CSEL 41, pp. 586–588).
[70] *Vita Augustini* 19 (PL 32.50).

The Greek bishop Epiphanius of Salamis is also known to have passed his entire mornings hearing legal cases.[71] Augustine persevered with this unpalatable duty, not only because the times thrust it upon him, but also because he understood that it was part of the apostolic duty of the bishop. Had not the Apostle Paul (1 Cor 6.1–6) commanded that disputes among the saints should be heard only among the saints without recourse to secular judges that did not follow the Gospel precepts? His attitude is explained in a reflection on judicial authority contained in his *Commentary on the Gospel of John Chapter 33*, written in 419 and also in his Sermon 302 *On the Feast of St Lawrence*.[72] In the latter reflection he makes his opinions felt robustly enough in a candid homily to his cathedral parish:

> Brothers, I am telling you plainly, and as far as the Lord allows me, I am telling you openly: Only bad men use violence, and will use it against other bad men. But you have to make a distinction with the violent actions of the authorities; for this is a different matter entirely. A judge usually will only unsheathe the sword when forced to it. When he strikes, he does so unwillingly . . . But why does our bishop keep on going to the civil authorities some of you are saying. And what does a Christian bishop have to do with the authorities anyway? Come on, you all know that it is your needs that force me to go there . . . If you are not happy then please put me out of a job. Let me off from all of this. It is not my choice to have dealings with the authorities. God knows I am forced into it.[73]

It was this precisely local context that formed and shaped Augustine's mind. His ambivalence remains tensely present all through his life. His general theory, that law is a very poor reflection of God's justice though a necessity in a society flawed by human greed and selfishness, is a view he hardly changes throughout his maturity as a Christian thinker.

Augustine Theorizing on the Role of Law

All in all, Augustine does not have a systematic treatment of the role of law in his theological work, although he leaves abundant reflections, many of them as acute as the situation he felt he was in that called forth his skills of legal adjudication. The most extensive set of reasoned reflections about the role of law in society come in the first book of his treatise *On Free Will* (*De Libero Arbitrio*) in which Augustine dialogues with his friend Evodius on the two types of law that exists the eternal and the

[71] *Vita Epiphanii* 55 (PG 41.93).
[72] Further see Atkins & Dodaro (2001) 128–173, translated political writings.
[73] Text in Atkins & Dodaro (2001) 116.

temporal.[74] This polarity sets the terms of all Augustine wishes to maintain about law's role in social affairs. Temporal law is that which strives after justice on earth, but in the course of time can change, according to human perception. This can negatively amount to a corruption of society by decadence of law; but it is also a positive factor in so far as this changeability is able to adapt the common principles of eternal law to various human cultural conditions across the ages; in fact, mediating eternal law to human society. The fallibility of temporal law can also work to mankind's advantage in many respects. For example, a good temporal law can take advantage of our race's propensity to selfish desires in order to limit them by regulating the personal possession of goods. Such regulation is a good thing, since humans are never free from cupidity and cannot act in that spiritual freedom necessary to apply possessions in accordance with Eternal Law; namely, that each should willingly distribute their goods to others according to need. Since we fall short of that standard, temporal law can regulate the individual's determination to hold on to what is his own regardless of the need of any other. To this extent, then, temporal law exists not for the sake of the perfect, but for the sake of the majority of faltering sinners who make up society and who will act justly largely only when compelled to do so by law.[75] It thus has its uses and its strict limits. Temporal law embodies a principle of justice which is only a dim reflection of the eternal standard of justice, and must never be mistaken for it or substituted for it. It is unable, on its own terms, to instill virtue in any human heart. This is why it always has to be inspired and complemented by the eternal law which is the archetypal and higher standard.[76]

To demonstrate the nature of temporal law's variability, Augustine takes the example of how a promulgation of democracy and of tyranny,[77] however mutually opposite in spirit, could both be instances of just laws according to the principles of temporal law.[78] His argument goes that if all citizens in a certain city were just and pure of heart they would naturally enact a democratic form of government and the law of that city, establishing that the magistrates should be elected by all the people, would *de facto* be a good and just law. But, he says, imagine a city where all the people were wicked and self-seeking. Their collective will expressed in laws promulgated according to majority will would reflect their wicked state and intentionality. On the other hand, if a law was promulgated that decreed that only a good and just person should lead society, only a person who was able to lead others to justice and

[74]See Fortin (1996) for a fuller analysis.

[75]*On Free Will* 1.5.12.

[76]*On Free Will* 1.5.13.

[77]In the ancient sense of single rule by one figure in time of emergency.

[78]*On Free Will* 1.6.14–15.

whose monarchical policy was aimed at teaching them how to do this, then this too would be a good and just law. Both laws, one installing democracy, one installing tyranny, would be just by reference, each in its own way, to the common principles of the eternal law that directs that the virtuous and not the wicked should distribute honors and punishments, set the tone for, and stand over, the affairs of social life. This alone is the proper order willed by God.

Eternal law, insofar as humans can attain to or understand this, is the manifestation of the highest reason (*summa ratio*) on earth. It is that factor in life which demands total and complete obedience and allegiance; it cannot suffer change or alteration and through it the good prosper and the evil suffer. It is eternal law which is properly the model for all temporal law. When the latter diverges from the standard of the former, corruption in society sets in. Augustine defines the eternal law as "That law in virtue of which it is just that all things should be perfectly ordered," and he identifies it with the will or wisdom of God which directs all things in creation to their God-given, naturally-constituted end.[79] Eternal law is the fountain of all justice and whatever is good in earthly laws takes its root in this. Whatever is opposed to this is not right, is exposed to be an unjust law which has no power to command the allegiance of the just. God has impressed his eternal law on the human mind as a universal charter for the happy life among human beings. All are capable of knowing it, and owe obedience to it. Such obedient allegiance is within the capacity of all people, but this becomes effective obedience only if they turn towards the good. It is by virtue of this ultimate standard of law and righteousness that all human beings, not simply Christians, will be judged on the last day. It is always the same everywhere and allows no variation.

Augustine admires Plato, from whom he learned much, as a wise teacher in relation to his understanding of law, and muses whether the ancient philosopher had actually come across the Hebrew Scriptures in his travels, as his moral teaching is so close to fundamental truths given in revelation.[80] Probably not, he reflects, but he certainly learned the truth from his study of the natural law which God has placed in the hearts of all. Nature itself is a God-given guide for human beings. "The laws of their nature" are inscribed by God into all beings.[81] In Augustine's conception, the eternal law covers the divine commands for all humanity, providence, and the physical laws that set terms to human nature. He describes it as "written in the hearts of the godly" in the form of our conscience; that standard by which all morality and justice is assessed.[82] The eternal law is also the will of God as manifested in the cos-

[79] *On Free Will* 1.6.15.
[80] *On the City of God* 8.
[81] *On the City of God* 19.12.
[82] *Confessions* 2.4.9; *On the Trinity* 12.15.24–25.

mos. It is the fundamental order subsisting within nature, as well as the operative law by which God rules all creation.[83] Since it is above all else a rational law it is knowable by all humans in and through the exercise of reason.[84] But its authority is greater than reason alone, for it stands over all living and rational creatures as the law of their governance.[85] If the temporal law shifts and bends, this inner spiritual law is a rock that knows no variation or deceit.[86] Only God is not subject to this law, as he is its source and Master.[87]

Augustine's ideas on law's authority, therefore, are clearly rooted in, and related to, the classical philosophic concepts of natural law, but with these two most deliberate and significant differences. In the first place, Augustine is profoundly directed in the *telos*, or scope, of his thought by the scriptural understanding of the law of God (particularly as that notion of "law as obedience" is found in the Psalms).[88] Second, Augustine dynamically replaces the root concept of natural law with that of the eternal law given directly from the hand of God into the constitutive instincts of Humankind. It is a profoundly theological anthropology which he substitutes, as a Christian. But that means his understanding of natural law is almost indistinguishable from conscience; and the rootedness of this inner spiritual guide in the human nature is a means of revelation of the divine presence. Neither law, nor society, nor humanity itself, can thus be properly understood without reference to their quintessentially religio-ethical foundations. In short, law in Augustine is profoundly a moral concept: at once intimately personal and collectively social. His emendation of the natural law tradition is an explicit correction of Cicero's argument about the role of Divine Providence in his treatise *Laws*. He obviously Christianizes Cicero's early attempt to remove law from the sacral domain to a certain kind of universal Deism that did not depend on any personal piety. But Augustine argues back with him that it is simply inconceivable that a just order can be established in a society without immense moral effort. Where does the energy and perseverance for this necessary moral effort come from? It is costly and difficult both at a personal level and at a societal level. It will demand conversion and sacrifice. For Augustine, well aware of the vagaries of human nature and the profound element of freedom that has been given to human nature, the establishment of a just order in the affairs of the world can only be secured by the notion of impending divine judgment, and the understanding that this life will be answered for in the eschaton.[89] His is a moral theory

[83] *Against Faustus the Manichean* 22:27, 30, 33.

[84] *On the City of God* 11.27; *Epistle* 157.3.15.

[85] *On Christian Doctrine* 1.26.27; *On the Literal Meaning of Genesis* 9.17.32.

[86] *Confessions* 3.7.13; *On the Trinity* 14.15.21; *Epistle* 138.1.4.

[87] *On the City of God* 21.8.

[88] See Ps 1.2; 40.8; 119 *passim*.

[89] *On the City of God* 5. 9–10.

rooted in personal realism that was dinned in to him not only by his own spiritual introspection, but by his constant interactions as a bishop with recalcitrant members of his flock. Augustine makes a point of noting how Cicero (an example for him of a learned thinker but essentially an agnostic) once affirmed the concept of Divine Providence in his treatise *On the Nature of the Gods*, and applied it for the purpose of the moral instruction of the simpler classes of society. His argument there was that the uneducated classes needed the basic notion of the stick and carrot of divine afterlife punishments to keep them on the straight and narrow, whereas the more philosophically learned types would arrive at an elevated ethical life through the refinements of their reflections. Augustine sardonically brushes aside the argument that the truly virtuous do not need the notion of divine correction to help them be moral. To expose Cicero's inconsistency he coined the memorable aphorism: "Wishing to make men free, he rendered them sacrilegious."[90]

Augustine's views on eternal and temporal law serve as the basis for all of his assessments of the value and success of past human efforts to create societies–whether they were just or not. He particularly assesses the record of Rome, which he regards as the apex of the world's empires and one of its most brilliant political achievements.[91] His dominant line of thought on the adjudication of the achievement of societies is that biblical archetype as set out in The *City of God*. The Two Cities thus describe all human activity as falling under one of two orientations: the choices of human cupidity, or the choice for God: the life of virtue in grace, or that of sin.[92] Both are spiritual powers more than they are spatial realities, although they exist really enough. The City of God is manifested in history by the pure Church of believers,[93] and manifested more clearly and gloriously in the energies of the angels and saints, and in the final day when it shall be fully completed and vindicated over all creation. Augustine's appreciation of law derives principally from the fact of its pedagogic value. The earthly city is the sum of all human selfishness and cupidity. It exists and flourishes on earth, constantly creating all manner of wickedness. The two cities therefore, co-exist on this earth, and cannot be separated from one another until the last day. Human beings can rarely tell the just apart from the wicked, for the hearts of men and women are devious, and kindness can even mask great malice. It is the situation Christ described in his parable of the Tares and Wheat, with corruption growing up in the very midst of good things.[94] Law can only attempt to mark off the limits of righteousness from wickedness, and serve as a crude

[90] *On the City of God* 5.9.

[91] *On the City of God* 5.12.

[92] *On the City of God* 14.1; 14.4.

[93] *On the City of God* 8.24; 13.16; 16.2

[94] *On the City of God* 20.9; 1.35; 11.1; 18.49; *Post Collationem Contra Donatistas* 8.11; *Contra Littera Petiliani* 2.21.46.

standard of protection and limitation. While Augustine was more or less content to leave the theory that way, governed by his strong sense of eschatological judgment belonging to God (and an allied sense of a certain desire to put some distance between himself as bishop and the state authorities), later medieval followers went further. They wished to begin a sifting out in this earthly society of the two cities, constituting an "earthly city of God" which would be the Church, and its opposite which would be the non-church. The theory was pushed even further to become a "Two Swords" theory of governance: where the Church, as the righteous plan for the world, was seen to have been given a God-blessed right to rule and dominate. The Two Swords mentioned in the Gospels (however accidentally[95]) was taken as being a legitimation of the Church extending its political dominion in the face of "secular" rulers. Such developments were to have a long afterlife in the Western Christian territories, and mark political theological culture to this day. But such grand conceptions played no part in Augustine's mind. His world was smaller. His task, as he saw it, more pastorally limited by his role as spiritual teacher, and pastoral protector of those who had been wronged in local and concrete ways, and who came to him for what redress he could make as a bishop.

In the *Confessions* Augustine describes law as being properly, and quintessentially, a constant factor in our variable lives.[96] It has power,[97] it seeks to be just.[98] Its energy is orientated towards the end of *Caritas,*[99] loving-kindness as a rule of life among society. This latter principle of social harmony is very important to him. It is derived from a *catena* of biblical injunctions[100] which he took as providing a digest and summary of how humans ought to conduct themselves in a just society. Since law tends to move towards *Caritas*, it is thus endowed with a character of what is right, and true, though it cannot be (as a human institution) identified with what is true, *per se*. There is always the distinction to be drawn between justice and law; between eternal and temporal law, between the fallibility of what humans attain to in their culture and moral life, and what God has called them to by the law of love.

[95]Lk 22.38.

[96]*Confessions* 3.7.13.

[97]*Confessions* 1.14.23; 2.2.

[98]*Confessions* 3.17.13; 5.9.16.

[99]*Confessions* 12.18.27; 12.25.35.

[100]1 Tim 1.5–11. "Our aim is that love which issues from a pure heart and a good conscience and sincere faith . . . The law is good if one uses it lawfully. But understand this, the law is not laid down for the just, but rather for the lawless and the disobedient, for the ungodly and sinners . . . "; See also 1 Jn 4. 7–10 and passim; and Rom 7.1–6 : "Love, and do what you will," Augustine concludes, since what you then desire will be the work of love.

Accordingly, St Augustine speaks of justice on numerous occasions.[101] In his approach he is heavily influenced by the classical Roman definition of justice in terms of distributive fairness (*aequitas*) and by classical philosophical reflections on justice as that habit of the soul (*virtus*) by which people in society "give to each one their due."[102] But although he has learned from the expected standard books, he is also clearly active in trying to introduce a more specific Christian alteration to this tradition which sees justice through the lenses of the New Testament and the earlier patristic writings which he has digested. His four mentors in this regard are Tertullian, Cyprian, Lactantius, and Ambrose.[103] The definition of justice which he forges and brings to later Christendom, therefore, is that justice is that virtue which is the giving of due love and respect to God, and correspondingly the offering of that love which is fitting to the neighbor.[104] His favorite exegetical proof text is that of Romans 13.8:[105] which elevates as its maxim: "Owe nothing to anyone, except to love one another." True love (*caritas*) consists in loving the neighbor either because he is just already, or so that he might become just.[106] For Augustine, to live in a just manner means to live in such a way that one's love for the neighbor assists them to love themselves and their fellows in the ways prescribed by divine law.[107] Justice is therefore a systemic part of what Augustine establishes as a hierarchy of loves (*ordo amoris*): that system of relative priorities in those things established by God as worthy objects of love and desire.[108] Justice thus establishes a series of right relationships, both within society and within the cosmos. Within his system, therefore, the volitional aspect of justice (just living as a series of righteous actions) is harmonized with the ontological order of natural law (the natural order of things established in the world).[109]

It was this system that was destined, more and more, throughout the early and high Middle Ages to rise to become the dominant frame of reference for all subsequent western ecclesiastical thinking on the relations of society, law, politics, justice

[101] *On Free Will* 1.27; *Discourse (Ennarratio) on Psalm* 83.11; *On the City of God* 19.4; 19.21; *Ord.* 1.19; *Div. Quaes.* 2.31.1.

[102] See Aristotle, *Nichomachean Ethics* 1129a; 1120a; Cicero, *Inv. Rhet.* 2.160; *Fin* 5.65; also Ulpian in the *Institutes of Justinian* 1.1.

[103] Tertullian, *Apologeticus, On the Soul*; Cyprian, *On Works and Almsgiving*; Lactantius, *Divine Institutes* 5; *Epitome* 54–55; Ambrose, *On the Offices of the Ministers* 1.20–23; 1.252; 1.130–136; 1.142; 1.188; 2.49; and *Exposition on Psalm 118* c. 35; *On the History of Naboth* 47–48

[104] Mt 22.40; *Div. Quaest.* 61.4.

[105] *On the Trinity* 8. 9–10.

[106] *On the Trinity* 8.9.

[107] *On the Trinity* 8.10.

[108] *Div. Quaes.* 36.1–3; *On Free Will* 1.11–15; *Against Faustus the Manichean* 22.2.7; *On Teaching the Uneducated* 14.1–2; *Epistle* 140.4; *On the Trinity* 9.14; *On the City of God* 11.17; 15.22.

[109] *Confessions* 13.9.10.

and culture. Augustine's influence was immense, altogether extraordinary, and for holding such a sway over the determination of massive structures of Christian thought in the Latin world, somewhat paradoxically disconnected: a matter more of instinctual attitudes than carefully elaborated theories of society; more the product of a very hard-pressed provincial bishop (of immense talent), than the carefully set out program of how a new religious world-order might deal with a massively complex social and political system that had fallen into its hands. In more ways than one Augustine's instincts on the relationship of Christian theology to its ancient forebears stood at some degree of separation from the attitudes that prevailed in the Eastern Christian provinces. The different political fortunes that would now deeply mark the western and eastern provinces of the empire would only underscore those differences and mark out very different trajectories for Christian Greek and Latin polity in the onset of the Middle Ages.

Further Reading

Primary Texts

M. Atkins & R. Dodaro. *Augustine: Political writings.* Cambridge: Cambridge University Press, 2001.

E. Barker. "St Augustine's Theory of Society," in *Essays on Government.* Oxford: Oxford University Press, 1945.

P. Schaff, tr. *Works of St Augustine.* NPNF, vols. 1–8. Grand Rapids, MI: Eerdmans, 1887–1892.

Studies

P. Brown. *Augustine of Hippo: A Biography.* Berkeley, CA, 1967.

H. Chadwick. *Augustine.* Oxford: Oxford University Press, 1986.

A.H. Chroust. "The Philosophy of Law of St Augustine." *Philosophical Review* 53 (1944) 195–202.

______. "The Philosophy of Law from St Augustine to St Thomas Aquinas." *New Scholasticism* 20 (1946) 27–41.

______. "The Fundamental Ideas of St Augustine's Philosophy of Law." *American Journal of Jurisprudence* 18 (1973) 57–79.

M.R. Cimma. *L' Episcopalis Audientia nelle Costituzioni Imperiali da Costantino a Giustiniano.* Turin, 1989.

H.A. Deane. *The Political and Social Ideas of St Augustine.* New York: Columbia University Press, 1963.

L. Dossey. "Judicial Violence and the Ecclesiastical Courts in Late Antique North Africa." Pp. 98–114 in R.W. Mathisen, ed. *Law, Society and Authority in Late Antiquity.*

Oxford: Oxford University Press, 2001.

J.B. Elshtain. *Augustine and the Limits of Politics.* Notre Dame, IN: University of Notre Dame Press, 1995.

J. Finnis. *Natural Law and Natural Rights.* Oxford: The Clarendon Press, 1980.

A. D. Fitzgerald, ed. *Augustine Through The Ages: An Encyclopedia.* Grand Rapids, MI: Eerdmans, 1999. *(Comprehensive reference guide to Augustine's life and work).*

E.L. Fortin. *Classical Christianity and the Political Order: Reflections on the Theologico-Political Problem.* Lanham, MD & London: Rowman & Littlefield, 1996.

______. "The New Rights Theory and the Natural Law." *Review of Politics* 44 (1982) 590–612. Repr. in Fortin (1996) 265–286.

J. Gaudemet. *Le Droit romain dans la littérature chrétienne occidentale de IIIième au Vième siècle.* Varese, 1978 (esp. pp. 127–16).

J.C. Lamoreaux. "Episcopal Courts in Late Antiquity." JECS 3 (1995) 143–167.

N.E. Lenski. "Evidence for the Audientia Episcopalis in the New Letters of St Augustine." Pp. 83–97 in R. Mathisen, ed. *Law, Society, and Authority in Late Antiquity.* Oxford: Oxford University Press, 2001.

R.W. Mathisen, ed. *Law,Society, and Authority in Late Antiquity.* Oxford: Oxford University Press, 2001.

A. Nonnoi. "San Agostino e il diritto romano." RISG 9 (1934) 531–545.

H. Rommen. *The Natural Law: A Study in Legal and Social History and Philosophy.* St Louis: Herder, 1964.

J. Scott. "Contemporary Influences of Augustine's Political Thought." P. 658 in A.D. Fitzgerald. *Augustine Through The Ages: An Encyclopedia.* Grand Rapids, MI: Eerdmans, 1999.

W.T. Smith. *Augustine: His Life and Thought.* Atlanta, 1980

F. Van der Meer. *Augustine the Bishop.* London, 1961.

CHAPTER 7

The Eastern Church's Early Synodical Process

The Developing Synodical System

When we see traces of one of the very first practical acts, or records, of an episcopal synod, as manifested, for example in the synod gathered by the Palestinian bishops in the early half of the third century to deal with the Arabian bishop Heracleides, we note how they functioned as *symposia* of the learned, exchanging opinions founded on argumentation, towards the goal of a common consensus. Heracleides seems to have wished to impose kosher food laws on his Church because of a literal reading of the Old Testament proscription against eating blood. It had alarmed members of his own Church and sufficiently alarmed the neighboring hierarchs of Caesarea Maritima and Jerusalem (two of Origen's admirers and protectors) that they asked the great theologian Origen to come and discourse on the right (allegorical) reading of the Bible, so as to demonstrate that the ceremonial legislation of the old covenant no longer had binding force. This meeting, contained in the recently discovered text *Dialogue With Heracleides*, is all about law; yet it masquerades as a Greek *symposium*, and actually amounts to an extended dialogue on the right forms of biblical interpretation. Perhaps we cannot differentiate the matters at this stage of Church history. Perhaps also the presence of Origen at this early synod, as a priest-expert, tipped the occasion over into becoming more like one of his own university seminars than a normal episcopal synod, where perhaps the usual attendees were not used to such elevated intellectual exchange. It is difficult to decide, for the extant remains of the earliest synods are thin on the ground until the fourth century, and by that time they are consciously modeling themselves more and more on senatorial procedure.

What is clear enough, however, is that the synodical gatherings soon left behind this earlier *symposium* model witnessed in third century Arabia; where ideas were presented, argued around, and a courteous seeking of a common mind was pursued. They became something else. Even in the time of Origen, it has to be admitted, for all his presentation of his case as a scholarly open-ended enquiry, and for all his exquisite rhetorical courtesy to the dissident bishop, it is nonetheless unarguable that the heavyweights of the Palestinian bishops had come in person to press a case against what they saw as Judaizing reversion. One suspects they were glad to arrive at their goal by persuasion rather than by decree, but were nevertheless fixed upon a course to reform Heracleides whether he wanted it or not.

What the episcopal synod was moving towards generally was a different model for the deliberations. It was to be increasingly based on a theory that the assembled bishops were the high priest and oracles (prophetically endowed) of the Church. Accordingly, when a matter disturbed the peace of the Church they were expected to meet and manifest a "common mind." This model of prophetic inspiration implied that when the senior hierarchs gathered they should already "know the faith," not be groping like novices to define what it was. Thus, when a crisis arose over a point of doctrine or discipline, the collective mind and faith of the bishops should be able to recognize immediately, and acclaim authoritatively, the true line of the Christian tradition. This was the whole point of God's endowing them with prophetic and priestly charisms. The conciliar outcome was not to be decided by majority vote, in this case, because the common recognition of the truth had to be unanimous. There was thus increasing pressure under this model to ensure that the final vote, when taken, was always unanimous. If this could not be achieved (certainly it was more common after the fourth century) the dissidents who refused to sign the conciliar acts were denounced by the synod as not having the "mind of the Church," and thus anathematized as having become heretics, and then deposed from office, a sentence usually confirmed (and enforced) by civil legislation.

By the late fourth century the nature of synodical debates was giving way to become more and more an issue that had been prejudged by the collection of authoritative voices from the ancient Christian "authority" of the Fathers (the beginning of the use of patristic authors as definitive witnesses to authentic tradition). Even so, and despite the advantage afforded to whatever particular episcopal chancery was organized enough to be able to take charge of the collection and arrangement of the texts,[1] all the large synods remained governed by Roman con-

[1]Rome and Alexandria had the advantage, and used it to great effect. Palestinian Caesarea partly did the same (with record keeping) though it lacked international prestige as a city, and even though it had a large scholarly archive it was not much listened to. After the fifth century the Imperial city, Constantinople, entirely eclipsed Alexandria, and outshone Rome. Most of the Oecumenical councils apart from the first (held before the city was built) were located here. Ephesus 431 was planned to be held here but since Nestorius, the city's archbishop, was under scrutiny it was held (geographically) halfway to Alexandria. Nicaea II was an exception to the capital's dominance also only because the first meeting of that synod, held in the Great Cathedral in 786, was interrupted by rebellious troops and the empress decided to relocate the second session outside the city's boundaries. Chalcedon, which seems an exception, is merely a suburb of Constantinople.

ventions regarding debates (the process of the Senate was increasingly taken as a model), and by Hellenistic ideas about how philosophical ideas could be exchanged (more propositional than informative). Some of these fourth century synods assume a sudden and dramatic significance, portending what is to come, anticipating as it were the model of the great synods that would assume "oecumenical" significance later.[2] Chief among these important meetings were the synods of Ancyra, Neo-Caesarea, Antioch, Gangra, and Laodicea. All of them were held in Asia Minor; and their deliberations were presented with a new-found voice, a determination to establish more visible and clearly delineated principles of church order. These meetings are very important in the developing notion of Christian canon law and we shall look at them briefly in due course.

After Constantine had achieved supreme power in the western part of the empire in 312, he determined that the Christians should be a force for cohesion, and his religious policy strongly advocated this. His religious policy throughout his reign was a rapidly developing and often spur-of-the-moment kind of thing. But he saw the importance for his New Empire of the Christians and their Church establishment. He wanted to use bishops as local forces for law and order, for the diffusing of moral standards and the advocacy of stable civic virtue. He would soon put this into civil law, giving bishops the status of a kind of parallel magistracy for Christian affairs, and a stand-in magistracy where the arm of the civic powers did not reach. But he demanded conformity of the Christians, he wanted a quiet house, and to gain this, he was determined to settle some long-running Christian controversies each time he entered and occupied territory in the course of the civil war that brought him to supreme power. He it was who especially encouraged a much wider assembly of Christian bishops, based on the model of the senatorial gatherings of the emperor's advisers. The first two examples of this "internationally conscient" kind of meeting (the seed, as it were, of what would later emerge as the system of Oecumenical Councils) were the Council of Elvira in 306, and the Council of Arles in 314, the latter called to resolve the Donatist crisis. It failed to do so, but it established a precedent for how Christian bishops would henceforth conduct synods under the shadow of a Christian emperor. When he summoned the Synod of Arles,

[2]The term "oecumenical" (or ecumenical) derives from the Greek for "world-wide." Its modern usage to denote inter-church polite discourse is a very modern application, not known in antiquity. It connotes a large geographical extent–with the subtext that for the Romans, the "world" always meant the civilized world of the Empire, both parts, Latin and Greek. So the Oecumenical Synod is very much an imperially fostered development of the provincial synodical process, with a view to keeping Christian affairs in tune in the Latin West and the Greek East. Those territories that did not fit into that mold of bi-lingual disposition (such as Armenia, Ethiopia, Syria) were also the first to "fall out of" that Oecumenical consensus. It was always presumed that a truly Oecumenical synod would not only be geographically representative, but of sufficient substance to command the attention of the Roman Oecumene.

Constantine was retreating from an earlier idea he had entertained of calling upon the Roman Pope Miltiades to resolve the Donatist crisis[3] by decree. He seems to have been given better intelligence, because he then moved to accept what the pope himself, observing canonical form more appropriately than the emperor, who was a new player on the Christian scene at this stage, had moved as a more useful alternative: the notion of calling together the leading "authoritative voices" (*auctoritates*) of the Western Christian world to resolve a thorny problem of communion that had massively disrupted Christian Africa. Constantine pushed ahead with this model once more in the East, almost as soon as he had assumed the monarchical leadership of the whole empire at the end of the civil war in 323, when he defeated Licinius and took the eastern territories.

This time he wanted to settle, quickly and definitively, the Arian crisis, so that he could move forward with his political policy of establishing the network of Christian bishops as his parallel "New Empire" magistrates. For this he needed unanimity and concord among the bishops themselves, and a proven way of settling inter-provincial disputes. He called a worldwide synod, the first designated "Oecumenical Council," at his palace at the town of Nicaea[4] in 325 to mark the occasion of the twentieth anniversary of his reign (his *Vicennalia*). This determined that a provincial council of bishops should be held in every local area at least twice a year (canon 5). Its theological decisions would later become the determinative standard of Orthodox theology and it also established the rule that the emperor was the one who should convoke a world-wide Council. Even so, the system and principle of the Oecumenical Synod did not "spring fully armed" into being. It took time to recognize it as a system that could be coordinated with the earlier pattern of smaller synods. Indeed, in the aftermath of Nicaea, its decisions were highly controverted and a whole series of councils held throughout the fourth century conflicted with one another. The disputes of this era, now known to us as the Arian crisis, stressed the synodical system almost to the point of destruction. Nicaea's role in the process of offering a solution to controversies at many times looked hopelessly compromised as it became itself a bone of contention. Synodical process looked as if it might not be the solution it promised. Constantine himself abandoned the policies he himself had set in motion at Nicaea 325, and for a whole generation until 381, the council was a focus of controversy as much as a clear guide to the Church at large. Things would change only when a strong emperor from the West (Theodosius I) established at the Council of Constantinople in 381 a radical reaffirmation of Nicaea 325 and a determination to protect that religious policy by force of civil law. At that meeting Nicaea was retrospectively given high honor. At the Council of Chalcedon

[3]Both sides of the African schism had appealed to him for legal redress.

[4]*Nikaia*, named "Victory City" after his recent successes in the war against Licinius.

in 451, the assembled bishops looked back and retrospectively declared that, of all these numerous synods that had taken place up to fifth century, only three had hitherto been truly "oecumenical" in stature; those of Nicaea 325, Constantinople 381, and Ephesus 431. After that point only momentously significant councils have earned the designation oecumenical, including (after several false starts) Chalcedon itself. These comprise a total of seven in the patristic era, all of them taking place in the Greek Christian world, and all commonly regarded as the supreme authority, under God, for settling matters in the ancient Christian Oecumene.

Given the embarrassment that numerous synods had publicly manifested conflicted views within the international episcopate at times of crisis such as the Arian dispute, the principle of synodical "inspiration," that is the notion that when Christian bishops assembled they would all speak the same message and sing the same reverent tune, took something of a battering in terms of popular faith. Increasingly, after the fifth century, the synods started to lose their inspirational quality as less reliance was placed on charismatic models and more stress was placed on juridical procedure. The synods started by the fifth century (Ephesus 431 is a prime example) to mutate into a collection of patristic evidences presented to the assembled hierarchs, after hearing which the bishops were expected to pass a sentence of agreement with the standard authorities of the past. By this stage, too, the earlier idea of the synod as symposium-like open sharing of ideas had largely passed, and it took on a predominantly forensic character. Even so, it is necessary to note that at no stage was the idea abandoned that a synod's decisions were especially governed by the Spirit of divine inspiration. So much then for a very rapid and cursory history of the rise of the synodical process.

Two things stand out from that as of significance for our tale of the ascent of law. The first is the two early Latin councils, Arles and Elvira, followed by that extraordinary series of Syrian and Asia Minor synods which seem to have had the idea of elaborating a code of canon law for the international Church. The second was the elaboration of this in the later fourth century under the protection and sponsorship of the Christian emperors who wished to see the synod assume the status of an Oecumenical Council for the resolution of truly international matters of dispute. Both sets of meetings, the early eastern synods and the Seven Oecumenical Councils, produced significant codifications of canons. It is now time to turn our attention to them both in a little greater detail. This chapter will first review the formative fourth century councils that were not afforded oecumenical status, but which were retrospectively elevated, sometimes at the later Oecumenical Councils, as having a paradigmatic canonical, legal status. The following chapter will deal with the Oecumenical Councils in their chronological sequence.

The Fourth Century Western, Syrian, and Asia Minor Synods

A body of decisions grew up in the fourth century deriving from the increasing pace of provincial bishops holding local councils to solve pressing local problems. The common denominator in this development was the desire to re-establish order in the aftermath of the fourth century extensive persecutions, when the emperors had used their expanding experience of suppressing the Church over several prior generations and had stopped simply slaughtering the less educated zealots who presented themselves as martyrs, seeing the unproductivity of this way forward, and had turned their attention to the purging and eradication of the higher clergy and the political leaders of the Christian movement. It was a policy that also targeted the wealthier business classes alongside the clerical leadership. This strategy, which Domitian started and which Diocletian and Galerius used to effect, had caused widespread lapses from Christian communion in the fourth century. The bishops knew that, in response, they had to relax the older rigorous rules that more or less cast aside people who had fallen in times of persecution and who then wished to be returned to Church life and communion in the times of peace. These fourth century councils are often taken as anticipatory drafts of the system of local and general councils that was soon to develop in the late fourth century after Nicaea. The first examples come from the West: the Spanish Council of Elvira (*c* 306), now Granada in Andalucía, and the Synod of Arles (*c* 314) in France. The concept of the collection of conciliar canons was given its future shape by the taking up of a regular process of collecting canonical decisions after synodical meetings; and for this we need to add to the two early Latin councils and the early fourth century Syrian and Asia Minor synods of Ancyra, Neo-Caesarea, Antioch, Laodicea, and Gangra. Several of this list of "formative" councils were officially elevated to paradigmatic legal status by the Oecumenical Council of Chalcedon and again by the fathers of the Quinisext Council in Trullo. The first canon of Chalcedon formally endorsed what must already have been traditional practice, that is, to see all the "traditional" canons that had earlier been collated into a collection,[5] when it said: "We have judged it right that the canons of the holy fathers made in every synod,[6] even until now, should remain in force." The second canon of the Council in Trullo is more specific. It reads: "We set our own seal upon all the rest of the canons which have been established by our holy and blessed fathers, that is to say the 318 God-inspired fathers who met at Nicaea, and by those who met at Ancyra, and by those who met

[5]Some have thought that the omission of a list of canons from Constantinople I in 381 was perhaps because this collection had recently been completed, and was generally recognized as serving the purpose.

[6]Of course it does not mean that literally; it signifies, rather, every major Orthodox synod—that is every synod held up until now to have had significant authority.

at Neo-Caesarea, as well as by those who met at Gangra; moreover the canons adopted by those who met at Syrian Antioch, and by those who met at Phrygian Laodicea, and the 150 fathers who gathered together in this God-preserved royal city,[7] and the 200 who were gathered in the Metropolis of Ephesus, and the 630 holy and blessed fathers who met at Chalcedon." In this decree the system of synodical rule is affirmed authoritatively, and most clearly delineated. But it was not created here. It was affirmed because it had already emerged and assumed high authority (*authentia*) in the Church's operative systems of government. By looking now at those synods we can see what characteristic drives and concerns shape them.

The Council of Elvira–306

The Elvira synod does not deal with many rules for the lapsed and maybe, given the very rigorous nature of the assembly, that was a good thing, for the first canon refuses communion to those who lapsed in the persecution even in times of danger of death, a stricture almost every other Church had relaxed. Elvira[8] enacts a large series of canons[9] in which moral and disciplinary matters begin to be managed much more closely than before. The synod is anxiously aniconic, worrying lest pagan converts will be led astray by the practice of Christian iconography.[10] One canon demands the celibacy of all Spanish clergy, whether currently married or not.[11] The decrees show that the clergy have already become a separate class in the Church. Higher moral standards are being required of them. The bishop's authority is now clearly much more elevated than that of any other clerical rank and presbyters and deacons are expected to obey him. Bishops, however, are not allowed to contradict one another's rulings: namely the excommunicate from one diocese is not to be received by another single bishop's more lenient decision, unless the matter is referred back to a synod for judgment.[12] Laity may baptize in times of emergency. But the faithful are forbidden any part in the cycle of pagan festive rites, and the tra-

[7]Council of Constantinople 1 381.

[8]Elvira, Canon 33.

[9]More than fifty. Meigne (1975) thinks the first twenty-one are authentic and the others were incrementally added later as successive Spanish synods accumulated a local "Code of Canon Law." Issues in the textual transmission of canonical collections are discussed in H. Hess, *The Early Development of Canon Law and the Council of Serdica,* Oxford Early Christian Studies (Oxford: Oxford University Press, 2002) 40–42.

[10]Canon 36. See Robert Grigg, "Aniconic Worship and the Apologetic Tradition: A Note on Canon 36 of the Council of Elvira," *Church History* 45.4 (December 1976) 428–433. Grigg notes how the synod reproduces the early Latin pre-Nicene apologetic arguments that spiritual worship precludes "material" iconography.

[11]The attempt to introduce this into the Eastern Church's canon law met with no success at all, but it is the first sign of the ruling that would become standard for the whole West in due course.

[12]Elvira, Canon 53.

ditional local political offices of *Flamen* and *Duumvir* are now expressly forbidden to Christians because of the pagan ritual aspects involved.

The Spanish decrees also try to make a strong line of demarcation between Christians on the one side, and Jews and pagans on the other, by passing canons forbidding intermarriage. Laeuchli, in a 1972 study devoted to this synod as a "tidal marker" moment in Church history, sees the focus on sexual canons as a tool of clerical control, tending to presume that sexual mores were in earlier times left to personal discretion. We do not have evidence to deduce that, of course, and the presupposition that the fourth century decrees reflect a stricter sense of control than what went beforehand seems a judgment that swims against the tide of what little we do know from the earlier ages, which seem to have had pretty severe standards of behavior expected as norms. Laeuchli is right, however, to note the stronger lines of division that are being drawn here between Christian and "secular" life. What this movement also shows is a profoundly altered sense of what Church canons ought to and will contain and what kind of oversight the episcopate ought to reflect. It is the first local synod that seems consciously aware that it has the obligation to present its identity as a Spanish synod, and identify how it will relate to wider areas of the Christian Church. Nineteen bishops and twenty-six presbyters were in attendance here. One of their intellectual leaders was Hosius, bishop of Cordoba. He had a genius for organizational matters and when he assumed the post of advisor to Constantine the Great, he brought this to bear as one of the chief arrangers of the synodical process that marked Constantine's early synodical judgments when he intervened in church order, notably his attempted resolution of the Donatist crisis, and his great Synod at Nicaea, where Hosius acted as the arranger of the agenda.

All kinds of disciplinary matters increasingly began to come under episcopal scrutiny during the fourth century. Lists of canons will now be the order of the day for episcopal provincial governance. Most prestigious of them all, of course, would be the international code of regulations appended to the Council of Nicaea's doctrinal statements in 325. The Nicene canons attempt to bring order and structure to a Church that had long endured the disruptions of persecution. After this point, reformatory canons, drawn up in this style, were regularly appended to all conciliar acts, whether in the West or the East, and collectively they grew to be the Church's code of canon law. In the Eastern Church they were never really rationalized, and, to this day, the ancient and more modern canons co-exist, often haphazardly, and sometimes in mutual contradiction. In the West there were regular movements to streamline and update the system of canon laws, especially after the fifth century, and the laws of the Roman Church came to have a wide circulation and influence. In the Western Patriarchate the decisions of the pope, independently from conciliar legislation, came to have a powerful authoritative status. These *decretals* greatly influenced the shape of canon law, whereas in the East the issuing of canons remained largely tied to synodical assemblies.

The Council of Arles–314

The Council of Arles in 314 is the other landmark moment. It started life as a direct legal petition from Donatus and his companions to the emperor as lawgiver and supreme judge in the empire. The Donatists were appealing against the ecclesiastical decisions of the Council of Rome in 313, which Constantine had encouraged as a way to reconcile the Donatist dissidents. Miltiades of Rome had communicated that decision to the emperor, and Donatus' personal appeal was the first time known that a Christian bishop had had recourse outside Church structures (the synodical process) to the civic system. Donatus' problem with the synodical process, of course, was related to his view that the very assembly of bishops around him had been corrupted by the presence in it of people of dubious reputation whose lukewarm behavior in the times of the African persecutions had effectively eradicated their priesthood. According to this view he did not accept them as clergy anyway, so he was not likely to be moved by their collective decisions in synod. The Donatist problem is an interesting example of how the synodical process, as it emerged as a major force for the organization of international Christianity, required a strong pro-Christian secular arm, not only legally to enforce decisions and curtail the cycle of endless appeal, but also to serve as legal consensus builder.

The classical synodical system, as it would soon emerge, is strongly tied to the presupposition of there being a stable series of Christian emperors who afford to the decrees of the assembled episcopate a parallel *auctoritas* to the secular laws superintended by the magistrates and judges. Constantine called the Synod of Arles together in order to avoid giving an imperial decision from his own authority. He was underlining his desire to establish the collective of Christian bishops as a legislative force in the new empire. The Council reaffirmed the Roman excommunication of Donatus, but went on to issue twenty-two canons regulating Church affairs. Some of them had reference to Donatism. Clergy who were proven to have been *traditores*[13] were to be deposed, but their clerical orders and thus their sacraments, were deemed to have been valid, *pace* Donatus. Which dissidents could be received back into the Church body and by which method (was Catholic baptism always required?) was a matter of discussion. Regulations were also passed for the observance of Pascha, against Christians taking part in pagan games and gladiatorial

[13]The word *traitor* derives from this, it refers to those clerics who "handed over" the Church's holy books to the persecuting authorities who demanded them to confiscate. It meant collaborator in time of persecution.

shows (involving death and prostitution), and against clergy absenteeism. The way this council and that of Elvira deal with regulatory matters shows the first glimmerings of the Constantinian "New Deal." Hosius of Cordoba, Constantine himself, and the appeal of the civic powers to the "established senior sees" are common factors here; and, indeed, we are probably faced with the external evidence (since internal memos no longer exist) of the very gestation of Constantine's policy to use structures of ecclesiastical governance to bring order into international Christianity, and then use that episcopal local system to extend the concept of good order, good religion, and good moral education widely across his imperial domains, all of which were high on his reformist agenda after the first quarter of the fourth century. It is this embryonic idea which is to grow dramatically after the Council of Nicaea into the system of the great General or Oecumenical Councils.

These western examples of formative councils are underlined even more in the eastern provinces by a series of synods that demonstrate, independently of Constantine and his own agenda, that the Christian bishops are themselves extending the synodical system of the Church to meet the new conditions of the post-persecution empire. There are five important synods that constitute this nexus: the synods of Ancyra (314), Neo-Caesarea (315?), Gangra (*c* 340), Antioch Encaeniis (341), and Laodicea (363, 365?). They each produce canonical lists of rules that henceforth have a dramatic effect on eastern canon law. These collections have weight because first of all, as it were, they survive in the lists as extant judgments, providing the grist to what will emerge as a recognized corpus of ecclesiastical law; like the grit in the pearl they form the substrate around which a concept of canonical law collection can assemble; and second, they set the pattern and precedent of how to compose canonical judgments: rules of the learned in corporate session, concerning matters of weight and matters of pressing import, all focused on the preservation or restoration of good order in the Churches.

The Synod of Ancyra–314

Ancyra was the capital city of Roman Galatia and the episcopal gathering which took place there happened at a very significant time. The persecuting Emperor Maximin had just been killed and Constantine and Licinius, his partner at that time, had established the peace of the Church in the eastern provinces. The bishops sensed an ending, or a near-ending, of the Roman civil war[14] and were ready to accede to the imperial suggestion that a large council should be called to set Christian affairs in order after generations of massive disruption. If Constantine's policy of using the

[14]In fact this would not happen until Constantine defeated Licinius and assumed monarchical power over the East in 324–the year before Nicaea.

Church hierarchy as a parallel magistracy was not yet wholly worked out, it is clear enough that the bringing of order into the Christian communities was legally desired so that the Christian religion could be formally constituted as a legal corporation: something necessary if it was now going to be recognized as *religio licita.*

The synod needed to repair much. Wealthy Christians had been targeted in the latest wave of persecutions as well as those who were the clerical leaders. The latter had been singled out for exemplary punishments meant to break the spirit of the others. Many of the laity had bribed officials to give them false certificates stating that they had fulfilled the imperial requirement to offer incense to the gods of Rome. These were known among the scandalized Church faithful as *libellatici.* While it was not the same as having offered sacrifice to the gods, it was widely regarded as a matter of publicly lying in the very core of one's baptismal confession, and as such meriting exclusion from the sacraments. The clergy who had suffered particularly heavy attack had also won their share of martyrs and their share of lapsed. Some had fallen because they could not endure the sophisticated and sustained tortures for which Rome was notorious. They had resisted at first and then had been broken. Some others had taken fright and broken quickly. Others still had run to the authorities scared out of their wits and conformed to their demands even before the first torture had commenced. The council clearly wishes to establish a wise form for a process of reconciliation: where points can be made that some did better than others, where the need for repentance can be underlined, and also where a system of face-saving degrees of penance can be established so that all could feel the Church was moving forward again, not continuing the evil work of the oppressors by indulging in self-recriminations. The canons established at Ancyra, therefore, deal with how the degrees of penance can be regulated. The first canon states that presbyters who lapsed can retain their places of honor in church but may not offer the oblation or preach, their basic liturgical functions. This sounds like a *non sequitur*, but in the standard liturgical context of the day it is a genuine face-saving solution, for the presbyters generally sat in the apse around the bishop, and he always offered the oblation as president in any case. With discretion one would not notice the lapsed presbyter "stood out" Sunday by Sunday, and the ruling allows the minister to continue serving the Church in other capacities. Those who had broken only after extensive torture were treated even more compassionately. Deacons who had lapsed under torture were instructed to retain their rank but not their functions in church. In this instance, the bishops are allowed individually to have leeway in cases where this debarment from liturgical service "causes distress of mind." It could not be clearer: the honorable who broke should be rehabilitated; the dishonorable should be relegated. The bishops should have discretion to test the character and caliber of the clergy. The second canon allows laity who had been literally carried to the altars of pagan sacrifice and physically forced to offer incense (there were many such cases, the pagans having an idea from the Christians themselves that sacrifice to the gods "washed out" the baptismal initiation) were allowed restitution to communion immediately. Even if they had been forced to make offerings to the gods, the worthy among these laity could still be ordained in the future. Other canons regulate the penance and readmission process in differing grades of severity for laity in different circumstances whether they had run to betray their faith, or whether they had only been cowed into it by torture or severe threats. In each case the bishops were given discretion to look to the "general character of their lives" not just their performance in the time of stress (canon 7).

Once it had dealt with the main and pressing item, the council was free to go on to signal ways ahead for church organization in the era of peace. The remaining canons demonstrate a sense of confidence. Three things arise that will be regularly descriptive of canonic lists in the East hereafter: establishing systems of pure worship, establishing protocols for good and ordered administration of the Churches, and establishing canons to elevate the moral ethos of the community, especially public morality.

Canon 10 of Ancyra establishes the eastern rules for married clergy with greater discretion than Elvira. If deacons before their ordination tell the bishop that they intend to get married, then the bishop will allow them to be married and remain as a deacon. If they did not tell him (that is, he thought he was ordaining a celibate deacon) and later decide to marry, he must depose them from office. This established the principle at large that eastern clerical orders were not incompatible with the married status, but that ordinands should be married first, before ordination occurs. Post-ordination marriage became generally precluded. Later in time the episcopate was restricted only to the celibate; but that ruling about married deacons and priests still holds force in the Eastern Church, whereas Elvira (symbolically) set the course for the Latin Church to move towards an all-celibate clergy. Canon 11 was an interesting reflection of the social disorder that occurs in the aftermath of war, and represents a compassionate move to assert the rights of women, who were so regularly victimized in time of hostilities and civil unrest. It legislated that, as far as the Church was concerned, a virgin who was betrothed remains contractually bonded to her fiancé even if she had been carried off and suffered ravishment in the time before she could be married. It asserted, therefore, the permanency of betrothal as a sacramental bond, a rule that still applies to the betrothal rite of the Eastern Church. This strongly suggests that the Church ruled to protect the honor of women returning from war captivity, in a social environment where, presumably, many fiancés were trying to break the engagement on the pretext of their own honor, i.e., that the fiancées were no longer virgins. Later church lawyers and commentators started, in Byzantine times, to weaken the force of this canon. Then the context was no longer war (we can imagine abductions in a village scene, family feuds and so on) and they started to add the *caveat* "provided the fiancé was still willing to receive her." But the original draft and intent was a signal defense of the honor of women setting the standards of honor according to the heart's intent, not the forced circumstances falling upon the innocent; something that rubbed against the grain of an ancient society that was predominantly organized around public standards of shame and honor.

Canon 13 of Ancyra demonstrates the attempt to establish systems of good order. Country bishops (*chorepiscopoi*) who were village church leaders, often simple men, were forbidden to ordain presbyters or deacons without the permission in writing of the ruling (city) bishop of the diocese. This clearly sets the precedent for ancient church organization of one city, one episcopal throne: one diocese, one leader. It also is the seed from which the devolved principle grows of metropolitan bishops; that is, bishops of the larger cities of the empire that held sway over a hinterland of smaller towns and tiny villages, all of which formed a chain, as it were, of local agricultural, military, and political association in the empire. Bishops are to have authority ranked according to the importance of their see, not simply as afforded to them by the caliber of their spiritual or intellectual attainments. From this time onwards the metropolitan bishops assume greater visibility and significance. It was also a move that immeasurably advanced the significance and stature of the synodical system itself, for the synods tended from this time onwards (Ancyra itself is an example, being the provincial capital) to be assemblies of the educated based around the imperial leading cities, where the protagonist senior clergy could assemble around them a staff of clerical *periti* (theologians and lawyers) and where archives could be stored and referred to. This movement takes us a long way towards the principle of the later Great Councils establishing enduring principles in doctrine and church law. The synod also dealt with a lot of smaller matters, establishing rules for good order in relation to alienation and use of church property,[15] and in terms of hierarchies of authority. We have already noticed how the chorepiscopoi are brought under the stricter control of the city bishops, and really reassigned the role as subordinate auxiliaries. Presbyters who had been ordained as bishops but who were, for some reason, not accepted by their intended Churches[16] could return to

[15]Canon 15 ordered that presbyters who had sold church property in the times of disruption when there was no bishop, should make restitution to the Church.

[16]This would be an increasing problem in the time of the Arian crisis, but we already see it operative in the sense that local Churches were still ready to throw over the choices of the metropolitan sees imposed on them, their own agreement still being a practical necessity before a bishop could presume to take over a foreign Church.

their originating Churches but had to accept the status of presbyters. If they acted as independent bishops they were to be deposed even from presbyteral rank. Here again the principle of one ruling bishop to a city is insisted on. It was greatly to strengthen the role and office of the *episkopos*, along the way it had been steadily advancing since the late second century.

Canons 16, 17, 19, 20, 21 and 25 of Ancyra are all focused on issues of personal sexual morality. They are set on establishing a sexual moral code within the Church that is distinctly higher than that prevalent in the external society. Some commentators have focused on this as an aspect of the increasing attempt by bishops to extend the remit of their power more and more into the domain of laity. But it is something that is seen as a characteristic of all of Constantine's New Empire deal. He, regardless of the Church, so it seems, but glad to affirm its efforts, was determined on setting higher and better standards of sexual ethics across the empire, believing that such a thing would call down the protection of heaven on his reign. Like Diocletian before him, Constantine was a puritan, not a cavalier. Scholars who see the development of these canonical regulations of sexuality in rather simple terms of episcopal power-flexing miss this historical moment where the empire, emerging from generations of civil chaos and war, was changing its ethos. The rise of Christianity itself is a sign of the change of times. To this I would also add that from time immemorial the approach to the altar for the reception of the sacraments had been closely tied to issues of purity of heart, so much so that the Syrian Church in the second century had demanded celibacy of those wishing to be baptized and to receive the Eucharist. The Syrians were an extreme example, admittedly, but they were not out of sorts with the larger Christian sensibility that approaching the altar had to be done only after significant efforts to establish a pure heart. Pagan religiosity is not that much different: rites were embarked on only after preparatory purification rituals had been accomplished.

What the increasing moral injunctions reflect, therefore, is not simply a matter of teaching moral standards; it is a sense that that the larger numbers filling the churches in times of peace have to be reminded of the ancient customs. The moral ethos devolves, so I believe, from the liturgical context that is being presumed. It is for the same reason that the "higher standards for clergy" movement is witnessed in the canons: the clergy are those who approach the altar most nearly and most frequently. The bishops are here once again reflecting what was their original and primary function, as presidents of the eucharistic assembly. Purity and compassion are prioritized in the Church. Alongside the high sexual ethic comes a compassionate response to the problem of murder and manslaughter (we must remember what a violent society antiquity was). The murderer who was repentant (and presumably who survived state punishment and family revenge) was only to be admitted back to communion on the point of death. The genuinely repentant man-slayer (which probably meant soldiers who had killed in time of war as much as civil manslaughter perpetrators) could be readmitted to communion after seven years, reduced to five at the bishop's discretion. While this looks severe to modern eyes, in the context of a growing reverence for the sacraments, where Eucharist might only be taken once or twice a year, the ban is not so severe as shutting out the culprits from the church premises. Christian sorcerers, soothsayers, and the like are penanced with a ban from communion for three years. This is clearly meant as an attempt to draw a line between Church and secular society where these practices were part of the fabric of daily life. It is targeting the professional Christian fortune tellers more than the larger circle of laity who presumably had recourse to them, thus showing the profession to be incompatible with life in the Church. It would take a long time indeed for the notion to bear general weight. Even Augustine, in the fifth century, admits as an older bishop that as a newly baptized Christian he still was popular among his *collegium* friends for casting good horoscopes.[17]

The Synod of Neo-Caesarea–315

The council of Neo-Caesarea took place in Pontus, the Black Sea region, at a time before the Council of Nicaea. Its precise date is not known. A good enough estimate might be circa 315. It is another example of the great rise of interest in the policing of matters of sexual morality in the early Constantinian era. The first canon[18] (always one to set the tone for the collection) demands that licentious priests should be deposed, excommunicated, and subject to enduring penance. The sense of shock that the penance system, meant for the most benighted members of the flock, should have to be invoked for the higher clergy, is palpable here. One of the problems of the era of peace, evidently, is that being a Christian presbyter is now socially rewarding. Now all sorts of types are moving forward to assume the office. When it carried a high chance of martyrdom, the morally lax stayed away. Canon 4 speaks around the bushes about "adultery intended but not accomplished." Given that this is probably referring to the Gospel injunctions about "committing adultery in the heart,"[19] I would read it as referring to erotic flirtations. Similarly in canon 2, marriage with kindred is debarred in the degree of consecutively marrying spousal siblings. Several successive marriages are heavily discouraged. When the early canons penalize digamy, the modern reader needs to understand that it is not the crime of

[17]*Confessions* 4.3.4; 7.6.8. See L. Ferrari, "Augustine and Astrology," *Laval théologique et philosophique* 33 (1977) 241–251.

[18]Canon 1: If a presbyter should marry [after ordination], let him be deposed from his order; but if he commits fornication or adultery, let him be altogether cast out (of the Church) and put to penance.

[19]Mt 5.28.

bigamy that is being referred to but the act of marrying for the second time after the death of the first spouse. The early Church regarded this as a very bad thing to do, and lays canonical penalties against it that are progressively abandoned and relaxed only into the fifth century. It is this council that finally establishes the rule for the Eastern Church that marriage after ordination will no longer be allowed.[20] Canons 9 through 11 come back to the same concern for the sexual probity of clergy, extending even into the times long before their ordination. Canon 11 finally directs that no presbyter should be ordained before the age of thirty. This, too, relates to the sexual ethic; for although this to us moderns is a very young age, in Late Antiquity it would be the equivalent of restricting ordination only to those over fifty, such was the relatively shorter average life span. Canon 8 is another prime representation of the "higher standard for clergy" ethic. If a lay Christian's wife has been openly convicted of having committed adultery, that fact debars the husband from entering orders. If the priest's wife commits adultery after his ordination he must set her aside publicly. If he does not, then he himself must stand down from active ministry. What Neo-Caesarea shows is the Church actively raising the profile of its clergy in the full glare of day. They are emerging at the level of the episcopate as city leaders of high significance in the structures of the empire, as well as the Church. So, too, the presbyteral and diaconal levels of the clergy are being professionalized in this time, offered to the secular city and the church community alike, as paradigms of the noble life: Christian Sophists whose teachings carry weight from reference to their lifestyle as well as their discourse. The presbyters at this period were more and more serving as independent parish priests, and thus to all intents and purposes acting *in persona episcopi* as tantamount to bishops, a single iconic leader of the local Christian community whose behavior attracts close scrutiny. The final canons (13–14) return to the theme of regulating the *chorepiscopoi* that we have seen elsewhere. The synod starts tolling the death knell for the institution of *chorepiscopoi* in Byzantium (they survive longer in the Syrian fringes of empire). They are classed not as belonging to the Twelve Apostles, but rather to the Seventy (Lk 10.1), clearly signaling that they are not of the apostolic order. Between the ascendancy of episcopate and presbyterate in the city churches, the country bishops did not really have a place to stand. In the end the notion of auxiliary, or non-ruling vicar bishops, would become the norm to replace them; though this itself was a paradox and contradiction (which is why *chorepiscopoi* began in the first place) because it ran against the grain of the canonical principle of one bishop in one city.

[20]Canon 1a.

The Synod of Gangra–340

This important synod took place in the far east of the Syrian diocese, on the Armenian border territory, in a Church under the administration of Palestinian Caesarea where Bishop Eusebius was the metropolitan. It was concerned with the problems caused by the young and charismatic churchman, the theologian and highly ascetic Eustathius of Armenian Sebaste. It has sometimes wrongly been read as an attack on Manichean practices. The asceticism it attacks is really a zealous form of nascent monasticism, at a time when the structures of the Churches were not "monasticized" in any significant degree. This would change by the end of the fourth century, after which point many leading bishops would be drawn from the monastic ranks or would be their sympathizers. Here at Gangra we see some real sense of alarm about the type of asceticism Eustathius was advocating and a stand by the city bishops against its implications for church order. Eustathius emerged from the council heavily censured but not rejected. He was ordained to the priesthood at Caesarea in the same year. But he earned the enmity of the powerful bishop Eusebius of Nicomedia, and was a thorn in the side of the Arian party throughout the fourth century. Eusebius of Nicomedia made it his personal business to ensure Eustathius was deposed at the Council of Antioch in 341, though the young man did not allow that to worry him as he dedicated himself to unseating any bishop of any town he felt was an Arian sympathizer by the strategy of sending in zealous monks to the place and gaining the support of the local townspeople, leading to the ousting of the heretical incumbent. He also became a mentor of St Basil the Great's family, though he and Basil had a spectacular falling out over theological issues in later life. Eustathius became bishop of Sebaste in Armenia in 357.

It was possibly this tactic of starting ascetical revivals that brought him into trouble at Gangra in 340. Eustathius was a son of a bishop, but his own father had censured him for excess of zeal. He preached a theology that God was calling all to the radical monastic life. This involved, as Jesus had said it would,[21] even the cutting of established social ties. No one who preferred mother or father or husband or wife to the Kingdom was a fit disciple. So Eustathius went on an ascetic itinerant lifestyle and preached a doctrine that said slaves were free and owed no responsibility to their slavers and women were equal to men in terms of discipleship and ought to leave their domestic situations, where husbands or fathers would lord it over them, and dedicate themselves as virgins in a free and equalized community, where there would be no social hierarchies (he made all of whatever class do the same manual work). Such ascetic women should cut their hair off to signify their radical throwing away of the old conventions. They should all, men and women alike, wear the

[21]Mt 8.22; Mk 3.33–35; Mk 8.34; Mk 10.28–31.

rough dark robe of the itinerant philosopher (the origins of the monastic black habit). Eustathius had an extraordinary career in the Church. It is, however, not our purpose here to recount it. Suffice it to say that among his most dedicated disciples was St Macrina, the sister of Basil the Great. In his first appearance in the region of Gangra, however, the city bishops rang the alarm bells. The canons they produced in their censure of him are a sustained defense of the city principle of church organization: a rejection of charismatic principles of organizing churches. Charisms wax and wane; even the most radiant charismatic individuals can turn cranky and falter. Proven structures endure and are refined by the test of time. At Gangra the synodical principle came of age: the Church would be governed more by law and precedence, with a view to social continuity, not radical discontinuity. Ascetical renunciation was one thing, and good; but it would not be the helmsman of the ship of the Church. Christian polity would be into the business of civilization building and the local structures of the Church would be forever welded to the imperial structures of the *polis*.

To arrive at a censure of Eustathius the synodical fathers made a rather extreme synopsis of his tendencies rather than an accurate digest of his views. They condemn the views that the sexes are equal; that marriage is to be despised (canon 1); that virginity is to be the only way; that familial and spousal authority can be flouted in the name of Christ (canons 15–16: young men and women leaving home to be ascetics without getting episcopal or parental approval, and a few cases of married people irresponsibly leaving their families in order to embark on monastic life). The synod attacks the ascetics for advocating that women should cut their hair (canon 17) and for suggesting that the eating of meat is evil (canon 2). It makes an extraordinary attack on women wearing men's clothes (which turns out only to be a disapproval of women adopting monastic garb under Eustathius' guidance, and thereby claiming the right to the itinerant life of the sophist community he led). The synodical canons get to the heart of matters regarding polity when they assert that church revenues must never be alienated from episcopal control. This ruling establishes a secure financial basis for the Church in all ages ahead. It stabilizes it as a corporation. What caused this reactive utterance is probably something simple: when Eustathius and his monastic party arrived in town the locals were probably amazed. An itinerant band of very fervent missionaries had descended on them and their dedication to Christ was highly impressive, but also challenging. It was a common practice for the Eustathians to hold prayer meetings in the houses of their admirers. In this way they did not have to submit to the control of the local clergy in the church buildings. They also collected alms and disciples before moving on. They never ate meat, practiced strict continence, and advocated social equality and the liberation of slaves. They taught that the ascetics should also work vigorously to alleviate the sufferings of the poor. Who could not admire them? Who would not like them? Well, city clergy for one, perhaps. The local people would much rather give their church alms to the itinerant zealots than perhaps to incumbent clergy who did not inspire them as much. So it was that the whole principle of stable city churches could be undermined; the principle of local communities under the single direction of a resident bishop could be overthrown. This is why we get such a strong reaction at Gangra. Christian assemblies are to be *leitourgia*, that is whole civic gatherings, not private conventicles. Christianity is at root a public matter, not a private religion. This notion is deeply embedded in all future church law; even in a time, after the sixth century, when the higher clergy are to be drawn only from the ranks of the monastics.

Gangra issued a list of twenty stinging canons. They have, for the first time in public, as it were, the character of emergency regulations issued to stamp out a particular local problem. The annoyance with the young radical Christian ascetic who had run rings around his more sedentary "elders and betters," and who would continue to be a church gadfly as long as he lived, led the Gangra synodists to adopt a tone of impressive authority. This, too, set the tone for future years. It gave the synod a real sense that it had the right to make the final decisions regarding church polity: not interest groups, or rich patrons, or even imperial overlords. The synod of resident city bishops, albeit a sedentary model by nature, clung to something different here: the idea that precedent and structure mattered, that revenues and systems had to be ordered and defended, and that synods of bishops were the way to do this, thus affirming the wisdom of the elders over the zeal of the young.

When we read today the claims of the Eustathian ascetics, and their rejection by the synodical canons, it is hard not to feel sorry for a group who so robustly stood up for equality among the sexes as part of a new world order under Christ; a group who so simply stated the principle that in Christ's Church there could be no room for institutions such as slavery or serfdom. But just as we may be ready to cheer for Eustathius, we perhaps ought to recall his later career and the chaos he caused as a figure who, all his life long, believed himself to be unqualifiedly right in every situation. Such larger-than-life figures are often as destructive as they are admirable. In this light, perhaps, we should save a little cheer for the more apparently grumpy bishops of Gangra who want to sustain the *status quo*. Not for all the *status quo* they asserted, of course, but for this one principle that lies hidden in the philosophy of the canons they issued: namely, that civilization is built in cities, and must be protected by systems; that Christianity is in the business of building civilization in real-world political communities, not in deserts on the fringes of cities; and that such a civilization can only be sustained by law and order. Gangra is perhaps the time when canonical lists first stand up, first start to change from being pastoral guidelines, to assume the status and significance of Christian practical law under the administration of Bishops now ready to act as judges of the *polis*. The Council of Chalcedon in 451 cited some of Gangra's canons as exemplary and retrospectively endorsed its authority.

Antioch in Encaeniis–341

The Synod of Antioch is another of the major fourth century local synods that set the tone for the establishment of the eastern law codes of the Church. The synod to which these canons are now attached[22] was held at Antioch the great capital of the Roman Orient in 341 on the occasion of the gathering of ninety-seven bishops in the city for the occasion of the dedication of the "Great and Golden Church" which had been commissioned by Constantine's family. It is known from this as Antioch *in Encaeniis* ("at the dedication"). In the larger canvas of Church history this was an odd council indeed. For most of those assembled were from the Syrian Archdiocese, and many of the leaders of the conciliar agenda had one thing in common, a profound dislike for St Athanasius of Alexandria and a determination to ruin his career. In the long view of church history, of course, Athanasius was the supreme defender of the Nicene creed and doctrinal orthodoxy about the person of Christ. This was not how the bishops assembled at Antioch in 341 saw it, however, believing Athanasius to be one of the troublemakers of the Eastern Church. Leaving the disputes about this council aside, where it stands in terms of pure Nicene Orthodoxy, or where it stands in terms of Athanasius' reputation,[23] we can simply note that even at the time many strong Nicene theologians felt that it had endorsed a proper expression of the faith. Hilary of Poitiers, a zealous Nicene theologian, called it a "synod of the saints" and regardless of the true theological sentiments of several of its leaders[24] all the early Church writers saw its canonical teachings as a classic model, which had a long influence. Some of them had undoubtedly been originated to hurt Athanasius, who was declared deposed from episcopal office at this meeting and was then suffering several exiles for the sake of his defense of truth. But in the

[22]Some scholars think the canons were originally part of a separate synod held a decade earlier at Antioch, and later confused with the more famous *In Encaeniis* synod.

[23]St Gregory of Nazianzus (Oration 18) asserted Athanasius as the true protagonist of Nicene Orthodoxy, and this sentiment came to be standard in later Church history. Gregory elevated the Athanasian doctrine at Constantinople 381, a council that endorsed Nicaea 325 as a definitive statement of Orthodox Christology.

[24]Eusebius of Nicomedia was one of them, known as a blatant Arian in Alexandria and the Latin West, and a constant enemy of St Athanasius. His reputation in the East was more varied, however. He was heavily protected and patronized by the imperial family, a significant theologian in his own right; and seen by many in the Syrian region as anti-homoousion and anti-Athanasius, not necessarily anti-Orthodox (though that was the clear position of Athanasius, of course; and Church history followed the latter in this regard).

longer term they did assert the principle once more of the superiority of the synod's judgment over that of a single, however charismatic, bishop. The canons were originated in the midst of the chaos of the post-Nicene environment when synod followed synod contradicting judgments on significant matters of faith. In setting out canons to regulate the reception of the judgments of synods, Antioch is attempting some form of remedial intervention so as to stabilize the synodical system in its infancy. Two of the Antiochene canons were cited and reaffirmed at Chalcedon in 451, and the Roman Popes John II, Zacharias, and Leo IV all approved this list of canons as "those of the holy fathers."

The first canon (again giving the tone for the whole set) asserts that all the Churches world-wide must observe the Nicene canons (Nicaea 325) concerning the establishment of an agreed date for Pascha. Anyone who communicates with an excommunicate person must be regarded as having incurred the same excommunication also.[25] This was meant to give synodical decisions of major councils some universal force in church law: powers that can determine good process for the body corporate. It followed up this attempt to subordinate individual charism to corporate wisdom by canon 4 which reiterated, for emphasis, that bishops who have been synodically deposed but who continue to act as if nothing had happened[26] are to be excommunicated "without hope of restoration," and those who shelter them are to be excommunicated also. This principle of establishing a due order of synodical decrees, and affirming their weight in the system of law, carried on with canon 9 asserting that the bishops of a province must acknowledge the metropolitan bishop (the bishop of the provincial capital, or the most important city) as their head and he ought to chair the synod; while the bishops in the synod, and the metropolitan should do "nothing whatsoever that is extraordinary" without mutual involvement. Canon 11 is also in the same camp, affirming synodical process when it declares that any bishop who appealed directly to imperial civic authority over the head of a synod so that they might be rehabilitated after ecclesiastical deposition, should never be restored to communion.[27] Another important regulation of synodical pro-

[25]Meant as a censure of the Roman Pope Julius who had sheltered Athanasius, defending him as a teacher of Orthodoxy. The pope wrote to the synod complaining about their censure of Athanasius, but still addressing them as "Dear Brethren." In this tension we can see the double principle operating: the power of the synod, rubbing against the power of the great metropolitan sees.

[26]Again Athanasius is in mind here. Since he regarded the Eusebian party who were orchestrating these hostile measures against him as both imperial stooges and Arian heretics, he refused to allow their synods (meetings where they set the agenda and posed the questions) any authority, as not being in the line of authentic synods of the Universal Church. It was one of the most dramatic (implicit) doctrines of Constantinople I in 381, retrospectively to draw the line of the proper lineage of general councils from Nicaea 325 straight to itself in 381.

[27]In the time of its issuing the harried Nicene party under Athanasius regarded it with scorn, as the leading Arians were heavily patronized by the eastern imperial family. The Athanasian party, alternatively

cedure appears in canon 14. Here it is decided that if a trial of a bishop has to take place in the context of a "controversial" synod,[28] the trial aspect, for the sake of preserving the appearance and character of justice, ought to be handed over to neighboring bishops to act as judges and their decisions ought to be accepted by the home synod. Canon 15 limited the reasons permissible for bishops of one province to be accused and tried by neighboring synods.[29] Canon 20 capped the series by reiterating Nicaea's call for the establishment of regular synodical meetings at least twice a year in each province on the fourth week of Pentecost, and on the Ides of October. The canon cited the reason for this commonality of the "synodical season" so that clergy with cases to present could know when and where to gather. To see how this heavy affirmation of good synodical order played out in the West at the same time, one needs to study the disastrous acts of the Council of Serdica 343, where the western bishops collectively demanded that the easterners revoke their condemnations of Athanasius and Marcellus of Ancyra who were the "elephants in the room" in relation to Antioch 341.

The other canons of the Antiochene Council, twenty-five in total, relate to very practical matters of establishing principles of good order in the Churches. Absenteeism was again a problem and was dealt with by refusing permission to presbyters to move around from church to church (canon 3). If presbyters clashed with their bishops publicly they ought to be deposed, and if they continued to make arguments they ought to be dealt with by civil authorities.[30] Laity who came late to the services and who left early were denounced as causing disruption to worship (canon 2). Travelling clergy ought to bear with them letters of introduction and validation from their own bishops (canons 7 and 8), or else should not be received in the foreign Churches. These letters (*eirenika*) were an old system of inter-Church introductions. Now in the Arian crisis they were being elevated as a way of controlling

found solace and support from the Roman Pope, and from the western imperial court. In later times of the Church, however, it gained a new venerability as a way of delineating strongly the proper domains of Church regulation and imperial law. The emperors had great influence over church policy, but in canons such as this the bishops show themselves ready to draw clear limits between themselves and imperial power. The ecclesiastical power of the Byzantine emperors always respected this limit in relation to synods. In their relations with individual patriarchs the emperors often acted high-handedly if they could get away with it. In relation to synods they did so usually at their own peril.

[28]A euphemistic way of looking at how the 4th century synod had become a war zone in the time of the Arians.

[29]The theological *animus* caused by the Arian crisis had led to a great deal of this type of accusation and counter-accusation. Truth to be told, the synodical process proved to have its limits of effectiveness in the course of the Arian period, and was "supplemented" by other systems. See McGuckin (1998).

[30]Again one suspects an original complaining Arian bias here; several presbyters had been high in the Nicene cause and had made things uncomfortable for incumbent Arian bishops by stirring up local opposition against them. Apollinaris' and Eustathius' disciples are examples that come to mind. In a later era the general principle is reinterpreted that presbyters should be duly obedient to bishops.

mobile, agitating, clergy. In less controverted times the canon settled into a way of regulating clergy who wanted to drift to the big cities to make fame and fortune there, rather than being content with quiet provincial life. The power of the chorepiscopoi is again brought into the light of day (canon 10) and once more circumscribed to the advantage of metropolitan (city) bishops who have ruling authority over them, whereas the metropolitan bishop did not have "ruling authority" (jurisdiction) over the other bishops comprising the synod, since the generic principle applied that each ruling bishop was jurisdictionally head of his own diocese. The metropolitan was chair of the synod, not its ruler and, accordingly, had *auctoritas* over the assembled bishops of his capital's province, not *potestas*.

Many of the canons not directly related to synodical process relate to the issue of regulating the episcopal order's exercise of power. Roving bishops are heavily discouraged (canons 16, 17, 18, & 21). Bishops must never appoint their own successors (canon 23); they must clearly delineate their personal finances from the church accounts (canon 24); and, while they are to enjoy supreme governance of the local Church's money, their duty is not to enrich themselves, but to help the poor, and the synod is to have supervisory oversight of their management of such things (canon 25). An episcopal ordination ought ideally to be performed with all the local synod's involvement. If this is not practical then letters of agreement can be assembled and the majority decision can be followed. This again sprang out of the Arian crisis context of vacant sees being heavily contested according to the theological persuasion of the contenders (Arian bishops put in over the wishes of Nicene locals as happened at Alexandria and Antioch) or vice versa (as happened at Constantinople in 380), and the practice of such as the Eustathians and the Apollinarists of deliberately travelling to contest vacant sees by putting forward a slate of qualified non-local candidates of their own. Once the charged theological environment of Arianism died away, however, these canons remained in a quieter ecclesiastical domain as good protocols, rules of the house that allowed a fair balance between a qualified monarchical episcopal rule within the diocese and provincial and inter-provincial governance by means of the synod. This is why the Antiochene canons were always highly regarded by the later Church. It is an impressive list of church laws that effectively establishes the future of church law as a synodical system: a moderated collegiality preserving good order through sets of agreed protocols that have binding force on the bishops who are otherwise the undisputed "canonical" rulers of church life in their dioceses.

The Synod of Laodicea–c 363

Laodicea was a major city of south Asia Minor (Phrygia). The superscription of the council canons describe it as "Pacatian Phrygia," a civic division of the imperial regions that took place in the mid-fourth century. Some scholars have thought the council was called earlier than this to deal with the ejection of the heretical theologian bishop Photinos who was reputed to have taught that Jesus was "only a man" (*Psilanthropism*). But the superscription, if authentic (and we have no reason to suppose otherwise), suggests a later date. When the Quinisext Council, three centuries later, made its retrospective listing of the major synodical decrees and put together the canons of important local synods before and after Nicaea, they set the Council of Laodicea in the series between Serdica 343 and Constantinople I 381. Most of the bishops assembled in Phrygia were from the Asia Minor province. They issued a total of fifty-nine canons. There is a sixtieth canon that was added later that presented the canonical list of Scriptures that could be read in the church worship services. The tone and focus of these canons is more generically about good liturgical order and the establishment of moral codes. The problem of reconciling divisions is again addressed. This time it is not to do with the return of those who lapsed under threat of persecution, but the administration of church unity when it concerns the reception of heretics who want to be received in the body of the Church. The sects listed are Novatians, Montanists, Photinians, Quartodecimans. These differed among themselves as being divergences from Catholic standards of belief and practice in several different degrees. Some were very close to the Church both doctrinally and liturgically; others were much further removed. The council establishes a variegated mode of receiving converts. Heretics shall be excluded from church worship (canon 6). The Orthodox shall not pray with them (canon 9). If they wish to enter the Church once more they shall be required to confess the Creed, and to be re-chrismated (canon 7).[31] Montanists, however, are not to be regarded as heretics at all but simply as pagans; and they shall be baptized, not as *de novo*, but as for the first time (canon 8). On the moral front, the rules against digamy (marrying again after the death of a spouse) are noticeably relaxed (canon 1) and the system of penance that had been so rigorous in the earlier two centuries of the Church shows signs of passing into a discretionary matter for the local bishop. This was because it was well on its way to passing out of the Church altogether. Nektarios, the Archbishop of Constantinople in 382, successor to St Gregory the Theologian, abolished the office of the last holder of the rank of "Grand Penitentiary." The old penance system (grades of weepers, standers, hearers) had all faded away and Nektarios was bowing to reality. Canon 2 of Laodicea says instead that, after a period of suitable

[31]This was the second part of ancient baptism; following after the baptism in water, it was the anointing with sacred chrism so as to confer "the seal of the gift of the Holy Spirit." Heresy was widely believed to have incurred the loss of the grace of the Holy Spirit in the soul of the dissident. So while baptism was not repeated (being once-for-all and unrepeatable) it was "partially" repeated, as Chrismation, as a form of readmission sacrament.

penance, sinners shall be restored to communion. The bishop now has full discretion. Public penance systems thus give way to private devotional confession.

Several of the canons turn their attention to insisting on the higher standards of moral code that ought to be expected of the clergy. Clerics are not to join together for nights out on the town (*symposia* where much drinking and discussion went on; canon 55), nor are they to frequent taverns or performances where actresses "display" (stage nudity in classically themed dramatic presentations, which were really erotic displays; canon 54). They were not to consort socially with dissidents or non-Christians (canons 37–39). They must never wear, let alone believe in, amulets or magical spells (canon 36). Their liturgical service should never be in a private house, but only in the main churches of the city under the bishop's jurisdiction (canon 58). The elections of presbyters should not be the primary responsibility of the town's people, the *demos* who acclaimed their potential priests according to how popular they were, but ought to be a system of promotion closely supervised by the bishop so that only men of proven quality would be advanced (canons 13, 12). Canon 11 forbids the old custom of appointing *presbytidae,* women presidents in the churches to deal with women's affairs. The ancient epitome of this canon reads this as referring to the order of widows. Others have seen it as one of the first public restrictions on the order of deaconesses, although the matter of the precise context is not clear. Female diaconal ordination continued for many centuries more at Constantinople where there were many highly-educated women. Perhaps it was in the provinces (such as Phrygia) that attitudes were hardening against female ministry, and partly from the cause that the voice to appoint ministers was passing more from the congregation to the bishop, many of whom were increasingly of the ranks of the monastic ascetics and who now had especial reason not to welcome women among the ranks of clerics in the Church orders.

Finally, rules for establishing a common practice of liturgical process in Asia Minor begin to be set in place. Church singers should be appointed who know the ritual (canon 15). The cantor's office should not be open to all indiscriminately. What Scriptures are permitted to be read is spelled out (canon 16) and Old Testament lessons ought be lightened with psalm singing interspersed between them, a standard matrix for what would grow to become the Church's service of Vespers (canon 17). The prayers of the Eucharist and the canonical hours should be brought into conformity and consonance, the beginning seeds of establishing a typikon of church services that were standardized in a large arc across the Church (canons 17–18). Laodicea is not a council whose rules are set out under the heavy pressures manifest at Antioch 341; but for this reason it allows us a more accurate glimpse, perhaps, of a late fourth century church system where canon law is now clearly emerging as an outreach of the synodical system of church governance. It bears the same marks and characteristics that have been prevalent in all the previous formative synods: a concern for establishing good order, a concern for elevating public morals especially by setting up the clergy as standard examples, a concern for the liturgical processes of the Church under the guidance of the clergy, and a desire to establish a code of good protocols under the supervision of bishops whose authority was reinforced by the synodical system. By this stage, at the end of the fourth century, everything is set in place for the final evolution of the synodical process into what we now know as the system of the Oecumenical Councils. We normally set Nicaea 325 in that line as the first and paradigmatic "General Council," but this is a retrospective. Throughout the fourth century Nicaea played too controversial a part to enjoy this status on its own merits. It was not until the Council of Constantinople 381 that Nicaea was retrospectively lifted up as the "Council of Councils" and given quasi-legendary status as the ark of Orthodox faith and its creed as the ultimate arbiter of catholicity. So it is really the late fourth century's growing sense of synodical and canonical order that actually sets up the final act of the *mise en scène* with the concept of the "Oecumenical" Council.

Further Reading

Primary Texts

Sts Nicodemos & Agapius, eds. *The Rudder (Pedalion) of the Holy Catholic and Apostolic Church.* Athens: Nicolaides Press, 1908. (English edition: D. Cummings, tr. Chicago, IL: Publications of the Orthodox Educational Society, 1957. Repr.: New York: Luna Printing Co., 1983.)

H.R. Percival. *The Seven Ecumenical Councils.* A Select Library of Nicene and Post Nicene Fathers, vol. 14. Grand Rapids, MI: Eerdmans, 1900.

N.P. Tanner. *The Decrees of the Ecumenical Councils.* London: Sheed and Ward, 1990.

Studies

P.R. Amidon. "The Procedure of St Cyprian's Synods." *Vigiliae Christianae* 37 (1983) 328–339.

H. Hess. *The Canons of the Council of Sardica, A.D. 343: A Landmark in the Early Development of Canon Law.* Oxford, 1958.

J.N.D. Kelly. *Early Christian Creeds* (3rd edn.). London: Longman, 1972.

S. Laeuchli. *Power and Sexuality: The Emergence of Canon Law at the Synod of Elvira.* Philadelphia: Temple University Press, 1972.

J. A. McGuckin. "Eschaton and Kerygma : The Future of the Past in the Present Kairos. The Concept of Living Tradition in Orthodox Theology." *St Vladimir's Theological Quarterly* 42, nos. 3 & 4 (Winter 1998) 225–271.

CHAPTER 8

The Seven Oecumenical Councils

The Great Councils

The seven Great Councils have predominantly been studied in Christian history for the theological content of their decisions. This is certainly because the decrees in each case affected monumental issues of theology, to do with Christology, Trinitarianism, and Sacramentalism. Our treatment here will sketch out only the merest guide to the context of the theological arguments, and instead look beyond those debates to the canons that each of the councils appended to their decrees. Since the Oecumenical Councils were afforded the highest juridical status in the governance structure of Christianity (incomparably greater in weight as far as the Eastern Church was concerned, than any emperor, patriarch, theologian, bishop, or local synod), it follows that their canonical, or legal, decisions assumed archetypal status in the formation of the systems of Christian law. The seven that are recognized in the Eastern Christian world are really, for canonical purposes, eight; for there is also a so-called Quinisext (Fifth-Sixth), the Synod in "Trullo," the domed hall of the Imperial Palace at Constantinople, that retrospectively attached a list of canons to the fifth and sixth Oecumenical Councils, thus using their authority, as it were, to effect a reformation of church discipline by means of canon law. We shall look at them in chronological order.

The Council of Nicaea–325

There is a cluster of surviving documentation from this council, but sadly no official *Acta*. The extant documents related to it include the Summons (imperial *sacra*) of Constantine calling the bishops to assemble; the letter of Eusebius of Caesarea in Palestine, of one of the bishops called there for judgment, who writes to his Church to explain why he acceded to the controversial term *homoousion*;[1] the con-

[1]Truth was he had to accede to it or suffer permanent deposition; but he had to put a better face on it than that for his home congregation before whom, in the lead-in to the council, he had often preached against the word "*homoousion*" as being far too materialist a term (i.e., substance-based) to describe the Godhead. Eusebius had a climb down and this letter is a face-saving device, so he plays down Nicaea's significance.

ciliar fathers' letter to the Church in Egypt informing them of their decisions supporting Alexander and censuring Arius; the letter of Constantine to the Church of Alexandria; and the letter of the emperor insisting on the establishment of the date of Pascha according to the Nicene computation. In addition, we have the synod's statement of faith (the original Nicene creed) and the list of canons of the council. St Athanasius of Alexandria has a lot to say about the conduct and doctrine of this council (and the conduct of his opponents at it). He was present at the synod as an attendant of Archbishop Alexander of Alexandria, one of the main protagonists. Tradition states that he was there as a deacon to Alexander. Afterwards he became Alexander's successor in the great Egyptian capital and throughout most of the first three quarters of the fourth century it was Athanasius who was the standard-bearer of the concept of the Council of Nicaea as the "establishment of core orthodoxy." To defend this view he was frequently at variance with many of the eastern bishops. Even his theological friends often regarded Athanasius' out and out fight to establish Nicene doctrine as sometimes bending canonical rules, as we have noted in discussing the Council of Antioch 341. His enemies on the other hand, those whom Church history has often collectively lumped in together as "Arians" but who were in reality a much more variegated group of theologian bishops, simply regarded him as an uncanonical renegade. He was exiled numerous times for his defense of the faith. By 362 he was the unrivalled "grand old man" of the bishops who stood together for the defense of the doctrine of the deity of the Son of God in the full sense of what that term implied (as opposed to an honorific or imputed deity).[2] Athanasius wrote about Nicaea in his treatises *Contra Arianos* and *De Synodis*. His detractors, both ancient and modern, have often held that his impassioned view of the truth does not lend to receiving his reflections on the council as a balanced and fair historical assessment. Unfortunately, our other sources of historical information come from equally biased (and later) sources from the other camp; such as the *Church History* of the writer Philostorgios.

History has now grown accustomed to seeing the Council of Nicaea as a theological debate of massive proportions. Its core theological question concerns the weight a Christian can place on the notion of the divinity of Jesus Christ. Both sides agreed that the Logos of God (the Word or Wisdom of God)[3] incarnated in Jesus Christ. One side took the status of the Logos as being "God of God, true God of True God." The Logos was fully divine in all that meant logically and religiously (eternal, uncreated, omnipotent and so on). This was the Nicene party: Alexandrian theologians gathered around the bishop Alexander, most of the western bishops

[2]The Arian creed held to the logic of a concept of "created deity," which Athanasius rejected as an impossibility.

[3]See, for example, 1 Cor 1.24.

who agreed with his viewpoint, and some significant theologians of the Eastern Church who were progressively "leaned on" by episcopal and imperial authorities so as to accept a less radical view for general consumption in the Churches, and who accordingly were frequently displaced and exiled by state intervention.[4] The other side was patronized by the Constantinian dynasty[5] and followed a doctrine advancing the notion of a "created divinity" for the Logos of God, seeing him not as the second person of a coequal and divine Trinity, but rather as a subordinate supreme angel of the One God who was used as God's medium of communication with the cosmos. He was divine, but not God in the same sense God was God. This theological argument roiled the entire fourth century in its fire. It was inevitable that anyone involved in it, or looking back on it, would see the start of the debate and, in a sense, its ending as the two pillars that defined the century. The first of those pillars therefore was the Council of Nicaea 325, the other was the Council of Constantinople I 381. In retrospect, both became the first two Oecumenical Councils. But this is a viewpoint conditioned by three things. First, it is the perspective of the victorious Nicene party; it is they who define Christian Orthodoxy henceforth in relation to Nicaea's understanding of what deity involves. Secondly, it is the perspective of those who set up the two pillars of this theology, in a historical way, as being bounded by those two Councils, which therefore are given a very high symbolic status. Thirdly, it is the perspective of those who look back and are overwhelmed by the intellectual troubles that this debate caused for the Church in so many different arenas (exegesis, organization, liturgical praxis to name only a few). In short, it is an important retrospective assessment which tells us what Nicaea was only in the aftermath of the passing of a generation. Instead of looking at Nicaea in this doctrinal light, we gain a different coloration altogether if we look at it in its own time and for what it set out to do canonically. This is not to set aside the doctrinal work of the council as unimportant. It has been and remains the classical exposition of Christian theology on the person of Christ. What it does allow us to do is to bypass the doctrinal argument and come into the debate from the canonical aspect. From a canonical standpoint, one may ask where Nicaea stands in the line of the formative councils that had preceded it, for it produces a list of twenty canons which, when Nicaea eventually rises to the surface of the ocean as the most important of all historical synods, are carried on the back of the council's prestige, so as to become almost the paradigmatic form of ecclesiastical law. Leaving aside the doctrinal angle, then, let us approach Nicaea from another route.

[4]Eusebius of Samosata, or Meletius of Antioch, for example.

[5]Although Constantine had first decreed that the Council of Nicaea was a standard guide to Christian central Orthodoxy, he was later persuaded that it could not play that role widely in the East, and was persuaded to abandon the conciliar creed and anathemas, to fall back on a softer, vaguer standard of doctrine for general consumption.

Constantine was not a serious theologian, but he did want the Church and its local bishops to play a serious part in his New Empire. To achieve that he needed a stable Church and one that had successfully reconciled after the trauma of the recent civil war and the preceding persecutions which had so disrupted internal Christian affairs. After he gained supreme monarchical power in the East, with the killing of his last rival the Emperor Licinius, he knew that he had to reward his Christian troops for their support, and so he moved decisively to favor the Church in the Greek provinces that he had newly conquered. He summoned the bishops predominantly to settle all internal divisions that were keeping them from functioning efficiently as a single *corpus*. He may even at this stage have imagined them as a parallel religious corporation for church affairs, akin to the Senate for political and civic affairs. After his analysis of Rome, with its pagan Senate fiercely opposed to him, he had already decided to move the Roman capital eastwards, and build a new Senate where Christians would feature largely. To make the Church work as a force in his new empire, he had to break the log jam of old resentments that had built up in the time of persecution. So it was that he learned that the main intellectual source of division for the East[6] was the Arian dispute. He himself thought it was a small matter of "niceties" and believed it could easily be settled. Constantine's elevation to supreme power had taken place in 305, and so, in 325, the year after his victory in the civil war, he used the occasion of his twentieth anniversary celebrations (a time of important political consolidation for someone who had lasted this long in Imperial office) to bring together the Christian bishops of the East. Western representatives were invited, but it was the easterners he wanted to galvanize into unity. Since it was his *Vicennalia,* Constantine brought them at public expense to his palace at "Victory City" (Nicaea) in Bithynia and wined and dined them there in a way that caused wonderment. Nowadays, as noted earlier, all eyes were on the doctrinal solution he offered there, a masterpiece of theological-political ambiguity that he had his religious advisor Hosius of Cordoba orchestrate. The council asserted that the divinity of the Logos was co-substantive with the divinity of the Father. This term could mean anything from "same stuff as" (generically alike) to "ontologically identical." With suitable elastic it could suit a whole range of theological creeds. The strategy for broad commonality was not destined to work on the intellectual level (because of the likes of St Athanasius), but let us pass over this for the moment.

What else was needed for unity? This is where the canons emerge into the light of day, probably what the original attendees of the Council of Nicaea thought had been their most important work. They had settled an apparently obscure theological dispute between the Egyptian archbishop and his recalcitrant priest Arius over

[6]Just as he had found out in the West that the cause of disruption was Donatism, as in the Synod of Arles 314.

the issue of whether the Logos was eternal or issued in time, but then they had got down to practical matters. The twenty Nicene canons, therefore, were offered as the first imperially validated charter for the structure of the Church, now poised, under a pro-Christian emperor, to emerge as a powerful Roman corporation, a major factor in establishing Roman legal and religious culture across the eastern empire. The fathers at this synod could not have guessed how monumentally right that presentiment was to be, but they did their work under the *afflatus,* or inspiration, of such an idea. The canons of Nicaea were promulgated with a resplendently robed emperor at the head of the chamber, and completed just before the first state banquet celebrating an imperial *Vicennalia* to which Christian priests had ever been invited.[7] They set the tone for a new world order, and in twenty short regulations they chart the rise of Christianity as a truly world-wide organization. It is for this reason that the series of major councils, which Nicaea heads, gained the epithet "Oecumenical" that is, having a "world-wide" remit.

On the premise that the first canon in a series reveals the tone of the meeting, we receive a surprise at Nicaea, for the first canon is deliberating whether *castrati* can continue in the clergy. One presumes at first sight that there have been some notable clerics present who have assumed holy orders and there is severe doubt being expressed about the validity of clerical status. The debate is chiefly about self-castrati, men who are otherwise in good health but have arranged to be surgically altered. The reasons for this are strongly related to the burgeoning ascetic movement, at the time especially prevalent in Palestine and Egypt. It was a *topos*, a commonplace of the sophic movement that the truly wise man, the sage, would be immune from the movements of the flesh and would enjoy philosophical *apatheia.* For such reasons the ancient philosophers did not marry (one remembers the anguish of Augustine expressed in his *Confessions* about the celibacy expected of the philosophical rhetorician). Christian sophists were expected to match the pagans. It is partly out of this context that the Christian monastic movement grows to subsume the episcopacy, and thus that the late fourth century bishops soon assume a celibate status that they did not have in the early part of that century. Here in this canon the conciliar fathers publicly censure any Christian sophist who undergoes castration in order to find an easy route to the life transcending fleshly desire. One important afterthought, however, is added on. People who are in holy orders who were slaves and had been castrated from infancy or in barbarian lands (the implication is strongly made that in "Christian culture" this barbaric practice ought to be disallowed) are not to be dismissed from orders.

[7]How different from the time they appeared at the Domus Aurea, Nero's palace at Rome, when they were used as pitch-covered living torches to illuminate his gardens!

This is a stronger statement than first appears because it explicitly rejects Old Testament paradigms for considering fitness for priestly office. Physical integrity was a major aspect of legitimacy of the ancient priesthood in both Jewish and Greco-Roman culture.[8] The Christian Church is setting new terms here. It is moral fitness that is more important than physical integrity. It also sends a large signal out about biblical interpretation. It is not the literalistic meaning of a text that matters. Christianity does not have to be fundamentalistic in order to be accurate, authentic, and true to its tradition. This was a clear statement that not every word in Scripture continues with binding legal force, a powerful statement against the Arians, for example, who had been heavily pushing texts such as Proverbs 8.22 to "prove" their theory that the Logos of God was a creature. It was a comforting canon also for the many bishops present at Nicaea who were missing noses, ears or lips. They had suffered the persecution of Emperor Maximin who had ordered physical mutilation instead of death for those Christian clerical leaders who refused to offer sacrifice to the gods. They bore their disfigurements in the imperial aula at Nicaea as signs of their status as confessors. But more than this, according to our rough and ready rule of thumb that the first canon "gets to the point" of a whole assembly, this statement is more than simply setting a standard and tone for Christian ordination (a common theme of the councils of the age which are determined to elevate the clergy as an example), it is rather a specific rhetorical statement about the Nicene doctrine of the faith. Its rhetorical "sting" has not often been recognized by commentators, but must have been widely recognized at the time as a snub to Eusebius of Caesarea, the bishop present at Nicaea who more than any other posed as the intellectual arbiter of the Christian faith and who, accordingly, had objections to the term *homoousion*.

Eusebius was under censure before Nicaea, and the Nicene fathers accepted him back into communion (leaned on for this cause by the emperor who wanted a general reconciliation to be effected). To afford him rehabilitation, they demanded a statement of his creed (for which he offered the baptismal creed of Jerusalem) which was a deliberate humiliation of this learned man.[9] They also required him to profess the utility of the term *homoousion*, which he had spoken against many times at his local Church, and to whom he had to write a face-saving *apologia* afterwards. The canon does not explicitly harry him anymore but it does send out a signal. For, truth to be told, no one who knew anything about medical practice would ever dream that a mature man in good health would actually go to a surgeon and seek castration in order to avoid sexual temptation and in order to live an ascetic and sophistic life. Post-adolescent castration does not have the same desire-reducing effect as prepubescent castration. On the contrary, it carries with it a high risk of death and

[8] Lev 21.21; See also M. Beard & J. North, *Pagan Priests* (London: Duckworth, 1990).

[9] Namely his sophisticated Origenian theology was not required, his baptismal faith was.

major recurring problems of health. No sage is ever known to have done this, except one; and that one in a famous literary fiction of Eusebius of Caesarea's own making. For in his *Church History*, Book Six, Eusebius presents the third century teacher Origen of Alexandria as the supreme theologian of the Church, the supreme sage and ascetic and a living example of pure doctrine and holy lifestyle. In order to offset growing rumbles against Origen in the Church of his own day, Eusebius (who was a devotee because he had inherited the school of Origen and his library, and was trying to make the Church of Caesarea the arbiter of proper doctrine) composed a *vita* of his hero which smoothed over every aspect where the theologian had caused controversy. In the face of the known facts that the Roman pope and the Alexandrian archbishop of the third century had both censured Origen's orthodoxy, Eusebius set off the rhetorical smokescreen that both bishops were annoyed at Origen only because of his excessive zeal for chastity and, possibly, their envy. Eusebius suggests that Origen must have castrated himself in order to "appropriately" teach both young women and young boys in his school[10] that he was a hero of *apatheia* in the service of theology (and on no account a controversial teacher!) and that it was this act of excessive zeal that had got him into trouble with the bishops. But everybody at Nicaea knew that it was Origen who, in the third century had said that *ousia*, "being," was a materialist category that only a fool would apply to the immaterial Godhead. He had also argued that *homoousion* was a term that signified one was foolishly unable to distinguish the Persons of the Trinity.[11] Neither position endeared him to the Nicene fathers. Origen is the deep intelligence behind Alexander and Athanasius, although they do not mention him, knowing that his legacy is now too controversial. But he is also the "authority" being cited by Eusebius of Nicomedia, Arius, and Eusebius of Caesarea. In canon 1, therefore, the fathers take a sardonic swipe at both Origen and Eusebius in a way that asserts quite clearly that a simplicity of faith and lifestyle is preferable to cleverness in theological argumentation if theological argumentativeness leads the person astray. In a world where

[10]The fact is that in Eusebius' day no sage would teach young women along with young boys; but in Origen's day most of his leading disciples were wealthy Christian women (and many of them were executed because of their profession). Origen however, taught in a different cosmopolitan social environment than Eusebius, and the latter is puzzling to think how his hero could have had women in his group. For this reason he "makes up" the story of the castration, thinking it would be edifying to the ascetics of the Palestinian desert whom he is trying to convert to Origen's cause. Origen himself, in his *Commentary on Matthew*, says that anyone who takes the story of Jesus in the Gospels about making oneself a eunuch, has to be foolish in the extreme. Further see: J.A. McGuckin, *The Westminster Handbook to Origen of Alexandria* (St Louis, KY: Westminster John Knox Press, 2004).

[11]It was a term that in Origen's time had only been used notably by Paul of Samosata, a renowned Monarchian thinker (there is only one undifferentiated Godhead; Father, Son and Spirit are just names for the same reality). Origen was a major opponent of Monarchianism and his attack on the word is an attack on them, a different context altogether.

rhetoric was carefully freighted, and "shame and honor" were major categories of social governance, this canon is a decided smack for Eusebius the theologian,[12] deliberately evoking his famed defense of Origen's orthodoxy and firmly putting it in its place.

Canon 2 of the council resumes the theme of elevating the status of the Christian clergy. Recently ordained persons, if their past lives are revealed not to be edifying, shall not continue in office. Ordaining bishops are strictly admonished to take more care with whom they ordain; the force of this is repeated in canons 9 and 10. The same concern to establish the superior status and reputation of Christian clergy is present in several more of the list of canons. Canon 3 forbids the houses of clergy to have single ascetic women living under the same roof. Only female relatives or aged women "beyond all suspicion" are to fulfill housekeeping duties. This effectively ended an earlier custom, especially prevalent in Syria, that Christian women left home to serve the Church as solitary virgins and found protection in the houses of the clergy. It appears at the same time that other ministerial avenues for women were also being restricted or were fading away (the office of widow, for example) or the discontinuance of the *presbytidae* as at Laodicea canon 11. Canon 17 orders that clergy serving as monetarist speculators (usurers) should be deposed. In canon 18, strict fences are set around the diaconal office. Never are deacons to "make an offering," that is to pray the priestly oblation that is reserved for bishops and presbyters.

At the core of the Nicene canons is a sequence of legislation to deal with synodical process. In this it resembles other councils of comparable age, especially Antioch in Encaeniis. Canons 4–7 and 15–16 especially relate to this theme. Canon 4 demands that bishops be appointed by all the bishops of a local synod, and, if this is impossible, the absent bishops should communicate agreement in writing. The metropolitan archbishop of the area shall have the final word. His ratification is necessary to confirm the legitimacy of an episcopal ordination. Once again this establishes the priority of governance order: bishops rule in their dioceses, but synodical process has weight over the head of individual bishops and the metropolitan is the president of the synod. This becomes the backbone of all Eastern Christian legal polity. It is this canon above all others that prohibits and thus prevents anything in the Orthodox world comparable to the rise of the western papacy. Canon 5 affirms that suspended bishops cannot be rehabilitated by single bishops, only by synods, and that synods shall be held twice each year, before Lent[13] and before the Autumn.[14] The sixth canon is an extremely important movement in church law. It takes the synodical system of the Church, hitherto conceived

[12]So too was canon 7 giving his canonically subordinate bishop at Jerusalem greater honors.

[13]So that no strife shall disturb the Paschal season.

[14]Canon 20 of Antioch; In Encaeniis repeats and adjusts this in 341.

in terms of province-wide consensus gathering, and imagines it in an imperial perspective, a world-wide way of managing Christian affairs across the Empire. It establishes principles which have ever afterwards been applied to Christian polity in the Christian East. Precedent is again cited as the guide: "Let the ancient customs as in Egypt, Libya, and Pentapolis prevail, namely that the bishop of Alexandria shall have jurisdiction[15] in all these, since the like is customary for the bishop of Rome also. Likewise in Antioch and the other provinces, let the Churches retain their privileges." This legislation acknowledged the rise of the super-city episcopal administrations: Rome, Alexandria, Antioch. Shortly after Constantine founded it five years later, after 330, Constantinople would be added to the super list, taking a territory of influence out of the traditional domains of Antioch and Alexandria, which both fought hard against its rise as can be seen in the struggles surrounding the Council of Ephesus 431.

Rome, too, would resent the rise of Constantinople to this list. It was a matter around which much Church history would hereafter be written. The canon, nevertheless, is historic, for it legitimates a principle that "large city" should mean "large weight" in Christian polity It also set the right tone for the establishment of Christian governance in the new Constantinian empire, that, in the future, beyond any Nicene bishop's possible imaginings, was going to become Christian in an amazing sense. Historic venerability is important (and Christians were nothing if not retrospectivists), but possessing it is not the same as being a real metropolitan city with political weight. In canon 7, therefore, Jerusalem is afforded an honorary metropolitan status, but not to the extent that it pre-empts Palestinian Caesarea under whose jurisdiction it had been placed for centuries, since Caesarea was the real metropolis, and Jerusalem more a place of pilgrimage and memories. Canons 15 and 16 lay down the law that no senior clergy shall "translate" from city to city. This canon has been much ignored in the course of history. It arose as a way of stopping the fluid movement of bishops roving around during the Arian crisis (Apollinarists and others) and agitating within local communities. It was invoked against Gregory of Nazianzus by Rome and Alexandria when he was duly elected as the Archbishop of Constantinople in 381. He made the reply in his historical poem *De Vita Sua* that the objections were a farce since everyone knew "this old rule was superseded." It was not raised against the translation of Eusebius of Nicomedia, a relative of the emperor, to the "new" eastern capital at Constantinople. It has always remained in the mind of the Church (especially for the way it castigates clerical ambition, or not being ready to stay in a backwater and serve the Church) but equally it has proven often not to be useful, for it prohibits the free movement of talent to where talent

[15]As Metropolitan or superintendent of a much larger ecclesiastical area.

can be most effectively used (the case of the movement of Gregory the Theologian from Nazianzus to Constantinople is a prime example). So this is one of many of the canons that are still "in force" in the East, but "not often observed."

Other rules in the list regulate the reception of converts. Canon 8 suggests how to deal with returning Novatianists (who broke communion on account of having a more severe discipline of dealing with the lapsed, and who censured the majority bishops for tolerating laxity, as they saw it). The canon establishes the important principle in church law of the difference between schism and heresy. The Novatianists (known ironically as the *katharoi* or "the pure ones") can be received by profession of faith. If their ministers return they retain their ordination, except that bishops among them shall be subordinate to the existing local bishop. In canon 19, the Paulian sect is mentioned. Here was a case of more than schism; deviant doctrine was involved. The Paulian converts are to be baptized as if for the first time. If there are worthy ministers among them, these people can be advanced to orders in rapid process. The distinction between schismatic disunity (where grace of sacraments can prevail) and heretical disunity (where all grace of sacraments disappears from the dissidents) became a major axiom of later Church life and a ready rule of thumb for local bishops to make decisions. It can be seen applied dramatically, and to high pastoral effect, in St Basil the Great's canonical rules.

The last major section of the twenty canons is comprised of that section which deals with the reconciliation of the lapsed in the aftermath of the persecutions and the Roman civil war. The Nicene fathers basically adopt an eirenic solution which was seen as mild and reconciliatory (though some aspects may strike us moderns as highly severe). Canon 11 sets out to punish the lapsed who, under a weak persecution, without any real threat to life or limb, succumbed and stood with the emperor, not with the Church. These false Christians, "who are offered clemency though they do not deserve it," must serve the whole path of public penance; after twelve years they may be readmitted to communion. This has specific reference to the faction around Licinius, Constantine's last rival in the civil war, whom he has just conquered. It is, in a sense, a purge from the Church of his archrival's faction in the aristocracy and army. The Nicene fathers were more than ready to go in that direction because of Licinius' final days on the throne when he started to show himself another of the hostile foes of Christianity. Canon 12 sets the real tone of the council. Those who lapsed in the persecutions because they were frightened for good cause or tortured shall go through penance in due degree. Their penance shall be set by the bishop who shall exercise discretion towards them, according to the level of genuine repentance and sorrow they demonstrate. Again discretion is rising to the fore. Canon 13 strongly moderates the severity of some rigorist local synods: no one, whatever their sin, is to be denied eucharistic reconciliation with the Church if they have a mortal illness. Catechumens who fell away because of the persecution are to be mildly disciplined: they shall stand as petitioners for three more years, before being restored to the catechumenal ranks. This mild solution made sure the Church retained the loyalty of the growing numbers who, before the last persecutions, were wanting to join. It also ensured that the late fourth century would be a period of massive conversions to the Christian religion.

The Council of Constantinople I–381

The Council of Constantinople was held in the Church of Divine Peace (St Eirene; the present church of the same name marks the site, now in the grounds of the Topkapi palace Istanbul) at the imperial capital between May and July of 381. It was called together on the occasion of the *adventus* of Theodosius to the city and was designed to signal the definitive proscription of Arianism after Theodosius exiled the incumbent Arian bishop Demophilos from the city when he and his party refused to "admit the faith of Peter of Alexandria and Damasus of Rome." The historical details of the Council of Constantinople are certainly as complex and dramatic as those surrounding Nicaea. The relation of the canons of this, the second in the listings of the Oecumenical Councils (as proclaimed at Chalcedon 451), is more complicated, however, as it is not certain when these were promulgated, possibly even a year later than the original conciliar meeting. It is difficult to tell precisely. St Gregory of Nazianzus was elected as second president of the council, after the sudden death of Meletios of Antioch, its first president and the acknowledged "Grand Old Man" of Nicene Orthodoxy who was still alive in the East.[16] But the council was highly controversial in its process. The Emperor Theodosius, a Spanish Nicene layman, wanted it to reaffirm the centrality of Nicaea as the major statement of Orthodoxy. The Nicene theologians gathered for that cause, and, when the state imperial support for Arian clergy (financial and political) was removed, the Arian movement withered away remarkably quickly afterwards.

There is no doubt that the general image of what Constantinople did is accurate enough: it set up Nicaea as the cornerstone of all councils and reaffirmed the wider Nicene tradition as the Orthodox faith. Its own creed is actually recited today in the churches under the simple designation of the "Nicene Creed" when it is really the Nicaea-Constantinopolitan creed. In making its theological resolution, the council of 381 opened up the Christological debate into its next extrapolation as a Trinitarian debate.[17] Gregory's sermons outline the main road to this, and these five ser-

[16]Athanasius had died by 381, as had Eusebius of Samosata, and Basil the Great.

[17]Further see McGuckin (1994).

mons known now as the *Five Theological Orations*[18] were endorsed at the Council of Chalcedon in 451 as central synopses of the faith. There were problems in 381, however, for Meletios was regarded with much suspicion in the West. Athanasius the Great had never trusted him, seeing him not as the leading eastern Nicene theologian, but rather as a tricky time-server. His presidency would have been contested by both Rome and Alexandria (who were weighing in at some geographical remove) had it not been for the fact that he suddenly died. His successor, Gregory, is now regarded as the finest theologian of the early Church, but his contemporaries at the council more or less forced his resignation and refused to listen to his demands that the *homoousion* of the Spirit of God should be added to the creed. He went home to Nazianzus muttering angrily to all would listen[19] that this synod was a muddle of "quacking geese who had dirtied the pure waters of the faith."

Our problems today in assessing the Constantinopolitan council result from the fact that Gregory is the main source of our detailed historical knowledge about what went on there.[20] No official *acta* are extant[21] beyond the creed and the canons, and Gregory's own memories are so jaundiced that he finds it hard to say anything good about the bishops assembled there. He systematically devoted himself in his last years to explaining the Constantinopolitan creed (which studiously avoids ascribing the *homoousion* to the Spirit) as "really meaning" that the Spirit is actually *homoousion*. The fact is that the Church in its greater wisdom has accepted him in that exegesis and elevated his Trinitarian doctrine as catholic Orthodoxy. It thus reads the conciliar creed in the "correct" interpretation of it offered by the conciliar president whose offices the conciliar fathers at the time dispensed with. One of the problems facing Gregory, of course, was the emperor. Theodosius wanted the council above all else to reconcile the group of thirty "Macedonian"[22] bishops who had been called there. Gregory was not keen to do so. He felt that the resisters of the clear affirmation of the Godhead of the Spirit were simply occult Arians, whether or not they confessed the *homoousion* of the Son. Gregory, however, was overruled more for political reasons than theological. But whatever the case, his retirement years, when he turned to poetry to recount episodes in his career, left him with little happy

[18]Orations 27–31.

[19]And repeated it, retrospectively, in writing in his *De Vita Sua*, and in his *Homily on the Bishops*. Further about the Council and Gregory's role in it: see McGuckin (2001).

[20]There are accounts from later historians. See: Socrates *Church History* 5.8, 9; Sozomen *Church History* 7.7–11; Theodoret *Church History* 5.6–8; Rufinus *Church History* 2.19.

[21]The bishop Demophilos (an Arian) had just gone off into self-imposed exile with his senior clergy, taking the accounts with him as Gregory tells us. The Council met in a chaotic environment shortly after the death of the Emperor Valens in a border skirmish with Gothic nomads. Everything was "up in the air." Major synods after this point will be heavily minuted by imperial stenographers.

[22]So named because they were disciples of Macedonius of Constantinople, a bishop who had passionately argued against the *homoousion* of the Spirit.

memory of the Council of Constantinople. In the aftermath of the conciliar events Theodosius appointed a small cadre of leading bishops to ensure the doctrinal message both went out to the wider Church, and was observed. The legate he appointed for the East was St Gregory of Nyssa.

The manuscripts attribute seven canons to the council. The more ancient Greek manuscript collections contain only four, however, and the old Latin versions that were made of the canonical list, similarly only know of the first four. The first three of these were read out word for word and endorsed at Chalcedon in 451. Canons 5 through 7 therefore appear as later addenda. In the sixth century the Byzantine canonist John Scholastikos added canons 5 and 6 to the recorded list of authoritative rulings, but he does not seem to know of the seventh which is a more elaborated form of the canon 8 of Nicaea detailing how to receive converts. The Constantinopolitan canons were either promulgated at the end of the synod in 381, or at the Synod of Constantinople in 382, which was called together in that following year as a kind of additional review body, and which, if it did originate the canons, appended them to the authority of the council of 381, not seeing itself as a separate *conciliabulum.* We know that something similar happened later in the seventh century in the case of the Council in Trullo (Quinisext) which added canons to the fifth and sixth Oecumenical Councils retrospectively.

The first canon again gives us the whole *ethos* in a nutshell. The faith of the Council of Nicaea shall stand firm. Every heresy is anathematized.[23] The second canon turned its attention to the affairs of Constantinople without explicitly naming it. The chaos that had reigned there for years was due to its imperial role as capital city. It had thus solidly represented the Arian faith of the imperial court for decades and had little respect in the minds of the Nicene attendees of the synod. Nevertheless in recent times there had been a fiasco in relation to who was the proper Nicene incumbent of the city. St Gregory of Nazianzus had been sent there out of his retirement at Seleukia by Meletios and Eusebius of Samosata. He was a bishop, but had refused to administer the see given to him (Sasima) and had recently left his father's see (Nazianzus) after the death of his bishop-father. Both things were flagrantly in disregard of the canons. Even so, he was the leading pro-Nicene theologian of the age; and he proved his worth in defending Nicene Orthodoxy in a time when the city was still Arian and still without Theodosius' imperial protection. Such things counted for much. But Meletios who had sponsored him was also widely regarded as an uncanonical bishop. And Peter of Alexandria had tried by force to secure his own candidate for the throne of Constantinople under Gregory's

[23]Specifically the Arians (Eudoxios of Constantinople's party), the Radical Arians (Heterousiasts such as Eunomios and Aetios), the Macedonians (Pneumatomachians), the Sabellians, the followers of Marcellus of Ancyra, the Photinians (Psilanthropists), and the Apollinarists.

eyes (the affair of Maximus the Cynic which is rendered void by canon 4). If the episcopal succession in the royal city could not be better managed, there was little hope for other places; so this canon tries to bring order into the chaos by setting out the generic principle that bishops should not go outside their own Churches "to bring confusion to other Churches." A system was clearly pointed up that was to follow historical precedent: "Let the bishop of Alexandria administer the affairs of Egypt strictly by the canons,[24] and let the bishops of the East administer the affairs of the East on their own."[25] Antioch was to retain its historic privileges, but the point is clear enough: "Let the Pontic bishops order only Pontic matters, and the Thracian bishops only Thracian." Let each synod mind its own business, first and foremost. The synodical principle is reaffirmed at the end of this canon, and those areas that do not have a traditional metropolitan structure are assigned to the "custom that has prevailed since the time of the fathers."

There is no trace in this second canon of any special privileges being wished upon Constantinople as a capital city: But the sense of the city's honor as a capital is certainly implicit in the way the interference of Rome and Alexandria is being deliberately slapped back and the affairs and independence of the East are affirmed. Reference is made to the sixth canon of Nicaea that sketched out the precedences of the ancient super-sees. This system should prevail as a general model. However, the very next decree makes a monumental step forward for the affairs of the capital city. It was a step too far for Rome and Alexandria who resented both canons 2 and 3 and resisted them for some time afterwards. They had seen the long-term implications all too clearly from the very beginning. The third canon establishes a new ordering of the system of the super-sees, and radically dislocates Alexandria. Canon 3 states: "The Bishop of Constantinople, however, shall have the prerogative of honor after the Bishop of Rome because Constantinople is the New Rome." Eventually Rome and Alexandria acceded to this ruling, but only after much tension. It effectively re-ordered the whole system of precedence in the East. But it can also be argued that it made a fault-line down the Church's international polity; and this because Rome (which had long understood itself as the senior see of the Christian world, with universal supervisory responsibilities and the right to hear legal appeal from all other Churches) understood this canon merely to be an impertinent one. It read it, therefore in the sense that New Rome would "come after" Old Rome as the second see of the world, displacing Alexandria from that role. But what many

[24]Implying as a canonical chairman but not as a prince-bishop.

[25]The bishop of Rome had intervened in the succession at Antioch and put in another contender under the nose of Meletios, greatly weakening the authority of this Nicene bishop by splitting his party with an ultra-Nicene and pro-western bishop. The Antioch affair was a very sore point at Constantinople I with most Greek-speaking bishops determined to punish this western intervention they resented very deeply.

in the East read it as proclaiming (necessitating a revisiting of that canon at Chalcedon in 451) was that Rome enjoyed its prestige and ecclesiastical rank mainly because it was the capital city of the empire. Now that Old Rome was no longer the imperial capital city, a rank that had passed to New Rome, it followed (did it not?) that the rank of Constantinople should now ascend to primary place, that is "come after" (succeed) Rome as the new leading see. However, these two interpretations of the phrase "come after" (immediate inferior ranking, and temporal succession/promotion) were to be matters that would mark all subsequent Church history and eventually would account for the great splitting apart of the Greek and Latin Churches. From this time onwards the city of Constantinople rose in prominence, attracting to itself a greater and greater ecclesiastical territory from the regions of Thrace and Asia Minor. By the time of Chalcedon less than a century later its undisputed imperial status was matched by an unrivalled ecclesiastical prestige and the privileges afforded to it in the synodical process were to be revisited significantly in canon 28 of Chalcedon 451.

Of the remaining canons attached to the council, canon 6 is an interesting and considered judgment on how to deal with accusations laid against bishops in their dioceses. It is decreed here that, if it concerns a matter of personal and simple justice (a bishop accused by someone of fraud or violent behavior or suchlike), then no enquiry shall be made as to the character of the accuser: For whether he is Christian or not, the synod states, matters of justice should be available to all freely and openly. But, if it concerns an ecclesiastical matter, and because so many heretics and dissidents are deliberately using the system to unsettle bishops whose theology they challenge, then the synod decrees that a careful investigation shall be made into the character of the complainer. If they are heretical, or under an ecclesiastical censure of any kind, their accusations shall not be forwarded directly. If they appear to have a genuine case, however, then their protests shall be forwarded to the local synod for discussion. The accusers shall also make a written promise to undergo the same canonical penalties that would have fallen on the accused bishop, if their case if found to be frivolous. The canon is an early and interesting study in limiting law as a political weapon by curtailing legal indemnity and instituting a prior process of scrutiny of cases.

The Council of Ephesus—431

The Council of Ephesus[26] was held in the summer of 431 in the magnificent city of Ephesus, Asia Minor. The ruins there are still a wonder of the ancient world. It was

[26]For a fuller historical account see McGuckin (1994, 2001).

occasioned by the dispute that arose between the Churches of Constantinople and Alexandria. Nestorius, the newly-appointed Archbishop of Constantinople, held to an Antiochene style of Christology which laid stress on the humanness of Jesus and the separateness of the human Jesus (and all his relevant human characteristics or *idiomata*) from the divine Logos who inhabited or indwelt the man Jesus. At its extreme form, the Antiochene Christology (as taught by Diodore of Tarsus or Theodore of Mopsuestia in the generation before Nestorius) had even suggested a distinction between the Logos and the man Jesus. This style of speaking was known as "Two Sons" Christology: that there was a way of speaking about the divine Son of God, and another way of speaking about the human Son of Man. Many who were not privy to this style of discourse felt this to be an alarming way of cutting off the "man" from the divine Logos, almost a revisiting of the ancient heresy of Adoptionism (the divinity inhabiting Jesus as if he were a human host for a short time). Cyril, the Archbishop of Alexandria found that Nestorius was propagating his doctrine all over the Middle East and reacted strongly against it. Cyril followed in the tradition of Athanasius, and taught a Christology which saw the divine Logos as so intimately united with the human condition that even the body of Jesus was in a real sense "divinized"; it was still a real human body that could (and did) die, but it was also a body that proved life-giving by its divine touch (miracles and so forth) and proved immortal by virtue of its resurrection. Where Nestorius above all else wanted a strict and severe separation of statements appropriate to the man Jesus, from those that were appropriate to the divine Logos, Cyril on the contrary delighted in stressing the paradoxical element of Christian thought about the indissoluble intimacy of divine and human in the One Lord Jesus: thoughts and utterances such as "God's death," and "God's flesh," thoughts that were contradictory on one level (God cannot die, God has no materiality) but which were to be understood, in the light of the incarnation, as essential statements of redemption theology. Cyril's more paradoxical Christology was evidently mystical in tone and inspiration, whereas that of Nestorius was dominated by logical semantic concerns. The argument between the two hierarchs took on an international aspect and the Emperor Theodosius II realized it was necessary to call another Oecumenical council to settle it.

The intellectual controversy fixed on some technical terms: one of the most famous was the issue of the *Theotokos*, or title "Mother of God." Nestorius had vetoed this as being at best, foolish, and at worst, heretical. Being eternal, God could not have a mother. Christians, he argued, must say instead that Mary was the "Mother of the Christ" or the "Mother of Jesus," but not the "Mother of God" because, "strictly speaking,"[27] it was not God who was born from her, but Jesus the Christ. Cyril countered by arguing that if Mary was not, strictly speaking, the

[27]His favorite phrase: *akribos*.

Mother of God, then the one who was born from her (Jesus) was not, strictly speaking, God. Thus he accused Nestorius of denying the divinity of Jesus. This was a new argument, because Nicaea had not clarified the relationship of Jesus to the divine, only the relation of the Logos to the divine by virtue of its term "homoousios" and its *anathemata.* Cyril maintained that the Logos assumed a human body, perfect in every regard, although it was not a distinct human person in its own right. In other words there were not two persons in the Christ; one the person of the divine Logos, the other the human person Jesus of Nazareth, but, rather, one single person. This was the divine and eternal person of God the Word, who in a specific time and place had assumed to himself a human body, and lived as a man by means of that body, for a specific purpose: to communicate with his human creation. When Nestorius said that this was a foolishly mythical view, Cyril countered by saying that it was an incomprehensible view, but clearly God's chosen plan of providential salvation which ought not to be mocked because it did not fit with the "wisdom of the world."

For his part, Nestorius taught that Jesus of Nazareth was a servant, a human being, who emptied himself out in the service of God the Logos who inhabited him. This is largely what he thought, but he did not wish to fall into the trap of agreeing to Cyril's hostile arguments that this meant he had resurrected Adoptionism. Nestorius did not support the Adoptionist heresy, but it might be fair to say that he did not have a really good argument to explain to his opponents why his views were different to Adoptionism. As a result his theology was obscure and less focused than Cyril's. He fell from grace at the Council of Ephesus, and after several years of further protests and refusals to be silent, the emperor condemned him to lifelong exile in the African desert. The council was so stormy and bad-tempered in its process that for years afterwards the Syrian and Alexandrian Churches would not speak with one another. The Syrian bishops arrived very late (weeks overdue) and, finding that Cyril had assumed the presidency and carried on without them, they held a separate council across the city, and anathematized all the majority council, who forthwith anathematized all the Syrian conciliarists. The imperial court had to cancel all conciliar sessions and hold the bishops in the city under supervision while it conducted a series of inquiries at the capital to see what had really happened. Later that year the emperor finally declared in favor of the majority council led by Cyril, and confirmed the deposition of Nestorius. For several years afterwards the court sponsored an international attempt to get Syria and Egypt to speak with one another again. A second attempt to patch up the quarrel by a large conciliar meeting went horribly wrong in 449. Flavian, the Archbishop of Constantinople, was beaten senseless on that occasion by rioting monks who felt he had disrespected their Alexandrian Archbishop, Dioscorus. Flavian subsequently died from his injuries. The resulting international scandal led to the immediate voiding of the decisions of

Ephesus 449 and the summoning of another council at Chalcedon in the year 451. Only Ephesus 431 would be retained in the listing of the truly Oecumenical Councils, while the Synod of Ephesus 449 was caustically described by St Jerome as *non concilium sed latrocinium*,[28] thus giving rise to its popular nomenclature as the "Brigandage of Ephesus."

The fraught nature of this large synod of 431, conceived first and foremost as a trial of major ideas and high ranking clergy (either Nestorius or Cyril was destined to be deposed from the most important offices in the Eastern Church), meant that all the vast effort expended tended to be on the clarification of highly technical theological positions. St Cyril put all the resources of the chancery of Alexandria to play in assembling a major dossier of patristic writings to defend the traditional nature of his doctrine. From this time onwards it became standard procedure in the Eastern Church to advance doctrinal points only in reference to patristic precedents. The canons are accordingly few in number, although the acts of the council that are extant now run to over a thousand pages, so careful were the imperial stenographers to get this all down since they saw that it was destined to become a legal nightmare.

There are eight canons emanating from the Council. Our rule of thumb applies still. The first canon in the series gives the *ethos* and is addressed against those clergy who have broken with the acts of the synod and gone over to support the condemned bishop Nestorius. It attacks bishop Celestios as one of the blatant "seceders." He was a pro-Syrian bishop who formed part of the main assembly that condemned Nestorius, but, when the Syrian bishops eventually arrived[29] and denounced the Cyrilline presidency, he literally went over the road to join the Syrian secessionists. The conciliar fathers proceeded to anathematize him for retracting his decision and judgment and to censure all who stood against their synodical decrees. If they were bishops or metropolitans they were to be held as automatically suspended from office and subject to their own local synod's decree of deposition. The canon sounds robust and firm. It was aimed at the Syrian Synod, however, and we see immediately a limit to legal decree: more or less the whole Syrian Archdiocese simply disregarded it. It was a point of learning: although the Council of Ephesus 431 already calls itself an "Oecumenical Council" in this canon, its effectiveness is not automatically assured. The extent of the imperial involvement in the conciliar aftermath, patiently brokering ecclesiastical agreements[30] and working on the premise all the time that this canon had never been enacted, demonstrates how much even an oecumenical synodical system needed the management and author-

[28]"Not a Council of the Church, rather a gathering of brigands."

[29]Cyril had accused them of deliberately dragging their feet so that the condemnation of their former colleague could be done before they arrived.

[30]Culminating in the *Formula of Reunion* in 433 (Cyril's Epistle: "Let the Heavens Rejoice").

ity of the civic legal system to support it. After this era of the Theodosian dynasty, it is established that the emperor alone can call an Oecumenical Synod by issuing an imperial *sacra*. His legal decree is necessary at the conclusion, so as to place the conciliar canons on the footing of imperial law. This foundation of Theodosius II's religious policy was to last throughout Byzantine times. It states the important *caveat* that in the middle of these two acts, the bishops themselves, not the court officials, are to have charge of the theological and canonical arguments.

Canons 2, 3, 4, 6, and 7 of Ephesus more or less simply reiterate the first. All senior clergy who were not present at the Ephesine council but who go over to the Syrian dissidents are to be held as deposed. All who have been deposed by Nestorius for their orthodox opinions are to be held as restored. In canon 5 all whom Nestorius and his supporters (meaning John of Antioch) attempt to rehabilitate will remain deposed. All of the canons are directly and primarily juridical in character, setting up anathematizations of those who had flouted its authority, i.e., the Syrian Archdiocese.

The eighth and last canon is slightly different in appearance but more or less on the same lines as the first and its echoes in the other six. It declares that Cyprus shall be an autocephalous Church. This is a privilege enjoyed even to this day by the Archbishops of Cyprus. The canon claims that this Church had an ancient apostolic foundation which had been illegitimately usurped: "an innovation contrary to ecclesiastical constitutions." What was at stake here was that John, the Archbishop of Antioch, had been asserting his rights as "super-see" to have metropolitan jurisdiction over the affairs of Cyprus which from time immemorial had fallen into the remit of the Syrian Church, but which did not feel they fitted there in present circumstances. The bishop of Cyprus, present at Ephesus and a close ally of Cyril's, saw his chance to detach his Church from the ambit of the Syrian archdiocese which they had so roundly been condemning. The Cyrilline council agreed gladly to their petition to be freed of the jurisdiction of Antioch, adopting it as another way of censuring Syrian behavior and practically reducing its ecclesiastical sway in the future.

The Council of Chalcedon–451

This major council was held immediately after the death of Theodosius II in an imperial palace at Chalcedon, a suburb of Constantinople, in 451. It was a serious effort to reconcile the divisions that had continued to plague the Church after the council of Ephesus I, 431, particularly after the exacerbation caused by the Synod of Ephesus in 449. Major rifts had continued between the Syrian Churches and

Alexandria. In the lifetime of Cyril, Rome had been very much on the side of Alexandria, but after his death in 444 his successor Dioscorus had alienated feeling on all sides by his methods and one-sided way of reading his predecessor. The Roman Church had come to agree with the Syrians that a decided stress on the two-natured reality of Christ was called for: that is, that the Christ had a divine nature and also a human nature, quite distinct. The Alexandrians and many other easterners felt that this created an intolerably divided and artificial view of Christ. The Council of Chalcedon studied the works of Cyril, and also a letter sent by Pope Leo (*Leo's Tome*[31]) which set out the doctrine of two natures. Cyril had preferred the concept of two natures (God and man) "before the Union" (the union that took place within the incarnation) but only one composite nature "after the Union," arguing that otherwise it could not be called a union at all.

By the time of Chalcedon, Cyril had been dead for seven years. The majority of bishops at the council wished to be loyal to his tradition, but were also pressed heavily by Emperor Marcian to represent the Roman and Syrian views (which had been forcibly ruled out of order at Ephesus 449) in so far as these could be reconciled. Eventually a compromise was worked out that met the terms of the Roman letter but was also in harmony with the doctrine of Ephesus 431: Christ had two natures, one divine and one human, but he only had one person. This person was wholly and utterly divine and pre-existent, and it was this person who adopted a human nature in the womb of Mary. There was thus, strictly speaking, no human person in Jesus: only a divine person made flesh. This definitive rejection of Adoptionism stated that at no time could Jesus be regarded as "merely a man" or "simply a man," for from his birth he was the Divine Word appearing in a human body. This remains the standard of Christological orthodoxy, although in the twentieth century it was again much controverted in western Christianity. Ostensibly, the council was called to settle the Eutychian or Monophysite heresy (those who maintained Jesus only had one, divine, nature). In reality it was called to reconcile the differing traditions of Rome, Syria and Alexandria. While adopting the *Tome of Leo* as an orthodox text, the council fathers clearly stated all their theology in phrases borrowed from Cyril's writings, and anathematized leading members of the Syrian tradition who were now dead, repeating the condemnation of Nestorius. The resentments left smoldering at Chalcedon were destined to flare into life again.

[31]A document that drew up traditional statements about Christ from the earlier Latin Fathers. It was offered by Pope Leo of Rome as the definitive text to resolve international Christological controversies: it never assumed that status in the East because its archaic formulation of the Christological problem seemed to most of the Greeks at Chalcedon a regressive step, and also because much of its terminology "sounded like" Nestorianism (though it was not).

The Canons of Chalcedon are thirty in number[32] and hold a high rank in the legal system of the Eastern Church. At Chalcedon the canonists were looking to the Antiochene corpus, which they refer to several times. The first of the Chalcedonian canons sets the tone for what the conciliar fathers specifically wanted to do in their legislation: "We have judged it proper that the canons of the holy fathers made in all the synods up to the present, should remain in force." The system of canon law as it had been developing throughout the fourth and early fifth centuries is here given affirmation by the highest synodical authority possible: a synod that already sees itself invested with the status of an "Oecumenical Council," summoned by the imperial authority from the world's highest sees to adjudicate matters of the highest importance and most pressing urgency. Their very first legislative decree is to rationalize the whole collation of laws that has been growing up organically as a "tradition of the holy fathers" and give it oecumenical endorsement. Of course, the terms of the decree are hopelessly vague. Although it endorses the synodical decrees, it omits specific reference to the canonical epistles and decrees of the holy fathers, which were also at the core of the "tradition of the fathers," and legislatively speaking it is indeterminately unfocused: did it really mean all the canons of every synod? What it meant to specify was primarily the formative fourth century synods we have previously reviewed; those synods that clustered around and before Nicaea, and enjoyed wide status in the fourth century Church, but which did not fall under the remit of the oecumenical synodical system. Their legislation had evidently attained high status and repute before Chalcedon vindicated it further. But the decree leaves things hanging. A century later the Emperor Justinian will give a heaver weight of law for the same motive as manifested here. His Novel 131 states "We honor the doctrinal decrees of the first four (oecumenical) councils as we honor Scripture. We honor the canons given or approved by them as we honor the [civil] laws." Another century on, at the Synod in Trullo, the ecclesiastical lawyers give precision to Chalcedon's vagueness, lifting up specifically which of the local synods' decrees are to be given an "enduring" status. What has emerged as a new issue, of course, is that the oecumenical synod, being the highest legislative assembly in the Church, ought to be the highest authority for sifting, collating, authorizing, and clarifying, all the legislation in the Church that is intended for universal application and to have enduring generic validity. Eastern canon law looks back to Chalcedon and the Council of Trullo as two specific moments when this oecumenical principle is enshrined.

[32]Canon 29, although accepted as a legislative rule of Chalcedon, is not part of the strict list of canons but an appendage from the acts of the fourth session of the council addressed to the cases of Photius of Tyre and Eustathius of Beirut. Photius had ordained bishops whose ordinations Eustathius, as metropolitan, had set aside, ordering them to return to the presbyteral status.

Most of the other canons of the council address abuses within the Church. The second deals with simoniacal ordinations. As high offices of state, as well as of the Church, it appears that bishop's ordinations were being dealt with as political and career moves, as early as the fourth century. Palladius in his *Dialogue on the Life of St John Chrysostom* tells his readers that the saint (acting as metropolitan of the Asian region) deposed the bishop of Ephesus and six other bishops on the charge of simony. "Antoninus of Ephesus," Palladius says, "had made it his business to sell off ordinations to the episcopate at a rate proportionate to the value of the see in question." The practice had continued with sufficient regularity as to merit a generic rule that all those proven to have ordained for financial reasons were to be deposed and those ordained in such contexts were to be held as not appointed at all. Clergy attempting to bribe[33] their way to office were to be deposed from whatever rank they did hold, and laity[34] were to be anathematized. The third canon addresses clergy and tries to regulate their behavior by forbidding them secular business careers, with the exception of state-ordered guardianships of minors and episcopally-ordered governance of the affairs of orphans and widows. All the clerical ranks and monastics were also forbidden to engage in secular business at the risk of ecclesiastical penalties. Throughout history, it was a canon that was weakly followed through, for it did not specify alongside its prohibition the terms of necessary balance: namely that the clergy ought to be provided for securely and sufficiently from the funds of the Church. In the great cities, such as Constantinople, this was presumably a simple matter of an imperial budget allotted to the clergy on the payroll of the "Great Church." In the provinces, however, it was far from clear that the local Church would ever have enough resources to fund all its clergy, without them having to undertake a trade or profession to support themselves and their families. In St Basil's time in Cappadocia (a very large see) we learn that most of the clergy worked in sedentary occupations in order to support themselves.[35] The canon, therefore, signals a principle that clergy ought not to be money-merchants, but does so in a less than clear manner in its specific legislative text. The seventh canon reasserts this in a slightly different form, ordering the censure of those who had once been enrolled as clergy but have since elected to follow a military career or accept a civic dignity; both being code words for taking high imperial office for personal gain. Here we see the underscoring of the desire to make the clergy stand apart as a sacral profession.

[33]The euphemism was to give "eulogiae" or blessings. The giving of eulogiae was a universal and constant custom of the Church in both East and West. The council, however, is signifying the penalty applicable for pushing that from a gift, towards being a significant financial incentive. By putting at risk the validity of all involved in simony, it made the likelihood of being totally de-legalized a radical disincentive to corruption.

[34]For the bishops of large sees held the keys to the access of several prestigious church-paid posts.

[35]Basil, Letter 198.1.

To ensure a proper standard of accounting and accountability in fiscal matters, Canon 26 demands that each bishop must appoint an *oikonomos* in his Church to administer the business affairs properly and to remove from the high priesthood the stigma of the least suspicion of financial maladministration. Canon 29 offers an important signal of the special role and authority of the episcopate. It had evidently been an occasional practice up until that time to discipline an offending cleric by deposing him in degree; that is, instead of entirely reducing him to lay status, to demote him. Some bishops had been reduced to the status of the presbyterate. The Council of Chalcedon decreed that it was henceforth a sacrilege to so reduce a bishop. If they had been disciplined for good cause, they were not to be accounted worthy of continuing exercise of priestly ministry in the ranks of the presbyters. If they had been so reduced for no good cause, they were to retain the status and function of the episcopate.

Monasticism and its governance by the episcopal order is also high on the agenda at Chalcedon. Canon 4 attempts to rein back the growing power of the monasteries by putting a limit on monastics who become politically powerful leaders. The foundation of monasteries is made subordinate to the will of the local bishop[36] who is also called upon to support them with due financial provision. The monks, however, are ordered not to engage in ecclesiastical or state politics, but to live in a stable way in the houses giving themselves over only to prayer and fasting. This too was a law that stated an intent (focusing all ecclesiastical precedence and significance in the local bishop) but it never had a real effect in Eastern Church history. Monastics always did (and still do) travel round a parallel network of ecclesiastical pathways, much more fluidly than bishops did. A highly intelligent and capable monastic could thus exercise a powerfully influential role at court and, if the emperor appreciated his talents, there was not much a bishop could do about it. What we witness here in the Chalcedonian decree is a first alarm at seeing the phenomenal rise of monastic power in the governance systems of the Church. In a short time the monastics were to wholly subsume the episcopate in any case. Throughout all Byzantine times monastics were far more free-ranging than their western equivalents. The dominant concept of *stabilitas loci* that Benedict imposed on his monks never applied to anything like the same degree. The fifth and sixth canons tried to enforce this rule of stability by once more asserting bishops should not roam; and as for clergy, no-one ought to be ordained "without a charge," that is without a specific post and occupation in mind. There must be no abstract ordinations or roving clerics. This decree has been of great use in Christian history for steering the priestly offices away from the ever-present temptation to become "ranks

[36]Later, provision will be made for patriarchal (*stavropegial*) monasteries independent of the local bishop.

and dignities" and to insist that they remain what they originally were, apostolic duties. To this day no one can be ordained *in abstractu*, without "title"[37] or altar. The same determination to stamp out roaming career clerics forms the substance of canon 10, canon 13 which demands that travelling clergy must carry commendatory letters from their local bishops, and canon 20 that forbids a bishop to receive a cleric assigned to the Church of another bishop (excepting the cases of genuine refugee necessity). This was a move that was directed against the slippage of clergy from the provinces and towards the great cities, especially Constantinople. Canon 23 likewise appeals to the state authorities to banish the growing number of clergy and monks who come to the capital on the grounds of seeking legal appeals, but who decide to remain there indefinitely, "raising disturbances and troubling the ecclesiastical condition, and turning men's houses upside down." The *Ekdikos*, or "Grand Advocate of the Church," is given the authority to notify them of their requirement to depart, and to expel them, if necessary.

Canon 8, asserting that all monks shall be subject to the bishop, gives further evidence of the anxiety that current tension between monastic and episcopal status was giving the hierarchs. Constantinople acted as a magnet to ascetics from the earliest times. There were numerous holy men in the city with large groups of disciples and with even larger circles of lay dependents and followers, many of whom held high office in the imperial service. Throughout the history of Constantinople (probably less so in other cities of the Greek world), this tension formed a significant dynamic in Church governance.[38] Canon 18 echoes it once more: forbidding all "ganging together" of clerics against their bishop, rattling the sabre that this is tantamount to the state crime of conspiracy (though it was not, and was not treated as such). This was a move that further underscored the authority of a bishop over the subordinate clergy of his diocese, and removed the *locus* of complaint against the bishop from the clerical assembly to the provincial synod.[39]

Canons 9 and 12 relate to the tension between civil law and developing ecclesiastic law. The establishment of dioceses in the Church followed the pattern of

[37] *Titulus beneficii* as it later came to be designated.

[38] Canon 24 sets a limit on lay patronage of monasteries, forbidding temporary gifts of property or money to monastic use (a significant tax advantage that was sometimes rescinded by the nobility–when they wanted their capital back for whatever reason). Capital endowment of monasteries had now to be legally permanent: the gift could not be rescinded. The canonist Joseph the Egyptian rendered this into Arabic in his collection of canons in the form: "If anyone turns a monastery into a private home for himself... let him be cursed and held anathema" (Percival [1900] 284). It has never seemed to trouble the English aristocracy, doubtless because of their small acquaintance with Arabic.

[39] Canon 21 similarly restricts the potentiality of individual clergy or laity to issue charges against a bishop. Those wishing to advance a complaint must subject themselves to "scrutiny" of character. It is a digest, in essence, of canon 6 of the Council of Constantinople 381, which sets out a more judicious version of the principle of scrutiny.

the civic dioceses, and had done so for a long time when Chalcedon became aware of the problems that this might raise. In the ninth canon a cleric is forbidden to have recourse to the civic system of legal redress, but has to follow the ecclesiastical system: appeals being made first to the bishop, and if the bishop is the cause of complaint, to the metropolitan, or the exarch of the diocese, or to the Archbishop of Constantinople. This is a clear indication of the emergence of the throne of Constantinople as a court of highest appeal. Later canons of Chalcedon will elevate the concept even higher. Canon 12 notes that certain bishops had successfully petitioned the imperial court to make divisions of the dioceses into smaller units and then claimed the title and jurisdiction of metropolitans of the new regions. The canon directs that if this happens independently of the initiation of the synod, then the new metropolitanate (since the clergy cannot control the political aspect of the decision) shall be a metropolitanate in name only, and the previous Church precedences shall hold force (again removing the incentive for individual bishops to initiate any appeal to civil law over the head of the canons).[40] Canon 17 underscores this in a highly influential way. Civic divisions are henceforth to carry ecclesiastic force as well, with the Church adapting to the new civic boundaries.[41] Country divisions are to remain subject to the large city to which they have been traditionally attached for the last thirty years, if this has been an undisputed relationship. If it is has been problematic in the last thirty years, the matter can be referred again to the judgment of local synod and then, if necessary, to the higher appeals process already instantiated: the diocesan exarch, then the throne of Constantinople. Here the issue of boundaries and jurisdictional principles is being clarified and ordered.

Several more canons relate to the governance of clergy, and the setting of standards for other orders. Readers and singers are specifically addressed in canon 14, with a view to regularizing their marriages and especially how their children marry. They must not marry "across the line of heresy," but even the minor clergy of the Church have to set a standard, and only allow their children to be baptized and communicate and marry within the Orthodox faith. The context for this decree was the widespread divisions then operating (especially in Syria, Palestine and Egypt) between the advocates of the "Eutychian Monophysites" and the advocates of the two-nature Christology defended by Chalcedon. Often the same families witnessed

[40]It was specifically referring to the case of Eustathius of Berytus who had taken advantage of an imperial honor given to his city to declare himself and six other bishops (whom he declared to be his new synod with him as Metropolitan) thereby freed of ecclesiastical obedience to Photios of Tyre. Photios had complained to the emperor, and Marcian referred the judgment to the Council.

[41]A principle that was to cause significant disruption among the Orthodox Churches after the fall of Byzantium and the rise of independent Orthodox nation states: to wit, who had the right to declare new civic boundaries?

divisions of faith within the immediate unit as well as the wider kin.[42] Canon 15 states that no deaconess shall be ordained by the laying on of hands who is less than forty,[43] and who has not "been subject to intense scrutiny"; a code for virginally upright life. If the deaconess is married after ordination ("despising the grace of God") both she and her husband are to be anathematized. The canon clearly shows that the female diaconate was an office open to senior ascetic women. In Constantinople, however, it was also an office sought after by many highly placed and wealthy noble women. Olympias, supporter and friend of St John Chrysostom, is an example. Such women may well have lived a significantly long life as dedicated virgins, but then have elected marriage for reasons of inheritance or political power. Pulcheria, the empress who jointly convened Chalcedon, was one such example: she sent shockwaves through the Church when, after years as a dedicated virgin, she married Marcian for dynastic reasons in order to stabilize the throne after the accidental death of her brother Theodosius II. Canon 16, which roundly declares the marrying of dedicated virgins is forbidden on pain of excommunication, wisely allows a let-out clause (surely with the empress in mind) that: "The bishop shall have the power of indulgence towards them." Canons 25 and 27 similarly relate to moral standards in clerical life.

It is canon 28 which is perhaps the most famous of all the canons of this council. It had a massive influence in the polity of the Eastern Church, and caused, at the time, much division (for Rome especially resisted it[44]) and some Syrian and Egyptian canonists[45] also simply decided not to list it at all. It concerns the special status of the see of Constantinople, which has already featured in several canons as having a role in the Christian East as final legal arbiter of canonical cases. The canon sets out clearly the basis for Constantinople's juridical status and thus its precedence. It begins by re-stating the terms of the third canon of the Council of Constantinople I 381, which originally had read "The Bishop of Constantinople,

[42]A century later even Justinian and Theodora his wife supported different sides of the Monophysite-Chalcedonian divide.

[43]Well past menopausal age in antiquity.

[44]It was for a long time the reason Rome had ambivalence over the council of Chalcedon: accepting its doctrinal decisions and quibbling over its canons. Pope Leo wrote to Pulcheria (Letter 105) about canon 28: "I declare it to be invalid and annul it by the authority of the holy Apostle Peter." But his neighbors the Illyrian bishops subscribed to it within the year, a fact Leo ruefully acknowledges in a second letter to Pulcheria (Letter 116), and no one took any notice of Rome's objections in the East, nor were they then (or afterwards) impressed that he had any special "Petrine" authority to annul or set aside a conciliar judgment.

[45]Resenting the triumph of Constantinople over Alexandria and Antioch, at a time when large areas of both patriarchates seceded from the Byzantine church world because of doctrinal issues arising out of Chalcedonian doctrine. Dionysius Exiguus omits it from his list of the canons (because of Roman antipathies), so too do the canonists Isidore, John of Antioch, and Joseph the Egyptian.

however, shall have the prerogative of honor after the Bishop of Rome; because Constantinople is the New Rome." But now the context is clearly and decidedly different. What had been a matter of honor and precedence (*proedria*) now becomes an issue of jurisdictional superiority (*prostasia*). Canon 28 reads:

> Following in all things the decisions of the holy fathers, and acknowledging the canon which has just been read of the 150 bishops beloved of God who assembled in the imperial city of Constantinople, which is New Rome, in the time of the Emperor Theodosius of blessed memory,[46] we also enact and decree the same things concerning the privileges of the most holy Church of Constantinople which is New Rome. For the fathers rightly granted privileges to the throne of Old Rome, because it was the royal city. And the 150 most religious bishops, moved by the same consideration, gave equal privileges[47] to the most holy throne of New Rome, judging most correctly that the city which is honored with the sovereignty and the Senate, and enjoys equal privileges with the old imperial Rome should also be magnified in ecclesiastical matters also, just as she is, and rank next after her. Accordingly in the Pontic, Asian, and Thracian dioceses the Metropolitans only (as well as those bishops of these dioceses who are among the barbarians) should be ordained by the aforementioned most holy throne of the most holy church of Constantinople. Every Metropolitan of these dioceses together with the bishops of his province should ordain their own province's bishops as has been set forth by the godly canons. But the Metropolitans of the aforementioned dioceses should be ordained by the Archbishop of Constantinople, after the proper elections have been held according to custom and have been reported to him.

The canon went far beyond the statute established by Canon 3 of Constantinople I, effectively giving to the imperial city a vast ecclesiastical hinterland of influence. When the city had been founded by Constantine in 330, it was ecclesiastically a parvenu. It had no territory of its own and was constantly subjected to the claims of the ancient sees of Alexandria and Antioch which ranked above it in canonical precedent. As it grew in major importance as a center of world affairs, the true seat of the Roman Empire, so it grew in weight as an ecclesiastical center. Such a development can be seen at the Council of Constantinople in 381, where it was reasserted as a center of Orthodoxy (to remain such ever after for the East). At Ephesus 431 the status of Antioch was seriously weakened because of the canonical and theological behavior of the so-called "Orientals." At Ephesus 449 and again at Chalcedon 451, the status and weight of Alexandria was equally weakened because of its canonical and theological behavior. Thus it was felt that the time had indeed come to remove

[46]Canon 3 of Constantinople 1.
[47]*isa presbeia.*

any doubt as the interpretation of Constantinople's ecclesiastical standing: the purpose of this present canon. There can be no doubt but that was the intention of canon 3 of Constantinople I. Even so, that rule was ambivalent, and capable of suggesting that Constantinople ranked second after Old Rome, that is, remained inferior and subject to her. The Chalcedonian iteration removes that possible interpretation, giving to New Rome the same rights and privileges of Old Rome (indeed far greater ones) in the matter of legal court of appeal and jurisdictional influence over large dioceses in the East. It retains for Old Rome only a priority of rank in precedence or honor, protocol as it were.

The Roman version of the super-episcopal authority which it enjoyed was already (since the time of Pope Damasus in the late fourth century) theologically based around the notion of Peter's mystical presence in his Church.[48] The Roman popes were super bishops because they were the "vicars of St Peter."[49] The East neither recognized nor understood this particular approach. As affirmed several times from Nicaea through Chalcedon, civic legal divisions of the empire should be reflected in the Church's administrative patterns. To this one had to add the force of canonical custom (meaning Nicaea). This, but nothing in the manner of a special Petrine office, was the context of the canonical judgment of Chalcedon. It drew protests from the Roman delegates present in the assembly, especially the next day when what had happened seemed to sink in to them; but these did not move the conciliar fathers to change their minds. Chalcedon's canon 28 reordered the precedences of the ancient sees so as to conform them to the new imperial division of affairs, with Constantinople as now the undisputed capital of the empire. It did not re-order them, as became the standard "reading" of this canon in the West, so as to be Old Rome first jurisdictionally, then New Rome, then Alexandria, Antioch and so on. It quite clearly orders them so that the affairs of the Eastern Church are under the single governance of New Rome as the last court of appeal. This is signified by the manner of ordaining the metropolitans of the vast surrounding hinterland of Pontus, Asia Minor and Thrace. Constantinople left Rome to supervise the affairs of the Latin Churches in its customary way, making no comment on the theory of Petrine privilege. This of course would be developed apace as a standard way of interpreting all canonical systems in the West, so that before long papal decretal ranked higher than synodical canon there. But this never happened in the East. And when the canonical and ecclesiological principles at stake because of the rise of the papacy first became universally visible (in the ninth century in the time of Photios the Great of Constantinople and Pope Nicholas of Rome) the collision course was

[48]A *theologoumenon* rising from the possession of the martyr's relics entombed in the city.

[49]A title only changed in the Middle Ages to being "Vicars of Christ."

set for what would even further down the road be the great parting of ways between the Christian Greek East and the Latin West.

Justinian gave canon 28 imperial legal force in his Novel 131; it was legally reaffirmed by the canon 36 of the Synod in Trullo, and again by Nicaea II in 787, which gave oecumenical sanction to all the canons of Trullo. The Roman Church refused to admit it after Leo's decision to annul it on the basis of the Petrine authority. But in 1215 the Fourth Lateran Council admitted its force in canon 5 of the same; moved to that end by the fact that Constantinople had fallen to the western crusader armies, and its patriarch was now, and would remain so for a generation, a Latin cleric.

The thirtieth and last of the Chalcedonian canons, like the twenty-ninth, is not a real canon at all, but a *notitia* from the synodical acts. It notes that the deposition of Dioscorus the Archbishop of Alexandria had taken place; but that then all the Egyptian bishops had claimed that they had no ecclesiastical precedent[50] to sign any canonical agreement without their "head."[51]

The Council of Constantinople II—553

The Fifth Oecumenical Council was again held in the capital city in 553, under the presidency of the Emperor Justinian, at a time when imperial affairs were being consolidated both civically and militarily, after years of decline. The Council was a reformation of church affairs, and specifically intended to bring an end to divisions that had sprung up in the aftermath of Chalcedon 451, with the consequent departure of large sections of Syrian and Egyptian Christianity from the confession of the "two natures" of Christ. The Christological divisions between "Chalcedonians" and "Monophysites" had blighted church unity in the East throughout the sixth century; Justinian was determined to resolve the conflict. The terms of this council largely veered away from the unsatisfactory compromise of Chalcedon and returned to the re-statement of Ephesus 431. The Council of 553 was always unpopular in the West because of its implied snub to Pope Leo. In the course of its deliberations the reluc-

[50]In the *fifth* century Alexandria retained a peculiar and ancient structure, unique to it in this age, that it had one effective archbishop (of the great city on the Mediterranean littoral) and hundreds of (more or less) suffragan bishops, who were country clergy bonded to the archbishop, often by oaths of loyalty. The synodical system elsewhere, presuming a chorus of learned city bishops with one Metropolitan in each region who was head of the large capital, simply did not apply in Late Antique Egypt.

[51]The conciliar fathers evidently did not wholly trust their decision not to sign the acts on this basis. The Roman delegates demanded that the Egyptians leave behind representatives and pledges in the capital until they returned with a new archbishop. The increasing departure from the remit of the Romano-Constantinopolitan axis of Orthodoxy of the anti-Chalcedonian Monophysites led to their ironic designation by the Byzantines as the *Akephaloi* the "headless ones."

tant Roman Pope Vigilius was dragged by the emperor to Constantinople to take part, and was there bullied into subservience. For such reasons the West took many years to recognize it as an Oecumenical Council. It eventually did so, but in western Church history most text books continued to stop their accounts at Chalcedon and often still continue to regard Chalcedon as the end of the story, whereas Constantinople II is a very significant readjustment of the theological argument. At Constantinople II the Syrian tradition was severely repressed and the Cyrilline doctrine of the single divine personhood of Christ was proclaimed as the definitive theology of the Church. Much of this bypassed western theological consciousness, then and now, which in antiquity and throughout the medieval period continued to read only the *Tome* of Pope Leo (an archaic and rather simplistic statement of Christological doctrine, but venerable in that it elevated only the ancient Latin fathers as its articulators) as its statement of belief.

There are no canons of Constantinople II as such. The conciliar business was taken up with the question of the retrospective condemnation of the leading Syrian Christological writers, the issue known now as the "Three Chapters;" that is, texts taken from Theodore of Mopsuestia, Theodoret of Cyrrh, and Ibas of Edessa. The theology of Cyril of Alexandria is elevated as the universal Church's surest guide, and a series of heresies is named and censured. This produced a series of fourteen *kephalaia* (*capitula* or chapters)[52] closely focused on theological matters. Justinian was also resolved to issue an empire-wide ban on the discussion or dissemination of the works of Origen, the great third century theologian, whose speculative mystical theories about preexistence of souls had caused immense controversy over several generations among the Church's international ascetic communities. Origen's name was probably[53] added to the eleventh *kephalaion*.[54] The emperor had decreed as early as 543 that Origen's works (in the conciliar *Acta* they are actually mainly excerpts from the treatises of Evagrius Pontikos) ought to be condemned and burned because they had been the basis of the heresy of the *Isochristoi*.[55] The acts of the Fifth Oecumenical Council, as we have them today, pass on from the *kephalaia* to a list of fifteen *anathemata* written against Origen (still conflating him with Evagrius). It is not at all sure whether these anathe-

[52]See Percival (1900) 312–316.

[53]Pope Vigilius cites the *Kephalaion* without seeming to know it mentions Origen; though the Imperial decree (the *Homonoia*) did mention him by name. Since the stenographers for the council were undoubtedly imperial scribes, the likelihood of conflation of agendas was of a very high order. But the conciliar fathers in session appear to have been predominantly concerned with the Christological heresy of the Syrians. We have no account of them discussing Origen's works.

[54]Some have thought it was added in to the list of heretics later; but early and widespread tradition existed that the council did censure Origen by name; and the Origenist monks of the Great Lavra in Palestine soon afterwards withdrew communion from the local bishops who signed the acts of this council, implying that the name was already there in *Kephalaion* 11.

[55]Evagrian ascetics who elevated the ideal of becoming as perfect as Christ.

mas issued from the conciliar fathers, were added later, or were appended by the imperial chancery as an afterthought. Scholarship is still divided on the matter. The lack of canons from the Fifth Oecumenical Council was retrospectively legislatively "repaired" by the Quinisext Council that attributed canons to the fifth and sixth, whose hierarchs were mainly concerned with dogmatic issues.

Constantinople III–681

This council, again held in the capital city, was the last of the seven great councils to be concerned wholly with Christological doctrine. It was in a sense a reopening of the Monophysite or Miaphysite dispute. These were the radical and uncompromising followers of St Cyril of Alexandria who regarded the adjustments he had made in his later and mature work as the lapses of a senile old man. They insisted that his earlier statement that the Word of God incarnate was "a single concrete reality /nature" (*mia physis*[56]) was definitive and ruled out the "two-nature" language of Chalcedon. In fact, the amendments Cyril made to his earliest thought were important realignments and adjustments he made to his vocabulary in the light of Syrian and Roman criticisms. By reverting to Cyril's early teaching, the Miaphysites utterly rejected the oecumenical status of Chalcedon. Even after Constantinople II they felt the point of the divinization of Christ's body, by virtue of its divine inhabitation, had been neglected. Their opponents felt that they in turn had underestimated the genuineness of the human condition of Jesus. The precise argument at this council was whether Christ had one will or two. That is, did he have one psychic center to his personality or a double center of motivation, namely a divine will (*thelema*) alongside a human one? If he had two this would explain how he could be tempted, and also how he could make genuinely human choices and entertain genuinely human feelings. If he only had one and it was asserted to be a human, then he could not be God. If he only had one and it was asserted to be divine, then the questions arose how he could be a real man, alongside men who are all fallible and capable of moral choices; whereas a divine will is fixed and incapable of variance. If avoiding this dilemma one asserted that the Christ had two psychic centers, then the implication was surely that he was not one person, but two: a God and a man fastened together in the same bodily shell. The "one-will" party was designated the "Monothelites." The two-will party had the name "Dyothelites." The argument would be settled in favor of the Dyothelite theologians. This was declared the posi-

[56]A phrase he used not more than half a dozen times in fact, and then abandoned when he saw its limits. *Mia physis* for Cyril did not mean "one nature" (*ousia*) but "one concrete reality" (*physis*) of the Christ.

tion closest to the spirit of the previous councils. Christ had to have two wills, in other words, otherwise he would not have possession of a perfect human nature. The earlier councils had defined that he had two natures: perfect manhood and perfect deity. On the other hand, the Council of Constantinople II insisted that these two wills only existed in theoretical distinction. In actuality, they were wholly united. In other words, just as Christ's humanity had never existed independently of the Divine Word (there was no human being called Jesus of Nazareth who had a separate life before the Logos took him over, but in fact the humanity only came into existence from the moment the Logos entered into the Virgin's womb and made for itself a human nature to represent it) so, too, the human will of Jesus (which was a fundamental part of that humanity) never had a separate existence from the divine will. It was a testimony to the perfect moral goodness of Jesus that the human will pertaining to his human nature always and at every moment served, and was subservient to, the will of God. Contemporary theologians argued much about the biblical text: "Not my will but thine be done,"[57] but the ultimate point was that the existence of two wills, always bound together in perfect harmony at each and every single moment, was a way of reaffirming Jesus' genuine manhood, while at the same time maintaining the doctrine from the Council of Ephesus 431 that there was only one divine person present in the Incarnate Logos, not a divine person alongside a human person. In the annals of later theology, Constantinople III is a little-known council that has not attracted much study despite its importance in terms of the difficulties of elaborating a Christian anthropology. It has grounds for being recognized as the first conciliar meeting of the Church where the principles of human freedom and individuation were laid out in principle and abstract.

The conciliar fathers anathematized the upholders of the Monothelite heresy across several decades previously, namely the Patriarchs of Constantinople Sergios, Pyrrhus, Paul and Peter; Honorius the Roman Pope, Cyrus the Pope and Patriarch of Alexandria, and Theodore, Bishop of Pharan in the Sinai. It issued no canons of its own, a deficiency that was repaired by the meeting of hierarchs at the Quinisext Council ten years later, held in the imperial city.

Constantinople–691
The Synod in Trullo–The Quinisext Council

The Quinisext Council,[58] held at Constantinople in 691, takes that name traditionally from not wishing (in the later reckoning of the lists of oecumenical synods) to

[57]Lk 22.42.
[58]See Ohme (2006).

be considered a separate council from the Fifth and Sixth Oecumenical Councils. It was assembled with the intention of being a reformist church synod, and added canons to the previous two great councils which lacked them. Many of the bishops who attended Constantinople III attended this meeting also. In its first canon, the Seventh Oecumenical Council designates this as the Sixth Oecumenical Council, considering it almost as an addendum (ten years later) to the acts of the synod of 681. Pope Hadrian II, in his letter to Patriarch Tarasius concerning the Seventh Oecumenical Council, accepts that designation also. The council took place in the same place as the Sixth Oecumenical, namely the great domed hall (*trullos*) of the imperial palace. From this it is also called the Synod "in Trullo."[59] More than three hundred bishops attended, with representation from all the Patriarchates and representatives from Rome.

It was summoned by Emperor Justinian II.[60] He was a highly effective military commander, intent on securing the borders of the Byzantine Empire and re-establishing Orthodoxy in its limits. He saw himself as a new Justinian the Great, and much of what he did can be understood in terms of that example of the earlier Justinianic policy (asserting strong guidance over the Church to bring it together, affirming the indivisible unity of the Latin and Greek provinces of the empire). Our following chapter, dedicated to the sixth century Justinianic revision of the imperial law, can give many insights into the seventh century mindset of Justinian II. Pressed by the Islamic Caliphate from outside, to whom he had to pay annual tribute, by Arabs and Slav rebels, and by dissensions within (he especially abhorred the Manichees and was determined to suppress them totally), Justinian II was the first emperor known to have had the image of Christ stamped on the imperial coinage. A few years before, in 689, he had successfully re-taken Thessalonike for the empire as its second city. It was his vision (since for almost all the Byzantine emperors religious Orthodoxy was the prime and direct cause of divine favor in political life) and his religious policy to fashion a strong moral renewal of Orthodoxy and reaffirm it as the univocal religious code for the united empire. To this end he summoned the bishops of the world to meet in the capital and systematize (that is, clear up some obscurities but basically affirm the tradition of) a code of canon law which would be the common standard of church life. In fact, more than reaffirming the ancient and ideal concept of "One Empire, One Church, One Faith," the gathering drew attention to the manner in which Western Church practice and customs and those of the East were already departing in significant ways. His response to Roman resist-

[59]Confusingly, so too, sometimes is the actual Sixth Council of 681.

[60]Known as *Rhinotmetos* "sliced nose" from the mutilation he suffered when he was first deposed. Regnant emperor from 685–695, and again 705–711, at which point he was executed by rebellious troops outside the walls of the capital, his son was murdered and so ended the dynasty of Heraclios.

ance to his determination to impose a single code of church law was to order the arrest of Pope Sergius I at Rome, but the imperial garrisons at Ravenna and Rome resisted him, refusing to enforce his decree. He would take revenge on them afterwards after securing his second accession to supreme power: subduing the Chersonese, and then turning his attention to the defeat of Ravenna, which fell to him in 709. Then he demanded papal obedience, from Pope John VII, to the decisions of the Council in Trullo. In 710 Justinian II commanded the new pope, Constantine, to come to Constantinople, where he publicly agreed to the acts of the Synod in Trullo. Constantine was to be the last of the popes until the twentieth century ever to set foot in the eastern capital again.

The Council in Trullo issued no fewer than one hundred and two canons. They are predominantly derivative from older established materials. The first of these is a long *proemium* that gives the tone and ethos in its preliminary statement: "We decree that the faith which has been handed down to us shall be, and shall remain, exempt from any and every innovation or mutilation, and shall be just as it was delivered to us by those who were eye-witnesses and servants of the God-approved Apostles; and moreover by the 318 holy and blessed fathers who convened at Nicaea . . . " It then goes on to list the heresies which each of the Oecumenical Councils fought against, the heretics who sustained them, and the leading fathers who stood against them. It thus lists the whole series of the first six Oecumenical Councils as standing in the series of that pre-eminent first, Nicaea, and like Nicaea as representing the Apostolic faith in all its purity. This first statement of the Synod in Trullo is immensely important in setting the seal, as it were, on the great synodical principle for the Eastern Church. It is meant, in all likelihood, to reassert it as the supreme principle for the governance of the West, too, and to bring back into alignment the two halves of the Church which were felt to be alarmingly growing apart in the seventh century, in a process of division which would reach a crisis point in the ninth century, when the significant differences in Trinitarian faith (not merely variant customs such as western clerical shaving of facial hair, compulsory clerical celibacy, ecclesiological differences in structure and theory, and worship practices) broke out into the open in the matter of the *filioque* controversy.[61]

The second canon also stands at the head of the list as a prelude with the effect of reviewing the whole series of which canons previously issued by the Churches ought to be recognized henceforward as authoritative and central to the processes of church law. This canon validates solemnly the eighty-five canons "handed down in

[61]The Latin addition to the Nicene-Constantinopolitan Creed, arising out of Spanish practices of confessing the Spirit of God as "proceeding from the Father and from the Son" (*filioque*) instead of "proceeding from the Father" as in the original. The "double-procession" eventually becoming the standard confession of the Western Christian Churches, configured fundamental matters of Trinitarian theology in a distinctly different way that became a matter of dispute between the Greek East and the West ever afterwards.

the name of the holy and glorious Apostles." It clearly shows awareness that much of this material is not historically demonstrable, but resolves the matter by reaffirming the "apostolicity" of the materials since the Fathers of the Church had accepted them as such, and also by deciding to expose and relegate the materials it acknowledged to have been "interpolated" by extraneous hands. In this it means the material in such books as the *Apostolic Constitutions* and so on, which by the seventh century have been generally recognized as having interpolated Arian liturgical canons within them. It is interesting as one of the first examples in the Church's formal documents showing an awareness of source criticism: "And so we have suitably weeded out such (spurious) ordinances in furtherance of the edification and security of the most holy Christian flock." The canon goes on to ratify "all the rest of the sacred canons promulgated by our holy and blessed fathers."[62] All other "pseudo-canons" not specifically listed are not to be accepted, and those who tamper with the canons in future are threatened with the penalty attached to that canon which they try to alter.

Now, having given stability of law to the system in a way that paralleled Justinian's work of coordinating the civil law, the canonical work of the hierarchs started in detail to address the contemporary problems. Many of the regulations concern clerical marriage laws. A range of civil liaisons are ruled out for the clergy. The Roman system of clerical celibacy, involving, in cases of married men, a promise before ordination to set the wives aside, is considered and twice rejected (canons 3 and 13) as not being permissible in the East; but a series of stricter rules concerning clerical marriage is introduced. Henceforth, no one who has been married twice shall be admitted to orders (canon 3) and no one who has married a widow, a divorcee, a former prostitute or actress, or a household servant is permitted to be advanced to orders. Canons 4–6 continue the argument that eastern clerical marriage standards have to be made stricter. Misbehaving clerics are to be deposed, and no one is allowed to be married at all after having received ordination. The issue of standards is contained in many other canons throughout the list.[63] Clearly it was a major concern of the council to regulate the standing and discipline of the clerical orders,[64] but there is also a determination to legislate more closely for the degrees

[62]It states: Nicaea 325, Ancyra, Neo-Caesarea, Gangra, Antioch, Laodicea, Constantinople 381, Ephesus 431, Chalcedon 451, Sardica 347 (issuing a large number of canons regulating episcopal mobility, their trials and process of appeals), Carthage 419, Constantinople 394; as well as the canons of the holy fathers–Dionysios, Peter, Gregory, Athanasius, Basil, Gregory of Nyssa, Gregory of Nazianzus, Amphilokios, Timothy, Theophilos, Cyril, Gennadios, and Cyprian (Carthage 257).

[63]Many of which expect a much higher standard of public morality from clergy: see for example canon 77 forbidding the clergy to use the bath houses on mixed days when women are present.

[64]Canons 9–10 forbid clergy to run taverns or lending houses. Canon 24 forbids clerical involvement in gambling of any sort. Canon 27 forbids clergy to wear "inappropriate" lay dress, but admonishes them to wear clerical costume. Canons 14–15 determine minimum ages for ordination. Canon 16 corrects the 15th canon of Neo-Caesarea that had set a limit of seven to the number of deacons in any church (the

of forbidden kinship that can or cannot constitute a civil marriage among the people.[65] We also notice a concern to restrict religious relations with the Jews of Constantinople, notably in the sharing of the Passover matzoth between the synagogues and the churches in some instances (canon 11), which is pressed to a further stricture for clergy to avoid business familiarity with Jewish merchants also—a sign of cooling relations for the future, certainly, but also one of the last witnesses to the lively interchange that must be presumed to have been happening in seventh century Constantinople and which, as in Alexandria in the fifth century, the hierarchs are concerned about as a source of potential religious fusion. Canon 19 determines that clerical preaching ought to be performed out of the texts of the fathers who have written on the Scriptures, a sign of the low level of general clerical education of the era. Men who do not belong to the clergy are forbidden to preach in church (canons 33 and 64). Several more canons regulate liturgical customs and innovations (canons 28, 29, and 31), while others reaffirm older canons regulating the rights and responsibilities of metropolitans, in which series canon 36 stands out, which reaffirms canon 28 of Chalcedon establishing the primacy of Constantinople in the East, and attributing to it equal canonical rights with Old Rome. The order of precedence of Churches is set out here in terms of the five ranking Patriarchates: Rome, Constantinople, Alexandria, Antioch, and Jerusalem. Their unanimity and concord, from this time onwards, was a major form of regulating canonical harmony in the international Church. Envisaged still, at this stage, as a truly empire-wide system of multi-ethic voices in the Church, the pentarchy system suffered immeasurably after the fall of Byzantine territories to the Arabs and Ottomans, by becoming more and more a simple extension of the Phanariot class of the throne of Constantinople.

Several canons regulated the refugee disruption that was being caused in the seventh century empire by loss of territories to the Arabs, particularly in the regions of Cyprus.[66] Others regulated the monastic life. It is determined in canon 43, for example, that no sin committed shall debar a person from adopting the monastic life, since it is a penitential one. In canon 40 the minimum age for accepting monastic applicants is set at ten,[67] and canon 41 insists that those wishing the anchoretic life

Cathedral of Constantinople in the time of Justinian had 100 of them). Canons 17–18 again regulate clerical mobility, forbidding clergy to move dioceses except with written permission from the bishop; and those who have had to flee because of war, must go back when possible.

[65]See canons 53–54 that list the forbidden degrees of kinship, a ruling that would enter Roman civil law thereafter; or canon 72 that forbids "mixed" marriages between an Orthodox and a heretic.

[66]Canons 18, 27–29.

[67]The council is aware that this is young (St Basil had decreed 17 a suitable age for a young woman seeking to enter monastic life), but decrees that at this tender age the habits and ascetic training can be more easily "sealed" on an eager and impressionable soul. The age for admission today, of course, is considerably elevated.

must first serve obedience under a hegumen in a regular coenobitic monastery so as to establish a basic training. Wandering ascetics, with long unkempt hair who choose to ply the streets of Constantinople (a feature of the city and popular with its people since its origins), are now admonished either to go to a monastery and settle there or else to be compelled go out into the desert regions (canon 42). Convents are censured in canon 45 for having allowed the custom to grow up of having a dramatic profession ceremony for nuns, in which the candidates wore expensive secular clothes (some of the entrants were high aristocrats) and just as dramatically laid them aside as they took up the monastic habit in the church. The council calls for a return to simple and sober ceremonies reminiscent of the fact that monasticism is a life of repentance. Monastic mobility is strictly regulated (canon 46): neither monks or nuns should wander the streets and never should they lodge elsewhere other than their own house. The earlier practice in force in which monastic institutions often returned back to secular use is forbidden in canon 49.

At canons 50 and 51 the fathers turned their minds towards social engineering. The first of this pair forbids all forms of gambling to all, both clerical and lay; and the second forbids animal spectacles as well as dancing on stage. The world of Byzantium in the previous ages, where the hippodrome was the center of all social life and where dancing acrobatics and gambling were a fundamental way of life for the populace, must now be presumed to be in massive flux. The shifting fortunes of the empire have put the luxurious "entertainment industry" into some form of crisis. The Hippodrome is never again to be the center of Byzantine affairs as it once was, and as it remained even up to the time of Justinian. Military reversals and economic distress had already put their mark on the life of the capital. Canon 62 of the council, issued without doubt with imperial approval and maybe even at the suggestion of the emperor, decrees that the last remaining pagan festivals at Constantinople will be abolished: the observance of the *Kalends*, the *Vota* and the *Brumalia*. The last vestiges of the Dionysian rites (ancient Greek mystery festivals involving bacchanalia and street carnivals) thus passed out of history. The clergy who continue to celebrate them (at that stage having only a symbolic connection with pagan religion, such as Halloween festivals might have today) are censured with the threat of deposition, and laity who do so will be excommunicated. The lighting of fires on the New Moon and fire leaping is also abolished as a heathen practice (canon 65).[68] In their place the Church accelerated the number and solemnity of saint's festivals, which also involved much public festivity outside the Church. Even so, the work of the fathers in these regulatory canons speaks volumes about a newly ascendant spirit of sobriety that is being advocated. Canon 100 actually seeks to ban all erotic art.

[68]It survives still as the popular summer festival for St John's day and is given a Christian explanation related to his asceticism.

Today one has to have a discriminating eye to see the several occasions in Greek public life where the ancient Greek rituals still endure[69] in a much changed form: Byzantium in the seventh century is determined to eradicate the obvious marks and in canon 62 it is specifically forbidden to Christian women to shout out "the execrable name of Dionysios" on the streets of Constantinople. In canon 66 it is decreed that the days following Pascha shall be days of peaceful leisure that will allow Christians to attend some of the post-paschal services and, for this reason, "let there be no horse races and other large public spectacles during these days." The extent of the successful obedience to the canons by the laity is, of course, a different matter altogether from their promulgation. But these canons addressed to the wider populace are significant; and they take a force among the clergy who are being used as instruments of social change. Canons are similarly aimed at the suppression of brothels (canon 86) and the strict censuring of those who procure abortions (canon 91), dealing with them as the same canonical penalty for homicide (many years of exclusion from communion).[70] Problems attendant on the regulation of marriages among the faithful are also treated, such as the issue of abductions preceding marriage, which were a widespread problem in the provinces in antiquity (canon 92), or the question of when and how a soldier's wife, or an abandoned spouse, could consider contracting another marriage (canon 93). The contracting of a betrothal is formally given the full status of a church marriage in canon 98. Those who break such an engagement (the *arrabon* was formally solemnized in church) are subject to the penalties of digamists. Canon 96 is apparently addressed to men who sport elaborately plaited hairstyles. It has often been taken as a generic condemnation of *fashionista* behavior, whereas sobriety ought to mark the Christian lifestyle; but it is more accurate to read it as a coded but quite specifically aimed censure against eunuchs in the imperial city, some of whose lifestyles also coincided with what many of the late Romans called "effeminate relationships" among men. This

[69]The Kalanda are still observed as the Greek New Year festival, and St Nicodemos the Hagiorite in his edition of the canons (Pedalion, 1841) is still complaining that: "These people are imitated in later times by Christians who go around on this first day of January dancing in front of the doors of private houses, rambling all over the place, uttering many nonsensical things and telling ludicrous stories, singing lines supposedly written by St Basil the Great (which indeed ought to be suppressed by the bishops and spiritual persons). People who do this should be penalized to stop them practicing Greek paganism." The wandering around was the vestige of the women's wild dances on the Dionysian festival; the telling of silly tales and staggering round, the vestige of the massive amounts of wine that were drunk. New Year in the Church's calendar was the feast of St Basil: so we see to this day a result of the seventh century canons trying to gain a purchase on public ceremonial: changing behavior by altering the motivation for celebrations, and introducing a higher note of sobriety into the occasion (admittedly difficult to do for the Dionysia).

[70]A length of excommunication significantly relaxed, for motives of pastoral care, in later times, though the legal synonymity of abortion and infanticide has been retained in the Eastern Church to this day.

is the force of the latter part of the canon that encourages the offenders to leave aside their plaited hair: "for the cause of following a life that is perennially calm, so that they might enjoy chaste associations in reverence, and approach God as closely as possible through their purity of life."

The conciliar canons which address rules of fasting in Lent and other liturgical matters[71] seem at first to have a specifically minor import. But some of these regulations (canons 29, 52, 55, 56, and 57) are deceptive, for in fact they are major statements of a new religious policy aimed at the Latin Churches of the West (canon 55, among others), and the Armenians in the East (canons 32, 33, 56, and 99) and more or less signaling that eastern canonical practice "ought" to prevail universally, being both a "middle way" and having the patristic sanction of history. The Latin customs that differ from the East in the rules of fasting are clearly disapproved of and the Armenian peculiarities of discipline (priesthood by family lineage among others) are ordered to be discontinued. This shows a determination on the part of the capital to bring the Churches into a harmony, and disallow the considerable disparity of liturgical, ascetical and canonical customs that had already grown up on the international front. History would show that the attempt to gather Rome and Armenia into the "flow" of the canonical life adopted by the four remaining great Churches of the Pentarchy, would not be successful. Both went their own way; to canonical dissonance was soon added the charge of doctrinal divergence. This council, in many ways, was the last major attempt of the still united Byzantine world to draw tight the circle of the Church serving as the spiritual unification of the international Oecumene: one world, one kingdom ruled by a common set of laws of the Romans, and a common church discipline. If it had worked we would perhaps remember Justinian II *Rhinotmetos* in the same way we recall Justinian, as one of the great legislators of history.

The church lawyers summed up their exhaustive list of regulations with the final canon (102) giving a short encomium to those whose duty it was to see to the application and enforcement of the canons. The text is an interesting reflection on the "philosophy" of canon law, subordinating it in its scope to the pastoral care and

[71]Forbidding the recycling of church books containing Scripture (canon 68); forbidding the non-ordained access to the sanctuary of the church (canon 69) with the exception of the emperor; forbidding the chatter of women in church (Canon 70–it does not imply that the men were paragons of silence, but they were nearer to the deacons in the main body of Hagia Sophia, who could silence them, whereas the women were upstairs in a separate great gallery); forbidding the engraving of the symbol of the cross on the floor (carpets or mosaics) where it could be walked on (canon 73); the abolition of the ancient *Agape* (canon 74); the forbidding of "disorderly music" in church in favor of ecclesiastical psalmody (canon 75); banning stalls and shops in the precincts of the church (canon 76); abolishing the festival of the *puerperium* of the Virgin (canon 79); regulating the exact words used at the Trisagion hymn (canon 81); animals shall never be stabled in a church except in temporary necessity to save the animal's life (canon 88); or refusing to give communion to those who presented golden receptacles for the eucharistic gifts instead of offering their hands as customary (canon 101).

development of the faithful. The legislator is called upon to be a physician, knowing when to administer a severe remedy and when to relax a strict regimen, because of the individual needs of each. The spirit and character of the individual person has to be taken into account: "For all that matters in the eyes of God and the one who undertakes pastoral leadership, is the recovery of the straying sheep, and the healing of someone who has been wounded by the serpent. Accordingly, the pastoral ruler ought neither to drive the patient to the verge of despair, nor slacken the reins to allow a dissolute or contemptuous life, but in one way or another, either by using stringent remedies or by resorting to milder and gentler ways, he should seek to curb the disease." The great list of regulations end, therefore, in the spirit in which they were begun, with the primacy of pastoral care to the fore and with a profound sense of legislative discretion afforded to the bishops as canonical adjudicators.

The Seventh Oecumenical Council: Nicaea II–787

The last of the Oecumenical Councils[72] was convened in 787 in the basilica church at Nicaea (still standing, though in ruins since the early twentieth century, at Iznik in modern Turkey). It had been removed there, largely for symbolic reasons (to give it the title of Council of Nicaea) after an earlier convocation, at Constantinople in the previous year, had been disrupted by rebellious soldiers.

Its fundamental point of argument was whether the Christ could be legitimately pictured in artistic forms or not, and whether icons were idolatrous. Those in favor of icons were called *iconodules* (icon venerators), those against, *iconoclasts* (icon smashers). It is a complicated council. In some ways its argumentation is deeply Christological, like the great fourth and fifth century councils. In other ways it represented the closest the Byzantine Church ever came to an experience similar to that of the Reformation in the West. The arguments ranged over a whole generation. In the end, the Eastern Church proclaimed that icons were a sacramental form of representing not only the image of Christ, not only a didactic aspect of the Gospel in art, but also in some mysterious sense were channels for actively representing his presence to his people who stood before him in prayer. The Western Church concurred with the doctrine, and accordingly, the practice of using icons in worship, praying over the relics of the saints (which was closely related to it in the argument of the council), and the

[72]Only the Roman Catholic Church has continued calling its major synods "Oecumenical"; Vatican II in the mid-*20th* century being listed in the Roman canons as the *21st* Oecumenical Council. But with the absence of the Roman Popes from the Pentarchy, a distance between the East and West accelerated after the rise of the Carolingians of the *9th* century, and formally fixed after the medieval schism between the Latin and Greek Churches, the Eastern Christian world has not named any synod subsequent to 787 as having oecumenical import.

understanding of the sacraments (such as the Eucharist) as representing a real presence of Christ (not just a symbolic representation) were all elements descriptive of both the Eastern and Western Churches until, in the West, the Reformation divided attitudes profoundly on all three issues of church life and worship. The Eastern Churches to this day still regard the place of icons in Christian prayer and worship as a "test of faith," that is, a matter of serious import in a person's understanding of the incarnation and of the sacraments. By the time of the later Medieval West iconography was understood in a significantly diminished fashion (useful as no more than an aid to devotion or a book for the unlettered), and certainly in the western Churches after the Reformation this understanding that Nicaea II promulgated, of a sacramental force in religious art, largely faded away in the Churches. There are still significant remnants of it in the different sacramental doctrines of the various Catholic and Protestant Churches and, to that extent, Nicaea II is still an important council in world-wide Christianity whose relevance goes beyond the mere surface argument over art and relics to fundamental matters of the relationship of spirit and matter, and how material forms can be genuine vehicles of divine grace.

The hierarchs, after concluding the doctrinal matters, were concerned with re-establishing order in the Churches after two prolonged periods of imperial persecution of the iconodules involving much disruption to the fabric and liturgical life of the Churches. They issued twenty-two canons. The first reaffirms the validity of the previous six Oecumenical Councils[73] along with the received local synods and canons of the holy fathers "for they are inspired with one and the same Holy Spirit." The second canon gets to the point, or the ethos of this collection: "Whoever is to be ordained a bishop, must firmly resolve to observe the canons, otherwise he cannot be ordained." From this time onwards there grew up the custom of requiring a written profession from episcopal candidates that they would be the zealous defenders of the canons of the Church. Canon 3 rejected imperial promotions of bishops (much used in the Iconoclastic era so that recalcitrant clergy could be ousted by imperial power) and reasserted the procedures of synodical election as set out many times before. Several canons (4, 5, and 19) weighed in against the practice of *eulogiae* expected, by patrons and others, of clerical candidates for ordination or monastic admission (as they were expected *de rigeur* from every candidate for secular office in Byzantium). Other canons have specific reference to the decrees in favor of the icons and relics of the saints. From this time onwards it is not permitted to consecrate a new church without the deposit of saints' relics in the altar (canon 7). Similarly, all the books written by the iconoclasts are called for deposit with the episcopal chancery at Constantinople, so that they shall cease circulating (canon 9).

[73]The canons of the Synod in Trullo already having been established and accepted as part of the Sixth Council.

Several canons deal with regulating the monastic life. Irregularities had sprung up since the monasteries were the particular target of attack by the Iconoclastic emperors. The practice of double monasteries (male and female monastics residing in the same monatery) is now ended (canon 20). The alienation of monasteries into public property is censured (canon 13) and the age-old complaint of wandering monastics is again brought up for censure (canon 21), with strictures being added against the practice of monks and clergy "eating alone with women," a ruling that echoes canon 18 that forbade monasteries or episcopal households from employing female servants, so that no suspicion of wrongdoing should attach to the bishop or the abbot. Many of the remaining canons deal with matters from previous legislation, such as the renewed stricture on wandering clergy, or those having more than one ecclesiastical charge (canons 10 and 15). The appointment of a skilled steward (*oikonomos*) for each Church is insisted on. If the Metropolitans resist this obligation it is reserved (in canon 11) for the Patriarch of Constantinople to send his own appointment to the Church in question. There is a sense in the list of the canons of the last oecumenical synod that the bishops are going through the motions here, that canons are expected from a great council, and so canons shall be delivered; but with the exception of a very few related to the consecration of church buildings in the post-iconoclastic phase, and admitting that there is an overall concern to re-establish order in monastic life, most the regulations have an archaizing air about them, and are frequently derivative from earlier canonical lists.

Afterthoughts

The Seven Oecumenical Councils not only stand as an historical chart of Christianity's intellectual and moral progress in the post-biblical era, they also represent the corpus of classical orthodoxy in Christian doctrine, especially in terms of its doctrine of God and its Christology. The canons of the council have often not been studied as closely as the ektheseis, or doctrinal statements of the protagonists. This is a pity in many ways for the contents of the canons not only witness to the vivid reality of the daily life of the Churches (what was held to be of pressing importance in any given generation) but also consistently set forth a philosophical and theological view of what constitutes the "sacred tradition" of Christianity. For the Eastern Church hierarchs it is abundantly clear from seeing the constant iteration and reiteration of the "patristic rules," that the canons are given status as elements revealing the "mind of the Church" as endowed with some sense of inspiration value, part of the deposit of Christian tradition, not alienated from it as sidelined matters of external rules and regulations. The canons of the great Councils significantly advance the concept of the Church as issuer and maintainer of law, and of the rule of law. The notion of good order that they consistently represent is always, so it seems to me, driven by deep pastoral concern and a constant desire to improve general morals and move social consensus to a *fundamentum* of merciful compassion built on Gospel principles as a charter. The force of this evolution of a sense of Church law (and indeed a massively growing *corpus* of the same) alongside Roman civil law, which marched to different tunes at many instances, cannot be overemphasized, for Roman civil law was softened, refined, and rendered attuned to master principles of compassion, justice, and reformation by the parallel presence of Church law in ways that other modern systems of law (considered on their own terms, or as having detached themselves from religious systems of inspiration) simply cannot attain to. Here in the Byzantine Church's system of juxtaposing two distinct but deeply conscient systems of law next to one another, almost as two wings of the imperial administration, a uniquely sensitized system that reflected both civic virtues and moral values could be promulgated. One last thing worthy of notice, as evidenced in the final postlude of the Council in Trullo of 691, but also witnessed throughout so many of the pages of the church legislation, is the highly developed sense of pastoral discretion that the Church law affords to the bishops considered as legal judges. Here again the Church elevates a major and noteworthy premise: law is not justice unless it is tempered with mercy and aimed at the establishment of good order through the improvement of the people.

Further Reading

Primary Texts

H. Ohme. *Das Konzil Quinisextum* (übersetzt und eingeleitet von H Ohme). Turnhout: Brepols, 2006.

H.R. Percival. *The Seven Ecumenical Councils.* NCNP vol. 14. Grand Rapids, MI: Eerdmans, 1900.

N.P. Tanner. *The Decrees of the Ecumenical Councils.* London: Sheed and Ward, 1990.

Studies

L. Davis. *The Seven Oecumenical Councils. Their History and Theology.* Wilmington: M. Glazier, 1987.

G. Florovsky. "The Authority of the Ancient Councils and the Tradition of the Fathers" in G Muller & W. Zeller. *Glaube, Geist, Geschichte.* Leiden: Brill, 1967.

W.H.C. Frend. *The Rise of the Monophysite Movement.* Cambridge: Cambridge University Press, 1979.

P.T.R. Gray. *The Defence of Chalcedon in the East. 451–553.* Leiden: Brill, 1979.

A. Grillmeier. *Christ in Christian Tradition.* vol. 1 2nd edn. London: Mowbray, 1975; pp. 520–557.

A. Grillmeier. *Christ in Christian Tradition.* vol. 2. Part 2. London: Mowbray, 1995

R.P.C. Hanson. *The Search for the Christian Doctrine of God.* Edinburgh: T. & T. Clark, 1988; ch. 23.

E.R. Hardy. *Christology of the Later Fathers.* Philadelphia: Westminster Press, 1954; pp. 378–381 (conciliar texts).

P.J. Henry. "Initial Eastern Assessments of the 7th Ecumenical Council." JTS, new series 25 (1974) 75–92.

M. Kalamaras. *He Pempte Oikoumenike Synodos.* Athens: Ekdosis Metropoleos Nikopoleos, 1985 (Greek text).

P. L'Huillier. *The Church of the Ancient Councils: The Disciplinary Work of the First Four Ecumenical Councils.* Crestwood, NY: St Vladimir's Seminary Press, 1995.

C. Luibheid. *The Council of Nicaea.* Galway: Galway University Press, 1982.

J.A. McGuckin. "Perceiving Light from Light in Light: The Trinitarian Theology of St Gregory The Theologian." Commemorative Volume for his Sixteenth Centenary. *Greek Orthodox Theological Review* 39, nos. 1–2 (1994) 7–32.

———. "Nestorius and the Political Factions of 5th Century Byzantium: Factors in his Downfall." In J.F. Coakley & K. Parry, eds. *The Church of the East: Life and Thought.* Special issue of the *Bulletin of the John Rylands University Library* 78.3 (1996) 7–21.

———. *St Cyril of Alexandria and the Christological Controversy.* Leiden: Brill, 1994 (reprinted Crestwood, NY: St Vladimir's Seminary Press, 2004).

———. *St Gregory of Nazianzus: An Intellectual Biography.* Crestwood, NY: St Vladimir's Seminary Press, 2001.

———. "Il Lungo Cammino Verso Calcedonia" (The Long Road to Chalcedon: The Unfolding Nexus of Christological Definition from Origen to Dioscorus). In A. Ducay, ed. *Il Concilio di Calcedonia 1550 Anni Dopo.* Rome: Libreria Editrice Vaticana, 2002; pp. 13- 41.

M. Meigne. "Concile ou collection d'Elvire." *Revue d'histoire ecclésiastique* 70 (1975) 361–387.

J. Meyendorff. *Byzantine Theology.* New York: Fordham University Press, 1983.

R.C. Mortimer. *Western Canon Law.* London: A&C Black, 1953.

K. Parry. *Depicting the Word. Byzantine Iconophile Thought of the 8th and 9th Centuries.* Leiden: Brill, 1996.

D.J. Sahas. *Icon and Logos: Sources in Eighth Century Iconoclasm.* Medieval Texts and Translations no. 4. Toronto, 1986.

R.V. Sellers. *The Council of Chalcedon: An Historical and Doctrinal Survey.* London: SPCK, 1953.

C. Stead. *Divine Substance.* Oxford: Oxford University Press, 1977; pp. 223–266.

N.P. Tanner. *The Councils of the Church: A Short History.* New York: Crossroad Press, 2001.

CHAPTER 9

Imperial Byzantine Codifications of State Law

Legal Crisis in the Time of the Principate

By the time of the late pre-Christian emperors it was widely agreed among the jurists and judges that the application of the sprawling system of Roman law had come into a major crisis. The principle of progression by traditional accumulations meant that the perennial problem of ancient Roman legal codification, namely what laws were still relevant and enforceable, was now felt acutely as Roman law assumed an international mantle, and the application of law under the emperors was expected, both by citizens and foreigners seeking redress at the throne, to be centrally efficient and secure. Nevertheless, within the legal record there were simply so many different types of enactment contracted in such widely different historical circumstances that interpretation had become immensely confused. Old laws that contradicted present legislation were still on the books of precedence. Where legal records were kept in authoritative reference collections, such as in the libraries of the law schools or the archives of the central and provincial imperial chanceries, it was becoming clear that imperial legislative decisions were detaching from any sense of useful grounding in the traditional precedents.[1] The situation of relevant citation had become so complicated that even the professional magistrates enjoyed only a loose hold on what constituted the correct legal parameters of many cases. And the situation was even worse for the many provincial towns across the empire where Roman law was often administered by an amateur squirearchy. The legal prescripts of the empire had by the late Principate amassed into a very unwieldy jungle. Roman law was by that time generically designated as "old law" and "new law." The first referred to three particular elements; namely, all the published statutes of the republic and early empire that were still regarded as holding force; the decrees of the senate that were held to have special and enduring significance; and lastly, the opinions of the professional jurists, particularly those whom the emperors had designated as having the authority to resolve dubious cases. The body of juristic opinion had been issued

[1]Mousourakis (2007) 179f.

in learned commentaries that sought to make an individual response to the growing mass of legislative chaos by setting material into a hierarchy of importance and by attempting the resolution of notable conflicts in the law. This meant that already by the early imperial period the jurists' writings had started to resolve the problem by incorporating most of what was regarded as enduringly important. They had become a heavily authoritative guide; but the problem remained that access to the statutes themselves was a hit and miss affair across the empire (difficult even in the capital since access to the imperial records was by no means a public affair). The legal records of statutes that existed were frequently partial, often corrupt, and hardly ever represented in the local libraries of the empire because of the great cost in copying them. Very few practicing lawyers were thus able to consult a wide record of the former juristic opinion.

Similar problems affected the new law, which, even though it was more recent in time, did not have a central organization (outside the relevant imperial chanceries, which had moved several times in the unstable years of the third century): it consisted of the ordinances of the emperors promulgated during the middle and later stages of the empire, but it was in a highly disorganized condition.

The emperors eventually responded to their role as chief magistrate (as devised by Augustus) by claiming the more elevated metaphysical title as *fons et origo legis*.[2] But it was in the early years, under the Principate, that the imperial protocols for governing legislative matters were established. There were four different types of imperial legal judgment, each one capable in a different way of establishing a new legal precedent as well as, in some cases, especially the more universal and public matter of the edicts, new policy for the empire. These were the imperial issuing of edicts, decretals, rescripts, and mandates. Imperial *edicta* were published in the major towns and cities and remained on display for over a month, before being held in the records of the town courts. *Decreta* were more private decisions given by the emperor as judge hearing appellate cases. These were not extensively collected in published form and would thus not be readily discernible except to the jurist who

[2]"The fount and origin of all law," thus making the emperor technically above the law, as its source. This probably originated from the orientalized Hellenistic "divine right of kings"; but although the Byzantine synthesis passed this on as a monarchical heritage to later Europe, it also heavily tempered the absolutism inherent in the idea, by refusing to admit the emperor, as a Christian, was ever free from, or above, the divine law as presented in the Gospel. Thus, his absolutism was a relative one, comparable to the Kings of Israel, validated by God only according to the manner in which the king as judge, and earthly icon of God's justice, affirmed and sustained the laws set out for the protection of the New Israel. It was this important aspect that explains why Byzantium set alongside a highly reverential attitude to the imperial charism as Law-Giver, a robust sense of political resistance to the emperors when they were seen to enact unjust, oppressive, or religiously unorthodox legislation. Alongside Byzantine regal subservience, therefore, must also be set the record of the regular imperial assassinations that have to be seen as qualifying any absolutist political theory in Byzantium.

studied them seeking to deduce from the decision under appeal, what the imperial interpretation of the law had been. *Rescripta* were imperial legal decisions that were recited in court and would be preserved also in the local court record of that case. These would have a local and immediate effect but unless they were professionally collated and preserved (such as by a scholarly jurist) their wider effect was very limited. Lastly, *mandata* were communicated privately to the provincial imperial officials to whom they were sent for various occasions. In Roman history they were collected only sporadically. From the second century of the Christian era, however, there is a discernible movement among the lawyers to start to make collections of all these imperial documents as case precedents for their own use. The famous jurist Paulus produced a collection of thirteen rescripts of the Emperor Septimius Severus in 200 A.D. and, in so doing, paved the way for the later architecture of both the Theodosian legal constitution and the Justinianic codification, his work featuring prominently in both. It was as part of Diocletian's generic reforms of the empire that the legal overhaul started systematically.

The lack of a generally applicable code of civil law was decided to be fixed by the publication of two unofficial (but weighty) collections of imperial adjudications, the first containing all the rescripts from the time of Hadrian up to the reign of Diocletian, which was issued as the *Codex Gregorianus* in 291 A.D.; and the second, the *Codex Hermogenianus* issued a few years later to collect the *Constitutions* issued by Diocletian himself. The depth and coverage of these publications was profound, because they could call on the whole resources of the central imperial palace archives, during the administration of one of the most efficient administrators the empire had ever seen. The legal-social ferment going on at this period can be seen also in the works of the Christian theorist, Lactantius, who was summoned by the imperial court to one of the court appointments at the capital of Nicomedia, for rhetoric-law, and whose major theoretical work, the *Divine Institutes,* in many ways reflects the "alternative" religious-legal vision of society that the court of Constantine would produce after Diocletian. Within a few years both of Diocletian's collections were widely used and cited as authorities in the courts. Neither has survived to the present but both were the foundation from which the *Codex Theodosianus* was built, and which incorporated them, as did the Code of Justinian.

The Theodosian Code

The Diocletianic publications were basically meant to offer guidance on current legislative policy. The underlying demonstration was meant to be what in the ancient laws could still be seen to have relevance and force, and what was simply archaically outdated. Between 321–322 the first Christian emperor, Constantine I, enacted a series of legislative statutes, once again meant to provide guidance to the court authorities on how to apply classical Roman law. His need to produce his own sets of guidelines came at a time when he also planned a widening of the base of the magistracies, extending the ability to function as a magistrate to a whole range of local dignitaries (including but not limited to Christian bishops) and thus bringing into the official processes another level of learned amateurs whose various levels of education could not be presumed to have delved deeply in history of law. The efforts under Constantine show that there was still widespread uncertainty as to which laws still applied, and which had been abrogated, despite the work of Diocletian.

In 426, the eastern emperor, Theodosius II, and Valentinian III, his western colleague, jointly issued the *Law of Citations*. This was intended to bring Constantine's more sporadic efforts to a new level of completion. What had been seen to be lacking in earlier efforts at reforming the obscurities of the law in terms of the publications issued to date, was some sense of learned legal commentary accompanying the text. To provide this, and to set the body of the laws into a framework of coherent interpretation, a working context, so to speak, the *Law of Citations* published a partial collection of juristic opinions to stand alongside the existing collections of imperial constitutions. The exercise was meant as an attempt to draw up a hierarchy of importance in the opinions of the jurists and the project is thought[3] to have all the signs of being a preliminary exercise for a much wider attack on the obscurities of the legal collections themselves, for only three years later the same emperors appointed a panel of internationally celebrated jurists to bring some order into the general codification of Roman civil law. They were given the task of compiling a single authoritative collection of all the imperial constitutions that had been produced since the time of Constantine which were still held to be in force and were instructed to combine these with the two Diocletianic codices, publishing the new definitive edition along with a comprehensive and ordered parallel set of juristic opinions on the laws. The new publication was meant to result in a definitive, exhaustive, up to date, and readily accessible code of Roman law, that could be universally and equitably applied across the international empire.

The whole plan was stillborn, however, doubtless because of the immense labor involved in drawing together a comprehensive new work, which would have involved collating disparate jurists' opinions, as well as the considerable labor involved in tabulating all the imperial chancery records across so many jurisdictions past. The commission, in the end, produced nothing of significance. Nevertheless, the idea was not abandoned, and, in 435, a second commission was established on

[3]Mousourakis (2007) 185.

the initiative of the eastern court and this time given the task of bringing together all the imperial constitutions since the time of Constantine into a single collection. This simpler, more narrowly focused task, was successfully managed this time round, completed within three years and published in 438 under the name of *Codex Theodosianus*, acquiring official force of law first in the East and subsequently in the western provinces. All constitutions that were not recorded in the Code, excepting those that were promulgated after it, were deemed after its date of publication to have no enduring force in Roman law.

The Theodosian Codex was a very large scale work indeed. It is predominantly concerned with public legal administration; which can be readily seen from a cursory examination of its contents. The first five of the sixteen books (*tomoi*) focus on private law. Books six through eight deal with constitutional matters and administrative law. Book nine arranges criminal law. Books ten through eleven pertain to laws regulating public revenue. Books twelve through fourteen concern laws regulating municipalities and civic corporations. Book fifteen is dedicated to legal matters concerning public works and games. And book sixteen is dedicated to ecclesiastical matters.

The Codex thus brought together more than three thousand imperial constitutions from the time of Constantine I (312) to the year 438. It was organized into sixteen books with each volume divided into working titles (*tituli*) concerning particular legal topics. Each Constitution was arranged in the order of the year it was issued, but this chronological sequencing was refined by the repeated division of prescripts under the various "titles." Accordingly, although the major arrangement was a chronological one massing all the data together, the researcher could very easily skim the text to see how later legislation had voided certain prescripts from an earlier time. The Code was to be a major source of, and influence on, the Justinianic code reforms. It has survived intact in two manuscripts of the fifth and sixth centuries. Scholars also see its handprint heavily apparent in the *Lex Romana Visigothorum* which became an important source of later medieval western law. But even despite the many advantages the Codex brought on its publication, it was still regarded by professional jurists as not having completed the required work sufficiently comprehensively. As a compromise exercise it had cut corners by omitting the one task that was felt to be mainly needed: providing a parallel commentary on the laws that offered digests of the works of the leading Roman jurists (selected opinions) so that a lawyer or judge could consult the work, and gain a preliminary idea of priorities of legislative importance on any given topic, before they went into court. It was to supply this perceived defect that the Justinianic projects of legal reform were initiated.

The Justinianic Reforms

This idea for continuing with the great renewal of the law, mastering its history and contemporary application, and reducing it to a single authoritative compendium, was fostered at the two great sixth century law schools of Byzantium: Beirut and Constantinople.[4] It struck a perfect note for the Byzantines who were highly conscious of their own role as the continuators of the *Imperium Romanum*. As Diocletian had reformed civil and military administration and begun the legal consolidation necessary from Nicomedia, the quondam eastern capital, just so it seemed under Justinian's administration that the final reform ought to proceed from the queen of cities, Constantinople. This legal consolidation was part and parcel of the Byzantine emperors' traditional perception of their civic and mystical role, as God's chosen ruler, to bring order to the Church and world by directing the ways of Rome towards the Gospel. Traditional Roman values (*Romanitas*, enduring even into the Greek term *Romaiosyne*) were thus a constant directing policy for Justinian; and it was this that governed his military campaigns under his general Belisarios to make the Mediterranean once more a Roman lake, as much as it was the governing force in his ideas about the state's direction of ecclesiastical affairs in the fraught aftermath of the Council of Chalcedon.

Justinian assumed the purple in 527, succeeding his uncle Justin I. For many years in the latter's administration Justinian had performed the role of great cultural patron and highly experienced political heir apparent. It was thus with many extensive plans in mind that he began his own reign with an energy from the outset that became more determinedly focused after his successful emergence from the Nika riots that almost toppled him at the beginning of his rule. The project to reform the law code was something that was dear to his heart as a major step in refurbishing essential elements of the past Roman greatness, in order to ensure its continuing vitality in the generations ahead. Its immediate moving spirit was undoubtedly Tribonian, a highly skilled historian of law and political leader at Constantinople, who was very close to Justinian and who occupied many of the highest and varied state offices in his administration.[5] Tribonian began his career with Justinian as *Magister Officiorum* (Secretary of State in the imperial administration). He was the Minister of Justice in 530 (*Quaestor Sacri Palatii*) but, on account of the strict measures taken by his agents against the populace after the Nika revolt, he lost the favor of the people and so was moved sideways by the emperor so as to become *Magister Officiorum* once again. After the publication of the first parts of the Codex he again resumed

[4]Zulueta, in Bailey (1923) 183.

[5]For a contemporary account, see Procopius *Anecdota* 13.12. and 20.16–17. For a wider consideration, see: T. Honoré, *Tribonian* (London 1978).

the post of *Quaestor Sacri Palatii*. After his death in 546 the continuing legal project lost much of its pace and energy. Another major contributor was Theophilos who was professor of law (*Antecessor*) in the school of Constantinople. The skills of Dorotheos and Anatolios were soon co-opted as chief members of the inner circle for planning the work. They were the chief professors of law in the prestigious school of Beirut.

On February 13, 528 Justinian issued the edict entitled *Constitutio Haec* which set up a ten member commission, including Tribonian, but chaired by the *Quaestor Sacri Palatii*. The task set to them was to bring to completion the work of Diocletian and Theodosius, and to codify all the still valid imperial constitutions into a single manageable collection. This basically meant that they were to collate together the Gregorian, Hermogenian, and Theodosian Codices and add in all the Constitutions issued between 438 and 539. They were empowered by the emperor to delete all perceived obsolete elements and eliminate contradictions or superfluities, adding whatever they thought necessary to bring the prescripts up to date, and reestablish their authority for the whole of the empire. Fourteen months later, on April 7, 529 the completed work was published under the title of *Codex Constitutionum* (often known just as *Codex Justinianus*) by the decree of the imperial *Constitutio Summa*, and was set to come into force on April 16th. Thereafter no Roman law that was not found within the Codex was permitted to be cited in any court of the empire. The chronological arrangement of earlier Codex models was again followed here, along with the listing under subject titles, making the Codex both comprehensive and easily negotiated by the legal researcher. The success of the project and its rapid completion gave encouragement to the Chancery of Justinian to press on with amplifications of the reform. So it was that in 534 a revised version was issued that has come to be called the New Code.[6]

The New Code of Justinian

Even at the time of the publication of the Code of 529, it was already clear to Justinian's Commission that a new and revised edition was badly needed if only because of the significant extent of Justinian's own legal decrees of recent years. More than this, however, the extensive scholarly sifting through the old source materials for the Code had clearly demonstrated to Justinian's Commission the stark need to address the problem the earlier generations of reforms had been systematically avoiding,

[6]The first edition being thus designated as *Codex Vetus* by scholars. A fragment of its Index was discovered in Egypt by Grenfell and Hunt in the 19th Century (Papyrus Oxyrhyncus XV. 1814). This is all that survives of the manuscripts.

namely the forceful bringing into some kind of order and coherence the teeming mass of legal opinion from the historical (and still revered) classical Roman jurists, which served as the contextual background for the interpretation of the legal enactments. The earlier systematization introduced by the *Law of Citations* had not managed to bring much order into this practical process of citing juristic opinion. Now having the texts in order made it all the more imperative to prioritize (and weed out) the body of juristic commentary which formed the main basis of practical legal pleading in the courts. Justinian himself saw the problem posed by the commentaries of the jurists (the weight of tradition in the handling of law) and resolved to attack it just as forcefully as he had the collation of the ancient enactments. As a preliminary measure he issued an imperial decree on November 17, 530, entitled *Quinquaginta Decisiones,* or "The Fifty Decisions." In this he formally noted the inconsistencies in the major authoritative source of the interpretation of Roman law and decreed resolutions to the major controversies that they had listed as open points of interpretation, simultaneously issuing definitive solutions. Having thus established his imperial credentials as the *Renovator Traditionum Romanorum,* that which was the quintessential role of the emperor as he saw it, namely to renew the springs of Roman culture, he set out on his own authority that this work of revision would be definitive: after it no alternative sets of sources would be admitted, no commentaries on his Codex would be allowed[7]. The implication was also given here that a similar all-inclusiveness (for example the forbidding of independent editions of his Code, or the publication of new independent legal books of legal philosophy) would mark his attack on the body of juristic opinions, though that work would take more time and effort on the part of his legal experts. *The Fifty Decisions,* nevertheless, is an early flare signal that he intended to take the minor revisions of the Code much further, a project that would eventually see the day as the Justinianic Digests.

The work of the first revision of the Code began in early 534. Tribonian and Dorotheos of Beirut, then resident in Constantinople, and three of the lawyers who prepared the *Codex Vetus* set to work to complete this. Their task was simply stated: to adapt the first Code by introducing the Justinianic decrees post-dating 529, and especially the terms of the 50 Decisions. But they also took the opportunity to repair perceived gaps in the historical coverage of The *Vetus Codex* and eliminate duplications. On November 16, 534 the New Code was published by the decree *Constitutio Cordi* under the title of *Codex Repetitae Praelectionis* and it came into force on December 29, 534.

The Code of Justinian is an impressive architectural work, like many of his state and church buildings in stone. It was meant to show even the casual observer the

[7]A few editions with Byzantine scholia (notes) did appear as time went on, however, mainly explaining the technical language of the Codex, and simplifying it for popular Greek usage.

glory and power of Roman culture, and in expressing it anew, perhaps to reiterate for the world of his own age, the precise vision of what the Christian imperium would offer as an enduring sequence of imperial dynasties stretching out from Constantine to himself. If so, the preponderant message was one of continuity with classical culture. The whole is structured as twelve books (a new Twelve Tables of Rome), each one being sub-divided into several titles relating to different legal topics. The titles present the Constitutions of the emperors in chronological sequence under the imperial name and that of the original addressee of the decree. The constitutions are further divided into paragraphs (propositional divisions that allow for easier citation). The first of these in each major heading is always designated the *principium*. Book 1 concerns jurisdictional and ecclesiastical matters. Books 2–8 treat private law. Book 9 sets out terms of criminal law. Books 10–12 relate to administrative law. The whole Code contains approximately forty-five hundred acts of law dating from the time of Hadrian in the early second century. The majority of the decrees emanate from Diocletian's reorganization in the late third and early fourth centuries.[8] Justinian's own decrees account for four hundred of the enactments, ten percent of the total.

The Digest (or Pandects) of Justinian

The rapid and efficient production of this first experiment encouraged the emperor to attempt the more difficult enterprise of simplifying and digesting the writings of the jurists. Thus, on December 15, 530, Justinian issued the Constitution *Deo Auctore* which instructed Tribonian, who had by then moved to become the *Quaestor Sacri Palatii*, or Justice Minister, to form a new commission of sixteen eminent experts with the charge of bringing order and system into the juristic texts and publishing a single supremely authoritative compendium within the space of ten years. It would, in fact, take them only three years to bring the work to completion.[9] The groundwork for this major compendium, which became known as the *Digest* or the *Pandects*,[10] had already been laid by the numerous annotations the compilers of the Code had made as to the inconsistencies that had to be dealt with in the mass of juristic opinions that comprised the traditional *Ius Romanum*.

[8]Twenty seven per cent of the total derive from Diocletian.

[9]The speed of the work was aided, doubtless, by the fact that the idea had already had a long gestation–in the air from the time of Theodosius. Also some of the later Roman jurists had already started to try to systematize the chaos. This can be seen for example in the work of Masurius Sabinus (*Libri tres iuris civilis*). Scholars surmise that the sixteen members undoubtedly split up into specializing sub committees. F. Bluhme argued a method of composition which has commanded widespread agreement: "Die Ordnung der fragmente in den Pandektentiteln." *Zeitschrift fur geschichtliche Rechtswissenschaft* 4 (1820) 257–472.

[10]Digest (derived from the Latin *digerere*) meant "systematization;" *Pandects* (derived from the Greek *pan dexesthe*) meant "encyclopedia."

Tribonian appointed as leading members Dorotheos and Anatolios, professors of the law school in Beirut, as well as Theophilos and Cratinos, chief teachers in the law school of Constantinople. He appointed also the palace official Constantinos, and eleven notable lawyers. The scope of their collating work was to be restricted to those Roman jurists who in times past had been afforded the highest rank and weight by preceding emperors, or, in other words, given the status of the *ius respondendi*. Their juridical opinions had for a long time enjoyed the force of custom at law. But there were others also whose names customarily carried weight. The commissioners were instructed not to allow custom to stand as a blind guide. The traditional fame of a jurist of the past was not to outweigh the practical value of his opinions; and all the collection was to be ordered in a coherent way according to the judgment of the panel, whose decisions were to have absolute and binding force.[11] Jurists who were not mentioned in *The Law of Citations* were able to be consulted, but those that the commissioners finally omitted from the *Pandects* were never to be cited again in Roman legal cases, nor were opinions of famous jurors to carry any more weight except as authorized in the *Digest ad locum*. Nor would there be any appeal against the commission's decisions on what had become obsolete in the law. The limit was set of not covering material that had already been sufficiently covered in the *Codex*. The *Digest* was thus the accompanying interpretative material for the *Codex*, which because of the support given to it by the *Digest*, was meant to be the final and definitive version of Roman law henceforth. Once it was published it was intended that any reference to the original treatises of the ancient jurors would be forbidden in the courts.

The seriousness of this centralizing work of reference was underlined by the emperor's forbidding any further creation of legal treatises commenting upon the *Digest* itself. Only cross translation from the original Latin to the vernacular Greek, short annotations (*scholia*), and brief quotations were to be allowed. An obvious reason for this was to avoid the problem of "accumulations" that had clogged up the reform attempts of Diocletian and Theodosius. It might also be the case that this very close encounter with the classical pagan Roman law sources revealed to Justinian's court just how much the early medieval Byzantines now moved within a different thought world. The old sources, interpreted in the light of the cult of the ancient gods of Rome, were primary guides to societal life, fundamentally social but far from secular. The Byzantine commissioners lived in a society where the religious parameters were significantly different; the very conceptions of justice and equity had moved in fundamental new ways. Modern commentators[12] sometimes express

[11]As to the conflicted material emerging in the review of old law, where the commissioners intruded decisions and made specific alterations, these instances have been known since the 16th century as the *Interpolationes Triboniani*.

[12]See for example: A. Watson, *The Spirit of Roman Law* (Athens: University of Georgia Press, 1995), p. 45.

surprise that, although Justinian himself was a profoundly religious Christian, a dedicated theologian whose vision of Rome's glory clearly depended on extending Christian Orthodoxy to the limits of his jurisdiction, the *Code* and *Digest* that bear his name seem incredibly "secular" in tone, almost devoid of any overtly Christian message. Two things can be borne in mind in relation to this. The first is that when one deals with a code of law rooted in ancient precedents one is not dealing with a direct mirror-reality of society in any case. Most reviewers now agree that the Justinianic Code is neither an accurate reflection of how law operated in the pagan imperial past, nor in his own day. It is not, to that extent, a clear reflecting mirror on either set of societies. It is more an attempt to secure a bridgehead between the world of Roman antiquity and the emerging world of the Christian early Middle Ages. It can be seen as a Roman Christian attempt to keep faith with the past, while moving energetically onwards. To this extent, Justinian's reordering of the classical Roman sources which he instinctively felt were the bedrock of Byzantine security precisely because they *were* Roman, is as much a determination to draw a line under the influence of ancient Roman values as it is a concern to reaffirm their authority. In more ways than geographical we have certainly moved from Old Rome to New Rome. The Byzantines, therefore, are trying to keep faith with a classical imperial past, without entirely committing to it; which is why Justinian fully asserts his own stamp, and affords his commissioners such total mastery of power over the "quality" of the classical record. The inevitable loss of historical resources that it signified (the varied historical contexts of individual antique jurors which it would cut loose from the legal history of Rome were *de facto* not liable to survive a further passage through time regardless of how venerable they were) was a fair price to pay for the way the Romans of Justinian's day reasserted themselves as masters of their own tradition, not slaves to it. And perhaps this may have been another reason why Justinian ordered a ban on further commentary on this work of review.

The second thing that has to be kept in mind if one muses over the apparent secularity of the Justinianic Code, is that the emperor had a very refined awareness of the massive legal codes that had already accumulated in relation to the religious law codes of the empire. These were fundamentally Christian in tone and spirit, and by the sixth century had become extensive, rising into a formal level of legal significance not merely at the local level, where the episcopal judgments bore force in Byzantine society, but even at international imperial level, when the canons of the councils (councils that could only be declared by imperial Constitution) were given force in Roman law by the emperor's decree subsequently acknowledging and accepting the work of the major synods of bishops. If one wonders at the relative absence of specific Christian legislation in the Code, one needs to bring alongside it what every Byzantine would have regarded as the parallel religious dimension to the law of Christian Rome, namely the collections of canons that were under the immediate concern of the hierarchy, as the functioning *quaestores ecclesiasticae*, the lawmakers of the *ekklesia*.

The *Digest's* authoritative status was announced and established by the imperial decree *Constitutio Tanta* (given in Latin) and duplicated in the Greek as *Dedoken*, which was issued on December 16 and set to become law from December 30, 533. Justinian notes in the preamble that the commission surveyed approximately two thousand books containing three million lines, reducing them to one hundred and fifty thousand lines of text, and altering "many things of the highest importance" in the process. The work of thirty-nine classical Roman jurists was abstracted in the *Digest*, ranging in time from 100 B.C. to 300 A.D. The earliest commentators were Quintus Mucius Scaevola and Aelius Gellus, the last was Arcadias Charisius who lived in the mid-fourth century. Eighty percent of the cited opinions were taken from the five leading Roman authorities of the late Principate (Ulpianus, Paulus, Papinianus, Gaius, and Modestinus); Ulpianus himself commanded forty percent of all the citations, and Paulus came a close second after him. The other thirty-four jurists mentioned in the work contributed collectively the remaining twenty percent. The leading five classical jurists, of course, had by that time already established an overwhelming level of authority and had the most complete editions of their work extant in the libraries of the law schools.

The *Digest* was comprised of fifty books. Almost each of them[13] was divided into titles (*tituli*) and then subdivided into *fragmenta* (also called *leges*) and in some cases then into sections, and also paragraphs (the first of the series of the latter being the *principium*). As Justinian had commanded, the titles were drawn up to reflect the titles used in the Codex. Cross-referencing was the heart of the matter. The beginning of each *fragmentum* in the *Digest* lists the name of the jurist in question, together with the legal title under discussion and the section of the original book from which the citation was taken.[14] The first four books, called the *Prota*, deal with generic matters such as how to conduct affairs in court, who the various public officials were and what were the proprieties of their rank, and what the limits of jurisdiction were. Books 5–11 were entitled *De Iudiciis*, and concerned judicial proceedings and cases. Books 12–19 set out contract law and personal actionable cases (*De Rebus*), while books 20–27 dealt with various more domestic issues such as marriages, guardianship, rights of mortgage-holders, and so on (*Umbilicus Pandectarum*). Books 28–36 (*De*

[13]The exception was books 30–32.

[14]This layout leads to the common way of citing material from the Justinianic *Digest*, in a fourfold numerical system: by book, by title, by fragment, by section. If there is no section because of the shortness of the fragment it reduces to a threefold reference. It is similarly reduced if only the *principium* of the fragment is being cited.

Testamentis) specifically legislated for wills and testamentary trusts. Books 37–44 concerned legal exceptions, ownership and property rights, and problems associated with intestacy. Books 45–50 dealt with obligations and civil injuries, the process of appeals, as well as local government processes and public works administration. At the heart of this section, in books 47–48 could be found the Byzantine criminal code, bearing the specific title of the "Awesome Volumes" (*Libri Terribili*). Eighty copies of the whole work were ordered to be made for use in the palace departments, the law schools, and throughout other sections of the capital's administration. Of these original eighty manuscripts, one has survived,[15] though most of the numerous copies of the work that we now possess[16] date to the eleventh century.

The Institutes of Justinian

While the Digest project was clearly also meant to serve as the future primary source of reference for trainees in the law schools of Beirut and Constantinople, the very size of the text made it necessary for the commissioners to think about a shorter, classroom-friendly project that could be expected to be part of the library of every provincial town as well as of every successful lawyer. For centuries past the classical text book the *Institutes of Gaius* had served this purpose. This was now determined to be overhauled and reissued in a form that corresponded to the arrangement of the *Codex* and *Digest*. In 533 Justinian commanded the text book should be revised so as to form a new book of instruction for the schools. A commission of three was appointed for the task. Tribonian led the panel and was accompanied by his long-standing colleagues, the law professors Theophilos from Constantinople and Dorotheos of Beirut. The remit was once more the same: to abbreviate, delete duplications, and cut what was obsolete from the record. The majority of the editorial work had already been completed as part of the process of dealing with the jurists in the *Digest*, and so the finished work, subsequently known as the *Institutes of Justinian*, was ratified by the imperial Constitution *Imperatoriam maiestatem* on November 21, 533 and published as law together with the *Digest* by the *Constitutio Tanta* (*Dedoken*) on December 30, 533.

Two thirds of the *Institutes* directly reproduces the *Institutes of Gaius*. The editors also introduced material from Gaius' other famous volume *Res Quotidianae* (Book of Daily Affairs) and various elementary materials were brought in from the other leading classical jurists Ulpianus, Paulus, Marcianus, and Florentinus. Some of the

[15]It came to Italy in the 10th century, and from the 12th century lodged at Pisa. It was captured by the Florentines in 1406. It is now known as the *Littera Florentina* or *Codex Florentinus*.

[16]The Latin versions that circulated were predominantly partial copies, usually omitting all the Greek material as a matter of course.

simpler materials from the Digest were also set out as test cases for students. The edited work retained the structure plan of Gaius' original in the main, making a threefold division in four books, related to law of persons, property, and actions, but now subdivided more consistently to reflect the contents of the sections in the titles and paragraphs of the *Codex* for ready reference. Where the *Digest* was composed basically of synopsized extracts, the *Institutes* was made up more from narrative essays on the topics in hand, making it much more relevant for educational use.

The Novels of Justinian

Between 534 and his death in 565, Justinian continued to issue a great number of ordinances that dealt with many subjects and which significantly altered the classical statement of the law on many points. These ordinances, falling as they did out of the scope of the *Codex*, came to be called the "New Constitutions" (*Novellae Constitutiones Post Codicem*). In recent English they have been customarily referred to as the *Novels*. By the time of his death they amounted to over one hundred and fifty Novels,[17] most of them concerning administrative or ecclesiastical law. He had intended, as announced in his *Constitutio Cordi* of 534, to bring these *Novels* into a systematic new volume when they had sufficiently accumulated, but it is probable that the intervening death of Tribonian in 546 took the energy out of this project.

The Corpus Iuris Civilis

All four parts of the entire Justinianic law program, namely the *Codex*, the *Digest*, the *Institutes* and *Novels*, are today collectively called the *Corpus Iuris Civilis*. It is a term invented by the renaissance scholar Dionysius Gothofredus (1549–1622) who produced one of the first early modern critical editions of Justinian's Code which remained a standard text until the nineteenth century. This *Corpus Juris* of Justinian, with a few additions from the ordinances of succeeding emperors, continued to be the center and focus of all legal ordinance and philosophy in what survived of the Roman world. The codification of the classical heritage and its emended adoption

[17]The *Collectio Graeca* manuscript contains 168 but extends into the reigns of Justin II (565–578) and Tiberius II (578–582). The manuscript tradition of the Novels now dates back to the 11th century at the earliest, but collections were first made in Justinian's time by Julianus, professor of law at Constantinople (*Epitome Juliani*), for export to the newly recaptured territories of Italy. There is also a separate version by an anonymous collator (the *Authenticum* containing 134 constitutions). The *Collectio Graeca* was the standard version known throughout all the history of Byzantium, but largely unknown to the West until fifteenth century refugees introduced it there after the collapse of 1453. It became a major source of inspiration for Renaissance scholars of the law thereafter. Further: see Mousourakis (2007) 190.

by the Byzantines allowed Roman law to be passed on as the common heritage of most later European cultures,[18], both eastern and western. By bringing the ancient Roman tradition into manageable order, and by showing in the civic sphere what the Church Fathers had already done in the fourth century, that the secular heritage of classical Rome could be adopted and adapted confidently by Christians, Justinian achieved an enduring legacy. Most significantly he was able to ensure that the ancient achievement of the concept of the rule of law, arguably the highest social philosophy of the ancients (however partially it had been applied in history), was able to pass alive into the ferment of the medieval world, in the process guaranteeing Roman law a foundational place in the ongoing history of Greco-Latin civilization.

Later Byzantine Imperial Adjustments of the Law

While Justinian's overarching work remained in Byzantium as the single authoritative source of reference, the passage of time and the progressive loss of the Latinate culture[19] increasingly made several parts of the language of Justinian's project inaccessible to the non-scholar. The later Byzantine legal adjustments, therefore, tend to be in the nature of simplifications and abridgements. They correspond, in terms of legal culture, with the fact that the empire after the eighth century was shrinking rapidly and losing much territory. What remained was no longer built around the premise of previous centuries of Eastern Roman social organization, where large landed estates held by largely absent aristocrat landowners fed into the tax system of local cities, which in turn supported the larger imperial cities, especially the capital. The old Byzantine system, still operative up to Justinian's time, like a stable and centralizing wheel, had given before the onset of the rise of the Arabs and incessant erosion of the borders. By the eighth century all imperial matters were conducted in Greek. It followed that at this time the Justinianic corpus began to be approached more and more through the medium of Byzantine digests of the *Digest*, always simplifying and popularizing the academic complexities and prolixities of the original work.

The earliest and perhaps most important of these Byzantine emendations was the *Ecloga Legum*, a collection of extracts from the Code of Justinian. It was issued

[18]Roman law had less impact on Saxon and Celtic cultures; the common law codes of England, Wales, and Ireland are much less indebted to it.

[19]The palace and law schools of Byzantium always conducted affairs in Latin until after the time of Justinian. The vernacular Greek, however, took over substantially. By the late fourth century few but scholars had any knowledge of Latin, and eventually the charade of continuing to use Latin as the official language of New Rome passed away.

by Emperor Leo III the Isaurian and published in 740. After this came the *Eisagoge* or *Epanagoge*, composed for use in the palace of Emperor Basil I (867–886). This was more or less a long preamble and theoretical introduction to a newly proposed law code which aspired to redo the Justinianic program, but never achieved its end.

From the late seventh and eighth centuries also comes the *Farmer's Law.* This, perhaps more than the magisterial work of the Justinianic system, was the law that generally applied in the medieval Byzantine hinterland. It reflects the radical change of the later Eastern Christian empire, from a system of interconnected fortified cities that guaranteed the security of the provincial landowners, to an era when the military cities were much fewer in number and local military units had to be organized and sustained by local landworkers themselves. In this smaller-scale world the notable factor is the disappearance of the great landowners of the past and the emergence of numerous peasant farmers who held their small-holdings generally on lease from local magnates. Law had become largely a matter of village border disputes and land contracts.[20] The scope and structure of the *Farmer's Law* had a great impact in determining local law codes throughout eastern Europe in later times. It is basically a "common man's" law.

In the early tenth century a new practical code known as the *Basilica* (or *Basilica Nomina*) was prepared by the Emperor *Leo VI* (the Wise). It was a Greek simplified version of parts of the *Codex* and parts of the *Digest* in sixty books. Alongside this main core it added in material from the *Novels* and imperial ordinances following after Justinian. It was entirely unknown in the Latin West which by this time had extensively detached from the Byzantine orbit. Here the law as settled by Justinian held its ground. The later tenth century also saw the issuing of the *Synopsis Basilicorum Maior,* which was not much more than an abridgement of the *Basilica.* One of the latest adjustments (though it was to have an enduring value in the post-Byzantine world) was the publication in 1345 of the *Hexabiblos*, a large six book manual of law written by Constantine Armenopoulos, who served as a judge in Thessaloniki and whom we shall meet again in the next chapter. The *Hexabiblos* was still used in the Greek courts during the Ottoman period and played a strong role in continuing the Byzantine Roman character of the law codes of Eastern Europe to the present day. In the West the memory of Justinian's work remained, but the manuscripts circulated only in partial form, in the main, almost always omitting the Greek consti-

[20]It has an apodeictic quality, consisting of homely adjudications meant to prevent local disputes. The following is a brief flavor: "If two farmers agree with the other before two or three witnesses to exchange lands and they agree for all time, let their determination and their exchange remain firm and secure and unassailable." Or again: "If two territories contend about a boundary or a field, let the judges consider it and they shall decide in favor of the territory which had the longer possession; but if there is an ancient landmark, let the ancient determination remain unassailed."

tutions. The dissolution of the grand idea of Roman imperium in the early western Middle Ages left little room for the presuppositions of Justinian's Christian sense of a transnational imperium based around Orthodox Christianity under God's single ruler on earth. Too much political dissolution and ferment was characterizing the West at this time for that notion to have a powerful influence any longer. After the eleventh century, however, things were different. The West rediscovered the concepts underlying Justinian's *Corpus Iuris Civilis* when Irnerius founded the University of Bologna and reintroduced the serious study of law there, which led the way throughout western Europe for a growing Romanization of the many local customs which had grown up during the Dark Ages, and had replaced Roman law with tribal custom of varying merit and sophistication.[21] A veritable legal reformation happened at that period, leading up to the sixteenth century, which saw the first European critical studies of the history and philosophy of Roman law, based again on Justinian's work. Commencing with the notion of the Justinianic Code as a great historical enterprise, its influence extended out from the merely historical so as to enter western Renaissance mentality as the potential *idée maitresse* of European political cohesion. The rule of law, based upon notions of equity and systematic reason, entered the early modern European consciousness along this track, bringing with it political concepts of a wider western legal civilization and with that the seminal notion of the rights of mankind. This connection of legal equitable association as a political bond in society was not that far removed from the springs which inspired the Christian Byzantines in refashioning the influence of the classical Roman law system. In their case, however, two centrally important theoretical principles undergirded the rationale of the social enterprise. The first was that society was bonded in common rights and obligations because of its primary bond under God. Thus for the Byzantines all social contract, however apparently "secular," was part of the sacral nature of a society caught up in God's work of the deification of humanity. The second was that this theoretical bonding together of the sacred community (the Byzantines saw themselves, as Orthodox Christians,[22] forming the ideal community on earth as God's Elect People) was made real and concrete by the supreme transnational power of the emperor, God's Vice-Gerent. In the West both principles, at various times,[23] have been set aside in the discourse about common human rights and rule of law, and to that extent the western philosophy of human rights as it has

[21]See De Zulueta, in Bailey (1923) 177; Mousourakis (2007) 192–195.

[22]Which is why Justinian's concern for social coherence under law was matched in his lifetime by a relentless attempt to impose Orthodox conformity among the subjects of the empire.

[23]Though part of the 11th century rekindling of interest in the Justinianic legal program was attributable to the way that emerging western monarchies saw in Byzantium's ideals of imperial unity and the sacred character of the ruler, good matrices to work from in fashioning their own dynastic ambitions.

emerged into the present day as a still vigorous notion has often lacked the theological foundations[24] from which it grew up in Byzantium, whose original "grand idea" it was.[25]

Further Reading

Primary Texts

J.A.C. Thomas. *The Institutes of Justinian: Text, Translation, and Commentary.* Amsterdam: North Holland Publishing Co., 1975

A. Watson et al., eds. *The Digest of Justinian.* Latin text edited by Theodor Mommsen with the aid of Paul Krueger; English translation edited by Alan Watson. Philadelphia: University of Pennsylvania Press, 1985.

C. Pharr, T.S. Davidson & M.B. Pharr, trs. *The Theodosian Code and Novels, and the Sirmondian Constitutions.* New York: Greenwood Press, 1969.

Studies

G.G. Archi. *Teodosio II e la sua codificazione.* Naples, 1976.

W. Ashburner, ed. "The Farmers' Law." *Journal of Hellenic Studies* 32 (1912) 87–95.

C. Gallagher. "Gratian and Theodore Balsamon: Two 12th Century Canonistic Methods Compared." In N. Oikonomides, ed. *Byzantium in the 12th Century: Canon Law, State & Society.* Athens, 1991; pp. 61–89 (Greek text).

L. De Giovanni. *Il libro XVI del Codice Teodosiano: alle origini della codificazione in tema di rapporti chiesa-stato.* Naples: M. D'Auria, 1985.

J. Harries and I. Wood, eds. *The Theodosian Code: Studies in the Imperial Law of Late Antiquity.* New York, 1993.

J. Harries. *Law and Empire in Late Antiquity.* Cambridge: Cambridge University Press, 1999.

T. Honoré. *Tribonian.* London, 1978.

______. *Law in the Crisis of Empire.* Oxford: Oxford University Press, 1998; chs. 5–7.

G. Mousourakis. *A Legal History of Rome.* London: Routledge, 2007; pp. 179–191.

P. Viscuso. "A Late Byzantine Theology of Canon Law." *Greek Orthodox Theological Review* 34 (1989) 203–219.

A. Schminck. *Studien zu mittelbyzantinischen Rechtsbüchern.* Frankfurt, 1986.

F. De Zulueta. "The Science of Law." In C. Bailey, ed. *The Legacy of Rome.* Oxford: The Clarendon Press, 1923.

[24]Western European thinkers from the late 16th century have often attempted to substitute a foundation of "natural law" (going back to Aristotle) in place of the Byzantine foundation of the deification of humanity.

[25]A biblicist extension of the concept of Law in the Old Testament, extended now among the Byzantines as the "New Israel" under the new Messiah, the *Basileus* of the Romans. This biblicizing macro-structure of thought can be seen in all the patristic writings (which grow from exegetical commentaries in almost every case) and is applied as a given in the Byzantine statesmen and theologians alike.

CHAPTER 10

Later Byzantine Canonists

The formative fourth century councils and the series of Great (Oecumenical) Councils that they initiated under imperial patronage were undoubtedly the major force in the collation and consolidation of eastern Christian canon law, especially as considered as a system of civil governance that was parallel to the civil law codes, for it goes without saying that the Byzantine Christians and the Slavs who followed them were a State Church. But precisely as the code of canon law developed its profile and was referred to more and more commonly as a living system of the guidance of the polity of church life, so, too, it followed, as a matter of course, that reference versions of the church laws were required in accessible form, chiefly by the episcopal chanceries of the cities. In this present section of our review, we will first consider two of the most important representatives of the medieval process of forming an accessible and coherently edited code of church law: the *Synagoge* of John Scholastikos, and the *Nomokanons* (of the Fifty and Fourteen Titles, respectively), the latter which was formerly attributed to St Photios the Great, but which was actually composed two generations before him and in his age given only an extended edition. The *Nomokanons* were, in a sense, the authoritative "cap" of the development of medieval Byzantine canon law, but as the work of the canonists certainly did not cease in the ninth century, the second section of the chapter will go on to look at some representative later Byzantine jurists.

Early Medieval Greek Canonical Collections: The Synagoge of Fifty Titles.

John Scholastikos[1] (his title means John the "lawyer") was the Patriarch of Constantinople between 565 and 577. He was a native of Antioch and was sent, in 548, as a priest-lawyer to the Byzantine capital by the leaders of the Syrian Church to serve as the official representative of the Antiochene Patriarchate at the imperial court where he occupied the post of *Apokrisiarios* (ambassador). He became a well-respected figure in Byzantium, and at the end of his reign the Emperor Justinian

[1]He has been tentatively identified as one and the same as John Malalas. See: Haury (1900).

nominated him to be the successor for the Constantinopolitan Patriarch Eutychios, whom he had deposed. John is traditionally asserted as the author of two very well-known hymns in the Greek liturgy: the *Cherubikon* ("We who in a mystery represent the Cherubim") and the *Koinonikon* ("At Your Mystical Supper").[2] He was a jurist, working at the law professionally both in Antioch and then in Constantinople after he relocated there; but he was known by his contemporaries first and foremost as a Christological theologian and was regarded by the hostile Monophysite writer John of Ephesus as one of the most vigorous defenders and promulgators of the Chalcedonian settlement. In his Christological researches the patriarch focused on showing the compatibility of St Cyril of Alexandria's thought with the *ekthesis* of the Council of Chalcedon (a main argument of the Monophysites was that Chalcedon contradicted St Cyril) and he was, in his day, the major opponent of the writing of Severus of Antioch. But his theological work is now more or less wholly unread. His larger Christian reputation hangs today on his authorship of a revision of Church law known as the *Synagoge of Fifty Titles*.[3] It is thought to have been a composition of his time in Antioch when he served as a leading canon lawyer for the Syrian Patriarch. In it John brought a systematic order into the canonical collections of the Church by arranging them (mimicking to some extent the same kind of systematizations that were being performed by the Justinianic revisers of the civil laws[4]) in an order based upon the content of what they referred to. Previously, of course, it had been a cataloger's nightmare to go through all the conciliar acts and find what one wanted in reference to any particular topic. An indexed and subject-referenced code of law was exactly what was missing in church affairs. John worked over the basic pre-existing collections of the Apostolic Canons; the synodical canons from the Councils of Nicaea, Ancyra, Neo-Caesarea, Sardica, Gangra, Antioch, Laodicea, Constantinople, Ephesus and Chalcedon;[5] and the Canonical Epistles of St Basil the Great. This collation is a major step towards the final form, albeit extended, that the whole corpus of eastern canon law would assume.

In the preface (*proioimion*) to the collection, the author states that he was moved to make this new edition because an earlier compilation along the same lines, but in sixty titles, had omitted St Basil's work altogether. There is no surviving trace of this earlier version from which he had worked. The authority of the Cappadocian fathers was mounting very high at this period and the omission of St Basil would have been regarded as a major fault even if the canonical content and utility of the

[2]He has also been suggested as the "real author" behind the pseudepigraphical works of St Dionysius the Areopagite, though there are several other contenders for that honor.

[3]*Synagoge kanonon ekklesiastikon eis n' titlous diermene* (A Compilation of Ecclesiastical Canons divided into 50 Titles). For the text see Benesevic (1937) or Pitra (1868) 375–385.

[4]The Justinianic *Pandects* served as a literary model.

[5]He predates the Synod in Trullo and the Seventh Oecumenical council, of course.

material[6] were not as significant as it is. It was John who took the two canonical epistles of St Basil[7] and edited them as a series of sixty-eight canon-propositions, arranged topically. This was the first time that the canonical authority of the fathers had been systematized, or formalized, in this way. It would grow into the larger system of the "Canonical Epistles of the Holy Fathers," a process already signaled by the Council of Ephesus in 431, when Cyril of Alexandria, in the year preceding the conciliar gathering, had dedicated the scribes of his chancery in Alexandria to producing authoritative digests of earlier patristic writers to serve as a guide to the conciliar hierarchs' adjudications. These collations were included in the acts of Ephesus. The concept of "father" by virtue of canonical wisdom (as distinct from one of the great ascetic or doctrinal teachers of the classical age) would be advanced in this way by Byzantine ecclesiastics, extending the notion of living authority in time, as it were, certainly to include the Photian age, before it again was capped in the medieval period and "patristic wisdom" was definitively relegated to the past, a matter fit only for commentary and *scholia*, not creation *de novo*.

John's own *Synagoge* amounted to three hundred and seventy-seven canons arranged under fifty discrete topics. After he became Constantinopolitan Patriarch, John produced an amplified edition of the *Synagoge in 50 Titles*. For this expansion he included in the work a compilation he made of the Justinianic civil law code in each instance where the latter had reference to ecclesiastical affairs. A total of eighty-seven excerpts from Justinian's *Novels* dealing with Church affairs[8] were included in the later edition. Towards the end of the century an unknown editor added to this edition a further twenty-five extra legislative decrees relating to the Church taken from both the Codex and Novels of Justinian. This was known as the *Collection of Twenty-Five Chapters*. A third example of the collation of state religious laws as a church enterprise, alongside the growing collations of the canons, was the production of the *Tripartite Collection* sometime in the last years of the Emperor Heraclios (610–641).[9] The *Synagoge* of John Scholastikos, however, was a major and primary step in the evo-

[6]It deals especially with ways of reconciling and distinguishing heretics and schismatics–very pertinent for the profound schisms the post-Chalcedonian aftermath had caused in the East.

[7]Second and third letters to Amphilokios. He only uses two of the three canonical epistles of St Basil as they were later accepted. It would be canon 2 of the Synod in Trullo which would authoritatively establish the concept of "patristic canons," adding in the Alexandrian writers to the Cappadocians.

[8]Laws the emperor issued subsequent to his *Corpus Iuris Civilis* (530–535), which begins with Church-related legislation and the standards expected of clergy. See Pitra (1868) 385–407.

[9]It is usually situated circa 580. Further see Rodopoulos (2007) 81. The *Tripartite Collection* was an anonymous mid-seventh century collection of the laws of state relating to the Church. It was the main civil source from which the author of the *Nomokanons in Fourteen Titles* would work. Both the *Tripartita* and the *Nomokanons* demonstrate the significant legal activity that was taking place during the reign of Heraclios: an era of renewed activity because it was at this time that Latin was finally replaced by Greek as the official legal language of the empire.

lution of eastern canon law, for it effectively put the state *nomoi* (laws) alongside the Church *kanones* (canons), to produce the exemplar of the next stage in eastern canon law: the books of *nomokanons*. The state and religious legislation of the bishops had, of course, been immensely close almost from the time of Constantine. His "New Empire" policy of involving the bishops in judicial administration within the state as a parallel magistracy for local and ethical matters has already been noted, and many leading and legally educated bishops made use of that legislation in the bishops' courts (*audientia episcopalis*). Augustine was a good example of this in North Africa. By the time of Byzantium in the sixth century the episcopal court was often preferred to that of the civil magistrate and its reputation had risen as more and more highly skilled church lawyers could be counted alongside their secular counterparts.

The development of the *nomokanons* was an obvious synthesis waiting to happen in Constantinople, where imperial and patriarchal chanceries were so close together. Even in the provinces the application of the canons could no longer proceed (from the point of view of the administration of law by episcopal chanceries) without a constant recourse to civil legislation relating to the Church. John Scholastikos refers in his introduction to the *Collection of Eighty-Seven Titles* to this growing closeness of the civic and canonical legislation; the Church's acceptance of the state's right to legislate for matters concerning the fabric of the Church, to which it gives its support and allegiance (for the canons were also afforded the support and sanction of civic authority).[10] He argued that this alignment was a legitimate development because of the manner in which the civil law had adopted the "spirit" of the canons; in other words, because of the way the two systems had entered into one another's thought worlds and ethical values by their common attachment to Orthodox Christianity as the charter of society. The state, under the emperors in patristic times, therefore, was seen by the Church as seeking the alignment of its laws with the values of the Gospel, and to that end the Church's voluntary coordination of its canons with those laws (always understood as being in the spirit of the canons) was legitimate for that time. In his preamble to the *Synagoge*, John Scholastikos preserves the distinction that while the laws are *politikoi* (civil), the canons are *theioi*, (divine, godly). While both the imperial power and the Church's authority proceed from the same fountain, the will of God for the salvation of humankind, the decrees of the Church have a more direct spiritual inspiration and aim at the inner life and moral quality of human beings more consistently, while the political power of the "Christ-loving Emperor" extends over a greater range of human affairs and ambitions. This, of course, is why the *nomokanons* never rolled together all the laws of the empire with the canons of the Church, only making nomocanonical books that pri-

[10]In 530 Justinian's *Codex* decreed that whatever was forbidden by the church canons should be forbidden also by the civil law (*Codex Justinianus* 1.3.45).

oritized the canons first and foremost (the decrees of the Oecumenical synods were always given preeminence), and then added solely the ecclesiastical legislation of the empire: information the adjudicating bishops and canonists absolutely needed for their day-to-day work.

The *Synagoge* thus became a master text for the later expansion of Eastern Church law in the form of the *Nomokanon of the Fifty Titles* and that single most important collection of Eastern Church law: the *Nomokanon in Fourteen Titles.*[11] The *Synagoge* did for the East, therefore, what those other canonists, Dionysius Exiguus and Cresconius, had done for the West merely fifty years previously; namely, make a codification that was accessible and far more useful in a bishop's chancery. It was to have immense influence as a guide for the production of all future Byzantine "books of canon law."

The Nomokanons

The success of the *Synagoge's* inclusion of civil legislation with religious canons led the way to the next significant development in Byzantine church law, namely the rise of the nomocanonical books. The first of these was the *Nomokanon of the Fifty Titles,*[12] heavily based upon the work of John Scholastikos and taking its cue from the larger amplification of it. This was edited in Antioch in the late sixth century by an anonymous collator working probably sometime during the reign of the Emperor Maurice (582–602). Once again, the principle is established of listing all the canons of various synods under topical headings.

It was the next collation, known as the *Nomokanon in Fourteen Titles*[13] that had the most influence on later eastern canon law. It was issued, probably in Constantinople, before the first half of the seventh century and was collated from a pre-existing work that supplied its structural main feature, the treatise called *Syntagma of Canons in Fourteen Titles.* The *Nomokanon* soon emerged as undoubtedly the primary text of the later Byzantine canonists. The collation was given a major second edition in 883 and received endorsement from the hand of the Patriarch Photios the Great. Because his name was attached to the second edition, the entire collection was long thought to have been entirely composed by him, and is still often called the *Nomokanons of Photios.*[14] This edition of the *Nomokanon in Fourteen Titles* was

[11]The precise relation and sequence between the two *Nomokanons* is not clear.

[12]Its indexed form, showing the titles and where the various canons were originally taken from, can be found in Pitra (1868) 416–420.

[13]See Pitra (1868) 433–640; Rodopoulos (2007) 82.

[14]The author describes himself (*Nomokanon* 4.10) as the composer of the book "On Apparent Contradictions" (*Enantiophaneion*).

translated into Slavonic in the tenth century and had a massive and determinative effect on all Slavic Church law thereafter.[15] The second edition not only incorporated all state legislation on ecclesiastical matters that had been issued since the seventh century, but also published the major synodical developments since that time: chiefly the decrees of the Synod in Trullo, the decisions of the Seventh Oecumenical Council, and the acts of the local synods of Constantinople in 861 and 879, together with the Canonical Epistle of Patriarch Tarasios (president of the Seventh Oecumenical Council) on the subject of simony, which is added to the list of *Canonical Epistles of the Fathers*. From this time onwards the *Nomokanon* prefaced the actual text of the canon itself with the list of topics (the indexed references to which synodical decree was relevant), making it a free-standing, single, authoritative and complete work of reference.

In the *Nomokanon in Fourteen Titles,* the patristic canons are noticeably gaining stature alongside the synodical decrees. The composer defends this in advance against potential critics, on the grounds that while the synods have unquestioned inspirational status, the fathers, too, can be thought of as God-inspired guides. He writes in his *proemium*:

> I thought it a good idea to record in the same collection also the reverent sayings of certain holy fathers in several letters, exhortations, and responses, which perhaps may supply the regulation of a canon. Of course I know very well, as is also the opinion of the Great Basil and Gregory, that we should select and prefer as ecclesiastical canons, those which were ordained by several holy fathers in assembly, on the basis of a common and carefully considered decision, rather than those composed by a single writer. Nevertheless I considered that these expositions of the (patristic) teachers either dealt with what had already been resolved in synod, and would add something useful in terms of clarification of things that many had rightly found difficult to comprehend, or that they were concerned with new problems which could not be found elsewhere among the recorded synodical debates and decisions; neither in the letter nor the spirit. It is my opinion that those who in this present time have the duty to decide on such problems, could make their decisions authoritative and laudable, on the grounds of the reliability of the persons of these fathers, and because of the spiritual light that flashed upon their words through the divine energies.[16]

By means of this defense the compiler was formally able to bring together in one work the three major strands of Byzantine canonical authority: the synodical decrees, the patristic ascetical rulings, and the imperial church legislation. All three

[15]Benesevic (1914); Schwartz (1933).
[16]Pitra (1868) 446.

"strands," as it were, forming a rope that specifically saw itself as commenting upon the Gospel charter for society. The comprehensiveness and general utility of this collection gave it a high standing, because the *Nomokanon* list of topics first assembled all the relevant canons from across the range of synods and fathers on any given topic, and then the actual text of the canons was presented in full. It has sometimes been said in modern studies that this presentation of the canons was solemnly endorsed by the decrees of the Synod of Constantinople in 920, but the evidence for this is controverted. In any case, the effort represents the high water mark of the formal canon law of the Orthodox Eastern Church, and is the basis from which modern editions of the Eastern Orthodox canons are still made.

Later Byzantine Canon Law

The later Byzantine canonists appear chiefly in the form of scholiasts and commentators. Two significant writers of the later eleventh century, the monks Nikon of the Roidios monastery on Black Mountain, and his later contemporary Symeon the Younger of the Miraculous Mountain in Syria, two important ascetical complexes of the late Byzantine world, began collections of the canons which tried to be even more complete than the Photian edition of the *Nomokanon*. Their works failed to get a wide dissemination, a fact that reflects the dire straits (political and financial) of the late Byzantine Empire, and the fact also that the application of canons was increasingly spreading outwards to the "spirituals," that is the priests and hegumens, and was no longer the chief preserve of the great episcopal chanceries (which had sponsored the earlier collections under imperial patronage). In this new environment of the "decentralization" of the lists of canons, it was not more and more amplification that was required, but more compact accessibility. So two things are particularly noteworthy of this final era of Byzantine development: first the synopsis and summary presentation of the canons, and secondly, their form of presentation with accompanying explanation from a jurist as if speaking over the shoulder of the clerical reader, suggesting ways to apply and adapt what was stated in the ancient text. In the same century the polymath Michael Psellos (*c* 1018–1081) produced his *Synopsis of the Nomokanon,* but this turned out to be little more than a list of synods without added commentary.

Alexios Aristenos

Alexios Aristenos, who lived in the mid- twelfth century in the time of Emperor John II Comnenos, at the emperor's request produced a commentary on the patristic material of the *Nomokanon*, and this work probably preceded those of John

Zonaras and Theodore Balsamon, his better known successors. He was a deacon who held many high positions in the imperial administration, both those directly serving the palace (the offices of *Nomophylax*, and *Orphanotrophos*) and those serving the patriarchal administration (the offices of *Skevophylax*, and *Megas Oikonomos*). He held both major positions of Legal Administrator of the time, the civil position of the imperial *Dikaiodotes*, and also simultaneously that of the Chief Canonical Judge of the Great Cathedral (*Protoekdikos*). This extreme fusion of the secular and ecclesiastic law functions caused some concern among his clerical contemporaries and the local Synod of Constantinople in 1157 demanded that he give up his Imperial post of *Dikaiodotes*. Alexios' *Epitome of All the Sacred Canons* also became known itself simply as the *Nomokanon*. It was basically in the form of an explanatory commentary on the laws, a late Byzantine approach that would set the tone for more famous commentators who followed. His work was based upon the earlier epitomizing canonical collections of Stephen of Ephesus and Symeon Metaphrastes.

Ioannes Zonaras

Ioannes Zonaras was another of the Byzantine commentators, who was active circa 1118 and worked during the reign of Emperor Alexios I Comnenos. He was first a notable Byzantine diplomat, serving as the *Megas Droungarios* of the Imperial Guard, and later as Chief Imperial Secretary (*Protoasecretis*) or Privy Councillor. Afterwards he became a monk in the monastery of Glykeria. The prelude of his *Commentary on the Canons* tells us that after his entrance into monastic life he was asked to explain difficulties in church legislation. His work covered the Canons of the Apostles, the Seven Oecumenical Councils, as well as the patristic canons. He was the first of all the commentators to apply a rhetorically high literary style to the work in hand. The elegance of his book won him wide renown and became a paradigmatic model for Theodore Balsamon who followed him and regarded him as a strong authority. Zonaras' comments on the patristic canons of Gregory of Nyssa, Timothy, Theophilos, and Cyril have not survived. His sense of what the canonical commentary ought to be gave precedence for seeking after clarity of exposition. He is noted for his focus and determination to get to the essential meaning of a given regulation, and how it can be applied to contemporary circumstances. His comments together with those of Balsamon were regularly collated and placed after a canon in several successive canonical editions, including the highly popularized one of Agapios and Nikodemos of the Holy Mountain (*The Pedalion*). To that extent, Balsamon and Zonaras are still regularly consulted by Orthodox clergy even to the present day for issues governing even the *minutiae* of parish life, as well as matters of larger moral questions.

Theodore Balsamon

Theodoros Balsamon[17] lived near the end of the twelfth century, during the reign of Manuel Comnenos and Patriarch Michael Anchialos. He was a deacon of Hagia Sophia in Constantinople, and held the position of Imperial *Nomophylax* (senior lawyer of the administration) as well as ecclesiastical *Chartophylax* (Chief Archivist). He headed the law school of Constantinople and was given senatorial status by the emperor, though he was a monk, and eventually served as abbot of the imperial monastery of Blachernae. While in the post of *Nomophylax*, around the year 1170, he was asked by the Patriarch Michael, as he himself tells in his prelude, to publish an *Exegesis of the Nomokanon in Fourteen Titles* which would be accompanied by his own explanatory annotations ("exegesis" in Byzantine Greek signifying "commentary"), giving special attention to the meaning of the imperial laws which had been published in the *Nomokanon*.[18] He intended in this extensive work to make a comment on all the synodical canons and patristic rules, first presenting the annotations of Zonaras upon everything, and then adding in his own clarifications and notes, especially in relation to recent imperial legislation and patriarchal decisions. To access what was still extant in imperial law he took as his main civil legal text the *Basilika*, the collection of state laws published in the early tenth century. If secular laws extant in the *Nomokanons* were not to be found repeated and validated in the *Basilika*, Balsamon followed civil legal precedent and considered them to also have been superseded and rendered defunct in canon law.[19] When he discovered contradictory elements in the ancient collections, Balsamon was willing to make critical interventions and suggestions for resolution. He particularly took care to note which of the canons had been superseded by other later canons and which ones were no longer to be considered as having force of law. His work was destined to assume a great authority and dissemination in the East, but several later canonists, particularly Neilos Cabasilas,[20] drew attention to a certain level of "inattentiveness' in some aspects of it, especially in those passages where he seemed to contradict even himself. In

[17]Pronounced Valsamon. Approximate date of birth between 1130 and 1140; died after 1195.

[18]PG 104.441f. The immediate cause of this new revision was a conflict between the Patriarch and the Metropolitan of Amaseia, over the former's decision to appoint to a vacant see that had not been filled by the local synod. The emperor had sided with the archbishop after the patriarch's intervention.

[19]The emperor's case against the patriarch's position that the ancient canons gave him the right to intervene was that the secular laws involved in this canon had not been confirmed in the *Basilika*, an abbreviating edition of the Roman laws. Balsamon, accordingly, elevates this principle, but while confirming that the emperor does have the right, as regnant Christian emperor, to determine what laws will hold sway over the Church as well as the state, he and the patriarch tell the ruler that this power must be exercised with great discretion and only rarely. The power to interfere in doctrinal matters, on the other hand, is stated to lie wholly outside the emperor's power.

[20]See A. Faillier, "Une réfutation de Balsamon par Nil Kabasilas," *Revue des Études Byzantines* 32 (1974) 211–223.

1195, Balsamon addressed a treatise to Patriarch Mark III of Alexandria in the form of canonical *Questions and Answers*. Later in life, as the backdrop of the fall of Constantinople to the Venetians and the exiling of many of the Constantinopolitan clergy, he was ordained as Patriarch of Antioch, though he never took up residence in that city.

Matthew Blastares

Matthew Blastares[21] (1280–1350) was a scholarly canonist, a monk of the monastery of St Isaac in Thessalonike. He saw himself as a follower of both Zonaras and Balsamon, but his work is of equal weight and his admiration for his predecessors has been a chief factor in effectively raising both men to a high canonical status in the subsequent tradition. Blastares himself produced an edition of the canons in 1335, entitled *Alphabetical Syntagma* (*syntagma kata stoicheon*). It has twenty-four divisions according to the Greek alphabet, each subdivided into sections totaling three hundred and three divisions into topical titles ("marriage," "ordination," and so on). Conceived as an "easy to use" edition of the *Nomokanon* in the later Photian extended version, one of the *Syntagma's* chief merits was to combine the canonical and legal texts with the sequenced commentaries of Balsamon and other canonists who had particular insights to offer on specific laws. Blastares followed the lead of civil law at this period, accepting only those laws of the state as presently valid which appeared in the tenth century *Basilika*. Soon after its appearance it had a wide dissemination in Byzantium, and also in the Slavic lands where it was enthusiastically received as one of the major sources of canon law for Serbia (after the fourteenth century), Bulgaria (after thesixteenth century), Russia (after the seventeenth century) and Romania (after the eighteenth century).

Constantine Armenopoulos

Constantine Armenopoulos (*c* 1320–1385) held the position of *Katholikos Krites* (Universal Judge) in Thessalonike. He made an encyclopedic edition of Christian civil code which was issued in six volumes, gaining it the title of *Hexabiblos*. The printed edition of this *Hexabiblos* was widely adopted as the state code of law for Christians in the Balkan states under Ottoman rule, and thereby came to be adopted also, for a short time, as the code of civil law in the newly established independent Greek state in the nineteenth century. Armenopoulos also composed an *Epitome of the Canons* founded upon the Photian revision of the *Nomokanon in Fourteen Titles*, which was brought to print in 1540 by Renaissance scholars in Paris and which was destined to have a long afterlife

[21]Pronounced Vlastares.

Two Late Byzantine Christian Judges in Session

The Byzantine Empire in the thirteenth and fourteenth centuries was in an immensely weakened state. Its territorial size, and consequently its available resources, had been diminished by centuries of losses to the advance of the Ottomans. The disastrous loss of the capital to the Crusaders in 1204, when the Fourth Crusade sailed into Constantinople for pillage there instead of the intended destination of the Holy Land, was a heavy nail in the coffin of its continuing imperial aspirations. Although Constantinople was eventually retaken and Byzantium had a last, late, and wondrous flowering in the time of the fourteenth century Paleologans, the imperial destiny was, throughout all this period, in steep decline. It is interesting, therefore, that the preservation of canonical works from two very late representatives of a Byzantine Church court functioning in this era give us a glimpse of the jurisprudence of this period and allow us to see that there were still highly specialized canonists who were maintaining legal standards and scholarly precedents in a highly impressive way.

Demetrios Chomatenos

The first of these was Demetrios Chomatenos[22] (also found as Chomatianos) who was born in the middle of the twelfth century and died sometime around 1236. In the late 1100's he was the clerical *apokrisiarios* (ambassador) to the palace of the Patriarch of Constantinople, on behalf of the Archbishop of Ohrid. Afterwards he became the *chartophylax* of the Archbishop in Ohrid, having charge of political matters and clerical administration, in all effect, a vice president's role to that of the archbishop. Part of his duties was the preparation of *eratopokriseis*, that is, statements resolving issues of canonical query, which the *chartophylax* published under his own name. According to the testimony of Theodore Balsamon, who wrote a treatise on the rights and duties of the offices of *chartophylax* and *protoekdikos* (the two highest ranking canonists in Byzantium) the *chartophylax* ran his own ecclesiastical court. So, even before 1216, when Chomatenos was himself appointed to the office of Archbishop of Ohrid, he had extensive legal and judicial experience. He owed his promotion to the patronage of Theodore Komnenos Doukas. Theodore was a high-ranking Byzantine prince of the house of the Angeloi[23] who ruled the Byzantine domains of Epiros in Greece after 1215. The Epirote dominions had been set up as an alternative Byzantine "government in exile" to that of Nicaea[24] after the Latin conquest of 1204. The Patriarch

[22]Pronounced in an aspirated way: Homatinos.

[23]His family line united all the major dynasties of the Byzantine aristocracy. He was the son of the Sebastokrator John Doukas.

[24]He ended his days in prison in Nicaea in 1253, captured by the Nicene *Basileus*, John III Vatatzes.

of Constantinople had gone with the Nicene imperial administration, so Theodore turned to the autocephalous see of Ohrid to secure ecclesiastical patronage for his imperial claims after he succeeded to the rule of the Epiros after the death of Michael Komnenos Doukas. Theodore captured Thessalonike in 1224 and Adrianople in 1225. This city was metaphorically at the gates of Constantinople itself, and expectations ran high that he would soon be able to capture the capital itself back from the Latins.[25] In this context he secured the agreement of Archbishop Demetrios to consecrate him as emperor in Thessalonike in 1225, a move that caused serious ecclesiastical estrangement between the Archbishop of Ohrid and the Constantinopolitan Patriarch Germanos at Nicaea, for it amounted to an ecclesiastical claim as well as a political one: that Epiros was the new Constantinople, and Demetrios the new patriarch to the new Emperor Theodore.

A whole dossier of writings, one hundred and fifty separate pieces, has survived from the hand of Chomatenos. They are what Foss (1991) describes as: "The main source of the administrative and ecclesiastical history of Epiros, Serbia, and Bulgaria in the first half of the thirteenth century."[26] Following in the steps of powerful patriarchal predecessors such as Michael Kaerularios in the eleventh century, Demetrios theorizes significantly on the limits of the power of the *basileus*. He introduces a strong sense of limit to the power of the *basileus*; not least that of the law of God and the canons of the Church, something that is stronger than in any Byzantine writing before; but which had been signaled by Balsamon, and is prophetic of what is to come in a few centuries when the Church itself is the only institution to survive the complete collapse of the Byzantine Empire in the face of Islamic conquest; and the Church alone thus had the task of transmitting Christian Roman values to the succeeding ages without the assistance of emperor, aristocracy, army, police force, or university.

The cases Chomatenos heard[27] and recorded for posterity relate to three serious regions of church jurisprudence: marriage legislation, homicide, and inheritance laws. The workings of a bishop's court are laid out very clearly here and the standards of jurisprudence are parallel to the state courts of the empire, though it is arguable that at this stage it is the church courts that have the strongest traditions of archival support and scholarship, because they had attracted the brightest intellectual lights of the day in a time of immense social disorder. In such dark times the Church shone more brightly than many of the parallel secular institutions.

[25]He did not achieve it, being captured by the Bulgarian Tsar in 1230, and having to scale back his ambitions once he secured his release.

[26]Foss (1991) 426.

[27]Texts in vol. 6 of L.B. Pitra, *Analecta Sacra et Classica Spicilegio Solesmensi Parata*; 7 vols. Paris, 1876–1882, & 1891; see also Macrides (1988).

Johannes Apokaukos

Another of the high clerical canonists related to the Epiros dynasty also gives us a glimpse into the functioning of the church courts in this same period. He is John Apokaukos[28] (born circa 1155, died in 1233). He followed a brilliant university career at Constantinople, and then served his uncle Constantine Manasses, who was Metropolitan Archbishop of Naupaktos, as a deacon. By 1186 John was once more back at Constantinople serving as legal Notary in the administration of Patriarch Niketas II. He succeeded to his uncle's see as Metropolitan Archbishop at Naupaktos in Aetolia, in 1200. He sided with Demetrios Chomatenos and the Epirote Emperor Theodore in the Nicene-Epiros schism following after Theodore's coronation. His legal judgments from his court at Naupaktos survive and have been used by historians to provide a lively picture of late Byzantine life.[29]

As a canonist he is less scholarly than Chomatenos. He passes decisions[30] that place a higher premium on the wisdom of the presiding judge, laying an emphasis on episcopal discretion, and "economy."[31] This too, in a different way, was prophetic of what was to come in later times when the Imperium fell, and the bishops, symbolically speaking, picked up the imperial mitre from the dust.[32] The episcopal administrators of law in this late Byzantine period are dealing with many cases of homicide and inheritance disputes (the two being closely related, doubtless), that is, the most serious cases referred to them from the Balkan tribal areas increasingly distanced from heavily policed and defensible areas of the empire. Blood feuds and land disputes are now important matters for church resolution. It is in such a context that pastoral discretion (never absent from church canons) begins to be seen more in evidence. As the presumption that there would be a heavily stocked legal library behind the court's decisions cannot just be presumed in future generations, and as the reliance on imperial power to enact and enforce legislation also fades, the episcopate turned more to its ancient Christian resources of moral authority, and rhetorical persuasion. The collections of canons themselves become more fixed, less re-edited and revised, more historically "canonized" in a sense, though largely from neglect and the lack of a common authoritative source after the fall of Byzantium. The Photian *Nomokanon* remains as a core authority to which countless newer edi-

[28]Pronounced "apokafkos."

[29]See Macrides (1991).

[30]See Bees (1974) 55–160; also: Wellnhofer (1913); and Macrides (1988).

[31]*Oikonomia*, the taking of a position that is less strict according to the letter of the law's rescripts, with the intention of thereby attaining to a better overall observance of the law, in circumstances that do not always admit of a strict (*akribos*) application of the prescripts. In later times it has often been more universally understood in a context of canon law as pastoral discretion on the part of "the Spirituals," the bishop or priest.

[32]The Orthodox bishop's mitre today is a deliberate evocation of the emperor's crown.

tions defer, adding in the major medieval commentators. The work of the two late medieval judges shows us all the typical trends in miniature.

Records from the patriarchal chancery at Constantinople also happen to survive from the period between 1315 to 1402. These also contain information relating to tried cases that came before the patriarchal *chartophylax*. They confirm what we see from the cases heard by Chomatenos and Apokaukos: that even in its twilight the main ecclesiastical courts functioned confidently and their decisions were supported by extensive and well maintained archives.

Much of the work throughout the later Byzantine era has consisted of cataloging and classifying. Such labor is often regarded as "secondary" in the scholarly life, but at many instances the Byzantines showed their retention of high academic standards and advanced the study of the law at the highest political level. To give them due credit and remove the slur often associated with this era, that it was dusty and disconnected, it is worthy of note that such cataloging labors so often repeated would never have been undertaken except for two primary and pressing beliefs the Byzantines fostered. The first was that this collection of laws of the Church was possessed of an inspired and sacred character. In the Byzantine mind, it bore with it the "energies of God" that shone in the minds of the saints illumined by grace (as the *proemium* to the *Nomokanon* states). It is an aspect which is easy to overlook, in so far as we often bring to our own study of the law the kind of contexts that usually illuminate later jurisprudence, with very strong distinctions between "ecclesiastic" and "secular" where the notion of "sacred" has disappeared. But we remember that law took its beginnings in the sacred (among the ancient Romans) and never lost those moorings in the hands of the Byzantines, whether civil court lawyers or church jurists. The second reason they expended so much energy, revising, synopsizing, simplifying, and even extending by commentary, the collation of the canons, was because it was a source of primary guidance in common life. The labors expended on it reflect, therefore, its massive utility. It was never an antiquarian subject. Even to the end of the Roman imperial era in the fifteenth century,[33] its concerns are those of real men and women in very real, often tortuous, situations.

It is difficult to abstract short conclusions from such a large body of evidence, but I will raise yet again what seems to me to be at the core here, in these large intellectual developments, for there are certain interests and philosophies at play very strongly in the manner in which the Church deals with Roman law. The first of these is the sentiment that might strike modern dwellers in "secular states" as alarming; both those who are religious and those who are not. It is the regularly repeated affirmation and acknowledgment that the God-Beloved *Autokrator* of the Romans has the right in the Christian imperium to determine laws that the Church (considered

[33]Traditionally marked by the Fall of Constantinople to the Ottomans in 1453.

in its instantiation as a body of citizens with specific moral and metaphysical values) is obliged to follow. Civil law and church law ought to be in harmony. That fundamental premise seemed to the Byzantines a starting point for all legal and moral judgment. It is a harmony that would be hard to envisage today, for many reasons, not least the most practical one that the age of monarchy has passed, and a univocal nature of Christian Orthodox society is a specter and a lost memory except in rare parts of Orthodox Eastern Europe today. But this is not without problems, for when the Byzantine synthesis was in place, law was philosophically a subset of justice, and justice was a subset of religious reverence. The rights of the citizens were rights of the children of God made in his image and afforded an unimpeachable status and honor. To remove the metaphysical foundations of this legal philosophy, and seek to divorce the issue of universal human rights from the concept of the divine (thus absolutized) worth of human beings, leads inexorably to a legal premise that has no metaphysical underpinning, and will eventually lose its credibility. The major collapses of legal polity in the late twentieth and twenty-first centuries have often been based on this very problem: that if governments do not believe that all humans are equal and possessed of rights, but rather believe that they are transient and subordinate masses, they will treat them as no more than cattle. Human rights today are not in an advancing state, as we often congratulate ourselves that they are: they are in a profoundly weak state philosophically and, because of that, the moral rhetoric of rights is fraught with the specter of failing before the many extant ideologies and regimes that do not give any transcendent respect to men or women.

Closely related to this first insight is the second macro conclusion. This massive interest of the medieval Church in the development of an authoritative code of law, reconciling the spiritual and material aspirations of its members, seems to be to be a sustained hymn to the concept of "the rule of law." This may seem too obvious to be worth stating; but base axioms often have that self-evident character which, on closer examination, is not at all self-evident. It tells me, for instance, that the Church is fundamentally, essentially committed to the notion of the rule of law. Bound to acknowledge that concept as a fundamental spiritual value, binding together believer and non-believer alike, the Church can never give its assent to random governance, tyranny, or a self-congratulatory governmental system that does not elevate the rights of the needy alongside the privileges of the rich, seeking a balance in polity according to its fundamentally "synodical mind." This synodical principle is witnessed powerfully throughout all the canons and the collations of those canons across eleven hundred years of Christian legislation. It is a monumental statement of value, and massively, overwhelmingly in favor of corporate polity. It stands against, at every instance, monarchical principles such as those witnessed in the papacy, or the Russian tsars who enslaved the Church when they had monarchical power over it, in contrast to the Byzantine emperors whose ecclesiastical remit was strictly curtailed and, in the main, most conscientiously observed. The "synodical mind" of the Church is the Christian baptism of the principle of the rule by *demos*, that root of democracy, although the ancient Greeks were never to rise to that concept since their democracy was built on the bones of their slaves and the silencing of women and the landless. The synodical mind of Christian legislation in the East projected a more fully Christian concept of conciliarity and commonality. God spoke more consistently in the wisdom of the assembly than in the inspirations of the individual, however gifted the individuals appeared to be. To this extent the slow and organically incremental pace of the change of Byzantine church law should not be held to them as a fault. It demonstrated a wisdom and balance that underlay a civilization that lasted for more than a millennium and passed on moral values and philosophical premises to the entire globe.

My third general conclusion from this evidence is something that I feel to have been apparent in every iteration of the Christian laws from the fourth century synods onwards: that is, they are dominated throughout by a concern for pastoral discretion. There are times, to be sure, when these ancient laws appear to a modern reader almost as inhumanely severe and unapproachable. Context determines how we read many of them. Some of them were issued in the aftermaths of periods of civil war and betrayal of communities by members still living in those communities, such as the canonical penalties put on those who had lapsed in times of persecutions. But many of them attempted to soften the rule of ancient law by elevating the idea of mercy to the level of having a legal force. The canons also progressively advance the concept of pastoral discretion (part of the fundamental priestly office of a judge who is a bishop, and not simply a civic judge) to the heart of Roman law. It was the canonists who, by the medieval period, became the leading legal theorists of the Eastern Christian world. This meant that after the appearance of the imperial *Basilika* in the tenth century, it was chiefly the canonists who collated, revised, and reproduced imperial law. Increasingly, therefore, the law came to be read in its reference to church concerns, moral and pastoral concerns. Law, even the state civil law, became deeply sacralized, but without ever leading to a priestocracy, a domination by clergy that is often the curse of ascendant religious law that does not have a parallel concept of the body politic such as that enjoyed by the Christian citizens of Rome. Eastern Christian law, therefore, grew up substantively in a religiously-orientated civilization and society, but never allowed the law to become mono-dimensional in the way Torah or Sharia developed for early Judaism and Islam.

The Byzantines thus had a legal system that protected civic and corporate values, that guarded both the state and Church from burdensome encroachment on the other's legitimate zones according to a viable system of subsidiarity, one that elevated communal wisdom alongside the divine right to rule, and which advocated pastoral discretion (mercy) as a core value in legal adjudication. It would be profoundly unfair to dismiss this monumental achievement as antiquarian. We have much to learn from it today.

Further Reading

Primary Texts

N.A. Bees. "Unedierte Schriftstucke aus der Kanzlei des Johannes Apookaukos des Metropoliten von Naupaktos (in Aetolien)." *Byzantinisch-neugriechische Jahrbucher* 21 (1971–1974) 55–160.

V. Benesevic, ed. *Ioannis Scholastici Synagoga L Titulorum.* Munich, 1937.

L.B. Pitra. *Iuris Ecclesiastici Graecorum Historia et Monumenta.* vol. 1. Rome: Propagandae Fidei, 1868.

Studies

L.B. Pitra. *Sinagoga v 50 titulov i drugie juridiceskie sborniki Ioanna Scholastika.* St Petersburg, 1914 (reprinted Leipzig, 1972).

C. Foss. "Demetrios Chomatenos." In A.P. Kazhdan, ed. *The Oxford Dictionary of Byzantium,* vol. 1. Oxford: Oxford University Press, 1991; p. 426.

C. Gallagher. *Church Law and Church Order in Rome and Byzantium: A Comparative Study.* Birmingham Byzantine and Ottoman Monographs, vol. 8. Aldershot: Ashgate Publ., 2002.

J. Haury. "Johannes Malalas identische mit dem Patriarchen Johannes Scholastikos?" *Byzantinische Zeitschrift* 9 (1900) 337–356.

R.J. Macrides. "Killing, Asylum, and the Law in Byzantium." *Speculum* 63 (1988) 509–538.

______. "Apokaukos, John." In A. Kazhdan, ed. *The Oxford Dictionary of Byzantium*, vol. 1. Oxford: Oxford University Press, 1991; p. 135.

P. Rodopoulos. *An Overview of Orthodox Canon Law.* Orthodox Theological Library. vol. 3. Rollinsford, NH: Orthodox Research Institute, 2007.

E. Schwartz. *Die Kanonessammlung des Johannes Scholastikos.* 1933. No. 6.

B.H. Stolte. "The Challenge of Change: Notes on the Legal History of the Reign of Heraclius." Pp. 191–204 in G.J. Reinink & B.H. Stolte, eds., *The Reign of Heraclius (610–641): Crisis and Confrontation.* Louvain: Peeters, 2001.

M. Wellnhofer. *Johannes Apokaukos, Metropolit von Naupaktos in Aetolien (c 1155–1233).* Freizing, 1913.

There are also very useful notes and text resources available for public access on the Internet, on the website of Catholic University of America, prepared by world class canonists Kenneth Pennington and Heinz Ohme.

See: *http://faculty.cua.edu/Pennington/Canon%20Law/ShortHistoryCanonLaw.htm*
And: *http://faculty.cua.edu/pennington/OhmeGreekCanonLaw.htm*

One of the leading Orthodox canonists of the younger generation is D.F. Wagschal. His exceptional dissertation on the Byzantine canons (*The Nature of Law and Legality in the Byzantine Canonical Collections: 381–883*) can be accessed at: *http://etheses.dur.ac.uk/468/*

Postludium

Our ending is entitled *Postludium* rather than *Conclusion* for the simple reason that, faced with the daunting array of the masses of Christian legislation the Church produced over almost two millennia, and the way they range over almost every aspect of life, it is too difficult to come up with simple conclusions. Even to set the terms of what a concluding review to such a book would be is difficult enough. I would like to have it pose the overarching question: "In terms of its approach to, and use of, law, did Christianity make any essential difference to the world?" But that is no easier a question than the one behind it, which it seeks to illuminate. Christianity's application of the law, both in terms of its own creation of guiding canons to direct its internal life, and its adaptation of the Roman civil law for use in Eastern and Western European societies from Late Antiquity almost into Modernity, has had an unarguable effect on the creation of the structures of society. Even in European societies where the common law was not so indebted to the Roman legal system,[1] the Church mediated the latter's influence by means of the canonical system that was so imbued with so many of its foundational ideas and presuppositions. It has thus had a determinative effect on the *ethos*, the fundamental character, of Western Civilization. In the western iterations of Christian tradition that trajectory of law has been encouraged by Catholic and Protestant theologies to follow a double road: one of a strong sense of separation of Church and State.[2] The Byzantine religious world regarded that dichotomous separation as a theological as well as a social error. The Church's episcopate was the custodian of its ecclesiastical law code; the emperor was the custodian and font of the civil code. As priests, the bishops also ruled their own courts to which the laity could have refuge, if they wished for a more pastoral hearing of their domestic cases, and they would abide by the episcopal decision without

[1]Such as in England, Ireland, and Wales (and subsequently the systems that were influenced therefrom, such as Canada, United States of America, Australia, & New Zealand).

[2]Under the rising papal monarchy, the "Two Swords Theory" originally develops not as a separation of Church and State. Take Pope Gelasius in the 5th century as an example, who tries to articulate the need to subordinate the imperial *regia potestas* (political dominion) to the superior papal *auctoritas* (moral ascendancy). Further see W. Ulmann, *Medieval Political Thought* (1975) 41. But with the rise of the later medieval nation-states, this theological theory of clerical subordination does develop into a deep-seated western political attitude of separation of the two powers. In the aftermath of the Protestant Reformation, especially with the latter's urgent attempts to shake papal authority root and branch, it is a separation that sometimes became politically enshrined as western default thinking.

recourse to appeal. As leader of the state, the emperor, however, was also regarded as exercising a sacral role. Neither locus of the law was "secular" in the Byzantine (or early Christian) understanding, for the law was fundamentally concerned with the moral structuring of society. The state officers would put that in terms of policing society and ensuring lawful conduct. The church authorities would put it in terms of ensuring moral purity in the worshipping community. But since the imperial and episcopal offices met together regularly in the ceremonies of the Great Cathedral of Hagia Sophia at Constantinople (or Kiev, Moscow, Sofia, Nicaea, Ohrid, or Lalibela, for that matter), then it was axiomatic in the Byzantine understanding of law that the Church and State were parallel realities that both, in "symphony," had the moral duty of the formation of their citizens. For both court and clergy, therefore, the law was an ethical construct. It is this primary *ethos* that marks Eastern Christian approaches to law more than anything else: a single premise that distinguishes it from the Greco-Roman theories about law that preceded the Church and from later iterations of the role of law in society that have abstracted (sometimes divorced) the concept of legality from the concept of justice.

Let us begin here, then, in stating this as the first of a series of small summations, rather than conclusions, about Eastern Christian attitudes to law. The first axiom derives from the teachings of Jesus which are retained among the Christians as the charter of a "New Society." His insistence that the actions of the heart are paramount,[3] that intention is the core of what ethical behavior means,[4] and that ethical behavior must never leave the simplest level of truth to seek refuge in obscurantism:[5] these things above all else have meant that Christians have tended, most profoundly, to connect law with ethics. The earliest beginnings of legal reflection in the New Testament, in the Apostolic Fathers, and in the later patristic writers, all show that Christians approach the law in utilitarian terms for the power it can have in effecting a moral elevation of social *mores*. To this extent it is inimical to the Christian philosophy of law that it can be secularized in the sense of being rendered morally neutral. Just so it is inimical to Christian philosophy of law that there can be a society that does not care to be a just and righteous society. The evangelical imperatives, therefore, provide a social charter from the outset, and it is not at

[3]Mk 7.14–16, 21–23. "He called the people to him once more and said: Listen to me, all of you, and understand this. Nothing that goes into a man from outside can make him unclean. It is the things that come out of a man that make him unclean . . . .for it is from within, from human hearts, that evil intentions emerge."

[4]See for example: Mt 5.20–22, 27–28, 33–37. Mt 5.43: "You have learned how it used to be said "You must love your neighbor and hate your enemy." But I say this to you: Love your enemies and pray for those who persecute you."

[5]See Mt 7.24. "Thus always treat other people as you would want them to treat you. This is the meaning of the Law and the Prophets."

all a matter of wonder that within three centuries of Christianity's appearance in the world, Christians took over the seat of power and set out on a long journey to effect change in society, creating a Christian civilization in the process. This can stand as our first summation: Christians understand law as a means of establishing a higher set of behaviors. It is not merely a matter of a penal or criminal code, but an indication for a society that will always contain within it levels of different moral agency (some good, some indifferent, some bad, some downright evil) that common standards cannot fall, while higher standards ought to prevail. The common "lower" standard ("below which not") established an ethic of no-harm (the outlawing of infanticide, the penalizing of manslaughter, the reiteration of its horror of murder, though with a simultaneous advocacy of the ending of automatic execution), while the standard of higher aspiration was set by the Church's ethic of pure altruistic love, self-renunciation, and the subordination of the power-principle to the ethic of service.[6] This as our first axiom sets the compass bearing for a new civilization that bonds together ancient civil premises about law and social governance with scriptural paradigms, all fashioned together in a community of worship that collectively elevated the teachings of Jesus as the charter authority of its polity. It is this master premise that determines most else of what will happen. Even when an individual Christian legislation is less than we might have expected it to be (and it certainly took a long time to liberate the slaves, and to raise the educational standards of women in antiquity), the axiomatic compass point is set at the outset. Men and women, of whatever race, or rank, both rich and poor, educated and illiterate, were given equality under the eye of God by this charter. Their lives were raised to infinite value as icons of the divinity, their rights and privileges as the divine icons could never be lost. Even when Christian law might lose its way temporarily in the welter of legislations, it never lost this sure compass setting. It is on this basis that Christian civilization was founded, one which remains untarnished in Christian theory today, and which one day may be used once more to rebuild a society's value system.

Our second summation also rises out of a long view over our subject. What this study of two millennia of law has suggested to me more than anything else appears almost banal to state, but the statement of it is something that is far from banal. Christianity endorses the rule of law. It does not have a grudging acceptance of law; it affirms it and lives by it and out of it, even at those times when it laments the limitations of the law and its inability to take society higher to the condition when law would truly no longer be necessary. This age of the transcendence of law, when all would live voluntarily in the spirit of compassion and truth was always a dream reserved for its eschatological hope of the "Next Age," the Age of the "Kingdom that

[6]Mk 9.34–37; Mk 10.42–45.

is to come." In this present age, however, the Church adopted and embraced the rule of law. This, albeit a simple conclusion when we look at how Christianity operated legally, is a major statement of *ethos*. Christianity is not a "legal religion" in the same sense that Judaism or Islam can be said to be such, but it nurtures a profoundly sacramental attitude to law. It endorses the rule of law, both civil and ecclesiastical. In reference to ecclesiastical law which it always controlled (it influenced Roman civil law, but did not originate it or ever control it fully), it shows something quite specific in reference to the principle of rule of law and that is that it must be conciliar and oecumenical. The Eastern Church refuses to allow a monarchical principle to be elevated in its ecclesiastical law. The Western Church departed from this rule in its own canonical systems, that ultimately became subordinated to the papacy. The East refused to allow any clergy, however important, to dominate the making or interpretation of law. Law thus belonged to the People of God collectively and was administered and refined by the whole *corpus* of the assembly of the bishops in synodical assembly. By insisting on this corporate and collective nature of the making and administration of law, Eastern Christianity, from ancient times, swam against the tide of Greco-Roman civilization, which valued autocracy. Even the much-vaunted Athenian democracy was in reality a narrowly-based government only of free male, slave-owning, property-owners. Not so in the Church. Christianity's legal system held up conciliarity as paradigmatic. Christian law theory rebuts the notion of tyranny as sacrilegious. Christ is the sole Lord of the "communion," and in his resurrected presence has not vacated the throne for any other to take it over, whether priest or king. The Byzantine imperial throne was always a double one: a "two-seater." But the other half was not reserved for the empress. One side was always allocated to Christ, and the emperor sat alongside him. When the emperor was not present the court clergy placed a Gospel book on the throne instead.

The Russian term for this sense of conciliarity is *sobornost* and it carries in it the precisely freighted nuances of communion and common aspiration. Insofar as law, if ethically conceived, is also the charter for the advancement of a society, this sense of conciliar instinct for what would be good legislation for the community meant that the body politic was always held up as a communion. There were not the rulers on one side and the mass of those to be governed, on the other, but a communion bonded in a worship that commonly expressed its values. The governance of the bishops, all of whom were regarded in Eastern Christian theology as equal to one another, meant that the application of law, strictly put, remained a local event, moving from the level of parish (however large or small), to the province (the provincial synod), thence to the regional or Oecumenical Council for matters of international weight. In Eastern Christian conciliar theory, however, a Council was not admitted as "oecumenical" unless it had the endorsement of the People of God, who accepted their bishops' judgments as truly expressing the mind of the Church.[7] So, at the heart of the endorsement of the rule of law is a profoundly local and communal principle; a principle of communion of values in the law that springs from the Christian notion of being a pure community of worship (a royal priesthood, a holy nation[8]). This too profoundly colored the Christian philosophy of law, and kept it accountable at the local domain.

Another summation for our list might be the manner in which so many of the Church's canons relate to clerical standards of behavior. As an historian, one is tempted to think that the more the clergy's behavior is regulated, the more they must have been misbehaving. We cannot rule that out, of course; but another aspect of this issue is the way in which church legislators are tuned and ready for the slightest aberrations in clerical behavior. What is clearly being stated is that Christianity wishes to elevate the clergy as practical moral examples in the ancient world. Their standards of behavior are to be higher than their neighbors. If they fall lower, the legislation attracts penalties to them rapidly. To this extent the Christian law codes are very much concerned to act in specific didactic ways, offering examples of a lifestyle, rather than theorizing about it. The clergy who apply the laws as a moral and elevating code are thus required to be the practical as well as theoretical leaders of the legal assembly. This, I think, is why there is such an obsessive concern throughout the ecclesiastical canons to ensure the highest moral standards among the clerical ranks; and, as a concomitant to that, why clerical moral lapses are regarded as so serious a scandal in the ancient Church that the complete removal of offending clerics is required so that the link between stated intent and practical reality is never severed by hypocrisy.

In the later Byzantine era, even in the larger cities, episcopal courts came to be preferred by the people to the civil alternative of a hearing before the magistrate, not only because the penalties were less severe for the offenders, but also for their deeper sense of pastoral care. It had been a deliberate policy of Constantine's New Empire to extend magisterial functions to local bishops, and by and large they fulfilled the charge most commendably. This I would like to elevate as another summation in our list: the concept Christianity brought to the law to make it a pastoral instrument. Penalty hitherto had been retributive. In Eastern Christian law it was not retributive (to God belonged the right of final retribution), but corrective. This was a dynamically new element that Christianity introduced to the ancient world. It reserved to the emperor and to the local magistrate acting in his name, the right

[7]This was usually elaborated retrospectively in history. But there were several attempts to orchestrate an Oecumenical council that were roundly rebuffed by the people.

[8]1 Pet 2.9.

of inflicting penalties on offenders, even up to death. The bishop who operated an ecclesiastical court also had the right to inflict beatings and fines for offenders. But, unquestionably, the ecclesiastical administration of law preferred to use persuasion and moral weight to effect a change in behavior rather than punish retributively. In this sense Christianity was one of the first major systems to advocate a pastorally formative influence to law. The laws that a state passes, in other words, are not simply marks of its current values, but ought to be signposts towards it higher aspirations.

Lastly, all of eastern church and civil law operated, while the Byzantine Empire existed (and long after it where Christian Orthodox rulers had survived), in a macro context where Church and state, though not one, were closely allied. The civil service was heavily populated by clergy and the leading intellectuals were men versed in theological literature in a way that would elude any modern. In this world where theoretically, theologically, and politically, the Christian Empire was a unified system, civil law was sacralized, and ecclesiastical law was afforded state support. And yet, Byzantium was no theocracy and never became a uniform or monolithic society: its linguistic range and ethnic diversity was always too great for that, albeit there was a remarkable theological unity to it all from Russia to Ethiopia. The Byzantines spoke of their ideal relation of Church and state as a "symphony" of powers. They meant this in the sense of two sounds, discretely separate, yet able to juxtapose themselves in harmony for the good of society. In this societal theology Eastern Christianity was quite distinct from ancient Judaism, from Islam with its policy of establishing Sharia, and even from Western Christianity where state and Church struggled for centuries to see which one could have the ascendancy over the other, with neither side being able to demonstrate their innate superiority.

The Byzantines advocated a moral unity among the forces of civil and religious values. They were well aware that the application of civil law and religious imperative could be a good force for social cohesion, and moral refinement, when both were applied harmoniously. They were equally well aware, from bitter experience, that the transgressing of the limits of religious freedom meant large-scale dissent and social disunity (of which the empire knew many examples in its long life) and generally speaking, they preferred a diverse harmonization policy rather than oppressive measures.[9] This last aspect, which they called *symphonia,* offers an interesting instance of a Christian civilization that endorsed the principle of political association and deal-making as an integral part of good order; compact, alignment, and alliance (between all the significant agents of social rule) thus being elevated as

[9]Suppressive religious measures were rarely taken, but are recorded in the cases of the Manichaeans and the Bogomils, and certainly the last vestiges of pagan cult were given a "hard push" in the 5th century East, with the confiscation of cult centers and the end of state salaries for pagan philosophers.

essential safeguards to the principle of the rule of law. In many other societies across history, these elements have been regarded with disdain and preference has been given to majority rule or, even worse, totalitarianism as the sole recipe for dramatic social change. For all its vaunted title as an "autocracy," the Byzantine empire never functioned in this way at all. It was only rhetorically an autocracy. In reality, the Church and state compacted to attempt to make for a profound harmony in the social order. The legal association of the Church and the court is one example of how seriously they took that. As a principle, what we might call the elevation of the idea of political communion, it retains its interest and its value.

Did Christianity make any difference with all its emphasis on law and order? I would think the conclusion must be unarguably that it did. It made a civilization out of large areas of barbarism, and altered the Greco Roman philosophical premises on many matters relating to human dignity and ethical constructs. It gave birth and voice to the principle of the sacred and inalienable dignity of the person. Its legal achievement is detailed, liberating in character, societally constructive and immensely prestigious; comparable in its range to the great achievements of the Roman world, which Eastern Christianity deliberately sets out to affirm, and yet refine. In terms of its accomplishment in the domains of ecclesiastical law, the Church's canonical philosophy is no less remarkable. Coherent and sober and focused across two millennia, accumulating to a vast body of literature that universally seeks to elevate human conduct in a pastoral and compassionate way, it tried to refine the body of society with the spirit of Christ's compassion. Christian polity will always, when it is alive and energized, seek to do the same. Its engagement with the forces of civilization building, legal refinement, and moral edification are not over. Even after two thousand years, it has hardly begun to establish the Kingdom of God on earth. And if contemporary western society detaches from its root inspiration substantively, the Church will simply begin over again in ways comparable to the energy it brought to the refinement of law and social morals when it was being persecuted and alienated by savage state powers. It has an innate drive to change society, a charter obligation to help it to transcend its own limitations. It has an unceasing determination to make law subordinate to justice, to elevate mercy and reconciliation as among the highest of human societal virtues. And it will do so for centuries to come, even if in so doing it calls down on its head the annoyance of contemporary cultures, rather than the former plaudits of a social establishment.